Computer Algebra in Scientific Computing

Computer Algebra in Scientific Computing

Special Issue Editor

Andreas Weber

MDPI • Basel • Beijing • Wuhan • Barcelona • Belgrade

Special Issue Editor
Andreas Weber
Bonn University
Germany

Editorial Office
MDPI
St. Alban-Anlage 66
4052 Basel, Switzerland

This is a reprint of articles from the Special Issue published online in the open access journal *Mathematics* (ISSN 2227-7390) from 2018 to 2019 (available at: https://www.mdpi.com/journal/mathematics/special_issues/Computer_Algebra)

For citation purposes, cite each article independently as indicated on the article page online and as indicated below:

LastName, A.A.; LastName, B.B.; LastName, C.C. Article Title. *Journal Name* **Year**, *Article Number*, Page Range.

ISBN 978-3-03921-730-4 (Pbk)
ISBN 978-3-03921-731-1 (PDF)

© 2019 by the authors. Articles in this book are Open Access and distributed under the Creative Commons Attribution (CC BY) license, which allows users to download, copy and build upon published articles, as long as the author and publisher are properly credited, which ensures maximum dissemination and a wider impact of our publications.
The book as a whole is distributed by MDPI under the terms and conditions of the Creative Commons license CC BY-NC-ND.

Contents

About the Special Issue Editor

Andreas Weber (Prof. Dr.) studied mathematics and computer science at the Universities of Tübingen, Germany, and Boulder, Colorado, U.S.A. He was awarded his MS in Mathematics (Dipl.-Math) in 1990 and his Ph.D. (Dr. rer. nat.) in computer science from the University of Tübingen in 1993. From 1995 to 1997, he was awarded a scholarship from Deutsche Forschungsgemeinschaft to conduct research as a postdoctoral fellow at the Computer Science Department, Cornell University. From 1997 to 1999 he was a member of the Symbolic Computation Group at the University of Tübingen, Germany. From 1999 to 2001, he was a member of the research group Animation and Image Communication at the Fraunhofer Institut for Computer Graphics. He has been Professor of computer science at the University of Bonn, Germany, since his appointment in April 2001. He has served as Chair of the Department of Computer Science from 2014 to 2016. During his academic career, he has written more than 100 papers for journals and refereed conference proceedings and has been the first supervisor of 9 completed Ph.D. theses and over 70 master's and bachelor's theses. He has served as a reviewer for more than 60 different journals and conferences. In 2013, he has been awarded the Teaching Award of the University of Bonn.

Preface to "Computer Algebra in Scientific Computing"

Although scientific computing is very often associated with numeric computations, the use of computer algebra methods in scientific computing has obtained considerable attention in the last two decades. Computer algebra methods are especially suitable for parametric analysis of the key properties of systems arising in scientific computing. The expression-based computational answers generally provided by these methods are very appealing as they directly relate properties to parameters and speed up testing and tuning of mathematical models through all their possible behaviors. The articles contained in this book cover a broad range of topics in the context of computer algebra in scientific computing. At the core of many computer algebra methods are algorithms for multivariate polynomials, and the first article on "Algorithms and Data Structures for Sparse Polynomial Arithmetic" is at the essence of this core, giving a comprehensive presentation of algorithms, data structures, and implementation techniques for high-performance sparse multivariate polynomial arithmetic over the integers and rational numbers as implemented in the freely available Basic Polynomial Algebra Subprograms (BPAS) library. "A Heuristic Method for Certifying Isolated Zeros of Polynomial Systems" deals with the fundamental problem of certifying the isolated zeros of polynomial systems. Computing Gröbner bases and other kind of bases is another core of computer algebra. In "Resolving Decompositions for Polynomial Modules", the authors deal with a fundamental task in "computational commutative algebra and algebraic geometry", namely, the determination of free resolutions for polynomial modules. They introduce the novel concept of resolving decomposition of a polynomial module as a combinatorial structure that allows for the effective construction of free resolutions and provide a unifying framework for recent results involving different types of bases. The analysis of certain invariants of a dynamical system—which are at the heart of many problems in scientific computing—is another major area for computer algebra research. In the article "First Integrals of the May–Leonard Asymmetric System", an important system arising in the life sciences is investigated, which is given by a quadratic system of the Lotka–Volterra type depending on six parameters. The authors look for subfamilies admitting invariant algebraic surfaces of degree two, and then for some such subfamilies, they construct first integrals of the Darboux type, identifying the systems with one first integral or with two independent first integrals. A problem based in physics, namely "Minkowski 4-space", is treated in the article "Dini-Type Helicoidal Hypersurfaces with Timelike Axis in Minkowski 4-Space". The authors consider Ulisse Dini-type helicoidal hypersurfaces with timelike axis in Minkowski 4-space, and by calculating the Gaussian and mean curvatures of the hypersurfaces, they demonstrate some special symmetries for the curvatures when they are flat and minimal. In the article "Implicit Equations of the Henneberg-Type Minimal Surface in the Four-Dimensional Euclidean Space" the authors find implicit algebraic equations of the Henneberg-type minimal surface of values (4,2). The exciting field of quantum computing has also lead to several problems in computer algebra. In "Quantum Information: A Brief Overview and Some Mathematical Aspects", not only is a review of the main ideas behind quantum computing and quantum information presented, but the focus is also on some mathematical problems related to the so-called mutually unbiased bases used in quantum computing and quantum information processing. In this direction, the construction of mutually unbiased bases is presented via two distinct approaches: one based on the group SU(2) and the other on Galois fields and Galois rings.

Andreas Weber
Special Issue Editor

mathematics

MDPI

Article

Algorithms and Data Structures for Sparse Polynomial Arithmetic

Mohammadali Asadi, Alexander Brandt *, Robert H. C. Moir and Marc Moreno Maza

Department of Computer Science, University of Western Ontario, London, ON N6A 5B7, Canada; masadi4@uwo.ca (M.A.); rmoir3@uwo.ca (R.H.C.M.); moreno@csd.uwo.ca (M.M.M.)
* Correspondence: abrandt5@uwo.ca

Received: 1 February 2019; Accepted: 12 May 2019; Published: 17 May 2019

Abstract: We provide a comprehensive presentation of algorithms, data structures, and implementation techniques for high-performance sparse multivariate polynomial arithmetic over the integers and rational numbers as implemented in the freely available Basic Polynomial Algebra Subprograms (BPAS) library. We report on an algorithm for sparse pseudo-division, based on the algorithms for division with remainder, multiplication, and addition, which are also examined herein. The pseudo-division and division with remainder operations are extended to multi-divisor pseudo-division and normal form algorithms, respectively, where the divisor set is assumed to form a triangular set. Our operations make use of two data structures for sparse distributed polynomials and sparse recursively viewed polynomials, with a keen focus on locality and memory usage for optimized performance on modern memory hierarchies. Experimentation shows that these new implementations compare favorably against competing implementations, performing between a factor of 3 better (for multiplication over the integers) to more than 4 orders of magnitude better (for pseudo-division with respect to a triangular set).

Keywords: sparse polynomials; polynomial arithmetic; normal form; pseudo-division; pseudo-remainder; sparse data structures

1. Introduction

Technological advances in computer hardware have allowed scientists to greatly expand the size and complexity of problems tackled by scientific computing. Only in the last decade have sparse polynomial arithmetic operations (Polynomial arithmetic operations here refers to addition, subtraction, multiplication, division with remainder, and pseudo-division) and data structures come under focus again in support of large problems which cannot be efficiently represented densely. Sparse polynomial representations was an active research topic many decades ago out of necessity; computing resources, particularly memory, were very limited. Computer algebra systems of the time (which handled multivariate polynomials) all made use of sparse representations, including ALTRAN [1], MACSYMA [2], and REDUCE [3]. More recent work can be categorized into two streams, the first dealing primarily with algebraic complexity [4,5] and the second focusing on implementation techniques [6,7]. Recent research on implementation techniques has been motivated by the *efficient* use of memory. Due to reasons such as the processor–memory gap ([8] Section 2.1) and the memory wall [9], program performance has become limited by the speed of memory. We consider these issues foremost in our algorithms, data structures, and implementations. An early version of this work appeared as [10].

Sparse polynomials, for example, arise in the world of polynomial system solving—a critical problem in nearly every scientific discipline. Polynomial systems generally come from real-life applications, consisting of multivariate polynomials with rational number coefficients. Core routines for determining solutions to polynomial systems (e.g., Gröbner bases, homotopy methods, or triangular decompositions) have driven a large body of work in computer algebra. Algorithms, data structures, and implementation techniques for polynomial and matrix data types have seen particular attention. We are motivated in our work on sparse polynomials by obtaining efficient implementations of triangular decomposition algorithms based on the theory of regular chains [11].

Our aim for the work presented in this paper is to provide highly optimized sparse multivariate polynomial arithmetic operations as a foundation for implementing high-level algorithms requiring such operations, including triangular decomposition. The implementations presented herein are freely available in the BPAS library [12] at www.bpaslib.org. The BPAS library is highly focused on performance, concerning itself not only with execution time but also memory usage and cache complexity [13]. The library is mainly written in the C language, for high-performance, with a simplified C++ interface for end-user usability and object-oriented programming. The BPAS library also makes use of parallelization (e.g., via the CILK extension [14]) for added performance on multi-core architectures, such as in dense polynomial arithmetic [15,16] and arithmetic for big prime fields based on Fast Fourier Transform (FFT) [17]. Despite these previous achievements, the work presented here is in active development and not yet been parallelized.

Indeed, parallelizing sparse arithmetic is an interesting problem and is much more difficult than parallelizing dense arithmetic. Many recent works have attempted to parallelize sparse polynomial arithmetic. Sub-linear parallel speed-up is obtained for the relatively more simple schemes of Monagan and Pearce [18,19] or Biscani [20], while Gastineau and Laskar [7,21] have obtained near-linear parallel speed-up but have a much more intricate parallelization scheme. Other works are quite limited: the implementation of Popescu and Garcia [22] is limited to floating point coefficients while the work of Ewart et al. [23] is limited to only 4 variables. We hope to tackle parallelization of sparse arithmetic in the future, however, we strongly believe that one should obtain an optimized serial implementation before attempting a parallel one.

Contributions and Paper Organization

Contained herein is a comprehensive treatment of the algorithms and data structures we have established for high-performance sparse multivariate polynomial arithmetic in the BPAS library. We present in Section 2 the well-known sparse addition and multiplication algorithms from [24] to provide the necessary background for discussing division with remainder (Section 3), an extension of the exact division also presented in [24]. In Section 4 we have extended division with remainder into a new algorithm for sparse pseudo-division. Our presentation of both division with remainder and pseudo-division has two levels: one which is abstract and independent of the supporting data structures (Algorithms 3 and 5); and one taking advantage of heap data structures (Algorithms 4 and 6). Section 5 extends division with remainder and pseudo-division to algorithms for computing normal forms and pseudo-division with respect to a triangular set; the former was first seen in [25] and here we extend it to the case of pseudo-division. All new algorithms are proved formally.

In support of all these arithmetic operations we have created a so-called alternating array representation for distributed sparse polynomials which focuses greatly on data locality and memory usage. When a recursive view of a polynomial (i.e., a representation as a univariate polynomial with multivariate polynomial coefficients) is needed, we have devised a succinct recursive representation which maintains the optimized distributed representation for the polynomial coefficients and whose conversion to and from the distributed sparse representation is highly efficient. Both representations are explained in detail in Section 6. The efficiency of our algorithms and implementations are highlighted beginning in Section 7, with implementation-specific optimizations, and then Section 8, which gathers our experimental results. We obtain speed-ups between a factor of 3 (for multiplication over the integers) and a factor of 18,141 (for pseudo-division with respect to a triangular set).

2. Background

2.1. Notation and Nomenclature

Throughout this paper we use the notation R to denote a ring (commutative with identity), $\mathbb{D}$ to denote an integral domain, and $\mathbb{K}$ to denote a field. Our treatment of sparse polynomial arithmetic requires both a distributed and recursive view of polynomials, depending on which operation is considered. For a distributed polynomial $a \in R[x_1, \ldots, x_v]$, a ring R, and variable ordering $x_1 < x_2 < \cdots < x_v$, we use the notation

$$a = \sum_{i=1}^{n_a} A_i = \sum_{i=1}^{n_a} a_i X^{\alpha_i},$$

where n_a is the number of (non-zero) terms, $0 \neq a_i \in R$, and α_i is an exponent vector for the variables $X = (x_1, \ldots, x_v)$. A term of a is represented by $A_i = a_i X^{\alpha_i}$. We use a lexicographical term order and assume that the terms are ordered decreasingly, thus $\mathrm{lc}(a) = a_1$ is the *leading coefficient* of a and $\mathrm{lt}(a) = a_1 X^{\alpha_1} = A_1$ is the *leading term* of a. If a is not constant the greatest variable appearing in a (denoted $\mathrm{mvar}(a)$) is the *main variable* of a. The maximum sum of the elements of α_i is the *total degree* (denoted $\mathrm{tdeg}(a)$). The maximum exponent of the variable x_i is the *degree with respect to* x_i (denoted $\deg(a, x_i)$). Given a term A_i of a, $\mathrm{coef}(A_i) = a_i$ is the coefficient, $\mathrm{expn}(A_i) = \alpha_i$ is the exponent vector, and $\deg(A_i, x_j)$ is the component of α_i corresponding to x_j. We also note the use of a simplified syntax for comparing monomials based on the term ordering; we denote $X^{\alpha_i} > X^{\alpha_j}$ as $\alpha_i > \alpha_j$.

To obtain a recursive view of a non-constant polynomial $a \in R[x_1, \ldots, x_v]$, we view a as a univariate polynomial in $\tilde{R}[x_j]$, with x_j called the *main variable* (denoted $\mathrm{mvar}(a)$) and where $\tilde{R} = R[x_1, \ldots, x_{j-1}, x_{j+1}, \ldots, x_v]$. Usually, x_j is chosen to be x_v and we have $a \in R[x_1, \ldots, x_{v-1}][x_v]$. Given a term A_i of $a \in \tilde{R}[x_j]$, $\mathrm{coef}(A_i) \in R[x_1, \ldots, x_{j-1}, x_{j+1}, \ldots, x_v]$ is the coefficient and $\mathrm{expn}(A_i) = \deg(A_i, x_j) = \deg(A_i)$ is the degree. Given $a \in \tilde{R}[x_j]$, an exponent e picks out the term A_i of a such that $\deg(A_i) = e$, so we define in this case $\mathrm{coef}(a, x_j, e) := \mathrm{coef}(A_i)$. Viewed specifically in the recursive way $\tilde{R}[x_j]$, the leading coefficient of a is an element of $\tilde{R}$ called the *initial* of a (denoted $\mathrm{init}(a)$) while the degree of a in the main variable x_j is called the *main degree* (denoted $\mathrm{mdeg}(a)$), or simply degree where the univariate view is understood by context.

2.2. Addition and Multiplication

Adding (or subtracting) two polynomials involves three operations: joining the terms of the two summands; combining terms with identical exponents (possibly with cancellation); and sorting of the terms in the sum. A naïve approach computes the sum $a + b$ term-by-term, adding a term of the addend (b) to the augend (a), and sorting the result at each step, in a manner similar to *insertion sort*. (This sorting of the result is a crucial step in any sparse operation. Certain optimizations and tricks can be used in the algorithms when it is known that the operands are in some sorted order, say in a *canonical form*. For example, obtaining the leading term and degree is much simpler, and, as is shown throughout this paper, arithmetic operations can exploit this sorting.) This method is inefficient and does not take advantage of the fact that both a and b are already ordered. We follow the observation of Johnson [24] that this can be accomplished efficiently in terms of operations and space by performing a single step of *merge sort* on the two summands, taking full advantage of initial sorting of the two summands. One slight difference from a typical merge sort step is that like terms (terms with identical exponent vectors) are combined as they are encountered. This scheme results in the sum (or difference) being automatically sorted and all like terms being combined. The algorithm is very straightforward for anyone familiar with merge sort. The details of the algorithm are presented in ([24], p. 65). However, for completeness we present the algorithm here using our notation (Algorithm 1).

Algorithm 1 AddPolynomials (a,b)
$a, b \in R[x_1, \ldots, x_v]$, $a = \sum_{i=1}^{n_a} a_i X^{\alpha_i}$, $b = \sum_{j=1}^{n_b} b_j X^{\beta_j}$;
return $c = a + b = \sum_{k=1}^{n_c} c_k X^{\gamma_k} \in R[x_1, \ldots, x_v]$

$(i, j, k) := 1$
while $i \le n_a$ **and** $j \le n_b$ **do**
  if $\alpha_i < \beta_j$ **then**
    $c_k := b_j;\ \gamma_k := \beta_j$
    $j := j + 1$
  else if $\alpha_i > \beta_j$ **then**
    $c_k := a_i;\ \gamma_k := \alpha_i$
    $i := i + 1$
  else
    $c_k := a_i + b_j;\ \gamma_k := \alpha_i$
    $i := i + 1;\ j := j + 1$
    if $c_k = 0$ **then**
      continue #Do not increment k
  $k := k + 1$
end
while $i \le n_a$ **do**
  $c_k := a_i;\ \gamma_k := \alpha_i$
  $i := i + 1;\ k := k + 1$
while $j \le n_b$ **do**
  $c_k := b_j;\ \gamma_k := \beta_j$
  $j := j + 1;\ k := k + 1$
return $c = \sum_{\ell=1}^{k-1} c_\ell X^{\gamma_\ell}$

Multiplication of two polynomials follows the same general idea of addition: Make use of the fact that the multiplier and multiplicand are already sorted. Under our sparse representation of polynomials multiplication requires production of the product terms, combining terms with equal exponents, and then sorting the product terms. A naïve method computes the product $a \cdot b$ (where a has n_a terms and b has n_b terms) by distributing each term of the multiplier (a) over the multiplicand (b) and combining like terms:

$$c = a \cdot b = (a_1 X^{\alpha_1} \cdot b) + (a_2 X^{\alpha_2} \cdot b) + \cdots .$$

This is inefficient because all $n_a n_b$ terms are generated, whether or not like terms are later combined, and then all $n_a n_b$ terms must be sorted, and like terms combined. Again, following Johnson [24], we can improve algorithmic efficiency by generating terms in sorted order.

We can make good use of the sparse data structure for

$$a = \sum_{i=1}^{n_a} a_i X^{\alpha_i}, \quad \text{and} \quad b = \sum_{j=1}^{n_b} b_j X^{\beta_j},$$

based on the observation that for given α_i and β_j, it is always the case that $X^{\alpha_{i+1}+\beta_j}$ and $X^{\alpha_i+\beta_{j+1}}$ are less than $X^{\alpha_i+\beta_j}$ in the term order. Since we always have $X^{\alpha_i+\beta_j} > X^{\alpha_i+\beta_{j+1}}$, it is possible to generate product terms in order by merging n_a "streams" of terms computed by multiplying a single term of a distributed over b,

$$a \cdot b = \begin{cases} (a_1 \cdot b_1)\, X^{\alpha_1+\beta_1} + (a_1 \cdot b_2)\, X^{\alpha_1+\beta_2} + (a_1 \cdot b_3)\, X^{\alpha_1+\beta_3} + \ldots \\ (a_2 \cdot b_1)\, X^{\alpha_2+\beta_1} + (a_2 \cdot b_2)\, X^{\alpha_2+\beta_2} + (a_2 \cdot b_3)\, X^{\alpha_2+\beta_3} + \ldots \\ \vdots \\ (a_{n_a} \cdot b_1)\, X^{\alpha_{n_a}+\beta_1} + (a_{n_a} \cdot b_2)\, X^{\alpha_{n_a}+\beta_2} + (a_{n_a} \cdot b_3)\, X^{\alpha_{n_a}+\beta_3} + \ldots \end{cases}$$

and then choosing the maximum term from the "heads" of the streams. We can consider this as an n_a-way merge where at each step, we select the maximum term from among the heads of the streams, making it the next product term, removing it from the stream in the process. The new head of the stream where a term is removed will then be the term to its right.

This sub-problem of selecting the maximum term among n_a different terms can be solved efficiently by making use of a priority queue data structure, which can be implemented as a heap (see Section 6.3 for implementation details). The virtue of using a heap was noticed by Johnson [24], but the description of his algorithm was left very abstract and did not make explicit use of a priority queue.

In Algorithm 2 we give our heap-based multiplication algorithm. This algorithm makes use of a few specialized functions to interface with the heap and the heads of streams contained therein. We provide here a simplified yet complete interface consisting of four functions. (Please note that algorithms for insertion and removal from a heap are standard and provided in any good reference on data structures and algorithms (see, e.g., [26]).) **heapInitialize**(a, B_1) initializes the heap by initiating n_a streams, where the head of the i-th stream is $A_i \cdot B_1$. Each of these heads are inserted into the heap. **heapInsert**(A_i, B_j) adds the product of the terms A_i and B_j to the heap. It is important to note, however, that the heap does not need to store the actual product terms but can store instead only the indices of the two factors, with their product only being computed when elements are removed from the heap. (This strategy is actually required in the case of pseudo-division (Section 7.4) where the streams themselves are updated over the course of the algorithm.) The exponent vector of the monomial must be computed on insertion, though, since this determines the insertion location (priority) in the heap. **heapPeek**() returns the exponent vector γ of the top element in the heap and the stream index s from which the product term was formed, i.e., s such that the top element comes from the stream $A_s \cdot B$. Please note that nothing is removed from the heap by **heapPeek**(). **heapExtract**() removes the top element of the heap, providing the product term. If the heap is empty **heapPeek**() will return $\gamma = (-1, 0, \ldots, 0)$, which is, by design, less than any exponent of any polynomial term because the first element is -1. We therefore abuse notation and write $\gamma = -1$ for an empty heap.

Algorithm 2 HEAPMULTIPLYPOLYNOMIALS(a,b)

$a, b \in R[x_1, \ldots, x_v]$, $a = \sum_{i=1}^{n_a} a_i X^{\alpha_i}$, $b = \sum_{j=1}^{n_b} b_j X^{\beta_j}$;
return $c = a \cdot b = \sum_{k=1}^{n_c} c_k X^{\gamma_k} \in R[x_1, \ldots, x_v]$

if $n_a = 0$ **or** $n_b = 0$ **then**
    return 0
$k := 1; C_1 := 0$
$s = 1$; $\gamma := \alpha_1 + \beta_1$ # Maximum possible value of γ
heapInitialize(a, B_1)
for $i = 1$ **to** n_a **do**
    $f_i := 1$ # Indices of the current head of each stream
while $\gamma > -1$ **do** # $\gamma = -1$ when the heap is exhausted
    if $\gamma \neq \text{expn}(C_k)$ **and** $\text{coef}(C_k) \neq 0$ **then**
        $k := k + 1$
        $C_k := 0$
    $C_k := C_k +$ **heapExtract**()
    $f_s := f_s + 1$
    if $f_s \le n_b$ **then**
        heapInsert(A_s, B_{f_s})
    $(\gamma, s) :=$ **heapPeek**() # Get degree and stream index of the top of the heap
end
if $C_k = 0$ **then** $k := k - 1$
return $c = \sum_{\ell=1}^{k} C_\ell = \sum_{\ell=1}^{k} c_\ell X^{\gamma_\ell}$

We note that while this algorithm seems simple in pseudo-code, its implementation, especially with respect to the heap, requires many subtle optimizations to achieve good performance. The discussions of such improvements are left to Section 7. Nonetheless the algorithm presented here is complete and correct.

Proposition 1. *Algorithm 2 terminates and is correct.*

Proof. Let $a, b \in R[x_1, \ldots, x_v]$. If either $n_a = 0$ or $n_b = 0$ then $a = 0$ or $b = 0$, in which case $c = 0$ and we are done. Otherwise, $c \neq 0$ and we initialize the heap with n_a pairs (A_i, B_1), $i = 1, \ldots, n_a$, we initialize the stream element indices f_i to 1, and we set $C_1 = 0$. We initially set $\gamma = \alpha_1 + \beta_1$, the maximum possible for polynomials a and b, and a guaranteed term of the product. This also serves to enter the loop for the first time. Since C_1 was initially set to 0, $C_k = 0$, so the first condition on line 9 is met, but not the second, so we move to line 12. Lines 12 through 15 extract the top of the heap, add it to C_k (giving $C_1 = A_1B_1$), and insert the next element of the first stream into the heap. This value of C_1 is correct. Since we add the top element of each stream to the heap, the remaining elements to be added to the heap are all less than at least one element in the heap. The next **heapPeek**() sets γ to one of $\alpha_2 + \beta_1$ or $\alpha_1 + \beta_2$ (or -1 if $n_a = n_b = 1$), and sets s accordingly. Subsequent passes through the loop must do one of the following: (1) if $C_k \neq 0$ and there exists another term with exponent $\text{expn}(C_k)$, add it to C_k; (2) if $C_k = 0$, add to C_k the next greatest element (since for sparse polynomials we store only non-zero terms); or (3) when $C_k \neq 0$ and the next term has lower degree ($\gamma_k > \gamma$), increase k and then begin building the next C_k term. Cases (1) and (2) are both handled by line 12, since the condition on line 9 fails in both cases, respectively because $\gamma = \text{expn}(C_k)$ or because $C_k = 0$. Case (3) is handled by lines 9–12, since $\gamma \neq \text{expn}(C_k)$ and $C_k \neq 0$ by assumption. Hence, the behavior is correct. The loop terminates because there are only n_b elements in each stream, and lines 14–15 only add an element to the heap if there is a new element to add, while every iteration of the loop always removes an element from the heap at line 12. □

3. Division with Remainder

3.1. Naïve Division with Remainder

We now consider the problem of multivariate division with remainder, where the input polynomials are $a, b \in \mathbb{D}[x_1, \ldots, x_v]$, with $b \neq 0$ being the divisor and a the dividend. While this operation is well-defined for $a, b \in \mathbb{D}[x_1, \ldots, x_v]$ for an arbitrary integral domain $\mathbb{D}$, provided that $\text{lc}(b)$ is a divisor of the content of both a and b, we rather assume, for simplicity, that the polynomials a and b are over a field. We can therefore specify this operation as having the inputs $a, b \in \mathbb{K}[x_1, \ldots, x_v]$, and outputs $q, r \in \mathbb{K}[x_1, \ldots, x_v]$, where q and r satisfy (We note due to its relevance for the algorithms presented in Section 5 that $\{b\}$ is a Gröbner basis of the ideal it generates and the stated condition here on the remainder r is equivalent to the condition that r is reduced with respect to the Gröbner basis $\{b\}$ (see [27] for further discussion of Gröbner bases and ideals)):

$$a = qb + r, \text{where } r = 0 \text{ or } \text{lt}(b) \text{ does not divide any term in } r.$$

In an effort to achieve performance, we continue to be motivated by the idea of producing terms of the result (quotient and remainder) in sorted order. However, this is much trickier in the case of division in comparison to multiplication. We must compute terms of both the quotient and remainder in order, while simultaneously producing terms of the product qb in order. We must also produce these product terms while q is being generated term-by-term throughout the algorithm. This is not so simple, especially in implementation.

In the general "long division" of polynomials (see Section 2.4 of [28]) one repeatedly obtains the product of a newly computed quotient term and the divisor, and then updates the dividend with the difference between it and this product. Of course, this is computationally wasteful and not ideal, since at each step of this long division one needs only the leading term of this updated dividend to compute the next quotient term. Thus, before concerning ourselves with a heap-based algorithm, we consider a computationally efficient division algorithm which does not perform this continued updating of the dividend. This algorithm, which is a special case of the algorithm in Theorem 3 of Section 2.3 in [27] , is presented as Algorithm 3.

Algorithm 3 DIVIDEPOLYNOMIALS(a,b)

$a, b \in \mathbb{K}[x_1, \ldots, x_v]$, $b \neq 0$; return $q, r \in \mathbb{K}[x_1, \ldots, x_v]$ such that $a = qb + r$ where $r = 0$ or $\text{lt}(b)$ does not divide any term in r (r is reduced with respect to the Gröbner basis $\{b\}$).

```
q := 0; r := 0
while (r̃ := lt(a − qb − r)) ≠ 0 do
    if lt(b) | r̃ then
        q := q + r̃/lt(b)
    else
        r := r + r̃
end
return (q, r)
```

In this algorithm, the quotient and remainder, q and r, are computed term-by-term by computing $\tilde{r} = \text{lt}(a - qb - r)$ at each step. This works for division by deciding whether $\tilde{r}$ should belong to the remainder or the quotient at each step. If $\text{lt}(b) \mid \tilde{r}$ then we perform this division and obtain a new quotient term. Otherwise, we obtain a new remainder term. In either case, this $\tilde{r}$ *was* the leading term of the expression $a - qb - r$ and now either belongs to q or r. Therefore, in the next step, the old $\tilde{r}$ which was added to either q or r will now cancel itself out, resulting in a new leading term of the expression $a - qb - r$. This new leading term is non-increasing (in the sense of its monomial) relative to the preceding $\tilde{r}$ and thus terms of the quotient and remainder are produced in order.

Proposition 2. *Algorithm 3 terminates and is correct. ([27], pp. 61–63)*

3.2. Heap-Based Division with Remainder

It is clear from Algorithm 3 that multivariate division reduces to polynomial multiplication (through the product qb) and polynomial subtraction. What is not obvious is the efficient computation of the term $\tilde{r} = \text{lt}(a - qb - r)$. Nonetheless, we can again use heap-based multiplication to keep track of the product qb. The principal difference from multiplication, where all terms of both factors are known from the input, is that the terms of q are computed as the algorithm proceeds. This idea of using a heap to monitor $q \cdot b$ follows that of Johnson [24] for his exact univariate division. We extend his algorithm to multivariate division with remainder.

In terms of the wording of the multiplication algorithm, we set q to the multiplier and b to the multiplicand, distributing q over b, so the streams are formed from a single term of q, while the stream moves along b. By having q in this position it becomes relatively easy to add new streams into the computation as new terms of q are computed. Using the notations of our heap-division algorithm (Algorithm 4), the crucial difference between heap-based multiplication and heap-based division is that each stream does not start with $Q_\ell B_1$. Rather, the stream begins at $Q_\ell B_2$ since the product term $Q_\ell B_1$ is cancelled out by construction.

The management of the heap to compute the product qb uses several of the functions described for Algorithm 2. Specifically **heapPeek**(), **heapInsert**($\cdot, \cdot$), and **heapExtract**(). However, **heapExtract**() is modified slightly from its definition in multiplication. For division it combines removal of the top heap element *and* insertion of the next element of the stream (if there is a next) from which the top element originated. In this algorithm we use δ to denote the exponent of the top term in the heap of $q \cdot b$. Similar to multiplication, we abuse notation and let $\delta = -1$ if the heap is empty.

Finally, having settled the details of the product qb, what remains is to efficiently compute the leading term of $a - qb - r$. This is handled by a case discussion between the maximum term (in the sense of the term order) of a which has yet to be cancelled out and the maximum term of the product qb which has yet to be used to cancel out something. Then, by construction, when a newly generated term goes to the remainder it exactly cancels out one term of $a - qb$. This case discussion is evident in lines 4, 7, and 10 of Algorithm 4, while Proposition 3 formally proves the correctness of this approach.

Algorithm 4 HEAPDIVIDEPOLYNOMIALS(a,b)

$a, b \in \mathbb{K}[x_1, \ldots, x_v]$, $a = \sum_{i=1}^{n_a} a_i X^{\alpha_i} = \sum_{i=1}^{n_a} A_i$, $b \neq 0 = \sum_{j=1}^{n_b} b_j X^{\beta_j} = \sum_{j=1}^{n_b} B_j$; return $q, r \in \mathbb{K}[x_1, \ldots, x_v]$ such that $a = qb + r$ where $r = 0$ or B_1 does not divide any term in r (r is reduced with respect to the Gröbner basis $\{b\}$).

```
 1: (q, r, l) := 0
 2: k := 1
 3: while (δ := heapPeek()) > -1 or k ≤ n_a do
 4:     if δ < α_k then
 5:         r̃ := A_k
 6:         k := k + 1
 7:     else if δ = α_k then
 8:         r̃ := A_k − heapExtract()
 9:         k := k + 1
10:     else
11:         r̃ := −heapExtract()

12:     if B_1 | r̃ then
13:         ℓ := ℓ + 1
14:         Q_ℓ := r̃ / B_1
15:         q := q + Q_ℓ
16:         heapInsert(Q_ℓ, B_2)
17:     else
18:         r := r + r̃

19: end
20: return (q, r)
```

Proposition 3. *Algorithm 4 terminates and is correct.*

Proof. Let $\mathbb{K}$ be a field and $a, b \in \mathbb{K}[x_1, \ldots, x_v]$ with $\operatorname{tdeg}(b) > 0$. If $b \in \mathbb{K}$ then this degenerate case is simply a scalar multiplication by b_1^{-1} and proceeds as in Proposition 2. Then $r = 0$ and we are done. Otherwise, $\operatorname{tdeg}(b) > 0$ and we begin by initializing $q, r = 0$, $k = 1$ (index into a), $\ell = 0$ (index into q), and $\delta = -1$ (heap empty condition) since the heap is initially empty. The key change from Algorithm 3 to obtain Algorithm 4 is to use terms of qb obtained from the heap to compute $\tilde{r} = \operatorname{lt}(a - qb - r)$. There are then three cases to track: (1) $\tilde{r}$ is an uncancelled term of a; (2) $\tilde{r}$ is a term from $(a - r) - (qb)$, i.e., the degree of the greatest uncancelled term of a is the same as the degree of the leading term of qb; and (3) $\tilde{r}$ is a term of $-qb$ with the property that the rest of the terms of $a - r$ are smaller in the term order. Let $a_k X^{\alpha_k} = A_k$ be the greatest uncancelled term of a. The three cases then correspond to conditions on the ordering of δ and α_k. The term $\tilde{r}$ is an uncancelled term of a (Case 1) either if the heap is empty (meaning either that no terms of q have yet been computed or all terms of qb have been removed), or if $\delta > -1$ but $\delta < \alpha_k$. In either of these two situations $\delta < \alpha_k$ holds and $\tilde{r}$ is chosen to be A_k. The term $\tilde{r}$ is a term from the difference $(a - r) - (qb)$ (Case 2) if both A_k and the top term in the heap have the same exponent vector ($\delta = \alpha_k$). Lastly, $\tilde{r}$ is a term of $-qb$ (Case 3) whenever $\delta > \alpha_k$ holds. Algorithm 4 uses the above observation to compute $\tilde{r}$ by adding conditional statements to compare the components of δ and α_k. Terms are only removed from the heap when $\delta \geq \alpha_k$ holds, and thus we "consume" a term of qb. Simultaneously, when a term is removed from the heap, the next term from the given stream, if it exists, is added to the heap (by the definition of **heapExtract**()). The updating of q and r with the new leading term $\tilde{r}$ is almost the same as Algorithm 3, with the exception that when we update the quotient, we also initialize a new stream with Q_ℓ in the multiplication of $q \cdot b$. This stream is initialized with a head of $Q_\ell B_2$ because $Q_\ell B_1$, by construction, cancels a unique term of the expression $a - qb - r$. In all three cases, either the quotient is updated, or the remainder is updated. It follows from the case discussion of δ and α_k that the leading term of $a - qb - r$ is non-increasing for each loop iteration and the algorithm therefore terminates by Proposition 2. Correctness is implied by the condition that $\tilde{r} = 0$ at the end of the algorithm together with the fact that all terms of r satisfy the condition $\operatorname{lt}(b) \nmid R_k$. □

4. Pseudo-Division

4.1. Naïve Pseudo-Division

The pseudo-division algorithm is essentially a univariate operation. Accordingly, we denote polynomials and terms in this section as being elements of $\tilde{\mathbb{D}}[x_1, \ldots, x_{v-1}][x_v] = \mathbb{D}[x]$ for an arbitrary integral domain $\tilde{\mathbb{D}}$. It is important to note that while the algorithms and discussion in this section are specified for univariate polynomials they are, in general, multivariate polynomials, and thus the coefficients of these univariate polynomials are in general themselves multivariate polynomials.

Pseudo-division is essentially a fraction-free division: instead of dividing a by $h = \mathrm{lc}(b)$ (once for each term of the quotient q), a is multiplied by h to ensure that the polynomial division can occur without being concerned with divisibility limitations of the ground ring. The outputs of a pseudo-division operation are the pseudo-quotient q and pseudo-remainder r satisfying

$$h^{\ell} a = qb + r, \ \deg(r) < \deg(b), \tag{1}$$

where ℓ satisfies the inequality $0 \le \ell \le \deg(a) - \deg(b) + 1$. When $\ell < \deg(a) - \deg(b) + 1$ the pseudo-division operation is called *lazy* or *sparse*.

Under this definition, the simple multivariate division algorithm (Algorithm 3) can be readily modified for pseudo-division by accounting for the required factors of h. This enters in two places: (i) each time a term of a is used, we must multiply the current term A_k of a by h^{ℓ}, where ℓ is the number of quotient terms computed so far, and (ii) each time a quotient term is computed we must multiply all the previous quotient terms by h to ensure that $h^{\ell} a = qb + r$ will be satisfied. Algorithm 5 presents this basic pseudo-division algorithm modified from the simple multivariate division algorithm.

Algorithm 5 PSEUDODIVIDEPOLYNOMIALS(a,b)
$a, b \in \mathbb{D}[x]$, $b \neq 0$, $h = \mathrm{lc}(b)$; return $q, r \in \mathbb{D}[x]$ and $\ell \in \mathbb{N}$ such that $h^{\ell} a = qb + r$, with $\deg(r) < \deg(b)$.

1: $(q, r, \ell) := 0$
2: $h := \mathrm{lc}(b)$; $\beta = \deg(b)$
3: **while** $(\tilde{r} := \mathrm{lt}(h^{\ell} a - qb - r)) \neq 0$ **do**
4:     **if** $x^{\beta} \mid \tilde{r}$ **then**
5:         $q := hq + \tilde{r}/x^{\beta}$
6:         $\ell := \ell + 1$
7:     **else**
8:         $r := r + \tilde{r}$
9: **end**
10: **return** (q, r, ℓ)

It is important to note that because pseudo-division is univariate, all of the quotient terms are computed before any remainder terms are computed. This is because we can always carry out a pseudo-division step, and produce a new quotient term, provided that $\deg(b) \le \deg(\mathrm{lt}(h^{\ell} a - qb - r))$, where $r = 0$. When $\deg(b) > \deg(\mathrm{lt}(h^{\ell} a - qb - r))$ then the quotient is done being computed and we have $r = h^{\ell} a - qb$, satisfying the conditions (1) of a pseudo-remainder. The following proposition proves the correctness of our pseudo-division algorithm.

Proposition 4. *Algorithm 5 terminates and is correct.*

Proof. Let $\mathbb{D}$ be an integral domain and let $a, b \in \mathbb{D}[x]$ with $\beta = \deg(b) > 0$. If $\deg(b) = 0$, $b = h$ and the divisibility test on line 4 always passes, all generated terms go to the quotient, and we get a remainder of 0 throughout the algorithm. Essentially this is a meaningless operation. q becomes $h^{n_a - 1} a$ and the formula (1) holds with $r = 0$ and the convention that $\deg(0) = -\infty$. We proceed assuming $\deg(b) > 0$. We initialize $q, r, \ell = 0$. It is enough to show that for each loop iteration, the degree of $\tilde{r}$ strictly decreases. Since the degree of $\tilde{r}$ is finite, $\tilde{r}$ is zero after finitely many iterations. We use superscripts to denote the values of the variables of Algorithm 5 on the i-th iteration. We have two possibilities for each i, depending on whether or not $x^{\beta} \mid \tilde{r}^{(i)}$ holds: (1) $Q_{\ell} = \tilde{r}^{(i)} / x^{\beta}$, Q_{ℓ} being a new quotient term; or (2) $R_k = \tilde{r}^{(i)}$, R_k being a new remainder term. In Case 1 we update only the quotient term so $r^{(i+1)} = r^{(i)}$; in Case 2 we update only the remainder term so $q^{(i+1)} = q^{(i)}$.

Suppose, then, that $\tilde{r}^{(i)}$ has just been used to compute a term of q or r, and we now look to compute $\tilde{r}^{(i+1)}$. Depending on whether or not $x^\beta \mid \tilde{r}^{(i)}$ we have:
Case 1: $x^\beta \mid \operatorname{lt}(h^\ell a - q^{(i)}b - r^{(i)})$ and $Q_\ell = \tilde{r}^{(i)}/x^\beta$. Here, because we are still computing quotient terms, $r^{(i+1)} = r^{(i)} = 0$. Thus,

$$\begin{aligned}
\tilde{r}^{(i+1)} = \operatorname{lt}(h^{\ell+1}a - q^{(i+1)}b - r^{(i+1)}) &= \operatorname{lt}(h^{\ell+1}a - ([hq^{(i)} + Q_\ell]b)) \\
&= \operatorname{lt}(h^{\ell+1}a - (hq^{(i)}b + Q_\ell b)) \\
&= \operatorname{lt}(h^{\ell+1}a - [hq^{(i)}b + (h\tilde{r}^{(i)} - h\tilde{r}^{(i)}) + Q_\ell b]) \\
&= \operatorname{lt}(h^{\ell+1}a - [hq^{(i)}b + h\tilde{r}^{(i)} + Q_\ell(b - hx^\beta)]) \\
&= \operatorname{lt}(h[h^\ell a - q^{(i)}b - \tilde{r}^{(i)}] - Q_\ell(b - B_1)) \\
&= \operatorname{lt}\Big((h[h^\ell a - q^{(i)}b - r^{(i)} - \tilde{r}^{(i)}]) - Q_\ell(b - B_1)\Big) \\
&< \operatorname{lt}(\tilde{r}^{(i)}) = \tilde{r}^{(i)}.
\end{aligned}$$

In the second last line, where $r^{(i)} = 0$ appears, notice that since $\tilde{r}^{(i)} = \operatorname{lt}(h^\ell a - q^{(i)}b - r^{(i)})$ and $h \in \mathbb{D}$, we can ignore h for the purposes of choosing a term with highest degree and we have therefore that $\operatorname{lt}(h^\ell a - q^{(i)}b - r^{(i)} - \tilde{r}^{(i)}) < \operatorname{lt}(\tilde{r}^{(i)})$. Also, the expression $Q_\ell(b - B_1)$ has leading term $Q_\ell B_2$ which is strictly less than $\tilde{r}^{(i)} = Q_\ell x^\beta$, by the ordering of the terms of b. Hence $\tilde{r}^{(i+1)}$ is strictly less than $\tilde{r}^{(i)}$.
Case 2: $x^\beta \nmid \operatorname{lt}(h^\ell a - q^{(i)}b - r^{(i)})$ and $R_k = \tilde{r}^{(i)}$

$$\begin{aligned}
\tilde{r}^{(i+1)} = \operatorname{lt}(h^\ell a - q^{(i+1)}b - r^{(i+1)}) &= \operatorname{lt}(h^\ell a - q^{(i)}b - (r^{(i)} + R_k)) \\
&= \operatorname{lt}((h^\ell a - q^{(i)}b - r^{(i)}) - \tilde{r}^{(i)}) \\
&< \operatorname{lt}(\tilde{r}^{(i)}) = \tilde{r}^{(i)}.
\end{aligned}$$

Similar to Case 1, $\tilde{r}^{(i)} = \operatorname{lt}(h^\ell a - q^{(i)}b - r^{(i)})$, thus the difference between $(h^\ell a - q^{(i)}b - r^{(i)})$ and $\tilde{r}^{(i)}$ must have a leading term strictly less than $\tilde{r}^{(i)}$. The loop therefore terminates. The correctness is implied by the condition that $\tilde{r} = 0$ at the end of the loop. The condition $\deg(r) < \deg(b)$ is met because the terms are only added to the remainder when $x^\beta \nmid \tilde{r}$ holds, i.e., when it is always the case that $\deg(h^\ell a - qb) < \deg(b)$. $\ell \le \deg(a) - \deg(b) + 1$ holds because ℓ is only incremented when a new quotient term is produced (i.e., $x^\beta \mid \tilde{r}$) and the maximum number of quotient terms is $\deg(a) - \deg(b) + 1$. □

4.2. Heap-Based Pseudo-Division

Optimization of Algorithm 5 using a heap proceeds in much the same way as for division. The only additional concern to handle to reach Algorithm 6 is how to account for factors of h in the computation of $\operatorname{lt}(h^\ell a - qb - r)$. Handling this requires adding the same number of factors of h to A_k that have been added to the quotient up to a given iteration, that is, h^ℓ. The number ℓ is incremented when the previous quotient terms are multiplied by h prior to adding a new quotient term. Other than this, the changes to Algorithm 5 to reach Algorithm 6 follow exactly the analogous changes to Algorithm 3 to reach Algorithm 4. These observations therefore yield the following algorithm and proposition.

Algorithm 6 HEAPPSEUDODIVIDEPOLYNOMIALS(a,b)

$a, b \in \mathbb{D}[x]$, $a = \sum_{i=1}^{n_a} a_i x^{\alpha_i} = \sum_{i=1}^{n_a} A_i$, $0 \neq b = \sum_{j=1}^{n_b} b_j x^{\beta_j} = \sum_{j=1}^{n_b} B_j$, $h = \mathrm{lc}(b)$;
return $q, r \in \mathbb{D}[x]$ and $\ell \in \mathbb{N}$ such that $h^\ell a = qb + r$, with $\deg(r) < \deg(b)$.

1: $(q, r, l) := 0$
2: $h := \mathrm{lc}(b)$; $\beta := \deg(b)$
3: $k := 1$
4: **while** ($\delta :=$ **heapPeek**()) > -1 **or** $k \leq n_a$ **do**
5:   **if** $\delta < \alpha_k$ **then**
6:     $\tilde{r} := h^\ell A_k$
7:     $k := k + 1$
8:   **else if** $\delta = \alpha_k$ **then**
9:     $\tilde{r} := h^\ell A_k -$ **heapExtract**()
10:     $k := k + 1$
11:   **else**
12:     $\tilde{r} := -$**heapExtract**()
13:   **if** $x^\beta \mid \tilde{r}$ **then**
14:     $q := hq$
15:     $\ell := \ell + 1$
16:     $Q_\ell := \tilde{r} / x^\beta$
17:     $q := q + Q_\ell$
18:     **heapInsert**(Q_ℓ, B_2)
19:   **else**
20:     $r := r + \tilde{r}$
21: **end**
22: **return** (q, r, ℓ)

Proposition 5. *Algorithm 6 terminates and is correct.*

Proof. Let $\mathbb{D}$ be an integral domain and $a, b \in \mathbb{D}[x]$ with $\deg(b) > 0$. If $b \in \mathbb{D}$ then this degenerate case proceeds as in Proposition 4. Then $r = 0$ with $\deg(r) = -\infty < 0 = \deg(b)$ and we are done. Observe that there are two main conditionals (lines 5–12 and 13–20) in the while loop. Given Proposition 4, it is enough to show that the first conditional computes $\mathrm{lt}(h^\ell a - qb - r)$ and the second uses $\tilde{r}$ to add terms to either q or r, depending on whether or not $x^\beta \mid \tilde{r}$. We initialize $q, r = 0$, $k = 1$ (index into a), $\ell = 0$ (index into q), $\delta = -1$ (heap empty condition) since the heap is initially empty. The central change to Algorithm 5 to reach Algorithm 6 is to take terms of qb from the heap to compute $\tilde{r} = \mathrm{lt}(h^\ell a - qb - r)$. Three cases must then be tracked: (1) $\tilde{r}$ is a term of $h^\ell a$ that has not yet been cancelled; (2) $\tilde{r}$ is a term from $(h^\ell a - r) - (qb)$; and (3) $\tilde{r}$ is a term of $-qb$ such that all remaining terms of $h^\ell a - r$ have smaller degree. Notice that all the terms of q are computed before the terms of r since this is essentially univariate division with respect to the monomials. Therefore, we can ignore r in the sub-expression $h^\ell a - r$. Thus, computing $\mathrm{lt}(h^\ell a - qb - r)$ in order simply requires computing terms of $(h^\ell a - qb)$ in order. These three cases for computing $\tilde{r}$ are handled by the first conditional. Let $a_k X^{\alpha_k} = A_k$ be the greatest uncancelled term of a. In Case 1, the heap is either empty (indicating that no terms of q have been computed yet or all terms of qb have been extracted) or $\deg(qb) = \delta > -1$ but $\delta < \alpha_k$. In either situation $\delta < \alpha_k$ holds and $\tilde{r}$ is chosen to be A_k. The term $\tilde{r}$ is a term from the difference $(h^\ell a - qb)$ (Case 2) if both A_k and the top term of the heap have the same degree ($\delta = \alpha_k$) and $\tilde{r}$ is chosen to be the difference of $h^\ell A_k$ and the greatest uncancelled term of qb. Lastly, $\tilde{r}$ is a term of $-qb$ (Case 3) in any other situation, i.e., $\delta > \alpha_k$. Thus, the first conditional computes $\mathrm{lt}(h^\ell a - qb - r)$, *provided* that the second conditional correctly adds terms to q and r. The second conditional adds terms to the quotient when $x^\beta \mid \mathrm{lt}(h^\ell a - qb)$ holds. Since each new quotient term adds another factor of h, we must first multiply all previous quotient terms by h. We then construct the new quotient term to cancel $\mathrm{lt}(h^\ell a - qb)$ by setting $Q_{\ell+1} = \mathrm{lt}(h^\ell a - qb)/x^\beta$, as in Algorithm 5. Since $Q_\ell B_1$ cancels a term of $(h^\ell a - qb)$ by construction, then line 18 initializing a new stream with $Q_\ell B_2$ is also correct. If, on the other hand, $x^\beta \nmid \mathrm{lt}(h^\ell a - qb)$, all remaining $\tilde{r}$ terms are remainder terms, which are correctly added by line 20. □

While the algorithmic shift between heap-based multivariate division (Algorithm 4) and heap-based pseudo-division (Algorithm 6) is very straight forward, the change of coefficient domain from simple numerical coefficients to full multivariate polynomials (when $\mathbb{D}$ is a polynomial ring) leads to many implementation challenges. This affects lines 6, 9 and 14 of Algorithm 6 in particular because they can involve multiplication of multivariate polynomials. These issues are discussed in Section 7.4.

5. Multi-Divisor Division and Pseudo-Division

One natural application of multivariate division with remainder is the computation of the normal form with respect to a Gröbner basis, which is a kind of multi-divisor division. Let $\mathbb{K}$ be a field and $\mathcal{B} = \{b_1, \ldots, b_k\}$ be a Gröbner basis with $b_j \in \mathbb{K}[x_1, \ldots, x_v]$ for $1 \leq i \leq k$. Then we can compute the normal form r of a polynomial $a \in \mathbb{K}[x_1, \ldots, x_v]$ (together with the quotients q_j) with respect to $\mathcal{B}$ by Algorithm 21.11 from [28], yielding $a = q_1 t_1 + \cdots + q_k t_k + r$, where r is reduced with respect to $\mathcal{B}$. This naïve normal form algorithm makes repeated calls to a multivariate division with remainder algorithm, thus we can take advantage of our optimized heap-based division (Algorithm 4).

We can offer algorithmic improvements in some cases where the set of divisors forms a triangular set, i.e., where the main variables of $t_j \in \{t_1, \ldots, t_k\}$ are pairwise different. Note that a triangular set $\mathsf{T} = \{t_1, \ldots, t_k\}$, with $t_j \in \mathbb{K}[x_1, \ldots, x_v]$ and $\mathrm{mvar}(t_k) > \cdots > \mathrm{mvar}(t_1)$, is called *normalized* if, for every polynomial of T, every variable appearing in its initial is free, i.e., is not the main variable of another polynomial of T. In the case where a normalized triangular set is also zero-dimensional (i.e., $k = v$) so that being normalized implies that $\mathrm{init}(t_i) \in \mathbb{K}$ holds, the triangular set T is actually a Gröbner basis for the ideal it generates.

For such zero-dimensional normalized (also known as Lazard) triangular sets it is possible to use a recursive algorithm (Algorithm 7) which is taken from [25]. Since the algorithm is recursive we appropriately use the recursive representation of the polynomials. If $v = 1$, the desired result is obtained by simply applying normal division with remainder. Otherwise the coefficients of a with respect to $x_v = \mathrm{mvar}(t_v)$ are polynomials belonging to $\mathbb{K}[x_1, \ldots, x_{v-1}]$ because T is a triangular set. The coefficients of a are reduced with respect to the set $\{t_1, t_2, \ldots, t_{v-1}\}$ by means of a recursive call, yielding a polynomial r. At this point, r is divided by t_v by applying the division algorithm. Since this operation can lead to an increase in degree of for the variables less than x_v, the coefficients of r are reduced with respect to $\{t_1, \ldots, t_{v-1}\}$ by means of a second recursive call.

Algorithm 7 TriangularSetNormalForm (a,T)
Given $a \in \mathbb{K}[x_1, \ldots, x_v]$, $\mathsf{T} = \{t_1, \ldots, t_v\} \subset \mathbb{K}[x_1, \ldots, x_v]$, with $x_1 = \mathrm{mvar}(t_1) < \cdots < x_v = \mathrm{mvar}(t_v)$ and $\mathrm{init}(t_1), \ldots, \mathrm{init}(t_v) \in \mathbb{K}$, returns $\mathbf{q} = \{q_1, \ldots, q_v\} \subset \mathbb{K}[x_1, \ldots, x_v]$ and $r \in \mathbb{K}[x_1, \ldots, x_v]$ such that $a = q_1 t_1 + \cdots + q_v t_v + r$, with r is reduced (in the Gröbner bas) with respect to the Lazard triangular set T.

```
1: if v = 1 then
2:     (q_1, r) := HeapDividePolynomials(a, t_1)
3: else
4:     for i = 0 to deg(a, x_v) do
5:         (q^(i) := {q_1^(i), ..., q_{v-1}^(i)}, r^(i)) := TriangularSetNormalForm(coef(a, x_v, i), {t_1, ..., t_{v-1}})
6:     end for
7:     q := 0
8:     r := Σ_i r^(i) x_v^i
9:     for j = 1 to v − 1 do
10:        q_j := q_j + Σ_i q_j^(i) x_v^i
11:    end for
12:    (q̃, r) := HeapDividePolynomials(r, t_v); q_v := q_v + q̃
13:    for i = 0 to deg(r, x_v) do
14:        (q^(i) := {q_1^(i), ..., q_{v-1}^(i)}, r^(i)) := TriangularSetNormalForm(coef(r, x_v, i), {t_1, ..., t_{v-1}})
15:    end for
16:    execute Lines 8–11
17: end if
18: return (q, r)
```

Proposition 6. *Algorithm 7 terminates and is correct [25].*

This approach can be extended to pseudo-division of a polynomial by a triangular set, an operation that is important in triangular decomposition algorithms, in the case that the triangular set is normalized. The pseudo-remainder r and pseudo-quotients q_j of a polynomial $a \in \mathbb{K}[x_1, \ldots, x_v]$ pseudo-divided by a triangular set $\mathsf{T} = \{t_1, \ldots, t_k\}$ must satisfy

$$ha = q_1 t_1 + \cdots + q_k t_k + r, \qquad \deg(r, \mathrm{mvar}(t_j)) < \deg(t_j, \mathrm{mvar}(t_j)) \text{ for } 1 \le j \le k, \tag{2}$$

where h is a product of powers of the initials (leading coefficients in the univariate sense) of the polynomials of T. If this condition is satisfied then r is said to be *reduced with respect to* T, again using the convention that $\deg(r) = -\infty$ if $r = 0$.

The pseudo-remainder r can be computed naïvely in k iterations where each iteration performs a single pseudo-division step with respect to each main variable in decreasing order $\mathrm{mvar}(t_k), \mathrm{mvar}(t_{k-1}), \ldots, \mathrm{mvar}(t_1)$. The remainder is initially set to a and is updated during each iteration. This naïve algorithm is inefficient for two reasons. First, since each pseudo-division step can increase the degree of lower variables in the order, if a is not already reduced with respect to T, the intermediate pseudo-remainders can experience significant coefficient swell. Second, it is inefficient in terms of data locality because each pseudo-division step requires performing operations on data distributed throughout the polynomial.

A less naïve approach is a recursive algorithm that replaces each of the k pseudo-division steps in the naïve algorithm with a recursive call, amounting to k iterations where multiple pseudo-division operations are performed at each step. This algorithm deals with the first inefficiency issue of coefficient swell, but still runs into the issue with data locality. To perform this operation more efficiently we conceive a recursive algorithm (Algorithm 8) based on the recursive normal form algorithm (Algorithm 7). Using a recursive call for each coefficient of the input polynomial a ensures that we work only on data stored locally, handling the second inefficiency of the naïve algorithm.

Algorithm 8 TRIANGULARSETPSEUDODIVIDE (a, T)

Given $a, t_1, \ldots, t_k \in \mathbb{K}[x_1, \ldots, x_v]$, $\mathsf{T} = \{t_1, \ldots, t_k\}$, with $\mathrm{mvar}(t_1) < \cdots < \mathrm{mvar}(t_k)$ and $\mathrm{init}(t_j) \notin \{\mathrm{mvar}(t_i) \mid t_i \in \mathsf{T}\}$ for $1 \le j \le k$, returns $\mathbf{q} = \{q_1, \ldots, q_k\} \subset \mathbb{K}[x_1, \ldots, x_v]$ and $r, h \in \mathbb{K}[x_1, \ldots, x_v]$ such that $ha = q_1 t_1 + \cdots + q_k t_k + r$, where r is reduced with respect to T.

1: **if** $k = 1$ **then**
2: $(q_1, r, e) :=$ HEAPPSEUDODIVIDEPOLYNOMIALS(a, t_1); $h = \mathrm{init}(t_1)^e$
3: **else**
4: $x_m := \mathrm{mvar}(t_k)$
5: **for** $i = 0$ **to** $\deg(a, x_m)$ **do**
6: $(\mathbf{q}^{(i)} := \{q_1^{(i)}, \ldots, q_{k-1}^{(i)}\}, r^{(i)}, h^{(i)}) :=$ TRIANGULARSETPSEUDODIVIDE$(\mathrm{coef}(a, x_m, i), \{t_1, \ldots, t_{k-1}\})$
7: **end for**
8: $\mathbf{q} = 0$
9: $h_1 := \mathrm{lcm}(h^{(i)}), 0 \le i \le \deg(a, x_m)$
10: $r := \sum_i (h_1 / h^{(i)})\, r^{(i)} x_m^i$
11: **for** $j = 1$ **to** $k - 1$ **do**
12: $q_j := q_j + \sum_i (h_1 / h^{(i)})\, q_j^{(i)} x_m^i$
13: **end for**
14: **if** $\mathrm{mvar}(r) = x_m$ **then**
15: $(\tilde{q}, r, \tilde{e}) :=$ HEAPPSEUDODIVIDEPOLYNOMIALS(r, t_k)
16: $\tilde{h} = \mathrm{init}(t_k)^{\tilde{e}}$
17: **for** $j = 1$ **to** $k - 1$ **do**
18: $q_j := q_j \tilde{h}$
19: **end for**
20: $q_k := \tilde{q}$
21: **for** $i = 0$ **to** $\deg(r, x_m)$ **do**
22: $(\mathbf{q}^{(i)} := \{q_1^{(i)}, \ldots, q_{k-1}^{(i)}\}, r^{(i)}, h^{(i)}) :=$ TRIANGULARSETPSEUDODIVIDE$(\mathrm{coef}(r, x_m, i), \{t_1, \ldots, t_{k-1}\})$
23: **end for**
24: $h_2 := \mathrm{lcm}(h^{(i)}), 0 \le i \le \deg(r, x_m)$
25: **for** $j = 1$ **to** k **do**
26: $q_j := q_j h_2$
27: **end for**
28: **execute** Lines 9–13 **with** h_2 replacing h_1
29: $h := h_1 \tilde{h} h_2$
30: **else**
31: $h := h_1$; $q_k = 0$
32: **end if**
33: **end if**
34: **return** $(\mathbf{q}, r, h)$

Proposition 7. *Algorithm 8 terminates and is correct.*

Proof. The central difference between this algorithm and Algorithm 7 is the change from division to pseudo-division. By Proposition 5 the computed pseudo-remainders are reduced with respect to their divisor. The fact that the loops of recursive calls are all for a triangular set with one fewer variables ensures that the total number of recursive calls is finite, and the algorithm terminates. If $k = 1$, then Proposition 5 proves correctness of this algorithm, so assume that $k > 1$.

We must first show that lines 4–13 correctly reduce a with respect to the polynomials $\{t_1, \ldots, t_{k-1}\}$. Let $c_i = \text{coef}(a, x_m, i)$, so $a = \sum_{i=0}^{\deg(a,x_m)} c_i x_m^i$. Assuming the correctness of the algorithm, the result of these recursive calls are $q_j^{(i)}$, $r^{(i)}$ and $h^{(i)}$ such that $h^{(i)} c_i = \sum_{j=1}^{k-1} q_j^{(i)} t_j + r^{(i)}$, where $\deg(r^{(i)}, \text{mvar}(t_j)) < \deg(t_j, \text{mvar}(t_j))$ and $h^{(i)} = \prod_{j=1}^{k-1} \text{init}(t_j)^{e_j}$ for some non-negative integers e_j. It follows that $c_i = \left(\sum_{j=1}^{k-1} q_j^{(i)} t_j + r^{(i)}\right) / h^{(i)}$. We seek a minimal h_1 such that $h_1 a = \sum_i h_1 c_i x_m^i = \sum_i (h_1/h^{(i)}) \left(\sum_{j=1}^{k-1} q_j^{(i)} t_j + r^{(i)}\right) x_m^i$ is denominator-free, which is easily seen to be $\text{lcm}(h^{(i)})$. This then satisfies the required relation of the form (2), with h_1 in place of h, by taking $q_j = \sum_i (h_1/h^{(i)}) q_j^{(i)} t_j x_m^i$ and $r = \sum_i (h_1/h^{(i)}) r_j^{(i)} x_m^i$. This follows from the conditions $\deg(r^{(i)}, \text{mvar}(t_j)) < \deg(t_j, \text{mvar}(t_j))$ since h_1 contains none of the main variables of $\{t_1, \ldots, t_{k-1}\}$ because T is normalized.

If at this point $\text{mvar}(r) \neq x_m$, then no further reduction needs to be done and the algorithm finishes with the correct result by returning $(q_1, \ldots, q_{k-1}, 0, r, h_1)$. This is handled by the else clause on lines 30 and 31 of the conditional on lines 14–32. If, on the other hand, $\text{mvar}(r) = x_m$, we must reduce r with respect to t_k. Proposition 5 proves that after executing line 15, $\deg(r, \text{mvar}(t_k)) < \deg(t_k, \text{mvar}(t_k))$, and together with lines 16–20 implies that with the updated pseudo-quotients

$$\tilde{h} h_1 a = \sum_{j=1}^{k} q_j t_j + r. \tag{3}$$

Since the pseudo-division step at line 15 may increase the degrees of the variables of r less than x_m in the variable ordering, we must issue a second set of recursive calls to ensure that (2) is satisfied. Again, given the correctness of the algorithm, it follows that the result of the recursive calls on lines 21–23 taking as input $r = \sum_{i=0}^{\deg(r,x_m)} c_i x_m^i$, with $c_i = \text{coef}(r, x_m, i)$, are $q_j^{(i)}$, $r^{(i)}$ and $h^{(i)}$ such that $h^{(i)} c_i = \sum_{j=1}^{k-1} q_j^{(i)} t_j + r^{(i)}$, where $\deg(r^{(i)}, \text{mvar}(t_j)) < \deg(t_j, \text{mvar}(t_j))$. Combining these results as before and taking $h_2 = \text{lcm}(h^{(i)})$ it follows that

$$h_2 r = \sum_{j=1}^{k-1} \tilde{q}_j t_j + \tilde{r} \tag{4}$$

satisfies a reduction condition of the form (2) with $\tilde{q} = \sum_i (h_2/h^{(i)}) q_j^{(i)} t_j x_m^i$ and $\tilde{r} = \sum_i (h_2/h^{(i)}) r_j^{(i)} x_m^i$, again because T is normalized. Multiplying (3) by h_2 and using Equation (4) yields $h_2 \tilde{h} h_1 a = \sum_{j=1}^{k} h_2 q_j t_j + h_2 r = \sum_{j=1}^{k} h_2 q_j t_j + \sum_{j=1}^{k-1} \tilde{q}_j t_j + \tilde{r} = \sum_{j=1}^{k-1} (h_2 q_j + \tilde{q}_j) t_j + h_2 q_k t_k + \tilde{r}$, which gives the correct conditions for updating the pseudo-quotients on lines 25–27, with the $\tilde{q}_j$ and $\tilde{r}$ computed at line 28. Now $\tilde{r}$ is reduced with respect to x_m because r is and with respect to $\text{mvar}(t_1), \ldots, \text{mvar}(t_{k-1})$ because of the above argument, so that the correct overall multiplier is $h = h_2 \tilde{h} h_1$, set on line 29. The algorithm is therefore correct. □

6. Data Structures

Polynomial arithmetic is fundamental to so many algorithms that it should naturally be optimized as much as possible. Although algorithm choice is important for this, so too is making use of appropriate data structures. When programming for modern computer architectures we must be concerned with the processor–memory gap: the exponentially increasing difference between processor speeds and memory-access time. We combat this gap with judicial memory usage and management. In particular, the *principle of locality* and cache complexity describe how to obtain performance by maximizing memory accesses that make best use of modern memory hierarchies (i.e., data locality). Basically, this means that the same memory address should be accessed frequently or, at the very least, accesses should be adjacent to those most recently accessed. Our implementation adheres to this principle through the use of memory-efficient data structures with optimal data locality. We see later (in Section 7) that our algorithms have implementation-specific optimizations to exploit this locality and minimize cache complexity.

This section begins by reviewing our memory-efficient data structures for both sparse distributed (Section 6.1) polynomials and sparse recursive polynomials (Section 6.2). The latter is interesting as the data structure is still flat and distributed but allows for the polynomial to be viewed recursively. Then, we discuss the implementation of our heap data structure (Section 6.3) which is specialized and optimized for use in polynomial multiplication.

6.1. A Sparse Distributed Polynomial Data Structure

The most simple and common scheme for sparsely representing a polynomial is a linked list, or some similar variation of data blocks linked together by pointers [6,29,30]. This representation allows for very easy manipulation of terms using simple pointer manipulation. However, the indirection created by pointers can lead to poor locality while the pointers themselves must occupy memory, resulting in memory wasted to encode the structure rather than the data itself. More efficient sparse data structures have been explored by Gastineau and Laskar [29], where *burst tries* store monomials in the TRIP computer algebra system, and Monagan and Peace [30], where the so-called POLY data structure for MAPLE closely stores monomials in a dense array. In both cases, the multi-precision coefficients corresponding to those monomials are stored in a secondary structure and accessed by either indices stored alongside the monomials (in the case of TRIP) or pointers (in the case of MAPLE).

Our distributed polynomial representation stores both coefficients and monomials side-by-side in the same array. This representation, aptly named an *alternating array*, improves upon data locality; the coefficient and monomial which together make a single polynomial term are optimally local with respect to each other. This decision is motivated by the fact that in arithmetic, coefficients are accessed alongside their associated monomials (say to perform a multiplication or combine like terms). In practice, this array structure is augmented by a simple C-struct holding three items: the number of terms; the number of variables; and a pointer to the actual array. This seemingly simple structure abstracts away some complexities in both the coefficients and monomials. We begin with the coefficients.

Due to the nature of arbitrary-precision coefficients, in our case either integers or rational numbers (We actually have two nearly identical yet distinct alternating array implementations. One implementation holds integer coefficients while the other holds rational number coefficients), we cannot say they are fully stored in the array. We make use of the GNU Multiple Precision Arithmetic (GMP) Library [31] for our coefficients. The implementation of arbitrary-precision numbers in this library is broken into two distinct parts, which we will call the *head* and the *tree*. The head contains metadata about the tree, as well as a pointer to the tree, while the tree itself is what holds the numerical data. By the design of the GMP library users only ever interact with the head. Thus, our alternating array representation holds the heads of the GMP numbers directly in the array rather than pointers or indices to some other structure, which in turn would hold the heads of the GMP numbers. Figure 1 depicts an arbitrary polynomial of n terms stored in an alternating array, highlighting the GMP tree structure.

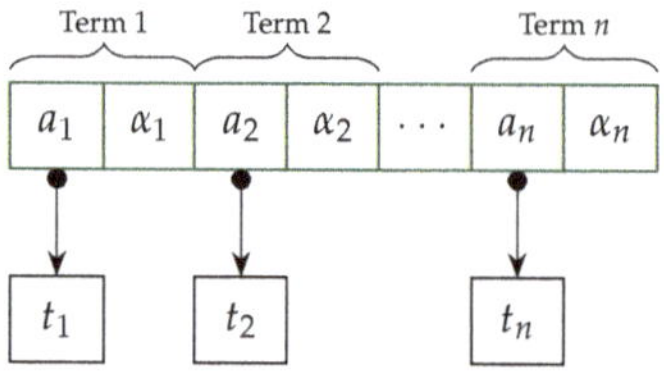

Figure 1. An alternating array representation of n terms showing GMP trees as $t_1, t_2, \ldots, t_n$, GMP heads as $a_1, a_2, \ldots, a_n$, and monomials as $\alpha_1, \alpha_2, \ldots, \alpha_n$. One head and tree together make a single arbitrary-precision number.

The alternating array diagram in Figure 1 may be misleading at first glance, since it appears that pointers are still being used; however, these pointers are completely internal to GMP and are unavoidable. Hence, where other structures use indices ([29], Figure 2) or pointers ([6], Figure 3) to a separate array of GMP coefficients, that coefficient array also further contains these pointers to GMP trees. Our implementation thus removes one level of indirection compared to these other schemes. We do note, however, that the data structure described in [6,30] includes an additional feature which automatically makes use of machine-precision integers stored directly in the data structure, rather than GMP integers, if coefficients are small enough.

Next, we discuss the implementation of monomials. Under a fixed variable ordering it becomes unnecessary to store the variables themselves with the monomial, and so we only store the exponent vector. This greatly reduces the required memory for a monomial. However, even more memory is saved via *exponent packing*. Using bit-masks and bit-shifts, multiple partial degrees, each taking a small non-negative value, can easily be stored in a single machine word (usually 64 bits). This fact should be obvious by looking at the binary representation of a non-negative integer on a computer. Integers are stored in some fixed size, typically 32 or 64 bits, and, when positive or unsigned, have many leading 0 bits. For example, 5 as a 32-bit integer is 0*b*00000000000000000000000000000101. By using a predetermined number of bits for each partial degree in an exponent vector, it becomes easy to partition the 64 bits to hold many integers. Our alternating array thus holds a single machine word directly in the array for packing each exponent vector.

Exponent packing has been in use at least since the 60s in ALTRAN [1], but also in more recent works such as [4,32]. Our implementation differs from others in that exponents are packed unevenly, i.e., each exponent is given a different number of bits in which to be encoded. This is motivated by two factors. First, 64 bits is rarely evenly divided among the number of variables, meaning some bits could be wasted. Second, throughout the process of operations such as pseudo-division or triangular decomposition the degrees of lower-ordered variables often increase more drastically than higher-ordered variables, and so we give more bits to the lower-ordered variables. This can allow for large computations to progress further without failing or having to revert to an *unpacked* exponent vector. One final highlight on exponent packing (first emphasized in [32]) is that monomial comparisons and monomial multiplications respectively reduce to a single machine-integer comparison and a single machine-integer addition. This result drastically reduces the time to complete monomial comparisons, and thus sort monomials, a huge part of sparse polynomial arithmetic.

6.2. A Sparse Polynomial Data Structure for Viewing Polynomials Recursively

We take this section to describe our recursive polynomial data structure. That is not to say that the data structure itself is recursive, rather the polynomial is viewed recursively, as a univariate polynomial with multivariate polynomial coefficients. In general, polynomials are stored using the distributed representation; however, some operations, such as pseudo-division, require a specifically univariate view of the polynomial. Thus, we have created an in-place, very fast conversion between the distributed and recursive representations, amounting to minimal overhead in both memory usage and time. As a result, we can use the same distributed representation everywhere, only converting as required. This recursive representation is shown in Figure 2.

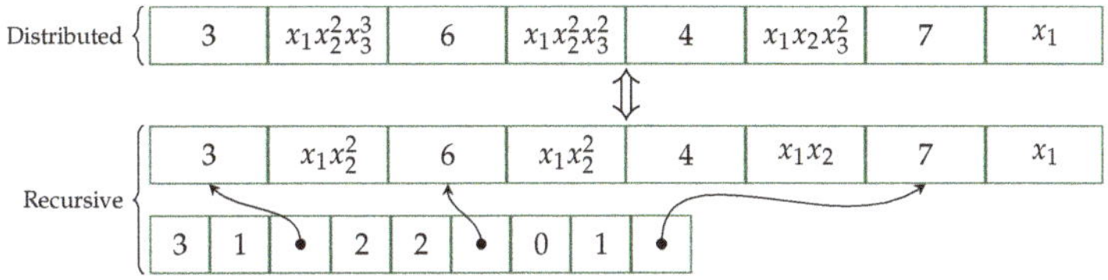

Figure 2. A distributed polynomial representation and its corresponding recursive polynomial representation, showing the additional secondary array. The secondary array alternates between: (1) degree of the main variable, (2) size of the coefficient polynomial, and (3) a pointer to the coefficient polynomial, which is simply an offset into the original distributed polynomial.

To view a polynomial recursively we begin by (conceptually) partitioning its terms into blocks based on the degree of the main (highest-ordered) variable. Since our polynomials are stored using a lexicographical term order, the terms of the polynomial are already sorted based on the degree of the main variable. Moreover, terms within the same block are already stored in lexicographical order with respect to the remaining variables. Therefore, each block will act as a multivariate polynomial coefficient of the univariate polynomial in the main variable. The partitioning is done in-place, without any memory movement, simply by maintaining an offset into the alternating array which signifies the beginning of a particular coefficient, in the recursive sense.

We create a secondary auxiliary array which holds these offsets, the number of terms in each polynomial coefficient, and the degree of the main variable. Simultaneously, the degree of the main variable in the original alternating array is set to 0. The degree of the main variable then does not pollute the polynomial coefficient arithmetic. This secondary array results in minimal overhead, particularly because its size is proportional to only the number of unique values of the degree of the main variable. Figure 2 highlights this secondary array as part of the recursive structure.

6.3. Heaps Optimized for Polynomial Multiplication

The largest effort required of our sparse multiplication algorithm (and thus also that of our division and pseudo-division algorithms) is to sort the terms of the product. Our algorithm makes use of a heap to do this sorting (much like heap sort), and thus arithmetic performance is largely dependent in the performance of the heap. Briefly, a heap is a data structure for efficiently obtaining the maximum (or minimum) from a continually updating collection of elements. This is achieved by using a binary tree, which stores key-value pairs, with a special *heap property*—children are always less than their parents in the tree. A more complete discussion of heaps can be found in ([26], Section 2.4).

The optimizations used in our heap implementation focus on two aspects, minimizing the working memory of the heap and minimizing the number of comparisons. The need for the latter should be obvious, while the need for the former is more subtle. Due to the encoding of a heap as a binary tree, parent nodes and child nodes are not adjacent to each other in memory; the heap must essentially perform random memory accesses across all its elements. In the sense of locality and cache usage, this is not ideal, yet unavoidable. Therefore, we look to minimize the size of the heap in hopes that it will entirely fit in cache and allow for quick access to all its elements.

The first optimization is due to [33] which reduces the number of comparisons required to remove the maximum element of the heap by a factor of two. The usual implementation of a heap removes the root node, swapping a leaf node into the hole, and then filtering it downward to re-establish the heap property. This requires two comparisons per level to determine which path to travel down. Instead, one can continuously promote the larger of the hole's two children until the hole is a leaf node. This requires only one comparison per level.

The second optimization called *chaining* reduces both the required number of comparisons and the amount of working memory for the heap. This technique is common in the implementation of hash tables for *conflict resolution* ([26], Chapter 3). Whenever a "conflict" occurs (when two elements are found to be equal) they form a *chain*, or linked list. Each node's key remains in the heap, but the values are now linked lists. Elements found to be equal simply add their value to the chain rather than insert a new element. This minimizes the number of elements in the heap but also allows extracting an entire chain, and therefore many elements, at the cost of removing a single element. This heap organization is presented in Figure 3.

In the context of polynomial multiplication, the exponent vector of the product term is the key while the value is a linked list of coefficients of the product. For our multiplication algorithm (Algorithm 2) we must also know from which stream a particular product term originated, and so should also store the stream index. However, to minimize the space required for the heap, while also storing the stream index (i.e., the multiplier term's index), we do not store the product term's coefficient at all and instead store the indices of the multiplier and multiplicand terms which together would produce a particular product term's coefficient. We do not need the coefficient of the product term to do the sorting, and so storing indices is more efficient. Moreover, delaying the multiplication of coefficients has benefits for locality. With chaining, removing the maximum element actually removes an entire chain of like terms, then the coefficient multiplication and addition of like terms can be done simultaneously.

Similar heap optimizations, including chaining, have been used in [6]. In contrast with our implementation, chaining in [32] used pointers to multiplier and multiplicand terms rather than indices. Integer indices (32 bits) are twice as efficient in memory usage as pointers on 64-bit machines, improving the overall memory and cache usage of the heap (and multiplication in general).

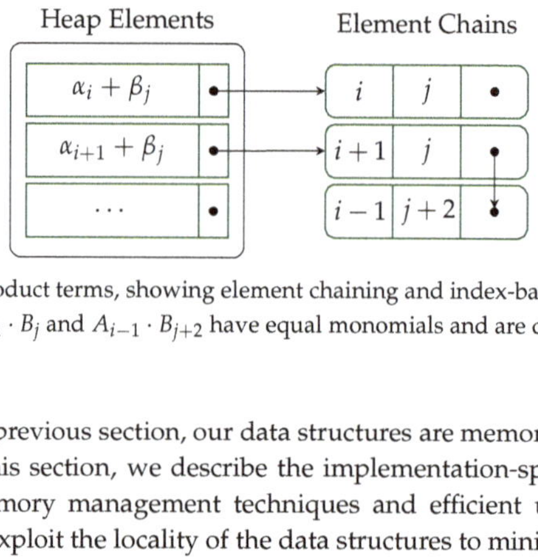

Figure 3. A heap of product terms, showing element chaining and index-based storing of coefficients. In this case, terms $A_{i+1} \cdot B_j$ and $A_{i-1} \cdot B_{j+2}$ have equal monomials and are chained together.

7. Implementation

As discussed in the previous section, our data structures are memory-efficient with exceptional data locality. Now, in this section, we describe the implementation-specific optimizations of our algorithms, such as memory management techniques and efficient use of our data structures. These implementations exploit the locality of the data structures to minimize cache complexity and improve performance. Formal cache complexity estimates of these algorithms are presented in [34]; we exclude them here and instead focus on motivations and techniques for reducing cache complexity in general.

We begin in Section 7.1 describing how to exploit our data structure for an optimized "in-place" addition (or subtraction) operation. Next, we discuss our implementations of multiplication (Section 7.2), division with remainder (Section 7.3), and pseudo-division (Section 7.4), all based on our heap data structure described above (Section 6.3). Lastly, we examine the application of these operations in our implementation of normal form and pseudo-division by a triangular set (Section 7.5).

7.1. In-Place Addition and Subtraction

An "in-place" algorithm suggests that the result is stored back into the same data structure as one of operands (or the only operand). This strategy is often motivated by either limited available memory resources or working with data that is too large to consider making a complete copy for the result. For our purposes, we are concerned with neither of these since our polynomial representations use relatively small amounts of memory. Hence, in-place operations are only of interest if they can improve running time. Generally speaking, in-place algorithms require more operations and more movement of data than out-of-place alternatives, making them most useful when the data set being sorted is so large that a copy cannot be afforded. For example, in-place merge sort has been a topic of discussion for decades, however, these implementations run 25–200% *slower* than an out-of-place implementation [35–37].

Due to the similarities between merge sort and polynomial addition (subtraction) it would seem unlikely that an in-place scheme would lead to performance benefits. However, our in-place addition becomes increasingly faster than out-of-place addition as coefficient sizes increase. This in-place addition scheme is not technically in-place, but it does exploit the structure of GMP numbers (as shown in Figure 1) for in-place coefficient arithmetic. In-place addition builds the resulting polynomial out-of-place but reuses the GMP *trees* of one of the operand polynomials. Rather than allocating a new GMP number—and thus a new GMP tree—in the resulting polynomial, we simply copy the head of one GMP number (and the pointer to its existing tree) into the new polynomial's alternating array, performing the coefficient arithmetic in-place. This saves on memory allocation and memory copying, and benefits from the improved performance of GMP when using in-place arithmetic ([31], Section 3.11).

These surprising results are highlighted in Figure 4 where out-of-place addition and its in-place counterpart are compared for various polynomial sizes with varying coefficient sizes. In-place addition has a speed-up factor of up to 3 for the coefficient sizes tested, with continued improvements as coefficient sizes grow larger. In-place arithmetic is put to use in pseudo-division to reduce the cost of polynomial coefficient arithmetic and improve the performance of pseudo-division itself. See Section 7.4 for this discussion.

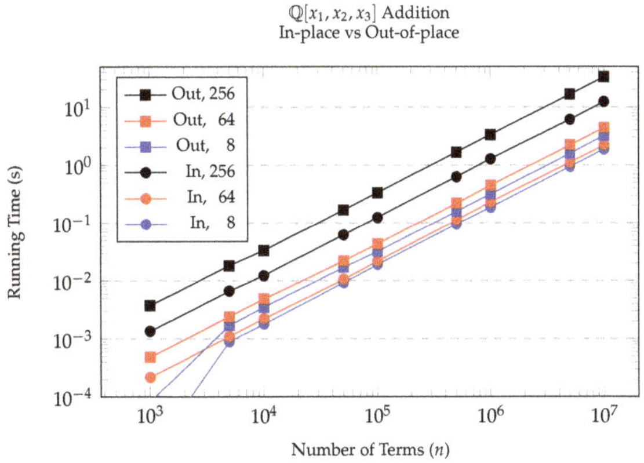

Figure 4. Comparing in-place and out-of-place polynomial addition. Random rational number polynomials in 3 variables are added together for various numbers of terms and for various coefficient sizes. The number of bits needed to encode the coefficients of the operands are shown in the legend. Notice this is a log-log plot.

7.2. Multiplication

The algorithm for polynomial multiplication (Algorithm 2) translates to code quite directly. However, we note some important implementation details to obtain better performance. Apart from the optimizations within the heap itself there are some implementation details concerning how the heap is used within multiplication to improve performance.

The first optimization makes use of the fact that multiplication is a commutative operation. Since the number of elements in the heap is equal to the number of streams, which is in turn equal to the number of terms in the multiplier (the factor a in $a \cdot b$), then we choose the multiplier to be the smaller operand, minimizing the size of the heap. The second optimization deals with the initialization of the heap. Due to the fact that for two terms A_i and B_j, $A_i \cdot B_j$ is always greater than $A_{i+1} \cdot B_j$ in the term order, then at the beginning of the multiplication algorithm it is only necessary to insert the term $A_{i+1} \cdot B_1$ after the term $A_i \cdot B_1$ has been removed from the heap.

A final optimization for multiplication deals with memory management. In particular, we know that for operands with n_a and n_b terms each, the maximum size of the product is $n_a \cdot n_b$. Therefore, we can pre-allocate this maximal size of the product (and similarly pre-allocate a maximal size n_a for the heap) before we begin computation. This eliminates any need for reallocation or memory movement, which can cause slowdowns. However, in the case where $n_a \cdot n_b$ is a very large number, say, exceeding 100 million, then we begin by only allocating 100 million terms for the product, doubling the allocation as needed in order amortize the cost of reallocation. Of course, any memory allocated in excess is freed at the end of the algorithm.

7.3. Division with Remainder

Polynomial division is essentially a direct application of polynomial multiplication. Again, we use heaps, with all the optimizations previously discussed, to produce the terms of the quotient-divisor product efficiently and in order. However, one important difference between division and multiplication is that the one of the operands of the quotient-divisor product, the quotient, is simultaneously being produced and consumed throughout the algorithm. Thus, we cannot pre-allocate space for the product or heap since the size of the quotient is unknown. Instead, we again follow a doubling of allocation strategy for the quotient and remainder to amortize the cost of reallocation. Moreover, we reallocate the space for the heap whenever we reallocate q since we know that the heap's maximum size will be equal to the number of terms in q. The added benefit of this is that the heap is guaranteed to have enough space to store all elements and does not need to check for overflow on each insert.

7.4. Pseudo-Division

As seen in Section 4.1 the algorithms for division (Algorithms 3 and 4) can easily be adapted to pseudo-division (Algorithms 5 and 6) by multiplying the dividend and quotient by the divisor's initial. However, the implementation between these two algorithms is very different. In essence, pseudo-division is a univariate operation, viewing the input multivariate polynomials recursively. That is, the dividend and divisor are seen as univariate polynomials over some arbitrary (polynomial) integral domain. Therefore, coefficients can be, and indeed are, entire polynomials themselves. Coefficient arithmetic becomes non-trivial. Moreover, the normal distributed polynomial representation would be inefficient to traverse and manipulate in this recursive way. Therefore, we use the recursive polynomial representation described in Section 6.1 with minimal overhead for conversion.

One of the largest performance concerns in this recursive view is the non-trivial coefficient arithmetic. As coefficients are now full polynomials there is more overhead in manipulating them and performing arithmetic. One important implementation detail is to perform the addition (and subtraction) of like terms in-place. Such combinations occur when computing the leading term of $h^\ell a - qb$ and when combining like terms in the quotient-divisor product. In-place addition, as described in Section 7.1, performs exceedingly better than out-of-place addition as the size of numerical coefficients grows, which occurs drastically during pseudo-division.

Similarly, the update of the quotient by multiplying by the initial of the divisor requires a multiplication of full polynomials. If we wish to save on memory movement we should perform this multiplication in-place as well. However, in our recursive representation (Figure 2), coefficient polynomials are tightly packed in a continuous array. To modify them in-place would require shifting all the following coefficients down the array to make room for the strictly large product polynomial. To avoid this unnecessary memory movement we modify the recursive data structure exclusively for the quotient polynomial; we break the continuous array of coefficients into many arrays, one for each coefficient. This allows them to grow without displacing the following coefficients. At the end of the algorithm, once the quotient has finished being produced, we collect and compact all of these disjoint polynomials into a single, packed array. In contrast, the remainder is never updated once its terms are produced, nor does it need to be viewed recursively, thus it is stored directly in the normal distributed representation, avoiding the unnecessary conversion out of the recursive representation.

7.5. Multi-Divisor (Pseudo-)Division

The performance of our normal form and multi-divisor pseudo-division algorithms primarily relies on the performance of the basic operations of division and pseudo-division, respectively. Hence, our normal form and multi-divisor pseudo-division algorithms gain significant performance benefits from the optimization of these lower-level operations. We only note two particular implementation details for these multi-divisor algorithms.

Firstly, the algorithms for normal form (Algorithm 7) and triangular set pseudo-division (Algorithm 8) use distributed and recursive polynomial representations, respectively, to manipulate operand polynomials appropriately for their operations. Secondly, we use in-place techniques, following the scheme of in-place addition (Section 7.1) to reduce the effects of GMP arithmetic and memory movement. Due to the recursive nature of these algorithms we can use a pre-allocation of memory as a destination to store both the final remainder and the remainder in each recursive call, continually reusing GMP coefficients.

8. Experimentation and Discussion

As we have seen in the previous two sections, our implementation has focused well on locality and memory usage in interest of obtaining performance. Indeed, as a result of the processor–memory gap this is highly important on modern architectures. The experimentation and benchmarks provided in this section substantiate our efforts where we will compare similar heap-based arithmetic algorithms provided in MAPLE [38].

Let us begin with a discussion on the quantification of sparsity with respect to polynomials. For univariate polynomials, sparsity can easily be defined as the maximum degree difference between any two successive non-zero terms. However, in the multivariate case, and in particular using lex ordering, there are infinitely many polynomial terms between x_1 and x_2, in the form of x_1^i. For multivariate polynomial, sparsity is less easily defined. Inspired by Kronecker substitution ([28], Section 8.4) we propose the following sparsity measure for multivariate polynomials adapted from the univariate case. Let $f \in R[x_1, \ldots, x_v]$ be non-zero and define $r = \max(\deg(f, x_i), 1 \le i \le v) + 1$. Then, every exponent vector $e := (e_1, \ldots, e_v)$ of a term of f can be viewed as an integer in a radix-r representation, $e_1 + e_2 r + \cdots + e_v r^{v-1}$. Viewing any two successive polynomial terms in f, say F_i and F_{i+1}, as integers in this radix-r representation, say c_i and c_{i+1}, we call the *sparsity* of f the smallest integer which is larger than the maximum value of $c_i - c_{i+1}$, for $1 \le i < n_f$.

Our experimentation uses randomly generated sparse polynomials whose generation is parameterized by several variables: the number of variables v, the number of terms n, the number of bits used to encode any coefficient (denoted coefficient bound), and a sparsity value s used to compute the radix $r = \lfloor \sqrt[v]{s \cdot n} \rfloor$ for use in generating exponent vectors as just defined. Our arithmetic algorithms, and code for generating random test instances, are openly available in the BPAS library [12].

We compare our arithmetic implementations against MAPLE for both integer polynomials and rational number polynomials. Thanks to the work by Monagan and Pearce [6,18,19,32] in recent years MAPLE has become the leader in integer polynomial arithmetic. Benchmarks there clearly show that their implementation outperforms many others including that of TRIP [39], MAGMA [40], SINGULAR [41], and PARI/GP [42]. Moreover, other common libraries like FLINT [43] and NTL [44] provide only univariate polynomials, so to compare our multivariate implementation against theirs would be unfair. Hence, we compare against MAPLE with its leading high-performance implementation. In particular, MAPLE 2017 with `kernelopts(numcpus = 1)` (which forces MAPLE to run serially.) Of course, the parallel arithmetic of MAPLE described in [18,19], which has been shown to achieve up to 17x parallel speed-up, could out-perform our serial implementation in some cases, such as multiplication and division over $\mathbb{Z}$. However, to be fair, we compare serial against serial.

Our benchmarks were collected on a machine running Ubuntu 14.04 using an Intel Xeon X560 processor (Intel, Santa Clara, CA, USA) at 2.67 GHz with 32 KB L1 data cache, 256 KB L2 cache, and 12288 KB L3 cache, with 12×4 GB of DDR3 RAM at 1333 MHz. In all the following timings we present the median time among 3 trials using 3 different sets of randomly generated input polynomials.

8.1. Multiplication and Division with Remainder

We compare multiplication and division with remainder against MAPLE for both polynomials over the rational numbers and the integers. For multiplication we call `expand` in MAPLE and for division with remainder we call `Groebner:-NormalForm`. Normal form is a more general algorithm for many divisors but reduces to division with remainder in the case of a single divisor. This operation appears to be the only documented algorithm for computing division with remainder in MAPLE. The optimized integer polynomial *exact* division of [6] appears in MAPLE as the `divide` operation. It would be unfair to use our division with remainder algorithm to compute exact divisions to compare against [6] directly (although, some examples of such are shown in Section 8.4). However, internally, `Groebner:-NormalForm` clears contents to work, at least temporarily, with integer polynomials for calls to `divide` and `expand` for division and multiplication operations, respectively, each of which is indeed optimized (Contents are cleared from (rational number) polynomials, to result in an integer polynomial, either via the basis computation or directly in the call to the underlying normal form function `Groebner:-Buchberger:-nfprocs`).

We begin by comparing our multiplication and division with remainder algorithms for polynomials over the rationals. MAPLE does not have an optimized data structure for polynomials with rational number coefficients [30], so this benchmark is meant to highlight the necessity of memory-efficient data structures for algorithmic performance. The plot in Figure 5a shows the performance of multiplication over $\mathbb{Q}$ for polynomials in 5 variables of varying sparsity and number of terms. The parameters specified determine how both the multiplier and multiplicand where randomly generated. The plot in Figure 5b shows the performance of division with remainder over $\mathbb{Q}$ for polynomials in 5 variables of varying sparsity and number of terms. For this division, we construct two polynomials f and g using the parameters specified and then perform the division $(f \cdot g + f)/g$. The disparity in running times between BPAS and MAPLE is very apparent, with multiple orders of magnitude separating the two. We see speed-ups of 333 for multiplication and 731 for division with remainder.

The same set of experiments were performed again for integer polynomials. Figure 6a,b shows multiplication and division with remainder, respectively, for polynomials over $\mathbb{Z}$. In this case, MAPLE features a more optimized data structure for polynomials over $\mathbb{Z}$ and performs relatively much better. However, BPAS still outperforms MAPLE with a speed-up factor of up to 3 for multiplication and 67 for division with remainder. The speed-up factors continue to grow as sparsity increases. This growth can be attributed to the fact that as sparsity increases, the number of like terms produced during a multiplication decreases. Hence, there is less coefficient arithmetic and many more terms in the product, highlighting the effects of better locality and memory management.

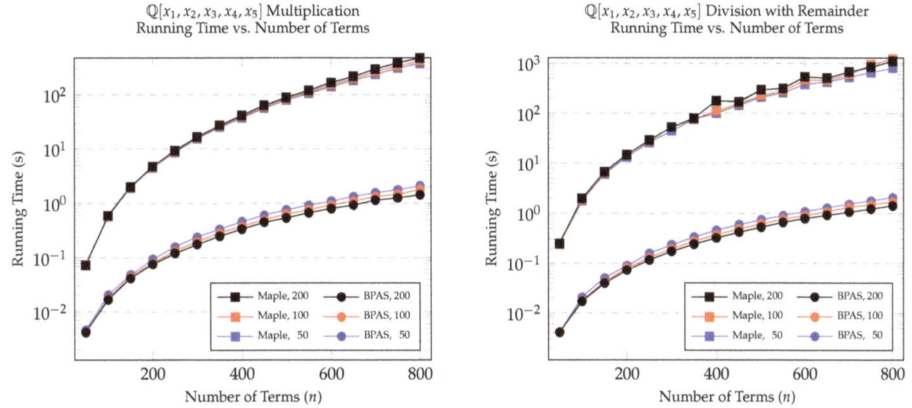

(**a**) Multiplication. (**b**) Division with remainder. $(fg + f)/g$ is performed.

Figure 5. Comparing multiplication and division with remainder over $\mathbb{Q}$. Polynomials are in 5 variables and the coefficient bound is 128. The sparsity varies as noted in the legend.

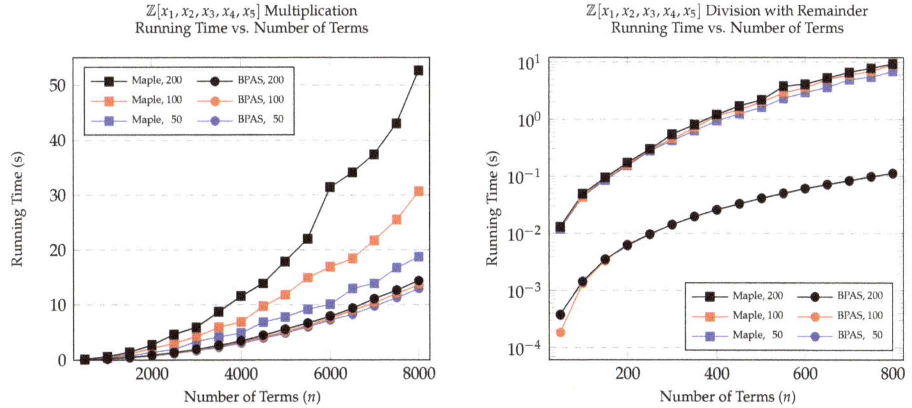

(**a**) Multiplication. (**b**) Division with remainder. $(fg + f)/g$ is performed.

Figure 6. Comparing multiplication and division with remainder over $\mathbb{Z}$. Polynomials are in 5 variables and the coefficient bound is 128. The sparsity varies as noted in the legend.

8.2. Pseudo-Division

We next compare the implementations of pseudo-division over $\mathbb{Z}$. We perform the pseudo-division of $(f \cdot g + f)$ by g for randomly generated f and g. However, since pseudo-division is essentially univariate, the randomly generated polynomials go through a secondary cleaning phase where the degree of the main variable is spread out evenly such that each polynomial coefficient, in the recursive sense, is the same size. This stabilizes the running time for randomly generated polynomials with the same number of terms. Figure 7b shows the running time of non-lazy pseudo-division, that is, ℓ is forced to be $\deg(a) - \deg(b) + 1$ in the pseudo-division equation $h^\ell a = qb + r$. Figure 7a shows a lazy pseudo-division, where ℓ is only as large as is needed to perform the pseudo-division. For lazy pseudo-division we see a speed-up factor of up to 2 while for non-lazy pseudo-division we see a speed-up factor of up to 178. A non-lazy pseudo-division's running time is usually dominated by coefficient polynomial arithmetic and performs much slower than the lazy version. Moreover, the gap between BPAS and MAPLE is much greater for non-lazy pseudo-division; increasing sparsity became a big problem in MAPLE, taking several hours to perform a single pseudo-division. Again, an increase in sparsity creates an increase in the number of terms in a polynomial product. Therefore, with our efficient memory management and use of data structures, increasing sparsity has little effect on our performance, in contrast to that of MAPLE. In MAPLE we call `prem` and `sprem` for non-lazy and lazy pseudo-division, respectively.

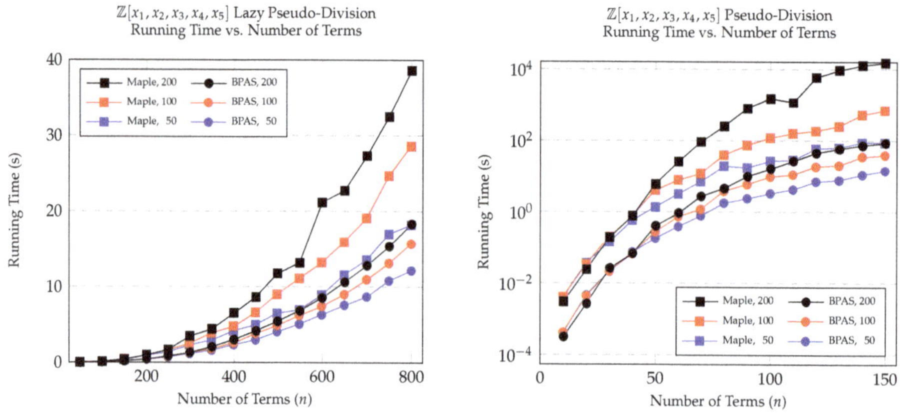

(**a**) Lazy pseudo-division of $fg + f$ by g. (**b**) Non-lazy pseudo-division of $fg + f$ by g.

Figure 7. Comparing lazy and non-lazy pseudo-division over $\mathbb{Z}$. Polynomials are in 5 variables and the coefficient bound is 128. The sparsity varies as noted in the legend.

8.3. Multi-Divisor Division and Pseudo-Division

For comparing multi-divisor division (normal form) and pseudo-division with respect to a triangular set, we require more structure to our operands. For these experiments we use a zero-dimensional normalized (Lazard) triangular set. For our benchmarks we use polynomials with 5 variables, say x_1, x_2, x_3, x_4, x_5, and thus a triangular set of size 5 ($\mathbf{T} = \{t_1, t_2, t_3, t_4, t_5\}$). The polynomials in the divisor set and dividend (a) are always fully dense and have the following degree pattern. For some positive integer Δ we let $\deg(a, x_1) = 2\Delta$, $\deg(a, x_i) = \lg(\Delta)$, $\deg(a, x_1) - \deg(t_1, x_1) = \Delta$ and $\deg(a, x_i) - \deg(t_i, x_i) = 1$ for $1 < i \leq 5$. There is a large gap in the lowest variable, but a small gap in the remaining variables, a common structure of which the recursive algorithms can take advantage. For both polynomials over $\mathbb{Q}$ (Figure 8a,b) and over $\mathbb{Z}$ (Figure 9a,b) we compare the naïve and recursive algorithms for both normal form and pseudo-division by a triangular set against MAPLE. For normal form we call MAPLE's `Groebner:-NormalForm` with respect to the `rem` while for triangular set pseudo-division we implement Algorithm 8 in MAPLE using `prem`. Since `prem` is a non-lazy pseudo-division, we similarly perform non-lazy pseudo-division in our implementations for a fair comparison. In general, the normal form results are relatively close, particularly in comparison to the differences between timings for pseudo-division. Our pseudo-division implementation sees several orders of magnitude speed-up against MAPLE thanks to our recursive scheme and optimized single-divisor pseudo-division.

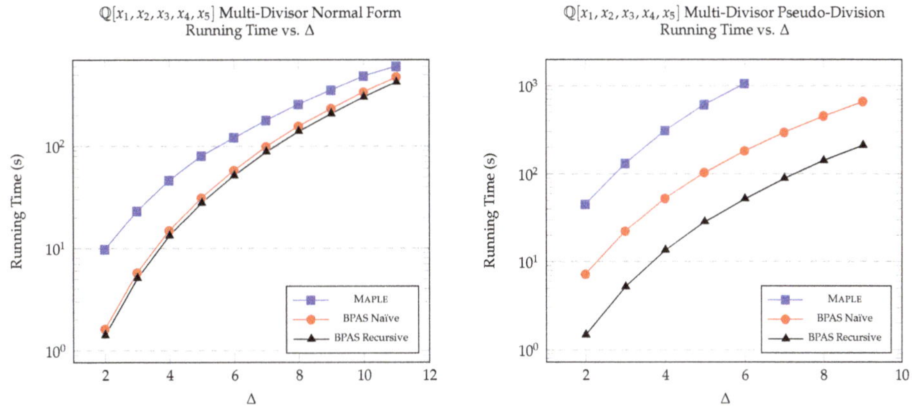

(**a**) Normal form. (**b**) Triangular set pseudo-division.

Figure 8. Comparing normal form and triangular set pseudo-division over $\mathbb{Q}$. For each, the naïve algorithm, the recursive algorithm, and the algorithm within MAPLE are compared. Polynomials are in 5 variables and the coefficient bound is 128.

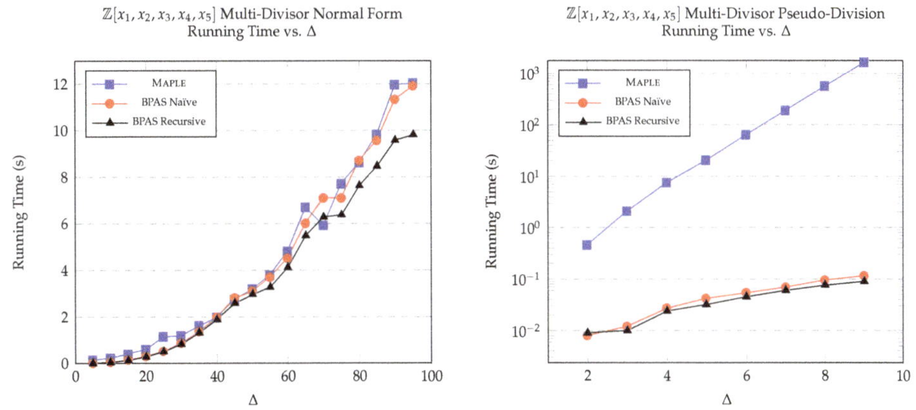

(**a**) Normal form. (**b**) Triangular set pseudo-division.

Figure 9. Comparing normal form and triangular set pseudo-division over $\mathbb{Z}$. For each, the naïve algorithm, the recursive algorithm, and the algorithm within MAPLE are compared. Polynomials are in 5 variables and the coefficient bound is 128.

8.4. Structured Problems

To further test our implementations on structured examples, rather than random, we look at two problems proposed by Monagan and Pearce in [6,45] and a classic third problem. First is the *sparse 10 variable problem*. In this problem $f_1 = (\sum_{i=1}^{9}(x_i x_{i+1} + x_i) + x_{10}x_1 + x_{10} + 1)^d$ and $g_1 = (\sum_{i=1}^{10}(x_i^2 + x_i) + 1)^d$. The multiplication $h_1 = f_1 \cdot g_1$ and the division $q_1 = h_1/f_1$ are performed. Second is the *very sparse 5 variable problem*. In this problem $f_2 = (1 + x_1 + x_2^2 + x_3^3 + x_4^5 + x_5^7)^d$ and $g_2 = (1 + x_1^7 + x_2^5 + x_3^3 + x_4^2 + x_5)^d$. The multiplication $h_2 = f_2 \cdot g_2$ and the division $q_2 = h_2/f_2$ are performed. Lastly, a classic problem in polynomial factorization and division, $f_3 = x^d - 1$ and $g_3 = x - 1$, performing f_3/g_3. Let us call this the dense quotient problem. The sparsity of the dividend is at a maximum, but the quotient produced is completely dense.

In these problems the coefficients are strictly machine-word sized, i.e., less than 64-bits. We concede that MAPLE uses more advanced techniques for coefficient arithmetic, using machine-word integers and arithmetic, if possible. This contrasts with our implementation which uses only arbitrary-precision integers. It is expected then for MAPLE to out-perform BPAS on these examples with machine-integer coefficients. However, this is only the case for the first two problems. To focus exclusively on the polynomial algorithms and not the integer arithmetic, we repeat the first two problems with arbitrary-precision coefficients, each term in f_1, g_1, f_2, g_2 is given a random positive integer coefficient using a coefficient bound. Table 1 shows the execution time and memory used (for all inputs and outputs) for these problems for various values of d. Multiplication again shows speed-up of a factor between 1.2 and 21.6, becoming increasingly better with increasing sparsity and number of terms. Division here is exact and, in comparison to division with remainder, MAPLE performs much better, likely thanks to their so-called *divisor heap* [32]. Only as sparsity increases does BPAS out-perform MAPLE. In all multi-precision cases, however, memory usage in BPAS is significantly better, being less than half that of MAPLE.

Table 1. Comparing multiplication and division on the three structured problems.

Operation	d	Coef. Bound	BPAS		MAPLE	
			Time (s)	Memory (MiB)	Time (s)	Memory (MiB)
Multiplication	4	1	4.28	172.11	1.78	79.31
$h_1 = f_1 \cdot g_1$	4	64	8.22	353.27	9.58	810.23
	5	64	155.51	2481.37	221.71	5569.25
Division	4	64	7.84	353.29	6.465	816.03
$q_1 = h_1 / f_1$	5	64	154.08	2509.42	124.37	5583.50
Multiplication	12	1	3.61	702.14	2.835	439.21
$h_2 = f_2 \cdot g_2$	12	32	7.62	1878.96	52.80	4026.29
	15	32	51.61	8605.52	1114.23	18,941.05
Division	12	32	8.09	1919.28	10.35	4033.57
$q_2 = h_2 / f_2$	15	32	57.09	8627.16	58.906	18,660.94
Division	1,000,000	1	0.18	38.59	1.505	164.54
$q_3 = f_3 / g_3$	10,000,000	1	1.87	522.65	23.63	1102.21

9. Conclusions and Future Work

In this paper, we have described algorithms and data structures for the high-performance sparse polynomial arithmetic as implemented in the freely available BPAS library. We have considered polynomials both over the integers and the rationals, where others have ignored the rationals; arithmetic over the rationals is important for areas such as Gröbner bases and polynomial system solving. The operations of multiplication, and division, have been extended from [24] to also include division with remainder and a new algorithm for sparse pseudo-division. We employ these fundamental algorithms for use in the mid-level algorithms of normal form and pseudo-division with respect to a triangular set. Our experimentation against MAPLE highlights how the proper treatment of locality and data structures can result huge improvements in memory usage and running time. We achieve orders of magnitude speed-up (for arithmetic over the rationals and non-lazy pseudo-division over the integers) or up to a factor of 67 (for other operations over the integers).

In the future we hope to apply these techniques for locality and arithmetic optimization to obtain efficient computations with regular chains and triangular decompositions. Following the design goals of the BPAS library we plan to apply parallelization to both the arithmetic operations presented in this paper and to upcoming work on triangular decompositions.

Author Contributions: Conceptualization, A.B. and M.M.M.; software, M.A. and A.B.; formal analysis, R.H.C.M.; investigation, M.A. and A.B.; writing—original draft preparation, M.A., A.B., R.H.C.M., M.M.M.; supervision, M.M.M.; project administration, M.M.M.; funding acquisition, M.M.M.

Funding: This research was funded by IBM Canada Ltd (CAS project 880) and Natural Sciences and Engineering Research Council of Canada (NSERC) CRD grant CRDPJ500717-16.

Conflicts of Interest: The authors declare no conflict of interest.

References

1. Hall, A.D., Jr. The ALTRAN system for rational function manipulation-a survey. In Proceedings of the Second ACM Symposium on Symbolic and Algebraic Manipulation, Los Angeles, CA, USA, 23–25 March 1971; ACM: New York, NY, USA, 1971; pp. 153–157.
2. Martin, W.A.; Fateman, R.J. The MACSYMA system. In Proceedings of the Second ACM Symposium on Symbolic and Algebraic Manipulation, Los Angeles, CA, USA, 23–25 March 1971; ACM: New York, NY, USA, 1971; pp. 59–75.
3. Hearn, A.C. REDUCE: A user-oriented interactive system for algebraic simplification. In *Symposium on Interactive Systems for Experimental Applied Mathematics, Proceedings of the Association for Computing Machinery Inc. Symposium, Washington, DC, USA, 1 August 1967*; ACM: New York, NY, USA, 1967; pp. 79–90.
4. Van der Hoeven, J.; Lecerf, G. On the bit-complexity of sparse polynomial and series multiplication. *J. Symb. Comput.* **2013**, *50*, 227–254, doi:10.1016/j.jsc.2012.06.004. [CrossRef]
5. Arnold, A.; Roche, D.S. Output-Sensitive Algorithms for Sumset and Sparse Polynomial Multiplication. In Proceedings of the ISSAC 2015, Bath, UK, 6–9 July 2015; pp. 29–36. [CrossRef]
6. Monagan, M.B.; Pearce, R. Sparse polynomial division using a heap. *J. Symb. Comput.* **2011**, *46*, 807–822. [CrossRef]
7. Gastineau, M.; Laskar, J. Highly Scalable Multiplication for Distributed Sparse Multivariate Polynomials on Many-Core Systems. In Proceedings of the CASC, Berlin, Germany, 9–13 September 2013; pp. 100–115.
8. Hennessy, J.L.; Patterson, D.A. *Computer Architecture: A Quantitative Approach*, 4th ed.; Morgan Kaufmann: San Francisco, CA, USA, 2007.
9. Wulf, W.A.; McKee, S.A. Hitting the memory wall: Implications of the obvious. *ACM SIGARCH Comput. Archit. News* **1995**, *23*, 20–24. [CrossRef]
10. Asadi, M.; Brandt, A.; Moir, R.H.C.; Moreno Maza, M. Sparse Polynomial Arithmetic with the BPAS Library. In Proceedings of the Computer Algebra in Scientific Computing—20th International Workshop (CASC 2018), Lille, France, 17–21 September 2018; pp. 32–50. [CrossRef]
11. Chen, C.; Moreno Maza, M. Algorithms for computing triangular decomposition of polynomial systems. *J. Symb. Comput.* **2012**, *47*, 610–642. [CrossRef]
12. Asadi, M.; Brandt, A.; Chen, C.; Covanov, S.; Mansouri, F.; Mohajerani, D.; Moir, R.H.C.; Moreno Maza, M.; Wang, L.X.; Xie, N.; et al. Basic Polynomial Algebra Subprograms (BPAS). 2018. Available online: http://www.bpaslib.org (accessed on 16 May 2019).
13. Frigo, M.; Leiserson, C.E.; Prokop, H.; Ramachandran, S. Cache-Oblivious Algorithms. *ACM Trans. Algorithms* **2012**, *8*, 4. [CrossRef]
14. Leiserson, C.E. Cilk. In *Encyclopedia of Parallel Computing*; Springer: Boston, MA, USA, 2011; pp. 273–288. [CrossRef]
15. Moreno Maza, M.; Xie, Y. Balanced Dense Polynomial Multiplication on Multi-Cores. *Int. J. Found. Comput. Sci.* **2011**, *22*, 1035–1055. [CrossRef]
16. Chen, C.; Covanov, S.; Mansouri, F.; Moreno Maza, M.; Xie, N.; Xie, Y. Parallel Integer Polynomial Multiplication. *arXiv* **2016**, arXiv:1612.05778.
17. Covanov, S.; Mohajerani, D.; Moreno Maza, M.; Wang, L.X. Big Prime Field FFT on Multi-core Processors. In Proceedings of the ISSAC, Beijing, China, 15–18 July 2019; ACM: New York, NY, USA, 2019.
18. Monagan, M.B.; Pearce, R. Parallel sparse polynomial multiplication using heaps. In Proceedings of the ISSAC, Seoul, Korea, 29–31 July 2009; pp. 263–270.

19. Monagan, M.; Pearce, R. Parallel sparse polynomial division using heaps. In Proceedings of the PASCO, Grenoble, France, 21–23 July 2010; ACM: New York, NY, USA, 2010; pp. 105–111.
20. Biscani, F. Parallel sparse polynomial multiplication on modern hardware architectures. In Proceedings of the 37th International Symposium on Symbolic and Algebraic Computation, Grenoble, France, 22–25 July 2012; ACM: New York, NY, USA, 2012; pp. 83–90.
21. Gastineau, M.; Laskar, J. Parallel sparse multivariate polynomial division. In Proceedings of the PASCO 2015, Bath, UK, 10–12 July 2015; pp. 25–33. [CrossRef]
22. Popescu, D.A.; Garcia, R.T. Multivariate polynomial multiplication on gpu. *Procedia Comput. Sci.* **2016**, *80*, 154–165. [CrossRef]
23. Ewart, T.; Hehn, A.; Troyer, M. VLI–A Library for High Precision Integer and Polynomial Arithmetic. In Proceedings of the International Supercomputing Conference, Leipzig, Germany, 16–20 June 2013; Springer: Berlin/Heidelberg, Germany, 2013; pp. 267–278.
24. Johnson, S.C. Sparse polynomial arithmetic. *ACM SIGSAM Bull.* **1974**, *8*, 63–71. [CrossRef]
25. Li, X.; Moreno Maza, M.; Schost, É. Fast arithmetic for triangular sets: From theory to practice. *J. Symb. Comput.* **2009**, *44*, 891–907. [CrossRef]
26. Sedgewick, R.; Wayne, K. *Algorithms*, 4th ed.; Addison-Wesley: Boston, MA, USA, 2011.
27. Cox, D.A.; Little, J.; O'shea, D. *Ideals, Varieties, and Algorithms*, 2 ed.; Springer: New York, NY, USA, 1997.
28. Von zur Gathen, J.; Gerhard, J. *Modern Computer Algebra*, 2 ed.; Cambridge University Press: New York, NY, USA, 2003.
29. Gastineau, M.; Laskar, J. Development of TRIP: Fast Sparse Multivariate Polynomial Multiplication Using Burst Tries. In Proceedings of the Computational Science—ICCS 2006, 6th International Conference, Reading, UK, 28–31 May 2006; Part II, pp. 446–453. [CrossRef]
30. Monagan, M.; Pearce, R. The design of Maple's sum-of-products and POLY data structures for representing mathematical objects. *ACM Commun. Comput. Algebra* **2015**, *48*, 166–186. [CrossRef]
31. Granlund, T.; others. *GNU MP 6.0 Multiple Precision Arithmetic Library*; Samurai Media Limited: Surrey, UK, 2015.
32. Monagan, M.; Pearce, R. Polynomial division using dynamic arrays, heaps, and packed exponent vectors. In Proceedings of the CASC 2007, Bonn, Germany, 16–20 September 2007; Springer: Berlin/Heidelberg, Germany, 2007; pp. 295–315.
33. Gonnet, G.H.; Munro, J.I. Heaps on heaps. *SIAM J. Comput.* **1986**, *15*, 964–971. [CrossRef]
34. Brandt, A. High Performance Sparse Multivariate Polynomials: Fundamental Data Structures and Algorithms. Master's Thesis, The University of Western Ontario, London, ON, Canada, 2018.
35. Huang, B.C.; Langston, M.A. Practical in-place merging. *Commun. ACM* **1988**, *31*, 348–352. [CrossRef]
36. Katajainen, J.; Pasanen, T.; Teuhola, J. Practical in-place mergesort. *Nord. J. Comput.* **1996**, *3*, 27–40.
37. Dalkilic, M.E.; Acar, E.; Tokatli, G. A simple shuffle-based stable in-place merge algorithm. *Procedia Comput. Sci.* **2011**, *3*, 1049–1054. [CrossRef]
38. Waterloo Maple Inc. MAPLE *2017—The Essential Tool for Mathematics*; Waterloo Maple Inc.: Waterloo, ON, Canada, 2017.
39. Gastineau, M.; Laskar, J. TRIP: A Computer Algebra System Dedicated to Celestial Mechanics and Perturbation Series. *ACM Commun. Comput. Algebra* **2011**, *44*, 194–197. [CrossRef]
40. Bosma, W.; Cannon, J.; Playoust, C. The Magma algebra system. I. The user language. *J. Symb. Comput.* **1997**, *24*, 235–265. [CrossRef]
41. Decker, W.; Greuel, G.M.; Pfister, G.; Schönemann, H. SINGULAR 4-1-1—A Computer Algebra System for Polynomial Computations. 2018 Available online: http://www.singular.uni-kl.de (accessed on 15 March 2019).
42. The PARI Group, Univ. Bordeaux. *PARI/GP Version* 2.3.3. 2008. Available online: http://pari.math.u-bordeaux.fr/ (accessed on 15 March 2019).
43. Hart, W.; Johansson, F.; Pancratz, S. FLINT: Fast Library for Number Theory. V. 2.4.3. Available online: http://flintlib.org (accessed on 15 March 2019).

44. Shoup, V. NTL: A Library for Doing Number Theory. Available online: www.shoup.net/ntl/ (accessed on 15 March 2019).
45. Monagan, M.B.; Pearce, R. Sparse polynomial multiplication and division in Maple 14. *ACM Commun. Comput. Algebra* **2010**, *44*, 205–209. [CrossRef]

© 2019 by the authors. Licensee MDPI, Basel, Switzerland. This article is an open access article distributed under the terms and conditions of the Creative Commons Attribution (CC BY) license (http://creativecommons.org/licenses/by/4.0/).

mathematics MDPI

Article

A Heuristic Method for Certifying Isolated Zeros of Polynomial Systems

Xiaojie Dou [1] and Jin-San Cheng [2,*]

[1] College of Science, Civil Aviation University of China, Tianjin 300300, China; xjdou@amss.ac.cn
[2] KLMM, Academy of Mathematics and Systems Science, Chinese Academy of Sciences, Beijing 100190, China
* Correspondence: jcheng@amss.ac.cn

Received: 12 July 2018; Accepted: 3 September; Published: 11 September 2018

Abstract: In this paper, by transforming the given over-determined system into a square system, we prove a necessary and sufficient condition to certify the simple real zeros of the over-determined system by certifying the simple real zeros of the square system. After certifying a simple real zero of the related square system with the interval methods, we assert that the certified zero is a local minimum of sum of squares of the input polynomials. If the value of sum of squares of the input polynomials at the certified zero is equal to zero, it is a zero of the input system. As an application, we also consider the heuristic verification of isolated zeros of polynomial systems and their multiplicity structures.

Keywords: over-determined polynomial system; isolated zeros; minimum point; sum of squares; interval methods

1. Introduction

Finding zeros of polynomial systems is a fundamental problem in scientific computing. Newton's method is widely used to solve this problem. For a fixed approximate solution of a system, we can use the α-theory [1–3], the interval methods or the optimization methods [4–9] to completely determine whether it is related to a zero of the system. However, the α-theory or the interval methods focuses mainly on a simple zero of a square system, that is, a system with n equations and n unknowns.

Some special certifications of a rational solution of rational polynomials with certified sum of squares decompositions are considered [10–16].

What about singular zeros of a well-constrained polynomial system? Usually, an over-determined system which contains the same zero as a simple one is constructed by introducing new equations. The basic idea is the deflation techniques [17–24]. In some studies [25–30], new variables are also included. Moreover, some authors verify that a perturbed system possesses an isolated singular solution within a narrow and computed error bound. The multiplicity structures of singular zeros of a polynomial system are also studied [18,21,29]. Although it is in a theoretical sense and global sense, the method in [17] provides a sufficient condition that a zero is exactly a zero of a zero-dimensional polynomial system with rational coefficients.

For the deflation methods mentioned above, on the one hand, to be a zero of the perturbed systems does not mean being a zero of the input system considering the difference between the two systems; on the other hand, although the over-determined systems without introducing new variables have the same zeros as the input systems, the verification methods, such as the α-theory or the interval methods, could not be used directly on the over-determined systems in general.

In [31], the authors extended the α-theory from well-constrained systems to over-determined systems. A main result about Newton's method given in their paper is their Theorem 4 [31], which says that under the condition of $2\alpha_1(g,\zeta) < 1$, where $g = (g_1,\ldots,g_m) \in (\mathbb{C}[x_1,\ldots,x_n])^m (m \geq n)$, $\mathbf{J}(g)(x)^\dagger$ is the Moore–Penrose inverse of the Jacobian matrix $\mathbf{J}(g)(x)$ of g and

$$\alpha_1(g,x) = \beta_1(g,x)\gamma_1(g,x),$$
$$\beta_1(g,x) = \|\mathbf{J}(g)(x)^\dagger\|\|g(x)\|,$$
$$\gamma_1(g,x) = \sup_{k\geq 2}\left(\|\mathbf{J}(g)(x)^\dagger\|\frac{\mathbf{J}^k(g)(x)}{k!}\right)^{\frac{1}{k-1}},$$

ζ is an attractive fixed point for Newton's method and, simultaneously, a strict local minimum for $\|g\|^2 = \sum_{j=1}^{m} \|g_j\|^2$. However, as they stated, whether the attracting fixed points for Newton's method are always local minima of $\|g\|^2$, or the zeros of the input system, is unknown.

In this paper, we consider the problem of certifying the simple real zeros of an over-determined polynomial system. Given $\Sigma = \{f_1,\ldots,f_m\} \in (\mathbb{R}[x_1,\ldots,x_n])^m (m \geq n)$, we construct a new square system $\Sigma' = \{\frac{\partial f}{\partial x_1},\ldots,\frac{\partial f}{\partial x_n}\}$ with $f = \sum_{i=1}^{m} f_i^2$. After transforming the input over-determined system into a square one, we can use both the α-theory and the interval methods to certify its simple zeros. In this paper, we only consider using the interval methods to certify the simple real zeros of the over-determined system. We prove that the simple real zeros of the input system are local minima of sum of squares of the input polynomials. We also give the condition that the local minimum is a simple zero of the input system.

Let $\mathbb{R}$ be the field of real numbers. Denote $\mathbb{R}[\mathbf{x}] = \mathbb{R}[x_1,\ldots,x_n]$ as the polynomial ring. Let $\mathbf{F} = \{f_1,\ldots,f_m\} \subset \mathbb{R}[\mathbf{x}]$ be a polynomial system. Let $\mathbf{p} = (p_1,\ldots,p_n) \in \mathbb{R}^n$.

The following theorem is the main result of this paper.

Theorem 1. *Let $\Sigma = \{f_1,\ldots,f_m\} \subset \mathbb{R}[\mathbf{x}]$ $(m \geq n)$ and $f = \sum_{i=1}^{m} f_i^2$. Then, we have:*

1. *If $\mathbf{p} \in \mathbb{R}^n$ is an isolated simple real zero of Σ, $\mathbf{p}$ is a local minimum of f.*
2. *$\mathbf{p}$ is a simple real zero of Σ if and only if $(\mathbf{p},0)$ is a simple real zero of the square system $\Sigma_r = \{\mathbf{J}_1(f),\ldots,\mathbf{J}_n(f), f-r\}$, where $\mathbf{J}_i(f) = \frac{\partial f}{\partial x_i}$ and r is a new variable.*

In the above theorem, we get a necessary and sufficient condition to certify the simple real zeros of the input system Σ by certifying the simple real zeros of the square system Σ_r. Therefore, to certify that $\mathbf{p}$ is a simple real zero of Σ, the key point is verifying that $f(\mathbf{p}) = 0$.

However, it is difficult to decide numerically if a point is a zero of a polynomial. Thus, we cannot use the necessary and sufficient condition to certify the simple real zeros of Σ by certifying the simple real zeros of Σ_r.

As an alternative, we refine and certify the simple real zeros of Σ by refining and certifying a new square system $\Sigma' = \{\mathbf{J}_1(f),\ldots,\mathbf{J}_n(f)\}$ with the interval methods and get a verified inclusion $\mathbf{X}$, which contains a unique simple real zero $\hat{\mathbf{x}}$ of Σ'. In fact, $\hat{\mathbf{x}}$ is a local minimum of f, which also is a necessary condition for the certification. On the one hand, if $f(\hat{\mathbf{x}}) = 0$, by Theorem 1, $(\hat{\mathbf{x}},0)$ is a simple real zero of Σ_r, and then $\hat{\mathbf{x}}$ is a simple real zero of Σ. Thus, we certified the input system Σ. On the other hand, if $f(\hat{\mathbf{x}}) \neq 0$, we can only assert that Σ_r has a unique zero in the verified inclusion $\mathbf{X} \times [0, f(\hat{\mathbf{x}})]$, which means we certified the system Σ_r.

A big difference between this paper and our pervious work [32] is that we do not merely consider certifying simple zeros of over-determined polynomial systems, but also consider the certification of the general isolated zeros. Specifically, as an application of our method, we give a heuristic method for certifying not only the isolated singular zeros of polynomial systems, but also the multiplicity structures of the isolated singular zeros of polynomial systems.

This paper is an extended version of the CASC'17 conference paper [32].

The paper is organized as follows. We introduce some notations and preliminaries in the next section. In Section 3, we give a method to show how to transform an over-determined system into a square one. The interval verification method on the obtained square system is considered in Section 4. We give two applications of our method in Section 5 and draw conclusions in Section 6.

2. Preliminaries

Let $\mathbb{C}$ be the field of complex numbers. Denote $\mathbb{C}[\mathbf{x}] = \mathbb{C}[x_1, \ldots, x_n]$ as the polynomial ring. Let $\mathbf{F} = \{f_1, \ldots, f_m\} \subset \mathbb{C}[\mathbf{x}]$ be a polynomial system. Let $\mathbf{p} = (p_1, \ldots, p_n) \in \mathbb{C}^n$. $\mathbf{F}(\mathbf{p}) = \mathbf{0}$ denote that $\mathbf{p}$ is a zero of $\mathbf{F}(\mathbf{x}) = \mathbf{0}$.

Let A be a matrix. Denote A^T as the transpose of A and $\mathrm{rank}(A)$ as the rank of A. Let $\mathrm{M}at(a_{i,j})$ denote the matrix whose i-th row j-th column element is $a_{i,j}$.

Let $\Sigma = \{f_1, \ldots, f_m\} \subset \mathbb{C}[\mathbf{x}]$ be a polynomial system. Denote $\mathbf{J}(\Sigma)$ as the Jacobian matrix of Σ. That is,

$$\mathbf{J}(\Sigma) = \begin{pmatrix} \frac{\partial f_1}{\partial x_1} & \cdots & \frac{\partial f_1}{\partial x_n} \\ \vdots & \ddots & \vdots \\ \frac{\partial f_m}{\partial x_1} & \cdots & \frac{\partial f_m}{\partial x_n} \end{pmatrix}.$$

For a polynomial $f \in \mathbb{C}[\mathbf{x}]$, let $\mathbf{J}(f)$ denote $(\frac{\partial f}{\partial x_1}, \frac{\partial f}{\partial x_2}, \ldots, \frac{\partial f}{\partial x_n})$, $\mathbf{J}_i(f) = \frac{\partial f}{\partial x_i}$ and $\mathbf{J}_{i,j}(f) = \mathbf{J}_j(\mathbf{J}_i(f)) = \frac{\partial^2 f}{\partial x_j \partial x_i}$. Denote $\Sigma_r = \{\mathbf{J}_1(f), \ldots, \mathbf{J}_n(f), f - r\}$ with $f = \sum_{j=1}^{m} f_j^2$.

We denote the value of a function matrix $A \in \mathbb{C}[\mathbf{x}]^{n \times n}$ at a point $\mathbf{p} \in \mathbb{C}^n$ as $A(\mathbf{p})$. Let $\mathbf{J}(\mathbf{F})(\mathbf{p})$ denote the value of a function matrix $\mathbf{J}(\mathbf{F})$ at a point $\mathbf{p}$, similarly for $\mathbf{J}(f)(\mathbf{p})$.

Definition 1. *An* **isolated solution** *of* $\mathbf{F}(\mathbf{x}) = \mathbf{0}$ *is a point* $\mathbf{p} \in \mathbb{C}^n$ *which satisfies:*

$$\exists\, \varepsilon > 0 : \{\mathbf{y} \in \mathbb{C}^n : \|\mathbf{y} - \mathbf{p}\| < \varepsilon\} \cap \mathbf{F}^{-1}(\mathbf{0}) = \{\mathbf{p}\}.$$

Definition 2. *We call an isolated solution* $\mathbf{p} \in \mathbb{C}^n$ *of* $\mathbf{F}(\mathbf{x}) = \mathbf{0}$ *a* **singular solution** *if and only if*

$$\mathrm{rank}(\mathbf{J}(\mathbf{F})(\mathbf{p})) < n.$$

Otherwise, we call $\mathbf{p}$ *a* **simple solution**.

Definition 3. *A* **stationary point** *of a polynomial function* $f(\mathbf{x}) \in \mathbb{C}[\mathbf{x}]$ *is a point* $\mathbf{p} \in \mathbb{C}^n$, *which satisfies:*

$$\frac{\partial f}{\partial x_i}(\mathbf{p}) = 0,\ \forall\, i = 1, \ldots, n.$$

We can find the following lemma in many undergraduate textbooks about linear algebra (see Example 7 on page 224 in [33] for example).

Lemma 1. *Let $A \in \mathbb{R}^{m\times n}$ be a real matrix with $m \geq n$ and $B = A^T A$. Then, the ranks of A and B are the same, especially for the case that A is of full rank.*

In the following, we consider the real zeros of the systems with real coefficients. It is reasonable since, for a system (m equations and n unknowns) with complex coefficients, we can rewrite the system into a new one with $2\,m$ equations and $2\,n$ unknowns by splitting the unknowns $x_i = x_{i,1} + \mathbf{i}\, x_{i,2}$ and equations $f_j(x_1, \ldots, x_n) = g_{j,1}(x_{1,1}, x_{1,2}, \ldots, x_{n,1}, x_{n,2}) + \mathbf{i}\, g_{j,2}(x_{1,1}, x_{1,2}, \ldots, x_{n,1}, x_{n,2})$, where $\mathbf{i}^2 = -1$, $f_j \in \mathbb{C}[\mathbf{x}]$, $g_{j,1}, g_{j,2} \in \mathbb{R}[\mathbf{x}]$, $j = 1, \ldots, m$, and find the complex zeros of the original system by finding out the real zeros of the new system.

3. Transforming Over-determined Polynomial Systems into Square Ones

In this section, we show how to transform an over-determined polynomial system into a square one with their zeros having a one-to-one correspondence, especially for the simple zeros.

By Definition 3, we have the following lemma:

Lemma 2. *Given a polynomial system $\Sigma = \{f_1, \ldots, f_m\} \subset \mathbb{R}[\mathbf{x}]$ ($m \geq n$). Let $f = \sum_{i=1}^{m} f_i^2$ and $\Sigma' = \{\mathbf{J}_1(f), \mathbf{J}_2(f), \ldots, \mathbf{J}_n(f)\}$. If $\mathbf{p} \in \mathbb{R}^n$ is an isolated real zero of Σ', then $\mathbf{p}$ is a stationary point of f.*

Lemma 3. *Let $\Sigma = \{f_1, \ldots, f_m\} \subset \mathbb{R}[\mathbf{x}]$ ($m \geq n$), $\Sigma' = \{\mathbf{J}_1(f), \mathbf{J}_2(f), \ldots, \mathbf{J}_n(f)\}$ with $f = \sum_{i=1}^{m} f_i^2$. If $\mathbf{p} \in \mathbb{R}^n$ is an isolated real zero of Σ, then we have:*

1. *$\mathbf{p}$ is an isolated real zero of Σ'.*
2. $\operatorname{rank}(\mathbf{J}(\Sigma)(\mathbf{p})) = \operatorname{rank}(\mathbf{J}(\Sigma')(\mathbf{p}))$.

Proof. It is clear that $\mathbf{p}$ is an isolated real zero of Σ' providing that $\mathbf{p}$ is an isolated real zero of Σ, since $\mathbf{J}_i(f) = 2 \sum_{k=1}^{m} f_k \mathbf{J}_i(f_k)$.

To prove the second part of this lemma, we rewrite $\mathbf{J}_i(f)$ as follows.

$$\mathbf{J}_i(f) = 2\,\langle f_1, \ldots, f_m\rangle\,\langle \mathbf{J}_i(f_1), \ldots, \mathbf{J}_i(f_m)\rangle^T, \tag{1}$$

where $\langle\,\cdot\,\rangle^T$ is the transpose of a vector or a matrix $\langle\,\cdot\,\rangle$. Then,

$$\begin{aligned} \mathbf{J}_{i,j}(f) &= \mathbf{J}_j(\mathbf{J}_i(f)) = \mathbf{J}_j(2\sum_{k=1}^{m} f_k \mathbf{J}_i(f_k)) = 2\sum_{k=1}^{m}(\mathbf{J}_j(f_k)\mathbf{J}_i(f_k) + f_k \mathbf{J}_{i,j}(f_k)) \\ &= 2\,\langle \mathbf{J}_j(f_1), \ldots, \mathbf{J}_j(f_m)\rangle\,\langle \mathbf{J}_i(f_1), \ldots, \mathbf{J}_i(f_m)\rangle^T + 2\sum_{k=1}^{m} f_k \mathbf{J}_{i,j}(f_k). \end{aligned} \tag{2}$$

Then, the Jacobian matrix of Σ' is

$$\mathbf{J}(\Sigma') = \begin{pmatrix} \mathbf{J}_{1,1}(f) & \cdots & \mathbf{J}_{1,n}(f) \\ \vdots & \ddots & \vdots \\ \mathbf{J}_{n,1}(f) & \cdots & \mathbf{J}_{n,n}(f) \end{pmatrix} = \operatorname{Mat}(\mathbf{J}_{i,j}(f)).$$

We rewrite

$$\text{Mat}(\mathbf{J}_{i,j}(f)) = 2\,A^T A + 2\,\text{Mat}(\sum_{k=1}^{m} f_k \mathbf{J}_{i,j}(f_k)), \tag{3}$$

where

$$A = \begin{pmatrix} \mathbf{J}_1(f_1) & \cdots & \mathbf{J}_n(f_1) \\ \vdots & \ddots & \vdots \\ \mathbf{J}_1(f_m) & \cdots & \mathbf{J}_n(f_m) \end{pmatrix}$$

is an $m \times n$ matrix which is exactly the Jacobian matrix of Σ, that is, $\mathbf{J}(\Sigma) = A$. Then, we have

$$\mathbf{J}(\Sigma')(\mathbf{p}) = 2A(\mathbf{p})^T A(\mathbf{p}). \tag{4}$$

By Lemma 1, the second part of the lemma is true. This ends the proof. □

Remark 1. *In our construction of f and Σ', the degrees of the polynomials almost be doubled compared to the original one. However, to evaluate the Jacobian matrix of Σ', we evaluate the Jacobian matrix of the original system with $m^2 n$ numerical products. One can find it from Equation (4) in the above proof. In fact, to get $\mathbf{J}(\Sigma')(\mathbf{p})$, we only need to compute $A(\mathbf{p})$, which does not increase our actual computing degree.*

As a byproduct, thanks to the doubled degree of the polynomials, our final certified accuracy is also improved in Lemma 4.

The following is the proof of Theorem 1:

Proof. In fact, by fixing the real zero $\mathbf{p}$ as an isolated simple zero in Lemma 3, we have $\mathbf{p}$ is an isolated simple real zero of $\Sigma' = \{\mathbf{J}_1(f), \ldots, \mathbf{J}_n(f)\}$. Since $\mathbf{p}$ is an isolated simple zero of Σ, $A(\mathbf{p})$ is a column full rank matrix. Therefore, it is easy to verify that $\mathbf{J}(\Sigma')(\mathbf{p}) = 2\,A(\mathbf{p})^T A(\mathbf{p})$ is a positive definite matrix. Thus, $\mathbf{p}$ is a local minimum of f and the first part of the theorem is true. Now, we consider the second part.

First, it is easy to verify that $\mathbf{p}$ is the real zero of Σ if and only if $(\mathbf{p}, 0)$ is the real zero of Σ_r. Notice that $\Sigma_r = \{\Sigma', f - r\}$. Thus, with the same method as proving Lemma 3, we can compute easily that

$$\mathbf{J}(\Sigma_r)(\mathbf{p}, 0) = \begin{pmatrix} \mathbf{J}(\Sigma')(\mathbf{p}) & 0 \\ 0 & -1 \end{pmatrix} = \begin{pmatrix} 2\mathbf{J}(\Sigma)(\mathbf{p})^T\mathbf{J}(\Sigma)(\mathbf{p}) & 0 \\ 0 & -1 \end{pmatrix},$$

which implies that

$$\text{rank}(\mathbf{J}(\Sigma)(\mathbf{p})) = \text{rank}(\mathbf{J}(\Sigma')(\mathbf{p})) = \text{rank}(\mathbf{J}(\Sigma_r)(\mathbf{p}, 0)) - 1, \tag{5}$$

which means that $\mathbf{J}(\Sigma_r)(\mathbf{p}, 0)$ is of full rank if and only if $\mathbf{J}(\Sigma)(\mathbf{p})$ is of full rank. Thus, $\mathbf{p}$ is an isolated simple zero of Σ if and only if $(\mathbf{p}, 0)$ is an isolated simple zero of Σ_r. The second part is true. We have finished the proof. □

From Theorem 1, we know that the simple real zeros of Σ and Σ_r are in one-to-one correspondence with the constraint that the value of the sum of squares of the polynomials in Σ at the simple real zeros is identically zero. Thus, we can transform an over-determined polynomial system into a square system Σ_r.

We show a simple example to illustrate the theorem below.

Example 1. *The simple zero* $\mathbf{p} = (0,0)$ *of the over-determined system* $\Sigma = \{f_1, f_2, f_3\}$ *corresponds to a simple zero of a square system* $\Sigma_r = \{\mathbf{J}_1(f), \mathbf{J}_2(f), f - r\}$, *where* $f = f_1^2 + f_2^2 + f_3^2$ *with*

$$f_1 = x^2 - 2y, f_2 = y^2 - x, f_3 = x^2 - 2x + y^2 - 2y.$$

We can verify simply that $(\mathbf{p}, 0)$ *is a simple zero of* Σ_r.

Although the simple real zeros of Σ and Σ_r have a one-to-one correspondence, it cannot be used directly to do certification of the simple zeros of Σ since we cannot certify $r = 0$ numerically. However, we can certify the zeros of $\Sigma' = \{\mathbf{J}_1(f), \mathbf{J}_2(f), \ldots, \mathbf{J}_n(f)\}$ as an alternative, which is a necessary condition for the certification.

We discuss it in next section.

4. Certifying Simple Zeros of Over-determined Systems

In this section, we consider certifying the over-determined system with the interval methods. We prove the same local minimum result as [31].

The classical interval verification methods are based on the following theorem:

Theorem 2 ([5,6,8,30]). *Let* $\mathbf{f} = (f_1, \ldots, f_n) \in (\mathbb{R}[\mathbf{x}])^n$ *be a polynomial system,* $\tilde{x} \in \mathbb{R}^n$, *real interval vector* $X \in \mathbb{IR}^n$ *with* $\mathbf{0} \in X$ *and real matrix* $R \in \mathbb{R}^{n \times n}$ *be given. Let an interval matrix* $M \in \mathbb{IR}^{n \times n}$ *be given whose i-th row* M_i *satisfies*

$$\{\nabla f_i(\zeta) : \zeta \in \tilde{x} + X\} \subseteq M_i.$$

Denote by I the $n \times n$ *identity matrix and assume*

$$-R\mathbf{f}(\tilde{x}) + (I - RM)X \subseteq int(X),$$

where $int(X)$ *denotes the interior of X. Then, there is a unique* $\hat{x} \in \tilde{x} + X$ *with* $\mathbf{f}(\hat{x}) = \mathbf{0}$. *Moreover, every matrix* $\tilde{M} \in M$ *is nonsingular. In particular, the Jacobian* $\mathbf{J}(\mathbf{f})(\hat{x})$ *is nonsingular.*

About interval matrices, there is an important property in the following theorem.

Theorem 3 ([34]). *A symmetric interval matrix* A^I *is positive definite if and only if it is regular and contains at least one positive definite matrix.*

Given an over-determined polynomial system $\Sigma = \{f_1, \ldots, f_m\} \subset \mathbb{R}[\mathbf{x}]$ with an isolated simple real zero, we can compute a related square system

$$\Sigma' = \{\frac{\partial f}{\partial x_1}, \frac{\partial f}{\partial x_2}, \ldots, \frac{\partial f}{\partial x_n}\} \text{ with } f = \sum_{j=1}^{m} f_j^2.$$

Based on Lemma 3, a simple zero of Σ is a simple zero of Σ'. Thus, we can compute the approximate simple zero of Σ by computing the approximate simple zero of Σ'. Using Newton's method, we can refine these approximate simple zeros with quadratic convergence to a relative higher accuracy. Then, we can certify them with the interval method mentioned before and get a verified inclusion $\mathbf{X}$, which possesses a unique certified simple zero of the system Σ' by Theorem 2, denoting as $\hat{\mathbf{x}} \in \mathbf{X}$.

However, even though we get a certified zero $\hat{\mathbf{x}}$ of the system Σ', considering Lemma 2, we cannot say $\hat{\mathbf{x}}$ is a zero of the input system Σ. Because the certified zero $\hat{\mathbf{x}}$ is just a stationary point of f. Considering Theorem 1 and the difference between Σ' and Σ_r, we have the following theorem.

Theorem 4. *Let Σ, Σ', Σ_r, f, $\hat{\mathbf{x}}$ and the interval $\mathbf{X}$ be given as above. Then, we have:*

1. *$\hat{\mathbf{x}}$ is a local minimum of f.*
2. *There exists a verified inclusion $\mathbf{X} \times [0, f(\hat{\mathbf{x}})]$ that possesses a unique simple zero of the system Σ_r. Especially, if $f(\hat{\mathbf{x}}) = 0$, the verified inclusion $\mathbf{X}$ possesses a unique simple zero of the input system Σ.*

Proof. First, it is easy to see that computing the value of the matrix $\mathbf{J}(\Sigma')$ at the interval $\mathbf{X}$ will give a symmetric interval matrix, denoting as $\mathbf{J}(\Sigma')(\mathbf{X})$. By Theorem 2, we know that, for every matrix $M \in \mathbf{J}(\Sigma')(\mathbf{X})$, M is nonsingular. Therefore, the interval matrix $\mathbf{J}(\Sigma')(\mathbf{X})$ is regular. Especially, the matrix $\mathbf{J}(\Sigma')(\hat{\mathbf{x}})$, which is the Hessian matrix of f, is full rank and, therefore, is positive definite. Thus, $\hat{\mathbf{x}}$ is a local minimum of f. By Theorem 3, we know that $\mathbf{J}(\Sigma')(\mathbf{X})$ is positive definite. Thus, for every point $\mathbf{q} \in \mathbf{X}$, $\mathbf{J}(\Sigma')(\mathbf{q})$ is a positive definite matrix. Considering Theorem 2, it is trivial that, for the verified inclusion $\mathbf{X} \times [0, f(\hat{\mathbf{x}})]$, there exists a unique simple zero of the system Σ_r. If $f(\hat{\mathbf{x}}) = 0$, by Theorem 1, the verified inclusion $\mathbf{X}$ of the system Σ' is a verified inclusion of the original system Σ. □

Remark 2. 1. *In the above proof, we know that, for every point $\mathbf{q} \in \mathbf{X}$, $\mathbf{J}(\Sigma')(\mathbf{q})$ is a positive definite matrix.*

2. *By Theorem 2, we know that there is a unique $\hat{\mathbf{x}} \in \mathbf{X}$ with $\Sigma'(\hat{\mathbf{x}}) = \mathbf{0}$. However, we could not know what the exact $\hat{\mathbf{x}}$ is. According to the usual practice, in actual computation, we take the midpoint $\hat{\mathbf{p}}$ of the inclusion $\mathbf{X}$ as $\hat{\mathbf{x}}$ and verify whether $f(\hat{\mathbf{p}}) = 0$. Considering the uniqueness of $\hat{\mathbf{x}}$ in $\mathbf{X}$, therefore, if $f(\hat{\mathbf{p}}) = 0$, we are sure that the verified inclusion $\mathbf{X}$ possesses a unique simple zero of the input system Σ. If $f(\hat{\mathbf{p}}) \neq 0$, we can only claim that there is a local minimum of f in the inclusion $\mathbf{X}$ and $\mathbf{X} \times [0, f(\hat{\mathbf{p}})]$ is a verified inclusion for the system Σ_r.*

Considering the expression of Σ and f and for the midpoint $\hat{\mathbf{p}}$ of $\mathbf{X}$, we have a trivial result below.

Lemma 4. *Denote $\epsilon = \max_{j=1}^{m} |f_j(\hat{\mathbf{p}})|$. Under the conditions of Theorem 4, we have $|f(\hat{\mathbf{p}})| \leq m\epsilon^2$.*

Based on the above idea, we give an algorithm below. In the verification steps, we apply algorithm **verifynlss** in INTLAB [30], which is based on Theorem 2, to compute a verified inclusion $\mathbf{X}$ for the related square system Σ'. For simplicity, denote the interval $\mathbf{X} = [\underline{x}_1, \overline{x}_1], \cdots, [\underline{x}_m, \overline{x}_m]$ and the midpoint of $\mathbf{X}$ as $\hat{\mathbf{p}} = [(\underline{x}_1 + \overline{x}_1)/2, \ldots, (\underline{x}_m + \overline{x}_m)/2]$.

The correctness and the termination of the algorithm is obvious by the above analysis.

We give two examples to illustrate our algorithm.

Example 2. *Continue Example 1. Given an approximate zero $\tilde{\mathbf{p}} = (0.0003528, 0.0008131)$, using Newton's method, we get a higher accuracy approximate zero*

$$\tilde{\mathbf{p}}' = 10^{-11} \cdot (-0.104224090958505, -0.005858368844383).$$

Compute $f = f_1^2 + f_2^2 + f_3^2$ *and* $\Sigma' = \{\mathbf{J}_1(f), \mathbf{J}_2(f)\}$. *After applying algorithm* **verifynlss** *on* Σ', *we have a verified inclusion:*

$$\mathbf{X} = \begin{pmatrix} [-0.11330049261083, \ 0.11330049261083] \\ [-0.08866995073891, \ 0.08866995073891] \end{pmatrix} \cdot 10^{-321}.$$

Based on Theorem 2, we know that there exists a unique $\hat{\mathbf{x}} \in \mathbf{X}$, *such that* $\Sigma'(\hat{\mathbf{x}}) = \mathbf{0}$.

Let $\Sigma_r = \{\mathbf{J}_1(f), \mathbf{J}_2(f), f - r\}$. *By Theorem 1, we can certify the simple zero of* Σ *by certifying the simple zero of* Σ_r *theoretically. Considering the difference between* Σ' *and* Σ_r, *we check first whether the value of* f *at some point in the interval* $\mathbf{X}$ *is zero. According to the usual practice, we consider the midpoint* $\hat{\mathbf{p}}$ *of* $\mathbf{X}$, *which equals* $(0, 0)$ *and, further,* $f(\hat{\mathbf{p}})$ *is zero. Therefore, we are sure that there exists a unique* $\hat{\mathbf{x}} = (\hat{x}, \hat{y}) \in \mathbf{X}$, *s.t.* $\Sigma_r((\hat{\mathbf{x}}, 0)) = \mathbf{0}$ *and, then, there exists a unique simple zero* $(\hat{x}, \hat{y}) \in \mathbf{X}$ *of the input system* Σ, *which means we certified the input system* Σ.

Example 3. *Let* $\Sigma = \{f_1 = x_1^2 + 3\,x_1x_2 + 3\,x_1x_3 - 3\,x_3^2 + 2\,x_2 + 2\,x_3, f_2 = -3\,x_1x_2 + x_1x_3 - 2\,x_2^2 + x_3^2 + 3\,x_1 + x_2, f_3 = 2\,x_2x_3 + 3\,x_1 - 3\,x_3 + 2, f_4 = -6\,x_2^2x_3 + 2\,x_2x_3^2 + 6\,x_2^2 + 15\,x_2x_3 - 6\,x_3^2 - 9\,x_2 - 7\,x_3 + 6\}$ *be an over-determined system. Consider an approximate zero*

$$\tilde{\mathbf{p}} = (-1.29655, 0.47055, -0.91761).$$

Using Newton's method, we get a higher accuracy zero

$$\tilde{\mathbf{p}}' = (-1.296687216045438, 0.470344502045004, -0.917812633399457).$$

Compute

$$f = f_1^2 + f_2^2 + f_3^2 + f_4^2 \text{ and } \Sigma' = \{\mathbf{J}_1(f), \mathbf{J}_2(f), \mathbf{J}_3(f)\}.$$

After applying algorithm **verifynlss** *on* Σ', *we have a verified inclusion:*

$$\mathbf{X} = \begin{pmatrix} [-1.29668721603974, \ -1.29668721603967] \\ [\ \ 0.47034450205107, \ \ 0.47034450205114] \\ [-0.91781263339256, \ -0.91781263339247] \end{pmatrix}.$$

Similarly, based on Theorem 2, we know that there exists a unique $\hat{\mathbf{x}} \in \mathbf{X}$, *such that* $\Sigma'(\hat{\mathbf{x}}) = \mathbf{0}$.

Proceeding as in the above example, we consider the midpoint $\hat{\mathbf{p}}$ *of* $\mathbf{X}$ *and compute* $f(\hat{\mathbf{p}}) = 3.94 \cdot 10^{-31} \neq 0$. *Thus, by Theorem 4, we get a verified inclusion* $\mathbf{X} \times [0, f(\hat{\mathbf{p}})]$, *which contains a unique simple zero of the system* Σ_r. *It means that* $\mathbf{X}$ *may contain a zero of* Σ. *Even if* $\mathbf{X}$ *does not contain a zero of* Σ, *it contains a local minimum of* f, *which has a minimum value no larger than* $f(\hat{\mathbf{p}})$.

5. Two Applications

As an application, we consider certifying isolated singular zeros of over-determined systems heuristically. Generally, dealing with the multiple zeros of polynomial systems directly is difficult. The classical method to deal with the isolated singular zeros of polynomial systems is the deflation technique, which constructs a new system owning the same singular zero as an isolated simple one. Although the deflation method can be used to refine or verify the isolated zero of the original system, it is a pity that the multiplicity information of the isolated zero is missed. In this section, as an application of the method of converting an over-determined system into a square system in previous section, we give a heuristic method for certifying isolated singular zeros of polynomial systems and their multiplicity structures.

5.1. Certifying Isolated Singular Zeros of Polynomial Systems

Recently, Cheng et al. [35] proposed a new deflation method to reduce the multiplicity of an isolated singular zero of a polynomial system to get a final system, which owns the isolated singular zero of the input system as a simple one. Different from the previous deflation methods, they considered the deflation of isolated singular zeros of polynomial systems from the perspective of linear combination.

In this section, we first give a brief introduction of their deflation method and, then, show how our method is applied to certify the isolated singular zeros of the input system in a heuristic way.

Definition 4. *Let* $f \in \mathbb{C}[\mathbf{x}]$, $\tilde{\mathbf{p}} \in \mathbb{C}^n$ *and a tolerance* $\theta > 0$, *s.t.* $|f(\tilde{\mathbf{p}})| < \theta$. *We say* f *is* **θ-singular** *at* $\tilde{\mathbf{p}}$ *if*

$$\left|\frac{\partial f(\tilde{\mathbf{p}})}{\partial x_j}\right| < \theta, \forall 1 \le j \le n.$$

Otherwise, we say f *is* **θ-regular** *at* $\tilde{\mathbf{p}}$.

Let $\mathbf{F} = \{f_1, \ldots, f_n\} \subset \mathbb{C}[\mathbf{x}]$ be a polynomial system. $\tilde{\mathbf{p}} \in \mathbb{C}^n$ is an approximate isolated zero of $\mathbf{F} = \mathbf{0}$. Consider a tolerance θ. First, we can compute the polynomials of all $f_i (i = 1, \ldots, n)$, which is θ-regular at the approximate zero $\tilde{\mathbf{p}}$. That is, we compute a polynomial set

$$\mathbf{G} = \{\mathbf{d}_{\mathbf{x}}^{\gamma}(f) | \mathbf{d}_{\mathbf{x}}^{\gamma}(f) \text{ is } \theta\text{-regular at } \tilde{\mathbf{p}}, f \in \mathbf{F}\}.$$

Then, put $\mathbf{G}$ and $\mathbf{F}$ together and compute a subsystem $\mathbf{H} = \{h_1, \ldots, h_s\} \subset \mathbf{G} \cup \mathbf{F}$, whose Jacobian matrix at $\tilde{\mathbf{p}}$ has a maximal rank s. If $s = n$, we get the final system $\widetilde{\mathbf{F}}' = \mathbf{H}$. Otherwise, we choose a new polynomial $h \in \mathbf{G} \cup \mathbf{F} \setminus \mathbf{H}$ and compute

$$g = h + \sum_{i=1}^{s} \alpha_i h_i,\ g_j = \frac{\partial h}{\partial x_j},\ j = 1, \ldots, n,$$

where α_j, $j = 1, \ldots, n$ are new introduced variables. Next, we check if

$$\operatorname{rank}(\mathbf{J}(\mathbf{H}, g_1, \ldots, g_n)(\tilde{\mathbf{p}})) = n + s. \tag{6}$$

If Equation (6) holds, we get the final system $\widetilde{\mathbf{F}}' = \mathbf{H} \cup \{g_1, \ldots, g_n\}$. Otherwise, let $\mathbf{H} := \mathbf{H} \cup \{g_1, \ldots, g_n\} \subset \mathbb{C}[\mathbf{x}, \boldsymbol{\alpha}]$ and repeat again until Equation (6) holds.

Now, we give an example to illustrate the above idea.

Example 4. *Consider a polynomial system* $\mathbf{F} = \{f_1 = -\frac{9}{4} + \frac{3}{2}x_1 + 2x_2 + 3x_3 + 4x_4 - \frac{1}{4}x_1^2, f_2 = x_1 - 2x_2 - 2x_3 - 4x_4 + 2x_1x_2 + 3x_1x_3 + 4x_1x_4, f_3 = 8 - 4x_1 - 8x_4 + 2x_4^2 + 4x_1x_4 - x_1x_4^2, f_4 = -3 + 3x_1 + 2x_2 + 4x_3 + 4x_4\}$. *Consider an approximate singular zero*

$$\tilde{\mathbf{p}} = (\tilde{p}_1, \tilde{p}_2, \tilde{p}_3, \tilde{p}_4) = (1.00004659, -1.99995813, -0.99991547, 2.00005261)$$

of $\mathbf{F} = \mathbf{0}$ *and the tolerance* $\varepsilon = 0.005$.

First, we have the Taylor expansion of f_3 *at* $\tilde{\mathbf{p}}$*:*

$$f_3 = 3\times 10^{-9} - 3\times 10^{-9}(x_1-\tilde{p}_1) + 0.00010522(x_4-\tilde{p}_4) + 0.99995341(x_4-\tilde{p}_4)^2$$
$$-0.00010522(x_1-\tilde{p}_1)(x_4-\tilde{p}_4) - (x_1-\tilde{p}_1)(x_4-\tilde{p}_4)^2.$$

Consider the tolerance $\theta = 0.05$*. Since*

$$|f_3(\tilde{\mathbf{p}})| < \theta,\ \left|\frac{\partial f_3}{\partial x_i}(\tilde{\mathbf{p}})\right| < \theta (i=1,2,3,4),\ \left|\frac{\partial^2 f_3}{\partial x_4^2}(\tilde{\mathbf{p}})\right| > \theta,$$

we get a polynomial

$$\frac{\partial f_3}{\partial x_4} = -8 + 4\,x_1 + 4\,x_4 - 2\,x_1x_4,$$

which is θ*-regular at* $\tilde{\mathbf{p}}$*. Similarly, by the Taylor expansion of* f_1, f_2, f_4 *at* $\tilde{\mathbf{p}}$*, we have that* f_1, f_2, f_4 *are all* θ*-regular at* $\tilde{\mathbf{p}}$*.*

Thus, we have

$$\mathbf{G} = \{f_1, f_2, -8 + 4\,x_1 + 4\,x_4 - 2\,x_1x_4, f_4\}.$$

Compute

$$r = \mathrm{rank}(\mathbf{J}(\mathbf{G})(\tilde{\mathbf{p}}), \varepsilon) = 3.$$

We can choose

$$\mathbf{H} = \{h_1 = f_1, h_2 = f_2, h_3 = -8 + 4\,x_1 + 4\,x_4 - 2\,x_1x_4\}$$

from $\mathbf{G}\cup\mathbf{F}$*. To* $h = f_4 \in \mathbf{G}\cup\mathbf{F}\setminus\mathbf{H}$*, let*

$$g = h + \alpha_1 h_1 + \alpha_2 h_2 + \alpha_3 h_3.$$

By solving a Least Square problem:

$$LeastSquares((\mathbf{J}(\mathbf{H},h)(\tilde{\mathbf{p}}))^T[\alpha_1,\alpha_2,\alpha_3,-1]^T = 0),$$

we get an approximate value:

$$(\tilde{\alpha}_1, \tilde{\alpha}_2, \tilde{\alpha}_3) = (-1.000006509, -0.9997557989, 0.000106178711).$$

Then, compute

$$\begin{cases} g_1 = \dfrac{\partial g}{\partial x_1} = 3 + \dfrac{3}{2}\alpha_1 + \alpha_2 + 4\alpha_3 - \dfrac{1}{2}\alpha_1 x_1 + 2\alpha_2 x_2 + 3\alpha_2 x_3 + 4\alpha_2 x_4 - 2\alpha_3 x_4, \\ g_2 = \dfrac{\partial g}{\partial x_2} = 2 + 2\alpha_1 - 2\alpha_2 + 2\alpha_2 x_1, \\ g_3 = \dfrac{\partial g}{\partial x_3} = 4 + 3\alpha_1 - 2\alpha_2 + 3\alpha_2 x_1, \\ g_4 = \dfrac{\partial g}{\partial x_4} = 4 + 4\alpha_1 - 4\alpha_2 + 4\alpha_3 + 4\alpha_2 x_1 - 2\alpha_3 x_1, \end{cases}$$

and we get a polynomial set

$$\mathbf{H}' = \{h_1, h_2, h_3, g_1, g_2, g_3, g_4\},$$

which satisfies

$$\text{rank}(\mathbf{J}(\mathbf{H}')(\tilde{\mathbf{p}}, \tilde{\alpha}_1, \tilde{\alpha}_2, \tilde{\alpha}_3), \varepsilon) = 7.$$

Thus, we get the final system $\widetilde{\mathbf{F}}'(\mathbf{x}, \boldsymbol{\alpha}) = \mathbf{H}'$.

In the above example, given a polynomial system $\mathbf{F}$ with an isolated singular zero $\mathbf{p}$, by computing the derivatives of the input polynomials directly or the linear combinations of the related polynomials, we compute a new system $\widetilde{\mathbf{F}}'$, which has a simple zero. However, generally, the final system $\widetilde{\mathbf{F}}'$ does not contain all $f_i (i = 1, \ldots, n)$. Thus, to ensure that the simple zero or parts of the simple zero of the square system $\widetilde{\mathbf{F}}'$ really correspond to the isolated singular zero of the original system, we put $\mathbf{F}$ and $\widetilde{\mathbf{F}}'$ together and consider certifying the over-determined system $\mathbf{F} \cup \widetilde{\mathbf{F}}'$ in the following.

Example 5. *Continue with Example 4. we put* $\mathbf{F}$ *and* $\widetilde{\mathbf{F}}'$ *together and get the over-determined system* $\Sigma = \mathbf{F} \cup \widetilde{\mathbf{F}}'$. *According to our method in Section 4, let*

$$f = \sum_{j=1}^{4} f_j^2 + h_3^2 + \sum_{j=1}^{4} g_j^2.$$

Then, we compute

$$\Sigma' = \{\frac{\partial f}{\partial x_1}, \ldots, \frac{\partial f}{\partial x_4}, \frac{\partial f}{\partial \alpha_1}, \ldots, \frac{\partial f}{\partial \alpha_3}\} \text{ and } \Sigma_r = \{\Sigma', \ f - r\}.$$

After applying algorithm **verifynlss** *on* Σ' *at* $(\tilde{\mathbf{p}}, \tilde{\alpha}_1, \tilde{\alpha}_2, \tilde{\alpha}_3)$, *we have a verified inclusion:*

$$\mathbf{X} = \begin{bmatrix} [\ 0.99999999999979, & 1.00000000000019] \\ [-2.00000000000060, & -1.99999999999945] \\ [-1.00000000000040, & -0.99999999999956] \\ [\ 1.99999999999998, & 2.00000000000002] \\ [-1.00000000000026, & -0.99999999999976] \\ [-1.00000000000022, & -0.99999999999975] \\ [-0.00000000000012, & 0.00000000000010] \end{bmatrix}$$

By Theorem 2, we affirm that there is a unique isolated simple zero $\hat{\mathbf{x}} \in \mathbf{X}$, *s.t.* $\Sigma'(\hat{\mathbf{x}}) = \mathbf{0}$.

Next, as in Examples 2 and 3, we consider the midpoint $(\hat{\mathbf{p}}, \hat{\boldsymbol{\alpha}})$ *of* $\mathbf{X}$ *and compute* $f(\hat{\mathbf{p}}, \hat{\boldsymbol{\alpha}}) = 4.0133 \times 10^{-28}$. *Thus, by Theorem 4, we get a verified inclusion* $\mathbf{X} \times [0, f(\hat{\mathbf{p}}, \hat{\boldsymbol{\alpha}})]$, *which contains a unique simple zero of the system* Σ_r. *It means that* $\mathbf{X}$ *may contain a zero of* Σ. *Even if* $\mathbf{X}$ *does not contain a zero of* Σ, *it contains a local minimum of* f, *which has a minimum value no larger than* $f(\hat{\mathbf{p}}, \hat{\boldsymbol{\alpha}})$.

In the above example, we get the verified inclusion $\mathbf{X} \times [0, f(\hat{\mathbf{p}}, \hat{\boldsymbol{\alpha}})]$ of the system Σ_r. Noticing that $f(\hat{\mathbf{p}}, \hat{\boldsymbol{\alpha}}) \neq 0$, according to Theorem 4, we are not sure if the verified inclusion $\mathbf{X}$ contains a unique simple zero of the system Σ. While, considering the value of $f(\hat{\mathbf{p}}, \hat{\boldsymbol{\alpha}})$ is very small, under certain numerical tolerance condition(for example 10^{-25}), we can deem that the verified inclusion $\mathbf{X}$ contains a simple zero of the system Σ. That is, we certified the over-determined system Σ and further certified the original system $\mathbf{F}$.

5.2. Certifying the Multiplicity Structures of Isolated Singular Zeros of Polynomial Systems

In recent years, Mourrain et al. [21,36] proposed a new deflation method, which can be used to refine the accuracy of an isolated singular zero and the parameters introduced simultaneously and, moreover, the parameters can describe the multiplicity structure at the zero. They also proved that the number of equations and variables in this deflation method depend polynomially on the number of variables and equations of the input system and the multiplicity of the singular zero. However, although they also showed that the isolated simple zeros of the extended polynomial system correspond to zeros of the input system, the extended system is usually an over-determined system. Therefore, the problem of knowing the multiplicity structure of the isolated singular zero exactly becomes the problem of solving or certifying the isolated simple zero of the over-determined system.

In this section, we first give a brief introduction of their deflation method and, then, show how our method is applied to certify the multiplicity structure of the isolated singular zero of the input system heuristically.

Let $\mathbf{F} = \{f_1, \ldots, f_m\} \subset \mathbb{C}[\mathbf{x}]$. Let $\mathbf{p} = (p_1, \ldots, p_n) \in \mathbb{C}^n$ be an isolated multiple zero of $\mathbf{F}$. Let $I = \langle f_1, \ldots, f_m \rangle$, $\mathfrak{m}_{\mathbf{p}}$ be the maximal ideal at $\mathbf{p}$ and Q be the primary component of I at $\mathbf{p}$ so that $\sqrt{Q} = \mathfrak{m}_{\mathbf{p}}$.

Consider the ring of power series $\mathbb{C}[[\boldsymbol{\partial}_{\mathbf{p}}]] := \mathbb{C}[[\partial_{1,\mathbf{p}}, \ldots, \partial_{n,\mathbf{p}}]]$ and we use the notation for $\beta = (\beta_1, \ldots, \beta_n) \in \mathbb{N}^n$:

$$\boldsymbol{\partial}_{\mathbf{p}}^{\beta}(f) := \partial_{1,\mathbf{p}}^{\beta_1} \cdots \partial_{n,\mathbf{p}}^{\beta_n} = \frac{\partial^{|\beta|} f}{\partial x_1^{\beta_1} \cdots \partial x_n^{\beta_n}}(\mathbf{p}), \text{ for } f \in \mathbb{C}[\mathbf{x}].$$

The deflation method based on the orthogonal primal-dual pairs of bases for the space $\mathbb{C}[\mathbf{x}]/Q$ and its dual $\mathscr{D} \subset \mathbb{C}[\boldsymbol{\partial}]$, which is illustrated in the following lemma.

Lemma 5. *Let* $\mathbf{F}$, $\mathbf{p}$, Q, $\mathscr{D}$ *be as in the above and* δ *be the multiplicity of* $\mathbf{F}$ *at* $\mathbf{p}$*. Then, there exists a primal-dual basis pair of the local ring* $\mathbb{C}[\mathbf{x}]/Q$ *with the following properties:*

1. *(a) The primal basis of the local ring* $\mathbb{C}[\mathbf{x}]/Q$ *has the form*

$$B := \{(\mathbf{x}-\mathbf{p})^{\alpha_0}, (\mathbf{x}-\mathbf{p})^{\alpha_1}, \ldots, (\mathbf{x}-\mathbf{p})^{\alpha_{\delta-1}}\}.$$

We can assume that $\alpha_0 = 0$ *and that the monomials in* B *are connected to 1. Define the set of exponents in* B

$$E := \{\alpha_0, \ldots, \alpha_{\delta-1}\}.$$

2. *The unique dual basis* $\boldsymbol{\Lambda} = \{\Lambda_0, \Lambda_1, \ldots, \Lambda_{\delta-1}\} \subset \mathscr{D}$ *orthogonal to* B *has the form:*

$$\begin{aligned}
\Lambda_0 &= \boldsymbol{\partial}_{\mathbf{p}}^{\alpha_0} = 1_{\mathbf{p}}, \\
\Lambda_1 &= \frac{1}{\alpha_1!}\boldsymbol{\partial}_{\mathbf{p}}^{\alpha_1} + \sum_{\substack{|\beta|<|\alpha_1| \\ \beta \notin E}} \nu_{\alpha_1,\beta} \frac{1}{\beta!}\boldsymbol{\partial}_{\mathbf{p}}^{\beta}, \\
&\;\vdots \\
\Lambda_{\delta-1} &= \frac{1}{\alpha_{\delta-1}!}\boldsymbol{\partial}_{\mathbf{p}}^{\alpha_{\delta-1}} + \sum_{\substack{|\beta|<|\alpha_{\delta-1}| \\ \beta \notin E}} \nu_{\alpha_{\delta-1},\beta} \frac{1}{\beta!}\boldsymbol{\partial}_{\mathbf{p}}^{\beta},
\end{aligned}$$

The above lemma says that, once given a primal basis B of the local ring $\mathbb{C}[\mathbf{x}]/Q$, there exists a unique dual basis $\mathbf{\Lambda}$, which can be used to determine the multiplicity structure of $\mathbf{p}$ in $\mathbf{F}$ and further the multiplicity δ of $\mathbf{p}$, orthogonal to B. Based on the known primal basis B, Mourrain et.al constructed the following parametric multiplication matrices, which can be used to determine the coefficients of the dual basis $\mathbf{\Lambda}$.

Definition 5. *Let B as defined in Lemma 5 and denote the exponents in B by $E := \{\alpha_0, \dots, \alpha_{\delta-1}\}$ as above. Let*

$$E^+ := \bigcup_{i=1}^{n} (E + \mathbf{e}_i)$$

with $E + \mathbf{e}_i = \{(\gamma_1, \dots, \gamma_i + 1, \dots, \gamma_n) : \gamma \in E\}$ and we denote $\partial(E) = E^+ \setminus E$. We define an array $\boldsymbol{\mu}$ of length $n\delta(\delta-1)/2$ consisting of 0s, 1s and the variables $\mu_{\alpha_i,\beta}$ as follows: for all α_i, $\alpha_k \in E$ and $j \in \{1, \dots, n\}$ the corresponding entry is

$$\mu_{\alpha_i,\alpha_l+\mathbf{e}_j} = \begin{cases} 1, & if\ \alpha_i = \alpha_k + \mathbf{e}_j \\ 0, & if\ \alpha_k + \mathbf{e}_j \in E,\ \alpha_i \neq \alpha_k + \mathbf{e}_j \\ \mu_{\alpha_i,\alpha_l+\mathbf{e}_j}, & if\ \alpha_k + \mathbf{e}_j \notin E. \end{cases}$$

The parametric multiplication matrices corresponding to E are defined for $i = 1, \dots, n$ by

$$\mathtt{M}_i^t(\boldsymbol{\mu}) := \begin{array}{|ccccc|} 0 & \mu_{\alpha_1,\mathbf{e}_i} & \mu_{\alpha_2,\mathbf{e}_i} & \cdots & \mu_{\alpha_{\delta-1},\mathbf{e}_i} \\ 0 & 0 & \mu_{\alpha_2,\alpha_1+\mathbf{e}_i} & \cdots & \mu_{\alpha_{\delta-1},\alpha_1+\mathbf{e}_i} \\ \vdots & \vdots & & & \vdots \\ 0 & 0 & 0 & \cdots & \mu_{\alpha_{\delta-1},\alpha_{\delta-2}+\mathbf{e}_i} \\ 0 & 0 & 0 & \cdots & 0 \end{array}.$$

Definition 6. *(Parametric normal form). Let $\mathbb{K} \subset \mathbb{C}$ be a field. We define*

$$\begin{aligned} \mathcal{N}_{z,\boldsymbol{\mu}} : \mathbb{K}[\mathbf{x}] &\longrightarrow \mathbb{K}[\mathbf{z}, \boldsymbol{\mu}]^\delta \\ f &\longmapsto \mathcal{N}_{\mathbf{z},\boldsymbol{\mu}}(f) := f(\mathbf{z} + \mathtt{M}(\boldsymbol{\mu}))[1] = \sum_{\gamma \in \mathbb{N}^n} \frac{1}{\gamma!} \partial_{\mathbf{z}}^{\gamma}(f) \mathtt{M}(\boldsymbol{\mu})^{\gamma}[1]. \end{aligned}$$

where $[1] = [1, 0, \dots, 0]$ is the coefficient vector of 1 in the basis B.

Based on the above lemma and definitions, the multiplicity structure are characterized by polynomial equations in the following theorem.

Theorem 5 ([36]). *Let $\mathbb{K} \subset \mathbb{C}$ be any field, $\mathbf{F} \subset \mathbb{K}[\mathbf{x}]$, and let $\mathbf{p} \in \mathbb{C}^n$ be an isolated zero of $\mathbf{F}$. Let Q be the primary ideal at $\mathbf{p}$ and assume that B is a basis for $\mathbb{K}[\mathbf{x}]/Q$ satisfying the conditions of Lemma 5. Let $E \subset \mathbb{N}^n$ be as in Lemma 5 and $\mathtt{M}_i(\boldsymbol{\mu})$ for $i = 1, \dots, n$ be the parametric multiplication matrices corresponding to E as in Definition 5 and $\mathcal{N}_{\mathbf{z},\boldsymbol{\mu}}$ be the parametric form as in Definition 6. Then, $(\mathbf{z}, \boldsymbol{\mu}) = (\mathbf{p}, \boldsymbol{\nu})$ is an isolated zero with multiplicity one of the polynomial system in $\mathbb{K}[\mathbf{z}, \boldsymbol{\mu}]$:*

$$\begin{cases} \mathcal{N}_{\mathbf{z},\boldsymbol{\mu}}(f_k) = 0,\ for\ k = 1, \dots, m, \\ \mathtt{M}_i(\boldsymbol{\mu}) \cdot \mathtt{M}_j(\boldsymbol{\mu}) - \mathtt{M}_j(\boldsymbol{\mu}) \cdot \mathtt{M}_i(\boldsymbol{\mu}) = 0,\ for\ i, j = 1, \dots, n. \end{cases} \tag{7}$$

The second part of Equation (7) gives a pairwise commutation relationship of the parametric multiplication matrices. Moreover, Theorem 5 makes sure that Equation (7) has an isolated zero $(\mathbf{p}, \boldsymbol{\nu})$ of multiplicity one. Thus, it can be used to deflate the isolated zero $\mathbf{p}$ of the input system $\mathbf{F}$ and simultaneously determine the multiplicity structure of $\mathbf{p}$.

Now, we show an example to illustrate how their method works.

Example 6. *Let* $\mathbf{F} = \{f_1 = x_1 + x_2 + x_1^2, f_2 = x_1 + x_2 + x_2^2\}$ *be a polynomial system with a three-fold isolated zero* $\mathbf{p} = (0,0)$. *Given the primal basis* $B = \{1, x_1, x_1^2\}$, *which satisfies the properties of Lemma 5, we can compute the parametric multiplication matrices:*

$$\mathtt{M}_1^t(\boldsymbol{\mu}) = \begin{bmatrix} 0 & 1 & 0 \\ 0 & 0 & 1 \\ 0 & 0 & 0 \end{bmatrix}, \ \mathtt{M}_2^t(\boldsymbol{\mu}) = \begin{bmatrix} 0 & \mu_1 & \mu_2 \\ 0 & 0 & \mu_3 \\ 0 & 0 & 0 \end{bmatrix}.$$

Thus, Equation (7) generates the following polynomials:

1. $\mathcal{N}(f_1) = 0$ *gives the polynomials* $x_1 + x_2 + x_1^2,\ 1 + 2x_1 + \mu_1,\ 1 + \mu_2$.
2. $\mathcal{N}(f_2) = 0$ *gives the polynomials* $x_1 + x_2 + x_2^2,\ 1 + (1 + 2x_2)\mu_1,\ (1 + 2x_2)\mu_2 + \mu_1\mu_3$.
3. $\mathtt{M}_1\mathtt{M}_2 - \mathtt{M}_2\mathtt{M}_1 = 0$ *gives the polynomial* $\mu_3 - \mu_1$.

Furthermore, Theorem 5 promises that $(\mathbf{p}, \nu_1, \nu_2, \nu_3)$ *is an isolated zero with multiplicity one of the system* $\mathbf{F}' = \{f_1,\ f_2,\ 1 + 2x_1 + \mu_1,\ 1 + \mu_2,\ 1 + (1 + 2x_2)\mu_1,\ (1 + 2x_2)\mu_2 + \mu_1\mu_3,\ \mu_3 - \mu_1\}$.

On the one hand, from the above example, we can see that given a polynomial system $\mathbf{F}$ with an isolated zero $\mathbf{p}$, by Theorem 5, we will get an extended system $\mathbf{F}' \subset \mathbb{C}[\mathbf{x}, \boldsymbol{\mu}]$, which owns an isolated zero $(\mathbf{p}, \boldsymbol{\nu})$ with multiplicity one. Moreover, by Lemma 5, we have the dual basis

$$\Lambda = \{1,\ \partial_1 + \nu_1\partial_2,\ \frac{1}{2}\partial_1^2 + \nu_2\partial_2 + \nu_3\partial_1\partial_2 + \frac{1}{2}\nu_1\nu_3\partial_2^2\},$$

which corresponds to the primal basis $B = \{1,\ x_1,\ x_1^2\}$.

On the other hand, it is not hard to see that Equation (7) defined in Theorem 5 usually gives an over-determined extended system $\mathbf{F}'$. Once given an approximate zero $(\tilde{\mathbf{p}}, \tilde{\nu})$, similar to in Corollary 4.12 in [29], we can use random linear combinations of the polynomials in $\mathbf{F}'$ to produce a square system, which has a simple zero at $(\mathbf{p}, \boldsymbol{\nu})$ with high probability. Furthermore, Newton's method can be used on this square system to refine $(\tilde{\mathbf{p}}, \tilde{\nu})$ to a higher accuracy. However, this operation can only return an approximate multiplicity structure of the input system $\mathbf{F}$ with a higher accuracy. Next, we consider employing our certification method to certify the multiplicity structure of $\mathbf{F}$.

Example 7. *Continue to consider Example 6. Let* $\Sigma = \mathbf{F}' = \{f_1,\ f_2,\ g_1 = 1 + 2x_1 + \mu_1, g_2 = 1 + \mu_2,\ g_3 = 1 + (1 + 2x_2)\mu_1,\ g_4 = (1 + 2x_2)\mu_2 + \mu_1\mu_3,\ g_5 = \mu_3 - \mu_1\}$. *Given an approximate zero*

$$(\tilde{\mathbf{p}}, \tilde{\nu}) = (0.15, 0.12, -1.13, -1.32, -1.47).$$

By Algorithm 1, with Newton's method, we get a higher accuracy zero

$$(\tilde{\mathbf{p}}', \tilde{\nu}') = (0.000000771, 0.000001256, -1.000002523, -1.000000587, -1.000001940).$$

Then, let

$$f = f_1^2 + f_2^2 + \sum_{j=1}^{5} g_j^2$$

and compute

$$\Sigma' = \{\mathbf{J}_1(f), \mathbf{J}_2(f), \mathbf{J}_{\mu_1}(f), \mathbf{J}_{\mu_2}(f), \mathbf{J}_{\mu_3}(f)\}.$$

After applying algorithm **verifynlss** *on Σ' at $(\tilde{\mathbf{p}}', \tilde{v}')$, we have a verified inclusion:*

$$\mathbf{X} = \begin{pmatrix} [-0.00000000000001, & 0.00000000000001] \\ [-0.00000000000001, & 0.00000000000001] \\ [-1.00000000000001, & -0.99999999999999] \\ [-1.00000000000001, & -0.99999999999999] \\ [-1.00000000000001, & -0.99999999999999] \end{pmatrix}.$$

Based on Theorem 2, we know that there exists a unique $(\hat{\mathbf{x}}, \hat{\boldsymbol{\mu}}) \in \mathbf{X}$, s.t. $\Sigma'(\hat{\mathbf{x}}, \hat{\boldsymbol{\mu}}) = \mathbf{0}$.

Similarly, as in Examples 2 and 3, we consider the midpoint $(\hat{\mathbf{p}}, \hat{v})$ of $\mathbf{X}$ and compute $f(\hat{\mathbf{p}}, \hat{v}) = 0$. Thus, by Theorem 4, we are sure that there exists a unique simple zero $(\hat{x}_1, \hat{x}_2, \hat{v}_1, \hat{v}_2, \hat{v}_3)$ of the input system Σ in the interval $\mathbf{X}$, which means we certified the input system Σ.

According to the analysis in the above example, we know that, after applying our Algorithm 1 on the extended system $\Sigma = \mathbf{F}'$, we get a verified inclusion $\mathbf{X}$, which possesses a unique simple zero of $\mathbf{F}'$. Noticing that the values of the variables μ_1, μ_2, μ_3 in $\mathbf{F}'$ determine the coefficients of the dual basis Λ, thus, certifying the extended system $\mathbf{F}'$ means certifying the multiplicity structure of the input system $\mathbf{F}$ at $\mathbf{p}$. Thus, by Theorem 4, as long as $f(\hat{\mathbf{x}}, \hat{\boldsymbol{\mu}}) = 0$, we are sure that we certified not only the isolated singular zero of the input system $\mathbf{F}$, but also its multiplicity structure.

Algorithm 1 VSPS: verifying a simple zero of a polynomial system.

Input: an over-determined polynomial system $\Sigma := \{f_1, \cdots, f_m\} \subset \mathbb{R}[\mathbf{x}]$ and an approximate simple zero $\tilde{\mathbf{p}} = (\tilde{p}_1, \cdots, \tilde{p}_n) \in \mathbb{R}^n$.
Output: a verified inclusion $\mathbf{X}$ and a small non-negative number.
1: Compute f and Σ';
2: Compute $\tilde{\mathbf{p}}' :=$ **Newton**$(\Sigma', \tilde{\mathbf{p}})$;
3: Compute $\mathbf{X} :=$ **verifynlss**$(\Sigma', \tilde{\mathbf{p}}')$ and $f(\hat{\mathbf{p}})$;
4: **if** $f(\hat{\mathbf{p}}) = 0$, **then**
5: return $(\mathbf{X}, 0)$;
6: **else**
7: return $(\mathbf{X}, f(\hat{\mathbf{p}}))$.
8: **end if**

6. Conclusions

In this paper, we introduce the following two main contributions. First, we consider certifying the simple zeros of over-determined systems. By transforming the given over-determined system into a square one, we prove a necessary and sufficient condition to certify the simple real zeros of the over-determined system Σ by certifying the simple real zeros of the square system Σ_r. However, noting that deciding numerically if a point is a zero of a polynomial is difficult, we refine and certify the simple real zeros of Σ by refining and certifying a new square system Σ' with the interval methods and get a verified inclusion $\mathbf{X}$, which contains a unique simple real zero $\hat{\mathbf{x}}$ of Σ'. In fact, $\hat{\mathbf{x}}$ is a local minimum of f, which is also a necessary condition for the certification. By the necessary and sufficient condition in Theorem 1, we know that, as long as $f(\hat{\mathbf{x}}) = 0$, we can say that $\hat{\mathbf{x}}$ is a simple real zero of Σ and we certified the input system Σ.

Second, based on our work [35] and the work of Mourrain et al. [21,36], as an application of our method, we give a heuristic method for certifying not only the isolated singular zeros of polynomial systems, but also the multiplicity structures of the isolated singular zeros of polynomial systems.

In the future, for the certified zero $\hat{\mathbf{x}}$, trying to give a sufficient condition for the certification is the direction of our effort.

Author Contributions: J.C. contributed for supervision, project administration, funding and conceived of the presented idea. X.D. developed the theory, performed the computations and wrote the initial draft of the paper. J.C. verified the analytical methods. Both authors read and approved the final version of the paper.

Funding: The work was partially supported by NSFC Grants 11471327.

Acknowledgments: The authors would like to thank the anonymous referees very much for their useful suggestions that improved this paper.

Conflicts of Interest: The authors declare no conflict of interest.

References

1. Blum, L.; Cucker, F.; Shub, M.; Smale, S. *Complexity and Real Computation*; Springer: New York, NY, USA, 1998.
2. Hauenstein, J.D.; Sottile, F. Algorithm 921: AlphaCertified: Certifying Solutions to Polynomial Systems. *ACM Trans. Math. Softw.* **2012**, *38*, 28. [CrossRef]
3. Smale, S. Newton's Method Estimates from Data at One Point. In *The Disciplines: New Directions in Pure, Applied and Computational Mathematics*; Ewing, R., Gross, K., Martin, C., Eds.; Springer: New York, NY, USA, 1986.
4. Kanzawa, Y.; Kashiwagi, M.; Oishi, S. An algorithm for finding all solutions of parameter-dependent nonlinear equations with guaranteed accuracy. *Electr. Commun. JPn.* **1999**, *82*, 33–39. [CrossRef]
5. Krawczyk, R. Newton-Algorithmen zur Bestimmung von Nullstellen mit Fehlherschranken. *Computing* **1969**, *4*, 247–293. [CrossRef]
6. Moore, R.E. A test for existence of solutions to nonlinear systems. *SIAM J. Numer. Anal.* **1977**, *14*, 611–615. [CrossRef]
7. Nakaya, Y.; Oishi, S.; Kashiwagi, M.; Kanzawa, Y. Numerical verification of nonexistence of solutions for separable nonlinear equations and its application to all solutions algorithm. *Electr. Commun. Jpn.* **2003**, *86*, 45–53. [CrossRef]
8. Rump, S.M. Solving algebraic problems with high accuracy. *Proceedings of the Symposium on A New Approach to Scientific Computation*; Academic Press Professional, Inc.: San Diego, CA, USA, 1983; pp. 51–120.
9. Yamamura, K.; Kawata, H.; Tokue, A. Interval solution of nonlinear equations using linear programming. *BIT Numer. Math.* **1998**, *38*, 186–199. [CrossRef]
10. Allamigeon, X.; Gaubert, S.; Magron, V.; Werner, B. Formal proofs for nonlinear optimization. *J. Form. Reason.* **2015**, *8*, 1–24.
11. Kaltofen, E.; Li, B.; Yang, Z.; Zhi, L. Exact certification of global optimality of approximate factorizations via rationalizing sums-of-squares with floating point scalars. In Proceedings of the

Twenty-first International Symposium on Symbolic and Algebraic Computation, ISSAC 08, Hagenberg, Austria, 20–23 July 2008; ACM: New York, NY, USA; pp. 155–164.
12. Kaltofen, E.L.; Li, B.; Yang, Z.; Zhi, L. Exact certification in global polynomial optimization via sums-of-squares of rational functions with rational coefficients. *J. Symb. Computat.* **2012**, *47*, 1–15. [CrossRef]
13. Monniaux, D.; Corbineau, P. On the generation of positivstellensatz witnesses in degenerate cases. In *Interactive Theorem Proving*; LNCS 6898; van Eekelen, M., Geuvers, H., Schmaltz, J., Wiedijk, F., Eds.; Springer: Berlin/Heidelberg, Germany, 2011; pp. 249–264.
14. Peyrl, H.; Parrilo, P.A. A Macaulay2 package for computing sum of squares decompositions of polynomials with rational coefficients. In Proceedings of the SNC 2007, Waterloo, AB, Canada, 2007; pp. 207–208.
15. Peyrl, H.; Parrilo, P.A. Computing sum of squares decompositions with rational coefficients. *Theor. Comput. Sci.* **2008**, *409*, 269–281. [CrossRef]
16. Safey, M.; Din, E.; Zhi, L. Computing rational points in convex semialgebraic sets and sum of squares decompositions. *SIAM J. Optim.* **2010**, *20*, 2876–2889.
17. Akogul, T.A.; Hauenstein, J.D.; Szanto, A. Certifying solutions to overdetermined and singular polynomial systems over $\mathbb{Q}$. *J. Symb. Comput.* **2018**, *84*, 147–171.
18. Dayton, B.; Zeng, Z. Computing the multiplicity structure in solving polynomial systems. In Proceedings of the 2005 International Symposium on Symbolic and Algebraic Computation, Beijing, China, 24–27 July 2005; Kauers, M., Ed.; ACM: New York, NY, USA, 2005; pp. 116–123.
19. Giusti, M.; Lecerf, G.; Salvy, B.; Yakoubsohn, J.-C. On location and approximation of clusters of zeros: case of embedding dimension one. *Found. Comput. Math.* **2007**, *7*, 1–58. [CrossRef]
20. Hauenstein, J.D.; Wampler, C.W. Isosingular sets and deflation. *Found. Computat. Math.* **2013**, *13*, 371–403. [CrossRef]
21. Hauenstein, J.D.; Mourrain, B.; Szant, A. Certifying isolated singular points and their multiplicity structure. In Proceedings of the Twenty-first International Symposium on Symbolic and Algebraic Computation, ISSAC' 15, Bath, UK, 6–9 July 2015; pp. 213–220.
22. Ojika, T. A numerical method for branch points of a system of nonlinear algebraic equations. *Appl. Numer. Math.* **1988**, *4*, 419–430. [CrossRef]
23. Ojika, T.; Watanabe, S.; Mitsui, T. Deflation algorithm for the multiple roots of a system of nonlinear equations. *J. Math. Anal. Appl.* **1983**, *96*, 463–479. [CrossRef]
24. Zeng, Z. Computing multiple roots of inexact polynomials. *Math. Comput.* **2005**, *74*, 869–903. [CrossRef]
25. Dayton, B.; Li, T.; Zeng, Z. Multiple zeros of nonlinear systems. *Math. Comput.* **2011**, *80*, 2143–2168. [CrossRef]
26. Kanzawa, Y.; Oishi, S. Approximate singular solutions of nonlinear equations and a numerical method of proving their existence. Theory and application of numerical calculation in science and technology, II (Japanese) (Kyoto, 1996). *Sūrikaisekikenkyūsho Kōkyūroku* **1997**, *990*, 216–223.
27. Leykin, A.; Verschelde, J.; Zhao, A. Newton's method with deflation for isolated singularities of polynomial systems. *Theor. Comput. Sci.* **2006**, *359*, 111–122. [CrossRef]
28. Li, N.; Zhi, L. Verified Error Bounds for Isolated Singular Solutions of Polynomial Systems. *SIAM J. Numer. Anal.* **2014**, *52*, 1623–1640. [CrossRef]
29. Mantzaflaris, A.; Mourrain, B. Deflation and certified isolation of singular zeros of polynomial systems. In Proceedings of the ISSAC 2011, San Jose, CA, USA, 17 January 2011; pp. 249–256.
30. Rump, S.M.; Graillat, S. Verified error bounds for multiple roots of systems of nonlinear equations. *Numer. Algorithms* **2010**, *54*, 359–377. [CrossRef]
31. Dedieu, J.P.; Shub, M. Newton's method for overdetermined systems of equations. *Math. Comput.* **1999**, *69*, 1099–1115. [CrossRef]

32. Cheng, J.S.; Dou, X. Certifying simple zeros of over-determined polynomial systems. In *Computer Algebra in Scientific Computing;* CASC'17 Lecture Notes in Computer Science; Gerdt, V., Koepf, W., Seiler W., Vorozhtsov E., Eds.; Springer: Cham, Switzerland, 2017; pp. 55–76.
33. Li, S. *Linear Algebra;* Higher Education Press: Beijing, China, 2006; ISBN 978-7-04-019870-6.
34. Rohn, J. Positive definiteness and stability of interval matrices. *SIAM J. Matrix Anal. Appl.* **1994**, *15*, 175–184. [CrossRef]
35. Cheng, J.S.; Dou, X.; Wen, J. A new deflation method for verifying the isolated singular zeros of polynomial systems. preprint 2018.
36. Hauenstein, J.D.; Mourrain, B.; Szanto, A. On deflation and multiplicity structure. *J. Symb. Comput.* **2017**, *83*, 228–253. [CrossRef]

© 2018 by the authors. Licensee MDPI, Basel, Switzerland. This article is an open access article distributed under the terms and conditions of the Creative Commons Attribution (CC BY) license (http://creativecommons.org/licenses/by/4.0/).

mathematics

MDPI

Article

Resolving Decompositions for Polynomial Modules

Mario Albert † and Werner M. Seiler *,†

Institut für Mathematik, Universität Kassel, 34132 Kassel, Germany; mario.albert@gmx.de
* Correspondence: seiler@mathematik.uni-kassel.de
† These authors contributed equally to this work.

Received: 12 July 2018; Accepted: 4 September 2018; Published: 7 September 2018

Abstract: We introduce the novel concept of a resolving decomposition of a polynomial module as a combinatorial structure that allows for the effective construction of free resolutions. It provides a unifying framework for recent results of the authors for different types of bases.

Keywords: polynomial modules; free resolutions; combinatorial decompositions

MSC: 13D02; 13P10; 68W30

1. Introduction

The determination of free resolutions for polynomial modules is a fundamental task in computational commutative algebra and algebraic geometry. Free resolutions are needed for derived functors like Ext and Tor and many important homological invariants like the projective dimension or the Castelnuovo-Mumford regularity are defined via the minimal resolution. Furthermore, already the Betti numbers, which measure the size of the minimal free resolution, give valuable information about the geometry and topology of varieties.

Unfortunately, resolutions are computationally rather expensive. A rough estimate says that a resolution of length ℓ requires to compute ℓ Gröbner bases. In many situations, partial information like the Betti numbers already suffice. However, all classical algorithms for the computation of Betti numbers require to always determine a full resolution. Indeed, one can observe in computer algebra systems like SINGULAR that computing the Betti numbers needs as much computation time as computing a full resolution.

In the recent work [1], we developed a novel approach to this question consisting of a combination of the theory of involutive bases—in the form of Pommaret bases—(see [2] for a general survey on involutive bases) and of algebraic discrete Morse theory (see [3,4]). We also implemented it in the CoCoALib [5]. To the best of our knowledge, this approach is the only one that is able to compute (even individual) Betti numbers without first determining a full resolution. For most ideals, it is therefore much faster than classical methods (see the detailed benchmarks given in [1,6]). Furthermore, the new approach can be easily parallelised and scales much better with the problem size.

Because of these advantages, a generalisation of our approach to other situations is of great interest. Furthermore, it should be noted that Pommaret bases exist only in generic coordinates. As a first step, we extended it therefore to Janet bases [6], as these can be computed more efficiently and always exist. While the proofs follow the same lines, the use of a different involutive division entailed the adaption of many technical points. Furthermore, we are currently considering the use of alternative ideal bases not necessarily coming from an involutive division, but inducing combinatorial decompositions of the ideal with essentially the same properties. The development of a syzygy theory for such bases again proceeds along the same ideas, but various proofs have to be modified in minor ways.

In a different line of work, we recently introduced the concept of a module marked on a quasi-stable submodule which is very useful for the explicit determination of equations for Hilbert and Quot schemes [7,8]. The marking induces a combinatorial decomposition based on Pommaret multiplicative variables, but this time the key issue is that the head terms are not chosen with respect to a term order. Nevertheless, we showed that the most important results on resolutions presented [1] still remain essentially true. Again the proofs follow the same basic ideas, but require smaller technical modifications at some places.

This article represents a revised and expanded version of [9] which was presented at the conference *Computer Algebra in Scientific Computing*. Its main objective is to unify all our above-mentioned works in a general axiomatic framework. It centers about the novel concept of a resolving decomposition of an ideal. It refines the classical Stanley decompositions by certain additional axioms implying the existence of standard representations and normal forms. We then discuss how a free resolution and Betti numbers can be determined from a resolving decomposition.

The goal of this unification is *not* the development of any new algorithms. In particular, no algorithm for the construction of resolving decomposition will be presented. Instead, our results should be considered as a "meta-machinery" which augments any concept of a basis that induces a resolving decomposition with an effective syzygy theory. As already mentioned above, we applied this "meta-machinery" already for the special case of Janet or Pommaret bases (including a concrete implementation in the CoCoALib) [1,6]. The case of marked bases is considered in great detail in [7,8] (the latter reference also describes a concrete implementation in CoCoALib for the case of ideals).

The article is structured as follows. The next section provides the definition of a resolving decomposition and shows explicitly that all the cases mentioned above are contained in it. The third section discusses the construction of a syzygy resolution out of a resolving decomposition and some of its properties. In the fourth section, an explicit formula for the differential of this resolution is derived by relating our construction with the work of Sköldberg [10]. Finally, some conclusions are given.

2. Resolving Decompositions

Throughout this article, we will use the following notations. Let $\Bbbk$ be a field and $\mathcal{P} = \Bbbk[\mathbf{x}]$ the polynomial ring in the variable $\mathbf{x} = (x_0, \dots, x_n)$. We write $\mathbb{T}$ for the set of terms $x^\mu \in \mathcal{P}$. Let $\mathcal{P}^m_{\mathbf{d}} = \bigoplus_{i=1}^m \mathcal{P}(-d_i)\mathbf{e}_i^{(0)}$ be a finitely generated free $\mathcal{P}$-module with grading $\mathbf{d} = (d_1, \dots, d_m)$ and free generators $\mathbf{e}_1^{(0)}, \dots, \mathbf{e}_m^{(0)}$. A module $\mathcal{U} \subseteq \mathcal{P}^m_{\mathbf{d}}$ is called *monomial module*, if it is of the form $\bigoplus_{k=1}^m J^{(k)}\mathbf{e}_k^{(0)}$ with each $J^{(k)}$ a monomial ideal in $\mathcal{P}$. A *module term (with index i)* is a term of the form $x^\mu \mathbf{e}_i^{(0)}$. If $J \subseteq \mathcal{P}$ is a monomial ideal, we denote by $\mathcal{N}(J) \subseteq \mathbb{T}$ the set of terms in $\mathbb{T}$ not belonging to J. In the case of monomial module $\mathcal{U}$, we analogously write $\mathcal{N}(\mathcal{U}) = \bigcup_{k=1}^m \mathcal{N}(J^{(k)})\mathbf{e}_k^{(0)}$. The *support* of an element $\mathbf{f} \in \mathcal{P}^m_{\mathbf{d}}$ is the set $\operatorname{supp}(\mathbf{f})$ of all module terms appearing in $\mathbf{f}$ with a non-zero coefficient, thus $\mathbf{f} = \sum_{x^\alpha \mathbf{e}_{i_\alpha}^{(0)} \in \operatorname{supp}(\mathbf{f})} c_\alpha x^\alpha \mathbf{e}_{i_\alpha}^{(0)}$. If $\mathcal{B}$ is a set of homogeneous elements of degree s in $\mathcal{P}^m_{\mathbf{d}}$, we write $\langle \mathcal{B} \rangle_\Bbbk$ for the $\Bbbk$-vector space generated by $\mathcal{B}$ in $(\mathcal{P}^m_{\mathbf{d}})_s$. For a module $\mathcal{U} \subseteq \mathcal{P}^m_{\mathbf{d}}$, we denote by $\operatorname{pd}(\mathcal{U})$ the *projective dimension* and by $\operatorname{reg}(\mathcal{U})$ the *(Castelnuovo-Mumford) regularity* of $\mathcal{U}$.

Let $\mathcal{B} = \{\mathbf{h}_1, \dots, \mathbf{h}_s\}$ be a finite set of homogeneous elements in $\mathcal{P}^m_{\mathbf{d}}$. We need the following data to define a resolving decomposition of the submodule $\mathcal{U}$ defined by $\mathcal{B}$. For every generator $\mathbf{h}_i \in \mathcal{B}$, we choose a term $x^{\mu_i}\mathbf{e}_{k_i}^{(0)} \in \operatorname{supp} \mathbf{h}_i$ denoted by $\operatorname{hm}(\mathbf{h}_i)$ and call it the *head module term* of $\mathbf{h}_i$. Furthermore, we define the *head module terms of* $\mathcal{B}$ by $\operatorname{hm}(\mathcal{B}) := \mathcal{B}igl\{\operatorname{hm}(\mathbf{h}) \mid \mathbf{h} \in \mathcal{B}\mathcal{B}igr\}$ and the *head module of* $\mathcal{U}$ by $\operatorname{hm}(\mathcal{U}) = \langle \operatorname{hm} \mathcal{B} \rangle$. Obviously, the monomial module $\operatorname{hm}(\mathcal{U})$ depends on the choice of both the generating set $\mathcal{B}$ and the head module terms $\operatorname{hm}(\mathcal{B})$. Furthermore, we assign to every head module term $\operatorname{hm}(\mathbf{h})$ with $\mathbf{h} \in \mathcal{B}$ a set of *multiplicative variables* $X_\mathcal{B}(\mathbf{h}) \subseteq \mathbf{x}$ and denote by $X_\mathcal{B}$ the set of all these sets. Finally, we choose a term order $\prec_\mathcal{B}$ on $\mathcal{P}^s$ with s the number of generators in $\mathcal{B}$.

Definition 1. *The above introduced quadruple* $(\mathcal{B}, \operatorname{hm}(\mathcal{B}), X_\mathcal{B}, \prec_\mathcal{B})$ *defines a* resolving decomposition *of a submodule* $\mathcal{U} \subseteq \mathcal{P}^m_{\mathbf{d}}$*, if the following five properties hold:*

(i) $\mathcal{U} = \langle \mathcal{B} \rangle$.

(ii) *Let* $\mathbf{h} \in \mathcal{B}$ *be an arbitrary generator. Each module term* $x^\mu \mathbf{e}_k^{(0)} \in \operatorname{supp}(\mathbf{h}) \setminus \{\operatorname{hm}(\mathbf{h})\}$ *must satisfy* $x^\mu \mathbf{e}_k^{(0)} \notin \operatorname{hm}(U)$.

(iii) *The assigned multiplicative variables induce direct sum decompositions of both the head module*

$$\operatorname{hm}(U) = \mathcal{B}igoplus_{\mathbf{h}\in\mathcal{B}} \Bbbk[X_{\mathcal{B}}(\mathbf{h})] \cdot \operatorname{hm}(\mathbf{h}) \tag{1}$$

and the module itself

$$U = \mathcal{B}igoplus_{\mathbf{h}\in\mathcal{B}} \Bbbk[X_{\mathcal{B}}(\mathbf{h})] \cdot \mathbf{h}\,. \tag{2}$$

(iv) *We have a direct sum decomposition* $(\mathcal{P}^m_{\mathbf{d}})_r = U_r \oplus \langle \mathcal{N}(\operatorname{hm}(U))_r \rangle_\Bbbk$ *for all degrees* $r \geq 0$.

(v) *Let* $\{\mathbf{e}_1^{(1)}, \ldots, \mathbf{e}_s^{(1)}\}$ *denote the canonical basis of the free module* $\mathcal{P}^s$. *Given an arbitrary term* $x^\delta \in \mathbb{T}$ *and an arbitrary generator* $\mathbf{h}_\alpha \in \mathcal{B}$, *we find for every term* $x^\epsilon \mathbf{e}_i^{(0)} \in \operatorname{supp}(x^\delta \mathbf{h}_\alpha) \cap \operatorname{hm}(U)$ *a unique* $\mathbf{h}_{\mathcal{B}eta} \in \operatorname{hm}(\mathcal{B})$ *such that* $x^\epsilon \mathbf{e}_i^{(0)} = x^{\delta'} \operatorname{hm}(\mathbf{h}_\beta)$ *with* $x^{\delta'} \in \Bbbk[X_{\mathcal{B}}(\mathbf{h}_{\mathcal{B}eta})]$ *by (iii). Then the inequality* $x^\delta \mathbf{e}_\alpha^{(1)} \succeq_{\mathcal{B}} x^{\delta'} \mathbf{e}_{\mathcal{B}eta}{}^{(1)}$ *holds with respect to the term order* $\prec_{\mathcal{B}}$.

In the sequel, we will always assume that $(\mathcal{B}, \operatorname{hm}(\mathcal{B}), X_{\mathcal{B}}, \prec_{\mathcal{B}})$ is a resolving decomposition of the finitely generated module $U = \langle \mathcal{B} \rangle \subseteq \mathcal{P}^m_{\mathbf{d}}$. In addition to the multiplicative variables, we define for $\mathbf{h} \in \mathcal{B}$ the *non-multiplicative variables* as $\overline{X}_{\mathcal{B}}(\mathbf{h}) = \{x_0, \ldots, x_n\} \setminus X_{\mathcal{B}}(\mathbf{h})$.

Remark 1. *Resolving decompositions refine the classical concept of Stanley decompositions [11]. Indeed, the equalities (1) and (2) simply represents Stanley decompositions of the head module of U and of U itself, respectively. This observation makes it straightforward to compute the Hilbert functions of* $\operatorname{hm}(U)$ *and of U, respectively. Since the two Stanley decompositions possess an identical structure, the arising Hilbert functions trivially coincides. This fact represents a built-in term order free version of the well-known Macaulay theorem for Gröbner bases—see e.g., [12]).*

Condition (iii) implies the existence of a unique standard representation

$$\mathbf{f} = \sum_{\alpha=1}^{s} P_\alpha \mathbf{h}_\alpha$$

with $P_\alpha \in \Bbbk[X_{\mathcal{B}}(\mathbf{h}_\alpha)]$ *for every* $\mathbf{f} \in U$. *Note that these representations are indeed unique due to the fact that each coefficient may only depend on the multiplicative variables. Condition (iv) implies the existence of unique* normal forms *modulo U for all homogeneous elements* $\mathbf{f} \in \mathcal{P}^m_{\mathbf{d}}$. *Due to it, we find a unique coefficient* $P_\alpha \in \Bbbk[X_{\mathcal{B}}(\mathbf{h}_\alpha)]$ *for each generator* $\mathbf{h}_\alpha \in \mathcal{B}$ *such that* $\mathbf{f}' = \mathbf{f} - \sum_{\alpha=1}^{s} P_\alpha \mathbf{h}_\alpha \in \langle \mathcal{N}(\operatorname{hm}(U)) \rangle_\Bbbk$. *It also follows trivially from (1) that for every generator in the basis* $\mathcal{B}$ *a different head module term is chosen.*

For the goals of this article, the mere existence of normal forms suffices. Nevertheless, we remark that Condition (v) entails that these normal forms can be effectively determined. The head terms and multiplicative variables inherent to a resolving decomposition allows for the definition of a natural reduction relation. If there exists a term $x^\epsilon \mathbf{e}_i^{(0)} \in \operatorname{supp}(\mathbf{f}) \cap \operatorname{hm}(U)$ for some module element $\mathbf{f} \in \mathcal{P}^m_{\mathbf{d}}$, then we find a unique head module term $\mathbf{h} \in \operatorname{hm}(\mathcal{B})$ such that $x^\epsilon \mathbf{e}_i^{(0)} = x^\delta \operatorname{hm}(\mathbf{h})$ with $x^\delta \in \Bbbk[X_{\mathcal{B}}(\mathbf{h})]$ and consequently a reduction $\mathbf{f} \xrightarrow{\mathcal{B}} \mathbf{f} - cx^\delta \mathbf{h}$ is possible for a suitably chosen scalar $c \in \Bbbk$.

Lemma 1. *For any resolving decomposition* $(\mathcal{B}, \operatorname{hm}(\mathcal{B}), X_{\mathcal{B}}, \prec_{\mathcal{B}})$ *the transitive closure* $\xrightarrow{\mathcal{B}}{}^{*}$ *of the reduction relation* $\xrightarrow{\mathcal{B}}$ *is Noetherian and confluent.*

Proof. It is sufficient to prove that for every term $x^\gamma \mathbf{e}_k^{(0)}$ in $\operatorname{hm}(U)$, there is a unique $g \in \mathcal{P}^m_{\mathbf{d}}$ such that $x^\gamma \mathbf{e}_k^{(0)} \xrightarrow{\mathcal{B}}{}^{*} g$ and $g \in \langle \mathcal{N}(\operatorname{hm}(U)) \rangle$. Since $x^\gamma \mathbf{e}_k^{(0)} \in \operatorname{hm}(U)$, there exists a unique $x^\delta \mathbf{h}_\alpha \in U$ such that $x^\delta \operatorname{hm}(\mathbf{h}_\alpha) = x^\gamma \mathbf{e}_k^{(0)}$ and $x^\delta \in X_{\mathcal{B}}(\mathbf{h}_\alpha)$. Hence, $x^\gamma \mathbf{e}_k^{(0)} \xrightarrow{\mathcal{B}} x^\gamma \mathbf{e}_k^{(0)} - cx^\delta \mathbf{h}_\alpha$ for a suitably chosen coefficient $c \in \Bbbk$. Denoting again the canonical basis of $\mathcal{P}^s$ by $\{\mathbf{e}_1^{(1)}, \ldots, \mathbf{e}_s^{(1)}\}$, we associate the term

$x^{\delta}\mathbf{e}_{\alpha}^{(1)}$ with this reduction step. If we could proceed infinitely with further reduction steps, then the reduction process would induce a sequence of terms in $\mathcal{P}^s$ containing an infinite chain which, by Condition (v) of Definition 1, is strictly descending for $\prec_{\mathcal{B}}$. However, this is impossible, since $\prec_{\mathcal{B}}$ is a well-ordering. Hence $\xrightarrow{\mathcal{B}}{}^*$ is Noetherian. Confluence is immediate by the uniqueness of the element that is used at each reduction step. □

The following examples show that involutive and marked bases, respectively, do indeed induce resolving decomposition as claimed in the introduction. In fact, one can say that the definition of resolving decompositions evolved from an abstraction and combination of these two basic examples: the emphasis on Stanley decompositions and unique normal forms represents a key feature of involutive bases and the somewhat convoluted last condition in Definition 1 stems from the theory of marked bases where it allows for the introduction of a Noetherian reduction relation without having head terms selected by a term order. The cited literature implicitly provides many concrete instances of resolving decompositions stemming either from involutive or marked bases. We refrain from repeating them, as this is, at least in the first case, rather standard now.

Example 1. *An involutive basis is a Gröbner basis with additional combinatorial properties (see [2] for a general introduction and a survey of their basic theoretical and algorithmic properties). It is defined with respect to a term order $\prec$ on the free module $\mathcal{P}_{\mathbf{d}}^m$ and an involutive division L (see ([2], Definition 2.1)). Given a finite set $\mathcal{B} \subset \mathcal{P}_{\mathbf{d}}^m$ of terms, an involutive division associates with each term in $\mathcal{B}$ a set of multiplicative variables. $\mathcal{B}$ is an L-involutive basis, if it suffices to multiply each term with terms in each multiplicative variable to obtain the whole module generated by $\mathcal{B}$. The extension to general polynomial modules is straightforward using the term order $\prec$ and normal form arguments. Note that the existence of Stanley decompositions induced by the multiplicative variables is thus a central part of the definition of involutive bases.*

Assume now that L is a continuous division, $\prec$ an arbitrary term order and $\mathcal{B} \subset \mathcal{P}_{\mathbf{d}}^m$ a finite, L-involutively autoreduced set ([2], Definition 5.8) which defines a strong L-involutive basis ([2], Definition 5.1) of the polynomial submodule $\mathcal{U} \subseteq \mathcal{P}_{\mathbf{d}}^m$ it generates. We choose the head module $\mathrm{hm}(\mathcal{B}) = \{\mathrm{lt}(\mathbf{h}_1), \dots, \mathrm{lt}(\mathbf{h}_s)\}$ via the leading terms for the given term order $\prec$. The multiplicative variables $X_{\mathcal{B}}$ are of course assigned according to the involutive division L. Finally, we take for the term order $\prec_{\mathcal{B}}$ the classical Schreyer order induced by $\mathcal{B}$ and $\prec$ as it appears in Schreyer's theorem (see e.g., ([13], Chapt. 5, Thm. 3.3)). Then the quadruple $(\mathcal{B}, \mathrm{hm}(\mathcal{B}), X_{\mathcal{B}}, \prec_{\mathcal{B}})$ defines a resolving decomposition of $\mathcal{U}$.

The proof that all conditions of Definition 1 are satisfied consists simply of recalling some basic results about involutive bases. Condition (i) is entailed by ([2], Corollary 5.5). Condition (ii) follows from the fact that the set $\mathcal{B}$ is assumed to be involutively autoreduced and Condition (iii) is a consequence of ([2], Lemma 5.12). Furthermore, by ([2], Proposition 5.13), every module element $\mathbf{f} \in \mathcal{P}_{\mathbf{d}}^m$ has a unique normal form with respect to $\mathcal{U}$. Remark 1 discusses that this property is equivalent to the fourth condition. Finally, Condition (v) is satisfied because of ([14], Lemma 5.5), asserting the existence of an L-ordering for any continuous division.

Example 2. *The key point about marked modules and marked bases, introduced in the first version of [8], is that no term order is used for the selection of the head terms. Given a basis $\mathcal{B}$ of the polynomial module $\mathcal{U} \subset \mathcal{P}_{\mathbf{d}}^m$, one can in principle choose any term in the support of a generator as head term. However, in general such a choice will not lead to a Noetherian reduction relation. Therefore, certain restrictions apply. The chosen head terms must define a quasi-stable module which is equivalent to saying that they form a Pommaret basis of the head module. This fact immediately entails that most polynomial modules do not possess a marked basis. Indeed, the point of marked bases is not that one wants to compute one for a given module $\mathcal{U} \subset \mathcal{P}_{\mathbf{d}}^m$, but that one prescribes a quasi-stable module $\mathcal{V} \subseteq \mathcal{P}_{\mathbf{d}}^m$ by giving its Pommaret basis and then constructs all possible marked bases where the set of head terms coincides with this Pommaret basis. This construction is a key step for obtaining local equations for Hilbert and Quot schemes modulo coordinate transformations (see [7,8] for more details).*

More precisely, let $\mathcal{H} = \{x^{\mu_1}\mathbf{e}_{k_1}^{(0)}, \dots x^{\mu_s}\mathbf{e}_{k_s}^{(0)}\}$ be a monomial Pommaret basis and $\mathcal{V} \subseteq \mathcal{P}_{\mathbf{d}}^m$ the quasi-stable module generated by $\mathcal{H}$. A marked basis $\mathcal{B} = \{\mathbf{h}_1, \dots, \mathbf{h}_s\}$ then firstly satisfies $\mathrm{hm}(\mathbf{h}_i) = x^{\mu_i}\mathbf{e}_{k_i}^{(0)}$

and $\operatorname{supp}(\mathbf{h}_i - x^{\mu_i}\mathbf{e}_{k_i}^{(0)}) \subseteq \langle \mathcal{N}(\mathcal{V})_{\deg(x^{\mu_i}\mathbf{e}_{k_i}^{(0)})}\rangle_{\Bbbk}$ *for each index* $1 \leq i \leq s$*. Secondly, we require that the homogeneous component* $\mathcal{N}(\mathcal{V})_r$ *of degree* r *induces a* $\Bbbk$*-linear basis of the factor module* $(\mathcal{P}^m_{\mathbf{d}})_r/\langle\mathcal{B}\rangle_r$ *for any* $r \geq 0$*. Note that this fact entails the decompositions* $(\mathcal{P}^m_{\mathbf{d}})_r = \langle\mathcal{B}\rangle_r \oplus \langle\mathcal{N}(\mathcal{V})_r\rangle_{\Bbbk}$ *for all* r*. For a more detailed discussion of marked bases, we refer to ([8], Section 2). For the desired resolving decomposition, we take as multiplicative variables* $X_{\mathcal{B}}$ *simply the multiplicative variables of the Pommaret basis* $\mathcal{H}$*. Recall that if* $1 \leq c \leq n$ *is the minimal index value such that the multi index* μ *has a non-zero entry at position* c *(this value is called the* class *of* μ*), then the variables* $x_1, \dots, x_c$ *are Pommaret multiplicative for* $x^\mu\mathbf{e}_k^{(0)}$*. Finally, we choose as module term order* $\prec_{\mathcal{B}}$ *the standard TOP lift of the classical lexicographic order [15].*

We claim now again that $(\mathcal{B}, \operatorname{hm}(\mathcal{B}), X_{\mathcal{B}}, \prec_{\mathcal{B}})$ *defines a resolving decomposition of* U*. Indeed, it follows immediately by construction that the Conditions (i), (ii) and (iv) are satisfied. The first part of Condition (iii) is a consequence of the fact that* $\mathcal{H} = \operatorname{hm}(\mathcal{B})$ *is a Pommaret basis and the second part of the uniqueness of the reduction process ([8], Lemma 5.1) (here it is crucial that in this particular case the reduction process is essentially the Pommaret normal form algorithm, as otherwise no Noetherian reduction relation would arise). Finally, Condition (v) is entailed by ([8], Lemma 3.6).*

The main obstacle in checking whether or not a given quadruple $(\mathcal{B}, \operatorname{hm}(\mathcal{B}), X_{\mathcal{B}}, \prec_{\mathcal{B}})$ defines a resolving decomposition is Condition (v). It can be tackled with the help of a directed graph induced by any decomposition $(\mathcal{B}, \operatorname{hm}(\mathcal{B}), X_{\mathcal{B}}, \prec_{\mathcal{B}})$ satisfying the first four conditions of Definition 1. Its vertices are given by the elements in $\mathcal{B}$. If $x_j \in \overline{X}_{\mathcal{B}}(\mathbf{h})$ for some $\mathbf{h} \in \mathcal{B}$, then, by definition, $\mathcal{B}$ contains a unique generator $\mathbf{h}'$ such that $x_j \operatorname{hm}(\mathbf{h}) = x^\mu \operatorname{hm}(\mathbf{h}')$ with $x^\mu \in \Bbbk[X_{\mathcal{B}}(\mathbf{h}')]$. In this case we include a directed edge from $\mathbf{h}$ to $\mathbf{h}'$. We call the thus defined graph the *$\mathcal{B}$-graph* and show now that acyclicity of it is a necessary condition for a resolving decomposition.

Proposition 1. *The $\mathcal{B}$-graph of a resolving decomposition* $(\mathcal{B}, \operatorname{hm}(\mathcal{B}), X_{\mathcal{B}}, \prec_{\mathcal{B}})$ *is always acyclic.*

Proof. Assume the $\mathcal{B}$-graph was cyclic. Then we can find pairwise distinct generators $\mathbf{h}_{k_1}, \dots, \mathbf{h}_{k_t} \in \mathcal{B}$ plus a non-multiplicative variable $x_{i_j} \in \overline{X}_{\mathcal{B}}(\operatorname{hm}(\mathbf{h}_{k_j}))$ and a multiplicative term $x^{\mu_j} \in \Bbbk[X_{\mathcal{B}}(\operatorname{hm}(\mathbf{h}_{k_j}))]$ for each $j \in \{1, \dots, t\}$ such that

$$
\begin{aligned}
x_{i_1} \operatorname{hm}(\mathbf{h}_{k_1}) &= x^{\mu_2} \operatorname{hm}(\mathbf{h}_{k_2}),\\
x_{i_2} \operatorname{hm}(\mathbf{h}_{k_2}) &= x^{\mu_3} \operatorname{hm}(\mathbf{h}_{k_3}),\\
&\vdots\\
x_{i_t} \operatorname{hm}(\mathbf{h}_{k_t}) &= x^{\mu_1} \operatorname{hm}(\mathbf{h}_{k_1}).
\end{aligned}
$$

Multiplying with some variables, we obtain the following chain of equations:

$$
\begin{aligned}
x_{i_1} \cdots x_{i_t} \operatorname{hm}(\mathbf{h}_{k_1}) &= x_{i_2} \cdots x_{i_t} x^{\mu_2} \operatorname{hm}(\mathbf{h}_{k_2})\\
&= x_{i_3} \cdots x_{i_t} x^{\mu_2} x^{\mu_3} \operatorname{hm}(\mathbf{h}_{k_3})\\
&\vdots\\
&= x_{i_t} x^{\mu_2} \cdots x^{\mu_t} \operatorname{hm}(\mathbf{h}_{k_t})\\
&= x^{\mu_1} \cdots x^{\mu_t} \operatorname{hm}(\mathbf{h}_{k_1})
\end{aligned}
$$

which implies that $x_{i_1} \cdots x_{i_t} = x^{\mu_1} \cdots x^{\mu_t}$. Furthermore, Condition (v) of Definition 1 implies in $\mathcal{P}^s$ the following chain:

$$
x_{i_1} \cdots x_{i_t} \mathbf{e}_{k_1}^{(1)} \succeq_{\mathcal{B}} x_{i_2} \cdots x_{i_t} x^{\mu_2} \mathbf{e}_{k_2}^{(1)} \succeq_{\mathcal{B}} \cdots \succeq_{\mathcal{B}} x^{\mu_1} \cdots x^{\mu_t} \mathbf{e}_{k_1}^{(1)}.
$$

Because of $x_{i_1} \cdots x_{i_t} = x^{\mu_1} \cdots x^{\mu_t}$, we must have throughout equality entailing that $k_1 = \cdots = k_t$ which contradicts our assumptions. □

The following two results provide a converse of this proposition for the special case of a monomial generating set $\mathcal{B}$ by showing that whenever the $\mathcal{B}$-graph of such a set is acyclic, then there exists a term order satisfying Condition (v).

Lemma 2. *Let $\mathcal{B}$ be a generating set consisting only of module terms. Assume that for the chosen multiplicative variables $X_\mathcal{B}$, the $\mathcal{B}$-graph is acyclic. Then it is not possible to find a chain of equalities of the form*

$$x^{\nu_1}\mathbf{h}_{k_1} = x^{\mu_2}\mathbf{h}_{k_2}, \tag{3a}$$
$$x^{\nu_2}\mathbf{h}_{k_2} = x^{\mu_3}\mathbf{h}_{k_3}, \tag{3b}$$
$$\vdots$$
$$x^{\nu_t}\mathbf{h}_{k_t} = x^{\mu_1}\mathbf{h}_{k_1} \tag{3c}$$

with multiplicative terms $x^{\mu_i} \in \Bbbk[X_\mathcal{B}(\mathbf{h}_{k_i})]$ and arbitrary terms $x^{\nu_i} \in \mathbb{T}$. Furthermore, whenever an equality $x^\nu \operatorname{hm}(\mathbf{h}_i) = x^\mu \operatorname{hm}(\mathbf{h}_j)$ holds with a multiplicative term $x^\mu \in \Bbbk[X_\mathcal{B}(\mathbf{h}_j)]$, then the $\mathcal{B}$-graph contains a directed path from $\mathbf{h}_i$ to $\mathbf{h}_j$.

Proof. We show that any chain of the form (3) induces a cycle in the $\mathcal{B}$-graph and thus violates the assumed acyclicity. Without loss of generality, we may assume that $\gcd(x^{\nu_i}, x^{\mu_{i+1}}) = 1$ and $x^{\nu_i} \notin \Bbbk[X_\mathcal{B}(\mathbf{h}_{k_i})]$. This implies the existence of a non-multiplicative variable $x_{i_0} \in \overline{X}_\mathcal{B}(\mathbf{h}_{k_1})$ dividing x^{ν_1}. Set $x^{\rho_0} = x^{\nu_1}/x_{i_0}$ and let the normal form of $x_{i_0}\mathbf{h}_{k_1}$ be $x^{\tau_1}\mathbf{h}_{l_1}$. Then $x^{\rho_0}x^{\tau_1}\mathbf{h}_{l_1} = x^{\mu_2}\mathbf{h}_{k_2}$. By assumption, there exists a non-multiplicative variable $x_{i_1} \in \overline{X}_\mathcal{B}(\mathbf{h}_{l_1})$ dividing $x^{\rho_0}x^{\tau_1}$. Now set $x_{\rho_1} = x^{\rho_0}x^{\tau_1}/x_{i_1}$ and repeat the procedure.

Due to the fact that the $\mathcal{B}$-graph is acyclic and that there are only finitely many terms x^ρ, x^τ and generators $\mathbf{h}_l$ such that $x^\rho x^\tau \mathbf{h}_l = x^{\mu_2}\mathbf{h}_{k_2}$, we find after finitely many steps x_{l_t} and $\mathbf{h}_{l_t}$ such that $x_{l_t} \in \overline{X}_\mathcal{B}(\mathbf{h}_{l_t})$ divides $x^{\rho_{t-1}}x^{\tau_t}$ and such that the normal form of $x_{l_t}\mathbf{h}_{l_t}$ is $x^{\mu_2}\mathbf{h}_{k_2}$. Now we do the same for $\mathbf{h}_{k_2}, \mathbf{h}_{k_3}, \ldots$ at the end we reach again $\mathbf{h}_{k_1}$. Hence, we have constructed a cycle in the $\mathcal{B}$-graph.

The final assertion follows immediately from the construction above. □

Lemma 3. *Let $\mathcal{B} = \{\mathbf{h}_1, \ldots, \mathbf{h}_s\}$ be a generating set consisting only of module terms. Assume that for the chosen multiplicative variables $X_\mathcal{B}$ Conditions (i) to (iv) of Definition 1 are satisfied. Furthermore, let the $\mathcal{B}$-graph be acyclic and the elements of $\mathcal{B}$ be numbered in such a way that for any path from $\mathbf{h}_i$ to $\mathbf{h}_j$ in the $\mathcal{B}$-graph we always have $i < j$. If $\prec_\mathcal{B}$ is an arbitrary term order on $\mathcal{P}^s$ such that $x^\alpha \mathbf{e}_i^{(0)} \succ_\mathcal{B} x^\mathcal{B}eta\mathbf{e}_j^{(0)}$ whenever $i < j$, then $(\mathcal{B}, \operatorname{hm}(\mathcal{B}), X_\mathcal{B}, \prec_\mathcal{B})$ is a resolving decomposition.*

Proof. We first remark that a numbering of the set $\mathcal{B}$ as assumed in the Lemma always exists for an acyclic graph. Now we only have to check Condition (v) of Definition 1. Take a generator $\mathbf{h}_i \in \mathcal{B}$ and an arbitrary term $x^\delta \in \mathbb{T}$. Then $x^\delta \mathbf{h}_i = x^\alpha \mathbf{h}_j$ for a suitable multiplicative term $x^\alpha \in \Bbbk[X_\mathcal{B}(\mathbf{h}_j)]$. By Lemma 2, there exists a path from $\mathbf{h}_i$ to $\mathbf{h}_j$ in the $\mathcal{B}$-graph and hence $i < j$. However, this implies $x^\delta \mathbf{e}_i^{(0)} \succ_\mathcal{B} x^\alpha \mathbf{e}_j^{(0)}$ proving the missing condition in the definition of a resolving decomposition. □

The last lemma provides us with a simple check whether a monomial generating set together with the chosen assignment of multiplicative variables can be used for defining a resolving decomposition: we only have to check whether the induced $\mathcal{B}$-graph is acyclic. If this is the case, then we can choose any term order satisfying the property of Lemma 3 to complete the definition of a resolving decomposition. The existence of such a term order is obvious, as every POT lift fulfils this property [16].

Example 3. *Set* $\mathcal{P} = \Bbbk[x_0, x_1, x_2, x_3]$ *with the standard grading and* $m = 1$. *Let* U *be the ideal generated by* $x_0 x_1, x_1^2, x_2 x_3, x_3^3$ *in* $\mathcal{P}$. *A Stanley decomposition of* U *is then given by the set*

$$\mathcal{B} = \{ \mathbf{h}_1 = x_0 x_1, \ \mathbf{h}_2 = x_0 x_1 x_2, \ \mathbf{h}_3 = x_0^2 x_1, \ \mathbf{h}_4 = x_1^2, \ \mathbf{h}_5 = x_1^2 x_3,$$
$$\mathbf{h}_6 = x_0 x_1 x_3, \ \mathbf{h}_7 = x_1^2 x_3^2, \ \mathbf{h}_8 = x_0 x_1 x_3^2, \ \mathbf{h}_9 = x_3^3, \ \mathbf{h}_{10} = x_2 x_3 \}$$

with multiplicative variables

$$\begin{array}{ll}
X_{\mathcal{B}}(\mathbf{h}_1) = \varnothing, & X_{\mathcal{B}}(\mathbf{h}_2) = \{x_0, x_2\} \\
X_{\mathcal{B}}(\mathbf{h}_3) = \{x_0, x_2\}, & X_{\mathcal{B}}(\mathbf{h}_4) = \{x_0, x_1, x_2\} \\
X_{\mathcal{B}}(\mathbf{h}_5) = \{x_1\}, & X_{\mathcal{B}}(\mathbf{h}_6) = \{x_0, x_1\} \\
X_{\mathcal{B}}(\mathbf{h}_7) = \{x_1\}, & X_{\mathcal{B}}(\mathbf{h}_8) = \{x_0, x_1\} \\
X_{\mathcal{B}}(\mathbf{h}_9) = \{x_0, x_1, x_3\}, & X_{\mathcal{B}}(\mathbf{h}_{10}) = \{x_0, x_1, x_2, x_3\}.
\end{array}$$

The corresponding $\mathcal{B}$-*graph is*

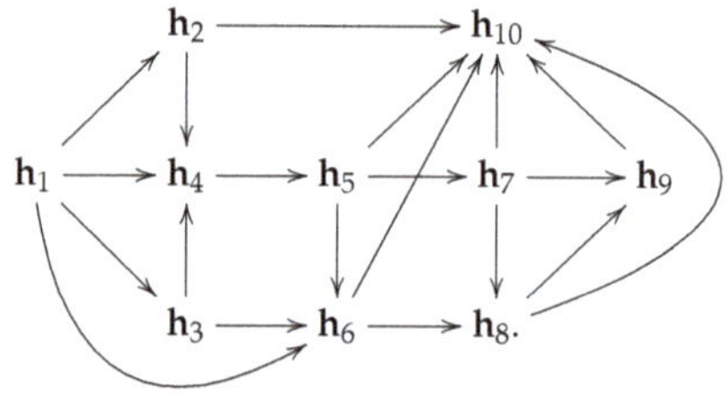

and obviously acyclic. Hence we can choose an arbitrary term order $\prec_{\mathcal{B}}$ *as described in Lemma 3 to complete the definition of a resolving decomposition* $(\mathcal{B}, \mathrm{hm}\,(\mathcal{B}), X_{\mathcal{B}}, \prec_{\mathcal{B}})$.

Example 4. *It should be emphasised that not even in the monomial case does every Stanley decomposition induce a resolving decomposition, i.e., we cannot always find a corresponding term order* $\prec_{\mathcal{B}}$. *A simple counterexample can already be given based on the homogeneous maximal ideal* U *in* $\mathcal{P}$ *for* $n = 4$ *and the standard grading. In ([17], Page 31), it is shown that a Stanley decomposition of* U *is defined by the set*

$$\mathcal{B} = \{ \mathbf{h}_1 = x_0, \quad \mathbf{h}_2 = x_1, \quad \mathbf{h}_3 = x_2, \quad \mathbf{h}_4 = x_3, \quad \mathbf{h}_5 = x_4, \quad \mathbf{h}_6 = x_0 x_1 x_3, \quad \mathbf{h}_7 = x_0 x_2 x_3,$$
$$\mathbf{h}_8 = x_0 x_2 x_4, \quad \mathbf{h}_9 = x_1 x_2 x_4, \quad \mathbf{h}_{10} = x_1 x_3 x_4, \quad \mathbf{h}_{11} = x_0 x_1 x_2 x_3 x_4 \}$$

with multiplicative variables

$$\begin{array}{ll}
X_{\mathcal{B}}(\mathbf{h}_1) = \{x_0, x_1, x_2\}, & X_{\mathcal{B}}(\mathbf{h}_2) = \{x_1, x_2, x_3\} \\
X_{\mathcal{B}}(\mathbf{h}_3) = \{x_2, x_3, x_4\}, & X_{\mathcal{B}}(\mathbf{h}_4) = \{x_0, x_3, x_4\} \\
X_{\mathcal{B}}(\mathbf{h}_5) = \{x_0, x_1, x_4\}, & X_{\mathcal{B}}(\mathbf{h}_6) = \{x_0, x_1, x_2, x_3\} \\
X_{\mathcal{B}}(\mathbf{h}_7) = \{x_0, x_2, x_3, x_4\}, & X_{\mathcal{B}}(\mathbf{h}_8) = \{x_0, x_1, x_2, x_4\} \\
X_{\mathcal{B}}(\mathbf{h}_9) = \{x_1, x_2, x_3, x_4\}, & X_{\mathcal{B}}(\mathbf{h}_{10}) = \{x_0, x_1, x_3, x_4\} \\
X_{\mathcal{B}}(\mathbf{h}_{11}) = \{x_0, x_1, x_2, x_3, x_4\}.
\end{array}$$

The $\mathcal{B}$-*graph corresponding to this basis is*

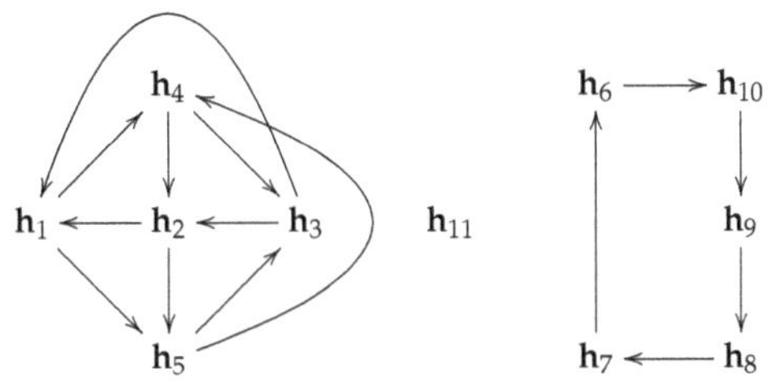

and obviously contains several cycles. Therefore, it is not possible to find a term order $\prec_{\mathcal{B}}$, which makes this Stanley decomposition into a resolving one.

This phenomenon is typical for Stanley decompositions considered in the context of the Stanley conjecture, i. e., for decompositions where one tries to maximise the Stanley depth which is given by the minimal number of multiplicative variables of a generator (see [17] and references therein for more details on the Stanley conjecture).

3. The Syzygy Resolutions Induced by a Resolving Decomposition

Let now $\mathcal{U} = \langle \mathcal{B}^{(0)} \rangle$ with $\mathcal{B}^{(0)} = \{\mathbf{h}_1, \dots, \mathbf{h}_{s_1}\}$ be a finitely generated graded submodule of $\mathcal{P}^m_{\mathbf{d}_0}$, the graded free polynomial module with canonical basis $\{\mathbf{e}^{(0)}_1, \dots, \mathbf{e}^{(0)}_m\}$ and grading defined by the vector $\mathbf{d}_0 = (d^{(0)}_1, \dots d^{(0)}_m)$. We assume that we have somehow obtained a resolving decomposition $(\mathcal{B}^{(0)}, \mathrm{hm}\,(\mathcal{B}^{(0)}), X_{\mathcal{B}^{(0)}}, \prec_{\mathcal{B}^{(0)}})$ of $\mathcal{U}$. Our first step consists of showing that it induces in a natural way a resolving decomposition $(\mathcal{B}^{(1)}, \mathrm{hm}\,(\mathcal{B}^{(1)}), X_{\mathcal{B}^{(1)}}, \prec_{\mathcal{B}^{(1)}})$ of the first syzygy module $\mathrm{Syz}(\mathcal{B}^{(0)}) \subseteq \mathcal{P}^{s_1}$. This result represents an extension or refinement of the classical Schreyer theorem providing a Gröbner basis $\mathcal{G}^{(1)}$ for the syzygy module $\mathrm{Syz}(\mathcal{G}^{(0)})$ of a Gröbner basis $\mathcal{G}^{(0)}$ (see e.g., ([13], Chapt. 5, Thm. 3.3)).

By the definition of a resolving decomposition, we have for every non-multiplicative variable x_k of each generator $\mathbf{h}_\alpha \in \mathcal{B}^{(0)}$ a unique standard representation $x_k \mathbf{h}_\alpha = \sum_{\beta=1}^{s_1} P^{(\alpha;k)}_\beta \mathbf{h}_\beta$ corresponding to the syzygy

$$\mathbf{S}_{\alpha;k} = x_k \mathbf{e}^{(1)}_\alpha - \sum_{\beta=1}^{s_1} P^{(\alpha;k)}_\beta \mathbf{e}^{(1)}_\beta \tag{4}$$

where $\{\mathbf{e}^{(1)}_1, \dots, \mathbf{e}^{(1)}_{s_1}\}$ denotes the canonical basis of the graded free polynomial module $\mathcal{P}^{s_1}_{\mathbf{d}_1}$ with grading defined by the degree vector $\mathbf{d}_1 = (\deg(\mathbf{h}_1), \dots, \deg(\mathbf{h}_s))$.

Lemma 4. *Let $S = \sum_{\alpha=1}^{s_1} S_\alpha \mathbf{e}^{(1)}_\alpha$ be an arbitrary syzygy of $\mathcal{B}^{(0)}$ with coefficients $S_\alpha \in \mathcal{P}$. Then we have $S_\alpha \in \Bbbk[X_{\mathcal{B}^{(0)}}(\mathbf{h}_\alpha)]$ for all $1 \leq \alpha \leq s_1$, if and only if $S = 0$.*

Proof. If $S \in \mathrm{Syz}(\mathcal{B}^{(0)})$, then $\sum_{\alpha=1}^{s_1} S_\alpha \mathbf{h}_\alpha = 0$. By definition of a resolving decomposition, each $\mathbf{f} \in \mathcal{U}$ can be uniquely written in the form $\mathbf{f} = \sum_{\alpha=1}^{s_1} P_\alpha \mathbf{h}_\alpha$ with $\mathbf{h}_\alpha \in \mathcal{B}^{(0)}$ and $P_\alpha \in \Bbbk[X_{\mathcal{B}^{(0)}}(\mathbf{h}_\alpha)]$. In particular, this holds for $0 \in \mathcal{U}$. Thus $0 = S_\alpha \in \Bbbk[X_{\mathcal{B}^{(0)}}(\mathbf{h}_l)]$ for all α and hence $S = 0$. $\square$

We denote the non-multiplicative variables of the generator $\mathbf{h}_\alpha \in \mathcal{B}^{(0)}$ by $\{x_{i^\alpha_1}, \dots, x_{i^\alpha_{r_\alpha}}\}$ where we assume that $i^\alpha_1 < \cdots < i^\alpha_{r_\alpha}$. Then we take as $\mathcal{B}^{(1)}$ the set $\{\mathbf{S}_{\alpha;i^\alpha_k} \mid 1 \leq \alpha \leq s_1,\ 1 \leq k \leq i^\alpha_{r_\alpha}\}$ consisting of all syzygies constructed as above from the products of generators by non-multiplicative variables.

Theorem 1. *For each syzygy $S_{\alpha;i^\alpha_k} \in \mathcal{B}^{(1)}$, we choose as head term*

$$\mathrm{hm}(S_{\alpha;i^\alpha_k}) = x_{i^\alpha_k} \mathbf{e}^{(1)}_\alpha$$

and as multiplicative variables

$$X_{\mathcal{B}^{(1)}}(\mathbf{S}_{\alpha;i^\alpha_k}) = \{x_0, \dots x_n\} \setminus \{x_{i^\alpha_1}, \dots, x_{i^\alpha_{k-1}}\}.$$

Furthermore, we take for $\prec_{\mathcal{B}^{(1)}}$ *the Schreyer order associated to* $\mathcal{B}^{(0)}$ *and* $\prec_{\mathcal{B}^{(0)}}$. *Then the quadruple* $(\mathcal{B}^{(1)}, \operatorname{hm}(\mathcal{B}^{(1)}), X_{\mathcal{B}^{(1)}}, \prec_{\mathcal{B}^{(1)}})$ *defines a resolving decomposition of the syzygy module* $\operatorname{Syz}(\mathcal{B}^{(0)})$.

Proof. We first show that $(\mathcal{B}^{(1)}, \operatorname{hm}(\mathcal{B}^{(1)}), X_{\mathcal{B}^{(1)}}, \prec_{\mathcal{B}^{(1)}})$ is a resolving decomposition of $\langle\mathcal{B}^{(1)}\rangle$. In a second step, we prove that furthermore $\langle\mathcal{B}^{(1)}\rangle = \operatorname{Syz}(\mathcal{B}^{(0)})$.

The first condition of Definition 1 is trivially satisfied. By construction, it is obvious that

$$\operatorname{hm}(\langle\mathcal{B}^{(1)}\rangle) = Bigoplus_{\alpha=1}^{s_1}\langle\overline{X}_{\mathcal{B}^{(0)}}(\mathbf{h}_\alpha)\rangle\mathbf{e}_\alpha^{(1)}\,. \tag{5}$$

It follows from (4) that any non head term $x^\mu\mathbf{e}_l^{(1)} \in \operatorname{supp}(\mathbf{S}_{\alpha;k} - x_k\mathbf{e}_\alpha^{(1)})$ must satisfy $x^\mu \in \Bbbk[X_{\mathcal{B}^{(0)}}(\mathbf{h}_l)]$ and hence we find $x^\mu\mathbf{e}_l^{(1)} \notin \operatorname{hm}(\langle\mathcal{B}^{(1)}\rangle)$ implying Condition (ii). Furthermore, it is obvious that

$$\langle\overline{X}_{\mathcal{B}^{(0)}}(\mathbf{h}_\alpha)\rangle\mathbf{e}_\alpha^{(1)} = \bigoplus_{k=1}^{r_\alpha}\Bbbk[X_{\mathcal{B}^{(1)}}(\mathbf{S}_{\alpha,i_k^\alpha})]x_{i_k^\alpha}\mathbf{e}_\alpha^{(1)}.$$

If we combine this equation with (5), then the first part of Condition (iii) follows immediately.

The second part of this condition is a bit harder to prove. We take an arbitrary module element $\mathbf{f} \in \langle\mathcal{B}^{(1)}\rangle$ and construct its standard representation using $\operatorname{hm}(\langle\mathcal{B}^{(1)}\rangle)$. Assume first that the support of $\mathbf{f}$ contains no multiple of a head term, i. e., $\operatorname{supp}(\mathbf{f}) \cap \operatorname{hm}(\langle\mathcal{B}^{(1)}\rangle) = \emptyset$. Then all terms $x^\epsilon\mathbf{e}_\alpha^{(1)} \in \operatorname{supp}(\mathbf{f})$ in the support must satisfy $x^\epsilon \in X_{\mathcal{B}^{(0)}}(\mathbf{h}_\alpha)$. Therefore, we get that $\mathbf{f} = 0$ due to Lemma 4.

We may thus assume that $\operatorname{supp}(\mathbf{f}) \cap \operatorname{hm}(\langle\mathcal{B}^{(1)}\rangle) \neq \emptyset$ and we take the biggest term $x^\mu\mathbf{e}_\alpha^{(1)}$ in this set with respect to the order $\prec_{\mathcal{B}^{(0)}}$. By the already proven first part of Condition (iii), there must be a syzygy $\mathbf{S}_{\alpha;i}$ such that $x_i \mid x^\mu$ and $x^\mu/x_i \in \Bbbk[X_{\mathcal{B}^{(1)}}(\mathbf{S}_{\alpha;i})]$. We reduce $\mathbf{f}$ by this syzygy and obtain the new module element

$$\mathbf{f}' = \mathbf{f} - c\frac{x^\mu}{x_i}\mathbf{S}_{\alpha;i}$$

for a suitable constant $c \in \Bbbk$ such that the term $x^\mu\mathbf{e}_\alpha^{(1)}$ is no longer in support of $\mathbf{f}'$. Every term $x^\lambda\mathbf{e}_\beta^{(1)} \in \operatorname{supp}(\mathbf{f}')$ that is newly introduced by the subtraction of $c\frac{x^\mu}{x_i}\mathbf{S}_{\alpha;i}$ and that also lies in $\operatorname{hm}(\langle\mathcal{B}^{(1)}\rangle)$ must be strictly less than the removed term $x^\mu\mathbf{e}_\alpha^{(1)}$ by Condition (v) of Definition 1 and by Equation (4) defining the syzygy $\mathbf{S}_{\alpha;i}$.

We repeat this reduction procedure until we eventually obtain a module element $\mathbf{f}''$ such that $\operatorname{supp}(\mathbf{f}'') \cap \operatorname{hm}(\langle\mathcal{B}^{(1)}\rangle) = \emptyset$. This will happen after a finite number of steps, since the reduced terms forms a decreasing sequence with respect to the well-order $\prec_{\mathcal{B}^{(0)}}$. By the same argument as above, this implies that we must have $\mathbf{f}'' = 0$, which concludes the proof of this condition.

The above procedure provides us with an algorithm to compute arbitrary normal forms and hence Condition (iv) follows immediately. For the last condition in Definition 1, we observe that the head term $x_i\mathbf{e}_\alpha^{(1)}$ is the leading term of the syzygy $\mathbf{S}_{\alpha;i}$ for the module term order $\prec_{\mathcal{B}^{(0)}}$. Thus the used Schreyer order indeed satisfies Condition (v). □

As is the case for the classical Schreyer theorem, this construction can now be iterated to obtain resolving decompositions of the second and higher syzygy modules. This iteration thus leads to a (generally non-minimal) free resolution of the submodule U where the constructed syzygies define the columns of the matrices of the differentials. Note that for actually writing down all these syzygies, we must compute many standard representations of products of generators by non-multiplicative variables. This fact does not change compared to the classical situation (where one considers S-polynomials instead of products by variables). However, since a resolving decomposition contains much more information than a Gröbner basis, it is now possible to make at least precise statements about the *shape* of the resolution. More precisely, it turns out that, without any further computations, it is now possible to predict solely on the basis of the resolving decomposition $(\mathcal{B}^{(0)}, \operatorname{hm}(\mathcal{B}^{(0)}), X_{\mathcal{B}^{(0)}}, \prec_{\mathcal{B}^{(0)}})$ the head terms of all higher syzygies and thus in particular their numbers corresponding to the ranks of the free modules appearing in the resolution. Furthermore, the length of the resolution can also be easily read off from $(\mathcal{B}^{(0)}, \operatorname{hm}(\mathcal{B}^{(0)}), X_{\mathcal{B}^{(0)}}, \prec_{\mathcal{B}^{(0)}})$.

Theorem 2. *Let* $(\mathcal{B}^{(0)}, \operatorname{hm}(\mathcal{B}^{(0)}), X_{\mathcal{B}^{(0)}}, \prec_{\mathcal{B}^{(0)}})$ *define a resolving decomposition of the graded submodule* $U \subset \mathcal{P}^m_{\mathbf{d}_0}$. *Denote by* $\beta^{(k)}_{0,j}$ *the number of generators* $\mathbf{h} \in \mathcal{B}^{(0)}$ *which are of degree* j *and have* k *multiplicative variables. Furthermore, we write* $d = \min\{k \mid \exists j : \beta^{(k)}_{0,j} > 0\}$ *for the minimal number of multiplicative variables of a generator. Then the submodule* U *possesses a graded free resolution of length* $n - d + 1$ *of the form*

$$0 \to \bigoplus_j \mathcal{P}(-j)^{r_{n+1-d,j}} \to \cdots \to \bigoplus_j \mathcal{P}(-j)^{r_{1,j}} \to \bigoplus_j \mathcal{P}(-j)^{r_{0,j}} \to U \to 0 \tag{6}$$

where the graded ranks of the appearing free modules are given by

$$r_{i,j} = \sum_{k=1}^{n+1-i} \binom{n+1-k}{i} \beta^{(k)}_{0,j-i}.$$

Proof. Iterating Theorem 1, we can construct a resolving decomposition $(\mathcal{B}^{(i)}, \operatorname{hm}(\mathcal{B}^{(i)}), X_{\mathcal{B}^{(i)}}, \prec_{\mathcal{B}^{(i)}})$ of the ith syzygy module $\operatorname{Syz}_i(U)$ for any i. Given an index $1 \leq l \leq m$ and a non-multiplicative variable $x_k \in \overline{X}_{\mathcal{B}^{(0)}}(\mathbf{h}_{\alpha(l)})$, we find $|\overline{X}_{\mathcal{B}^{(1)}}(S_{l;k})| < |\overline{X}_{\mathcal{B}^{(0)}}(\mathbf{h}_{\alpha(l)})|$.

If d_i denotes the minimal number of multiplicative variables assigned to a head module term in $\operatorname{hm}(\mathcal{B}^{(i)})$, then it is easy to see that the minimal number of multiplicative variables assigned to a head term in $\operatorname{hm}(\mathcal{B}^{(1)})$ is $d + 1$. This fact immediately entails the claimed length of the resolution (6). Furthermore, it follows from our construction of the basic syzygies via products of generators by non-multiplicative variables that $\deg(\mathbf{S}_{k;i}) = \deg(\mathbf{h}_k) + 1$.

The assertion about the graded ranks of the modules is obtained by a combinatorial calculation. We denote by $\beta^{(k)}_{i,j}$ the number of generators in $\mathcal{B}^{(i)}$ of degree j with k multiplicative variables. It follows from our construction, that we have

$$\beta^{(k)}_{i,j} = \sum_{t=1}^{k-1} \beta^{(t)}_{i-1,j-1},$$

as each generator in $\mathcal{B}^{(i-1)}$ of degree $j - 1$ with less than k multiplicative variables contributes one generator in $\mathcal{B}^{(i)}$ with k multiplicative variables. We will now show by induction how $\beta^{(k)}_{i,j}$ can be expressed in terms of $\beta^{(k)}_{0,j}$, namely that

$$\beta^{(k)}_{i,j} = \sum_{t=1}^{k-i} \binom{k-t-1}{i-1} \beta^{(t)}_{0,j-i}.$$

The base case $i = 1$ is trivial. For the inductive step, we first note that obviously $\beta^{(\ell)}_{i,j} = 0$ if $\ell < i + 1$. Using this observation and the inductive hypothesis, we get

$$\beta^{(k)}_{i+1,j} = \sum_{\ell=i+2}^{k-1} \beta^{(\ell)}_{i,j-1} = \sum_{\ell=i+2}^{k-1} \sum_{t=1}^{\ell-i} \binom{\ell-t-1}{i-1} \beta^{(t)}_{0,j-i} = \sum_{t=1}^{k-i-1} \left[\sum_{\ell=i+t}^{k-1} \binom{\ell-t-1}{i-1} \right] \beta^{t}_{0,j-i}.$$

A shift of the index in the inner sum by $t + 1$ proves our claim via the following identity obtained by summing over one column in the Pascal triangle:

$$\sum_{m=i-1}^{k-t-2} \binom{m}{i-1} = \binom{k-t-2}{i}.$$

For the ranks of the free modules, we compute

$$r_{i,j} = \sum_{k=1}^{n+1} \beta_{i,j}^{(k)} = \sum_{k=1}^{n+1} \sum_{t=1}^{k-i} \binom{k-t-1}{i-1} \beta_{0,j-i}^{(t)} = \sum_{k=1}^{n+1-i} \binom{n+1-k}{i} \beta_{0,j-i}^{(k)}$$

where we used again the above identity for binomial coefficients for obtaining the last equality. □

We now take a closer look at this iterative construction of the resolving decompositions $(\mathcal{B}^{(j)}, \operatorname{hm}(\mathcal{B}^{(j)}), X_{\mathcal{B}^{(j)}}, \prec_{\mathcal{B}^{(j)}})$ for the syzygy modules $\operatorname{Syz}_j(\mathcal{U})$. To define an element of $\mathcal{B}^{(j)}$, we consider for each generator $\mathbf{h}_\alpha \in \mathcal{B}^{(0)}$ all ordered integer sequences $\mathbf{k} = (k_1, \ldots, k_j)$ with $0 \leq k_1 < \cdots < k_j \leq n$ of length $|\mathbf{k}| = j$ such that $x_{k_i} \in \overline{X}_{\mathcal{B}^{(0)}}(\mathbf{h}_\alpha)$ for all $1 \leq i \leq j$. We denote for any $1 \leq i \leq j$ by $\mathbf{k}_i$ the sequence obtained by eliminating k_i from $\mathbf{k}$. Then the generator $\mathbf{S}_{\alpha;\mathbf{k}}$ arises recursively from the standard representation of $x_{k_j}\mathbf{S}_{\alpha;\mathbf{k}_j}$ according to the resolving decomposition $(\mathcal{B}^{(j-1)}, \operatorname{hm}(\mathcal{B}^{(j-1)}), X_{\mathcal{B}^{(j-1)}}, \prec_{\mathcal{B}^{(j-1)}})$:

$$x_{k_j}\mathbf{S}_{\alpha;\mathbf{k}_j} = \sum_{\beta=1}^{s_1} \sum_{\mathbf{l}} P_{\beta;\mathbf{l}}^{(\alpha;\mathbf{k})} \mathbf{S}_{\beta;\mathbf{l}}. \tag{7}$$

The second sum is over all ordered integer sequences $\mathbf{l}$ of length $j-1$ such that for each entry ℓ_i the variable x_{ℓ_i} is non-multiplicative for the generator $\mathbf{h}_{Beta} \in \mathcal{B}^{(0)}$. Denoting the free generators of the free module which contains the jth syzygy module by $\mathbf{e}_{\alpha,\mathbf{l}}^{(j)}$, such that $\alpha \in \{1, \ldots, s_1\}$ and $\mathbf{l}$ is an ordered subset of $\overline{X}_{\mathcal{B}^{(0)}}(\mathbf{h}_\alpha)$ of length $j-1$ we get the following representation for $\mathbf{S}_{\alpha,\mathbf{k}}$:

$$\mathbf{S}_{\alpha;\mathbf{k}} = x_{k_j}\mathbf{e}_{\alpha;\mathbf{k}_j}^{(j)} - \sum_{\beta=1}^{s_1} \sum_{\mathbf{l}} P_{\beta;\mathbf{l}}^{(\alpha;\mathbf{k})} \mathbf{e}_{\beta;\mathbf{l}}^{(j)}.$$

An important consequence of our construction is that it allows us to bound certain homological invariants of the submodule $\mathcal{U}$ in terms of data easily read off from the resolving decomposition $(\mathcal{B}^{(0)}, \operatorname{hm}(\mathcal{B}^{(0)}), X_{\mathcal{B}^{(0)}}, \prec_{\mathcal{B}^{(0)}})$. Note, however, that in contrast to the situation in [14] where the resolution induced by a Pommaret basis was considered, we obtain indeed only bounds, whereas a Pommaret basis gives directly the exact values of the invariants.

Corollary 1. *In the situation of Theorem 2, define*

$$d = \min\left\{k \mid \exists j : \beta_{0,j}^{(k)} > 0\right\}, \qquad q = \deg(\mathcal{B}^{(0)}) = \max Bigl\{\deg(\mathbf{h}) \mid \mathbf{h} \in \mathcal{B}^{(0)} Bigr\}.$$

Then we obtain the following bounds for the projective dimension, the Castelnuovo-Mumford regularity and the depth, respectively, of the submodule $\mathcal{U}$*:*

$$\operatorname{pd}(\mathcal{U}) \leq n+1-d, \qquad \operatorname{reg}(\mathcal{U}) \leq q, \qquad \operatorname{depth}(\mathcal{U}) \geq d.$$

Proof. The first estimate follows immediately from the resolution (6) induced by the resolving decomposition $(\mathcal{B}^{(0)}, \operatorname{hm}(\mathcal{B}^{(0)}), X_{\mathcal{B}^{(0)}}, \prec_{\mathcal{B}^{(0)}})$ of $\mathcal{U}$. The last estimate is a simple consequence of the first one and the graded form of the Auslander-Buchsbaum formula ([18], Ex. 19.8). By construction, the module $\operatorname{Syz}_i(\mathcal{B}^{(0)})$ is generated by syzygies of degree less than or equal to $q+i$. Hence $\mathcal{U}$ is q-regular which implies by definition the second estimate. □

Remark 2. *If one takes a closer look at the construction of the resolving decomposition* $(\mathcal{B}^{(1)}, \operatorname{hm}(\mathcal{B}^{(1)}), X_{\mathcal{B}^{(1)}}, \prec_{\mathcal{B}^{(1)}})$ *of* $\operatorname{Syz}(\mathcal{B}^{(0)})$ *provided in Theorem 1, then one notices that* $\mathcal{B}^{(1)}$ *is always a Janet basis of* $\operatorname{Syz}(\mathcal{B}^{(0)})$ *for the order* $\prec_{\mathcal{B}^{(0)}}$*. This follows simply from the fact that the way in which we choose in Theorem 1 the multiplicative variables for* $(B^{(1)}, \operatorname{hm}(B^{(1)}), X_{B^{(1)}}, \prec_{B^{(1)}})$ *is inspired by the definition of the Janet division. Thus, if the resolving decomposition* $(\mathcal{B}^{(0)}, \operatorname{hm}(\mathcal{B}^{(0)}), X_{\mathcal{B}^{(0)}}, \prec_{\mathcal{B}^{(0)}})$ *stems from a Pommaret or a Janet basis,* *then all the resolving decompositions* $(B^{(i)}, \mathrm{hm}\,(B^{(i)}), X_{B^{(i)}}, \prec_{B^{(i)}})$ *are actually also induced by Pommaret or Janet bases for a Schreyer order.*

Gerdt [19] introduced a new involutive division called alex, *since it is based on the anti degree lexicographic order (a local term order for which terms of higher degree are always smaller than those of lower degree). It is easy to see that a Janet basis which only consists of variables defines also an involutive basis for the* alex *division. Hence, the same assertions are true for resolving decompositions induced by* alex *bases.*

Such observations already demonstrate some advantages of the introduction of such a general framework, like resolving decomposition. In our previous works on the free resolutions induced by an involutive basis, we always needed the assumption that the used involutive division L is of Schreyer type to ensure that our construction yields at each step again an L-involutive basis for the syzygy module for a suitable Schreyer order. The construction in Theorem 1 always yields a Janet basis for $\mathrm{Syz}(\mathcal{B}^{(0)})$, *as in a resolving decomposition we can choose the head terms and the multiplicative variables as we like. This allows us to extend the results of [14] to involutive bases for arbitrary involutive divisions (not necessarily of Schreyer type), provided the L-graph of the L-involutive basis is acyclic (which is guaranteed for continuous division). Note that, in contrast to the old approach, the here presented construction will not necessarily lead to an L-involutive basis for each syzygy module, but for most applications this fact is irrelevant.*

4. Explicitly Determining the Differentials

As in the previous section, let $\mathcal{P}^m_{\mathbf{d}_0}$ be a graded free module with free generators $\mathbf{e}^{(0)}_1, \dots \mathbf{e}^{(0)}_m$ and a grading defined by the vector $\mathbf{d}_0 = (d^{(0)}_1, \dots d^{(0)}_m)$. We will always work with a finitely generated graded submodule $\mathcal{U} \subset \mathcal{P}^m_{\mathbf{d}_0}$ with a resolving decomposition $(\mathcal{B}^{(0)}, \mathrm{hm}\,(\mathcal{B}^{(0)}), X_{\mathcal{B}^{(0)}}, \prec_{\mathcal{B}^{(0)}})$ where $\mathcal{B}^{(0)} = \{\mathbf{h}_1, \dots, \mathbf{h}_{s_1}\}$.

While Theorem 2 provides us with the shape of the induced resolution 6, we cannot obtain explicit expressions for the differentials in the resolution. As discussed above, we only now the head term of each higher syzygy. Our goal in this section is to derive such explicit fomulae. We first describe the complex underlying the resolution (6) in a different manner. For this purpose, we introduce two free $\mathcal{P}$-modules, $\mathcal{W} = \bigoplus_{\alpha=1}^{s_1} \mathcal{P}\mathbf{w}_\alpha$ and $\mathcal{V} = \bigoplus_{i=0}^{n} \mathcal{P}\mathbf{v}_i$, the ranks of which are determined by the size of the resolving decomposition $(\mathcal{B}^{(0)}, \mathrm{hm}\,(\mathcal{B}^{(0)}), X_{\mathcal{B}^{(0)}}, \prec_{\mathcal{B}^{(0)}})$ and by the number of variables in the polynomial ring $\mathcal{P}$, respectively. Then we set $\mathcal{C}_i = \mathcal{W} \otimes_{\mathcal{P}} \Lambda_i \mathcal{V}$ where $\Lambda_\bullet$ denotes the exterior product. A $\mathcal{P}$-linear basis of $\mathcal{C}_i$ is provided by the elements $\mathbf{w}_\alpha \otimes \mathbf{v}_{\mathbf{k}}$ where $\mathbf{v}_{\mathbf{k}} = \mathbf{v}_{k_1} \wedge \cdots \wedge \mathbf{v}_{k_i}$ for an ordered sequence $\mathbf{k} = (k_1, \dots, k_i)$ with $0 \le k_1 < \cdots < k_i \le n$. Then the free subcomplex $\mathcal{S}_\bullet \subset \mathcal{C}_\bullet$ generated by all elements $\mathbf{w}_\alpha \otimes \mathbf{v}_{\mathbf{k}}$ with $\mathbf{k} \subseteq \overline{X}_{\mathcal{B}^{(0)}}(\mathbf{h}_\alpha)$ corresponds to (6), if we identify $\mathbf{e}^{(i+1)}_{\alpha;\mathbf{k}} \leftrightarrow \mathbf{w}_\alpha \otimes \mathbf{v}_{\mathbf{k}}$. Let $k_{i+1} \in \overline{X}_{\mathcal{B}^0}(\mathbf{h}_\alpha) \setminus \mathbf{k}$, then the differential comes from (7),

$$d_{\mathcal{S}}(\mathbf{w}_\alpha \otimes \mathbf{v}_{\mathbf{k},k_{i+1}}) = x_{k_{i+1}} \mathbf{w}_\alpha \otimes \mathbf{v}_{\mathbf{k}} - \sum_{\beta,\mathbf{l}} P^{(\alpha;\mathbf{k},k_{i+1})}_{\beta;\mathbf{l}} \mathbf{w}_\beta \otimes \mathbf{v}_{\mathbf{l}}\,,$$

and thus requires the explicit determination of all the higher syzygies (7).

We will now present a method to directly compute the differential without computing higher syzygies. It extends a construction of Sköldberg [10] using algebraic discrete Morse theory [3,4] and generalises our results in [1,6] for the resolution induced by a Pommaret or a Janet basis.

Definition 2. *The graded submodule $\mathcal{U}$ possesses* head linear syzygies, *if it has a finite presentation*

$$0 \longrightarrow \ker \eta \longrightarrow \mathcal{W} = \bigoplus_{\alpha=1}^{s} \mathcal{P}\mathbf{w}_\alpha \xrightarrow{\ \eta\ } \mathcal{U} \longrightarrow 0 \tag{8}$$

such that $\ker \eta$ *can be generated by a finite set* $\mathcal{H} = \{\mathbf{h}_1, \dots, \mathbf{h}_t\}$ *where one can choose for each generator* $\mathbf{h}_\alpha \in \mathcal{H}$ *a head module term* $\mathrm{hm}(\mathbf{h}_\alpha)$ *of the form* $x_i \mathbf{w}_\alpha$.

Sköldberg's construction begins with the following two-sided Koszul complex $(\mathcal{F}, d_{\mathcal{F}})$ defining a free resolution of $\mathcal{U}$. Let V be a $\Bbbk$-linear space with basis $\{\mathbf{v}_0, \dots, \mathbf{v}_n\}$ and introduce the free $\mathcal{P}$-module $\mathcal{F}_j = \mathcal{P} \otimes_{\Bbbk} \Lambda_j V \otimes_{\Bbbk} \mathcal{U}$. Any $\Bbbk$-linear basis $\{m_a \mid a \in A\}$ of $\mathcal{U}$ induces a $\mathcal{P}$-linear basis of $\mathcal{F}_j$ consisting of all elements of the form $1 \otimes v_{\mathbf{k}} \otimes m_a$ with ordered sequences $\mathbf{k}$ of length j. The differential $d_{\mathcal{F}}$ of the two-sided Koszul complex $\mathcal{F}$ is now defined as

$$d_{\mathcal{F}}(1 \otimes \mathbf{v}_{\mathbf{k}} \otimes m_a) = \sum_{i=1}^{j} (-1)^{i+1} \big(x_{k_i} \otimes \mathbf{v}_{\mathbf{k}_i} \otimes m_a - 1 \otimes \mathbf{v}_{\mathbf{k}_i} \otimes x_{k_i} m_a \big). \tag{9}$$

Note that the second term on the right hand side is not yet expressed in the chosen $\Bbbk$-linear basis of $\mathcal{U}$ and that this resolution is generally of infinite size, as the index set A is almost always infinite. For notational simplicity, we will drop in the sequel the tensor sign $\otimes$ and leading factors 1 when writing elements of $\mathcal{F}_\bullet$.

Sköldberg uses a specialisation of head linear terms. He requires that for a given term order $\prec$ the leading module of $\ker \eta$ in the presentation (8) must be generated by terms of the form $x_i \mathbf{w}_\alpha$. In this case, he says that $\mathcal{U}$ has *initially linear syzygies*. Our definition is term order free. Furthermore, Sköldberg considered exclusively the case that the presentation (8) is minimal. However, this represents a severe restriction, as the existence of such presentations cannot be guaranteed. As his construction needs this restriction only to ensure that the final resolution is minimal, we have dropped it.

For a module $\mathcal{U}$ with head linear syzygies via a presentation (8), we now construct a finite resolution $(\mathcal{G}, d_{\mathcal{G}})$ via a Morse matching. We call the variables

$$\operatorname{crit}(\mathbf{w}_\alpha) = \{x_j \mid x_j \mathbf{w}_\alpha \in \operatorname{hm}(\mathcal{H})\},$$

where $\mathcal{H}$ is chosen as in Definition 2, *critical* for the generator $\mathbf{w}_\alpha$; the remaining *non-critical* ones are contained in the set $\operatorname{ncrit}(\mathbf{w}_\alpha)$. Then a $\Bbbk$-linear basis of $\mathcal{U}$ is given by all elements $x^\mu \mathbf{h}_\alpha$ with $\mathbf{h}_\alpha = \eta(\mathbf{w}_\alpha)$ and $x^\mu \in \Bbbk[\operatorname{ncrit}(\mathbf{w}_\alpha)]$. Following [4], we define $\mathcal{G}_j \subseteq \mathcal{F}_j$ as the free submodule generated by those vertices $\mathbf{v}_{\mathbf{k}} \mathbf{h}_\alpha$ where the ordered sequences $\mathbf{k}$ are of length j and such that every entry k_i is critical for $\mathbf{w}_\alpha$. In particular $\mathcal{W} \cong \mathcal{G}_0$ with an isomorphism induced by $\mathbf{w}_\alpha \mapsto \mathbf{v}_\emptyset \mathbf{h}_\alpha$.

The description of the differential $d_{\mathcal{G}}$ is based on reduction paths in the associated Morse graph (for a detailed treatment of these notions, see [1,3,4]) and expresses the differential as a triple sum. If we assume that, after expanding the right hand side of (9) in the chosen $\Bbbk$-linear basis of $\mathcal{U}$, the differential of the complex $\mathcal{F}_\bullet$ can be expressed as

$$d_{\mathcal{F}}(\mathbf{v}_{\mathbf{k}} \mathbf{h}_\alpha) = \sum_{\mathbf{m}, \mu, \gamma} Q^{\mathbf{k}, \alpha}_{\mathbf{m}, \mu, \gamma} \mathbf{v}_{\mathbf{m}} (x^\mu \mathbf{h}_\gamma),$$

then $d_{\mathcal{G}}$ is defined by

$$d_{\mathcal{G}}(\mathbf{v}_{\mathbf{k}} \mathbf{h}_\alpha) = \sum_{\mathbf{l}, \beta} \sum_{\mathbf{m}, \mu, \gamma} \sum_{p} \rho_p \big(Q^{\mathbf{k}, \alpha}_{\mathbf{m}, \mu, \gamma} \mathbf{v}_{\mathbf{m}} (x^\mu \mathbf{h}_\gamma) \big) \tag{10}$$

where the first sum ranges over all ordered sequences $\mathbf{l}$ which consists entirely of critical indices for $\mathbf{w}_\beta$. Moreover, the second sum may be restricted to all values such that a polynomial multiple of $\mathbf{v}_{\mathbf{m}}(x^\mu \mathbf{h}_\gamma)$ effectively appears in $d_{\mathcal{F}}(\mathbf{v}_{\mathbf{k}} \mathbf{h}_\alpha)$ and the third sum ranges over all reduction paths p going from $\mathbf{v}_{\mathbf{m}}(x^\mu \mathbf{h}_\gamma)$ to $\mathbf{v}_{\mathbf{l}} \mathbf{h}_\beta$. Finally ρ_p is the reduction associated with the reduction path p satisfying

$$\rho_p \big(\mathbf{v}_{\mathbf{m}} (x^\mu \mathbf{h}_\gamma) \big) = q_p \mathbf{v}_{\mathbf{l}} \mathbf{h}_\beta$$

for some polynomial $q_p \in \mathcal{P}$.

Remark 3. *The explicit formula (10) with its complicated summation ranges obviously looks rather cumbersome and does not appear to be very useful for practical purposes. However, this first impression is misleading. In fact, (10) can be well exploited both theoretically and computationally. As shown by the* CoCoALib *implementations described in [1,6], it is for a computer rather straightforward to evaluate (10) for any concrete submodule U. Moreover, the most valuable feature of (10) is that it provides an explicit expression for each entry in the differential which is independent of all other entries of the differential. This observation will be the key for the efficient determination of Betti numbers (even individual ones).*

In the sequel, we will show that for a finitely generated graded module U with resolving decomposition $(\mathcal{B}^{(0)}, \mathrm{hm}(\mathcal{B}^{(0)}), X_{\mathcal{B}^{(0)}}, \prec_{\mathcal{B}^{(0)}})$ the resolution constructed by Sköldberg's method is isomorphic to the resolution which is induced by the resolving decomposition, if we choose the head linear syzygies properly. Firstly, we obtain the following trivial assertion.

Lemma 5. *If the graded submodule $U \subseteq \mathcal{P}^{s_1}_{\mathbf{d}_0}$ possesses a resolving decomposition $(\mathcal{B}^{(0)}, \mathrm{hm}(\mathcal{B}^{(0)}), X_{\mathcal{B}^{(0)}}, \prec_{\mathcal{B}^{(0)}})$, then it has head linear syzygies. More precisely, we can set $\mathrm{crit}(\mathbf{w}_\alpha) = \overline{X}_{\mathcal{B}^{(0)}}(\mathbf{h}_\alpha)$, i. e., the critical variables of the vector $\mathbf{w}_\alpha$ are simply the non-multiplicative variables of the generator $\mathbf{h}_\alpha = \eta(\mathbf{w}_\alpha)$.*

We will subsequently apply some lemmata from [1]. In this reference, they are formulated only for the special case that the resolution is induced by a Pommaret basis. Nevertheless, if not explicitly stated otherwise, we can still use them in our more general setting, as their proofs remain correct also for arbitrary resolving decompositions. This is due to the fact that the proofs only require the existence of unique standard representations and a separation of the variables into multiplicative and non-multiplicative ones. In some proofs, the notion of the class of a generator in $\mathcal{B}^{(0)}$ appears. As already mentioned above, it is used to assign multiplicative variables for the Pommaret division. When working with an arbitrary resolving decomposition, one must simply substitute it by the maximal index of a multiplicative variable of the considered generator.

We could see above that the explicit description of the differential $d_{\mathcal{G}}$ is based on reduction paths in the associated Morse graph. We now take a closer look at them and their properties. Any reduction path can be decomposed into so-called elementary ones which are always of length two. One can distinguish three different types of elementary reductions paths ([1], Section 4). Those of *type 0* are irrelevant ([1], Lemma 4.5); the other ones have the form

$$\mathbf{v_k}(x^\mu \mathbf{h}_\alpha) \longrightarrow \mathbf{v}_{\mathbf{k}\cup i}(\frac{x^\mu}{x_i}\mathbf{h}_\alpha) \longrightarrow \mathbf{v_l}(x^\nu \mathbf{h}_\beta)\,.$$

Here $\mathbf{k} \cup i$ denotes the ordered sequence arising when i is inserted into the sequence $\mathbf{k}$; likewise $\mathbf{k} \setminus i$ stands for the sequence obtained by removing an index $i \in \mathbf{k}$. Now we distinguish two further types of elementary reduction paths depending on the form of the associated reduction.

Type 1: This is the case where $\mathbf{l} = (\mathbf{k} \cup i)\backslash j$, $x^\nu = \frac{x^\mu}{x_i}$ and $\beta = \alpha$. Note that it is allowed that $i = j$. We define $\epsilon(i;\mathbf{k}) = (-1)^{|\{j \in \mathbf{k} | j > i\}|}$. Then the corresponding reduction is

$$\rho(\mathbf{v_k} x^\mu \mathbf{h}_\alpha) = \epsilon(i; \mathbf{k} \cup i)\epsilon(j; \mathbf{k} \cup i) x_j \mathbf{v}_{(\mathbf{k}\cup i)\backslash j}(\frac{x^\mu}{x_i}\mathbf{h}_\alpha)\,.$$

Type 2: In this case $\mathbf{l} = (\mathbf{k} \cup i) \setminus j$ and the term $x^\nu \mathbf{h}_\beta$ appears in the involutive standard representation of the product $\frac{x^\mu x_j}{x_i}\mathbf{h}_\alpha$ with the coefficient $\lambda_{j,i,\alpha,\mu,\nu,\beta} \in \Bbbk$. By the construction of the Morse matching, we now always find $i \neq j$. The corresponding reduction is

$$\rho(\mathbf{v_k} x^\mu \mathbf{h}_\alpha) = -\epsilon(i; \mathbf{k} \cup i)\epsilon(j; \mathbf{k} \cup i)\lambda_{j,i,\alpha,\mu,\nu,\beta} \mathbf{v}_{(\mathbf{k}\cup i)\backslash j}(x^\nu \mathbf{h}_\beta)\,.$$

This case distinction comes from the differential (9). Summands appearing in it possess one of the following two possible forms: $x_{k_i}\mathbf{v}_{\mathbf{k}_i} m_a$ or $\mathbf{v}_{\mathbf{k}_i}(x_{k_i} m_a)$. Each of these summands corresponds to a directed edge in the Morse graph $\Gamma^A_{\mathcal{F}_\bullet}$. Consider now an elementary reduction path

$$\mathbf{v_k}(x^\mu \mathbf{h}_\alpha) \longrightarrow \mathbf{v}_{\mathbf{k}\cup i}(\frac{x^\mu}{x_i}\mathbf{h}_\alpha) \longrightarrow \mathbf{v_l}(x^\nu \mathbf{h}_\beta)\,.$$

If the second edge starts at a summand of the first resp. second form, then the elementary reduction path is of type 1 resp. type 2.

For the proof of the existence of an isomorphism relating the resolution induced by a resolving decomposition to the resolution constructed via the above outlined method of Sköldberg, we recall a well-known result about the uniqueness of free resolutions.

Theorem 3. *([20], Theorem 1.6) Let U be a finitely generated graded $\mathcal{P}$-module. If $\mathcal{F}$ is the graded minimal free resolution of U and $\mathcal{G}$ an arbitrary graded free resolution of U, then $\mathcal{G}$ is isomorphic to the direct sum of $\mathcal{F}$ and a trivial complex.*

Theorem 4. *Let $U \subset \mathcal{P}^m_{\mathbf{d}}$ be a graded submodule. The graded free resolution $\mathcal{F}$ induced by a resolving decomposition $(\mathcal{B}^{(0)}, \operatorname{hm}(\mathcal{B}^{(0)}), X_{\mathcal{B}^{(0)}}, \prec_{\mathcal{B}^{(0)}})$ of U and the graded free resolution $\mathcal{G}$ obtained by the method of Sköldberg in the case that the head linear syzygies have been chosen in such a way that $\operatorname{crit}(\mathbf{h}_\alpha) = \overline{X}_{\mathcal{B}^{(0)}}(\mathbf{h}_\alpha)$ for every generator $\mathbf{h}_\alpha \in \mathcal{B}^{(0)}$ are isomorphic.*

Proof. It is not difficult to see that bases for the free modules in the resolution $\mathcal{G}$ constructed by Sköldberg's method consists of those generators $\mathbf{v_k}\mathbf{h}_\alpha$ with $x_k \in \overline{X}_{\mathcal{B}^{(0)}}(\mathbf{h}_\alpha)$ for all indices k contained in $\mathbf{k}$. In the discussion following the proof of Theorem 2, we showed that bases for the modules in the resolution $\mathcal{F}$ coming from the resolving decomposition are induced by the syzygies $\mathbf{S}_{\alpha,\mathbf{k}}$ and are thus of the same cardinality. Hence, the two resolutions considered possess the same shape, meaning that the homogeneous components of the contained free modules satisfy $\dim_{\Bbbk}(\mathcal{F}_i)_j = \dim_{\Bbbk}(\mathcal{G}_i)_j$. The made assertion is now a trivial consequence of Theorem 3. □

This proof already indicates that the two considered resolutions actually possess very similar differentials. To deepen the comparison of the resolutions a bit more, we now recall a few further simple observations made in [1]. It turns out that in the resolution $\mathcal{G}$ we may always choose as head module terms for the higher syzygies exactly the same terms that appear as head module terms in the resolving decompositions $(\mathcal{B}^{(i)}, \operatorname{hm}(\mathcal{B}^{(i)}), X_{\mathcal{B}^{(i)}}, \prec_{\mathcal{B}^{(i)}})$. In the case that we start with a resolving decomposition induced by an involutive bases and then obtain involutive bases for all syzygy modules (recall Remark 2), this entails that Sköldberg's method also actually constructs involutive bases.

Lemma 6. *([1], Lemma 4.3) Given an index i such that $x_i \in \operatorname{crit}(\mathbf{h}_\alpha)$, let $x_i\mathbf{h}_\alpha = \sum_{\beta=1}^{s_1} P_\beta^{(\alpha;i)}\mathbf{h}_\beta$ be the standard representation. Then we have $d_{\mathcal{G}}(\mathbf{v}_i\mathbf{h}_\alpha) = x_i\mathbf{v}_\emptyset\mathbf{h}_\alpha - \sum_{\beta=1}^{s_1} P_\beta^{(\alpha;i)}\mathbf{v}_\emptyset\mathbf{h}_\beta$.*

Our next statement may be interpreted in the following way. Assume that we choose in the Morse graph a vertex $\mathbf{v}_i(x^\mu\mathbf{h}_\alpha)$ having certain properties and then follow all possible reduction paths starting at it. Then we will never reach a point where it becomes necessary to calculate a standard representation. Assume furthermore that the chosen vertex possesses no critical (i.e., non-multiplicative) variables. Then no such variables will arise while we follow a reduction path. If we want to generalise this statement to higher homological degrees, then we must only replace the index conditions $x_i \in \operatorname{ncrit}(\mathbf{h}_\alpha)$ and $x_j \in \operatorname{ncrit}(\mathbf{h}_\beta)$ by the conditions $x_k \in \operatorname{ncrit}(\mathbf{h}_\alpha)$ and $x_\ell \in \operatorname{ncrit}(\mathbf{h}_\beta)$ for all indices k and ℓ contained in the ordered sequences $\mathbf{k}$ and $\mathbf{l}$, respectively.

Lemma 7. *([1], Lemma 4.4) Assume that $\{x_i\} \cup \operatorname{supp}(x^\mu) \subseteq \operatorname{ncrit}(\mathbf{h}_\alpha)$. Then for any reduction path $p = \mathbf{v}_i(x^\mu\mathbf{h}_\alpha) \to \cdots \to \mathbf{v}_j(x^\nu\mathbf{h}_\beta)$ we have $x_j \in \operatorname{ncrit}(\mathbf{h}_\beta)$. In particular, in this situation there is no reduction path $p = \mathbf{v}_i(x^\mu\mathbf{h}_\alpha) \to \cdots \to \mathbf{v}_k\mathbf{h}_\beta$ with $x_k \in \operatorname{crit}(\mathbf{h}_\beta)$.*

Our final corollary now asserts that we can indeed choose in the resolution $\mathcal{G}$ head module terms in such a way that there is a one-to-one correspondence to the head module terms in the resolution $\mathcal{F}$. It is a direct consequence of Lemma 7 and provides us with an alternative explicit proof of Theorem 4.

Corollary 2. *Let* $\mathbf{k} = (k_1, \ldots, k_j)$ *with* $x_{k_i} \in \operatorname{crit} \mathbf{h}_\alpha$ *for all i, then*

$$x_{k_l} \mathbf{v}_{\mathbf{k} \setminus k_l} \mathbf{h}_\alpha \in \operatorname{supp}(d_{\mathcal{G}}(\mathbf{v}_{\mathbf{k}} \mathbf{h}_\alpha)).$$

5. Conclusions

In this article, we introduced a framework that provides many different types of bases of graded polynomial submodules with an effective syzygy theory. The key is less the properties of the bases themselves and more the combinatorial decompositions induced by them via the choice of head terms and multiplicative variables. Effectivity is guaranteed through the required term order.

Given any basis that induces a resolving decomposition in the sense of Definition 1, we obtain with Theorem 1 a generalised version of the classical Schreyer theorem and iteration leads to a free resolution. One should, however, note the following crucial difference. The classical Schreyer theorem yields only "in principle" a resolution; without actually performing the computations required for every iteration step, no information about the final resolution can be obtained. By contrast, Theorem 2 describes already the full shape of the final resolution based only on the resolving decomposition of the given submodule. Thus we could give (usually quite sharp) bounds for important homological invariants in Corollary 1. In fact, the numbers $r_{i,j}$ given in Theorem 2 can also be interpreted as upper bounds for the Betti numbers.

In [1], we showed that with the help of Pommaret bases Sköldberg's method for the construction of an explicit resolution can be made fully effective and then yields essentially the same resolution, as the one induced by the Pommaret basis. In Section 4, we extended these results to arbitrary resolving decompositions and thus provided an approach for the explicit computation of free resolutions based on such a decomposition.

In [1,6], we presented a method to effectively compute graded Betti numbers via the induced free resolutions of Janet and Pommaret bases and the method of Sköldberg. It is well-known that one needs only the constant part of an arbitrary free resolution to determine the Betti numbers via linear algebra over the field $\Bbbk$. We showed that the method of Sköldberg allows us to compute directly only this constant part instead of the whole resolution which drastically improves the complexity of such a computation. With this approach, it is even possible to determine a single Betti number without computing the complete constant part of the free resolution. The reason for this is that Sköldberg's formula allows us to compute any entry of a differential in the free resolution independently of the rest of the free resolution. Furthermore, the theorem about the induced free resolution gives us a formula to compute the ranks of any homogeneous component appearing in the resolution. These methods are also applicable for an arbitrary resolving decomposition due to the fact that we proved Theorem 2 and the form of the differential (10).

Author Contributions: Both authors contributed equally to conceptualisation and writing of this article.

Funding: The research of the first author was funded by Otto Braun-Stiftung and the research of the second author partially by the European grant H2020-FETOPEN-2016-2017-CSA SC^2 (712689).

Conflicts of Interest: The authors declare no conflict of interest.

References

1. Albert, M.; Fetzer, M.; Sáenz-de Cabezón, E.; Seiler, W. On the free resolution induced by a Pommaret basis. *J. Symb. Comp.* **2015**, *68*, 4–26. [CrossRef]
2. Seiler, W. A Combinatorial Approach to Involution and δ-Regularity I: Involutive Bases in Polynomial Algebras of Solvable Type. *Appl. Algebr. Eng. Commun. Comput.* **2009**, *20*, 207–259. [CrossRef]
3. Jöllenbeck, M.; Welker, V. *Minimal Resolutions via Algebraic Discrete Morse Theory*; Memoirs American Mathematical Society (AMS): Providence, RI, USA, 2009; Volume 197.
4. Sköldberg, E. Morse Theory from an Algebraic Viewpoint. *Trans. Am. Math. Soc.* **2006**, *358*, 115–129. [CrossRef]
5. Abbott, J.; Bigatti, M. CoCoALib: A C++ Library for Doing Computations in Commutative Algebra. Available online: http://cocoa.dima.unige.it/cocoalib (accessed on 9 August 2018).
6. Albert, M.; Fetzer, M.; Seiler, W.M. Janet Bases and Resolutions in CoCoALib. In *Computer Algebra in Scientific Computing, Proceedings of the 17th International Workshop on Computer Algebra in Scientific Computing (CASC 2015), Aachen, Germany, 14–18 September 2015*; Gerdt, V.P., Koepf, W., Seiler, W.M., Vorozhtsov, E.V., Eds.; Springer International Publishing: Cham, Switzerland, 2015; pp. 15–29.
7. Albert, M. Computing Quot Schemes. Ph.D. Thesis, Institut für Mathematik, Universität Kassel, Kassel, Germany, 2017.
8. Albert, M.; Bertone, C.; Roggero, M.; Seiler, W.M. Computing Quot Schemes via Marked Bases over Quasi-Stable Modules. *arXiv* **2018**, arXiv:1511.03547v2 .
9. Albert, M.; Seiler, W. Resolving Decompositions for Polynomial Modules. In *Computer Algebra in Scientific Computing, Proceedings of the 18th International Workshop on Computer Algebra in Scientific Computing—CASC 2016, Bucharest, Romania, 19–23 September 2016*; Lecture Notes in Computer Science; Gerdt, V., Koepf, W., Seiler, W., Vorozhtsov, E., Eds.; Springer: Cham, Switzerland, 2016; Volume 9890, pp. 13–27.
10. Sköldberg, E. Resolutions of Modules with Initially Linear Syzygies. *arXiv* **2011**, arXiv:1106.1913.
11. Stanley, R. Hilbert Functions of Graded Algebras. *Adv. Math.* **1978**, *28*, 57–83. [CrossRef]
12. Cox, D.; Little, J.; O'Shea, D. *Ideals, Varieties, and Algorithms*; Undergraduate Texts in Mathematics; Springer: New York, NY, USA, 1992.
13. Cox, D.; Little, J.; O'Shea, D. *Using Algebraic Geometry*; Graduate Texts in Mathematics 185; Springer: New York, NY, USA, 1998.
14. Seiler, W. A Combinatorial Approach to Involution and δ-Regularity II: Structure Analysis of Polynomial Modules with Pommaret Bases. *Appl. Algebr. Eng. Commun. Comput.* **2009**, *20*, 261–338. [CrossRef]
15. Given a term order $\prec$ on $\mathcal{P}$, its term over position (TOP) lifts to a module term order $\prec_{TOP}$ on $\mathcal{P}^m_{\mathbf{d}}$ is defined as follows: let $x^\mu \mathbf{e}^{(0)}_k, x^\nu \mathbf{e}^{(0)}_l \in \mathcal{P}^m_{\mathbf{d}}$, then $x^\mu \mathbf{e}^{(0)}_k \succ_{TOP} x^\nu \mathbf{e}^{(0)}_l$ if $x^\mu \succ x^\nu$ or if $x^\mu = x^\nu$ and $k < l$.
16. Given a term order $\prec$ on $\mathcal{P}$, its position over term (POT) lift to a module term order $\prec_{POT}$ on $\mathcal{P}^m_{\mathbf{d}}$ is defined as follows: let $x^\mu \mathbf{e}^{(0)}_k, x^\nu \mathbf{e}^{(0)}_l \in \mathcal{P}^m_{\mathbf{d}}$, then $x^\mu \mathbf{e}^{(0)}_k \succ_{POT} x^\nu \mathbf{e}^{(0)}_l$ if $k < l$ or if $k = l$ and $x^\mu \succ x^\nu$.
17. Herzog, J. A Survey on Stanley Depth. In *Monomial Ideals, Computations and Applications*; Bigatti, A., Gimenez, P., Sáenz-de Cabezón, E., Eds.; Lecture Notes in Mathemmatics; Springer: Berlin/Heidelberg, Germany, 2013; Volume 2083, pp. 3–45.
18. Eisenbud, D. *Commutative Algebra with a View Toward Algebraic Geometry*; Graduate Texts in Mathematics 150; Springer: New York, NY, USA, 1995.
19. Gerdt, V.P.; Blinkov, Y.A. Involutive Division Generated by an Antigraded Monomial Ordering. In *Computer Algebra in Scientific Computing, Proceedings of the 13th International Workshop on Computer Algebra in Scientific Computing (CASC 2011), Kassel, Germany, 5–9 September 2011*; Gerdt, V.P., Koepf, W., Mayr, E.W., Vorozhtsov, E. V., Eds.; Springer: Berlin/Heidelberg, Germany, 2011; pp. 158–174.
20. Eisenbud, D. *The Geometry of Syzygies: A Second Course in Algebraic Geometry and Commutative Algebra (Graduate Texts in Mathematics)*; Springer: Berlin/Heidelberg, Germany, 2005.

© 2018 by the authors. Licensee MDPI, Basel, Switzerland. This article is an open access article distributed under the terms and conditions of the Creative Commons Attribution (CC BY) license (http://creativecommons.org/licenses/by/4.0/).

mathematics

MDPI

Article

First Integrals of the May–Leonard Asymmetric System

Valery Antonov [1], Wilker Fernandes [2], Valery G. Romanovski [3,4,5,*] and Natalie L. Shcheglova [6]

1. Department of Mathematics, Peter the Great St. Petersburg Polytechnic University, Polytechnicheskaya, 29, 195251 St. Petersburg, Russia; antonovvi@mail.ru
2. Departamento de Matemática e Estatística, Universidade Federal de São João del Rei, São João del Rei, Minas Gerais 36307-352, Brazil; wilker@ufsj.edu.br
3. Faculty of Electrical Engineering and Computer Science, University of Maribor, Koroška cesta 46, SI-2000 Maribor, Slovenia
4. Center for Applied Mathematics and Theoretical Physics, Mladinska 3, SI-2000 Maribor, Slovenia
5. Faculty of Natural Science and Mathematics, University of Maribor, Koroška cesta 160, SI-2000 Maribor, Slovenia
6. Faculty of Mechanics and Mathematics, Belarusian State University, Nezavisimosti avenue 4, 220030 Minsk, Belarus; shcheglova@tut.by

* Correspondence: valerij.romanovskij@um.si

Received: 8 January 2019 ; Accepted: 15 March 2019; Published: 21 March 2019

Abstract: For the May–Leonard asymmetric system, which is a quadratic system of the Lotka–Volterra type depending on six parameters, we first look for subfamilies admitting invariant algebraic surfaces of degree two. Then for some such subfamilies we construct first integrals of the Darboux type, identifying the systems with one first integral or with two independent first integrals.

Keywords: integrability; invariant surfaces; Lotka–Volterra system; computational algebra

---

1. Introduction

An important class of mathematical models describing different phenomena in biology, ecology and chemistry are the so-called Lotka–Volterra systems, which are written in the form

$$\dot{x}_i = x_i\Big(\sum_{j=1}^{n} a_{ij}x_j + b_i\Big) \qquad (i = 1, \dots, n). \tag{1}$$

They were introduced independently by Lotka and Volterra in the 1920s to model the interaction among species, see [1,2], and continue being intensively investigated. For the class of systems in Equation (1), most studies are devoted to the case $n = 3$. One of simplest models of such a type describing a competition of three species was introduced by May and Leonard in [3]. It is a model depending on two parameters and is written as the differential system

$$\begin{aligned} \dot{x} &= x(1 - x - \alpha y - \beta z), \\ \dot{y} &= y(1 - \beta x - y - \alpha z), \\ \dot{z} &= z(1 - \alpha x - \beta y - z), \end{aligned} \tag{2}$$

where $x, y, z \geq 0$, $0 < \alpha < 1 < \beta$, and

$$\alpha + \beta > 2. \tag{3}$$

It was shown in [3] that system (2) has four singular points in $\mathbb{R}^3_+ = \{(x,y,z) \in \mathbb{R}^3,\ x,y,z \geq 0\}$—three of them are on the boundary of $\mathbb{R}^3_+$ in

$$E_1 = (1,0,0),\ E_2 = (0,1,0),\ E_3 = (0,0,1)$$

and the fourth one in the interior point

$$C = ((1+\alpha+\beta)^{-1}, (1+\alpha+\beta)^{-1}, (1+\alpha+\beta)^{-1}).$$

There is a separatix cycle F formed by orbits connecting E_1, E_2 and E_3 on the boundary of $\mathbb{R}^3_+$ and every orbit in $\mathbb{R}^3_+$, except of the equilibrium point C, has F as ω-limit. It was shown in [3] that in the degenerate case $\alpha + \beta = 2$, the cycle F becomes a triangle on the invariant plane

$$x + y + z = 1,$$

all orbits inside the triangle are closed and every orbit in the interior of $\mathbb{R}^3_+$ has one of these closed orbits as an ω-limit. Latter on, the dynamics of Equation (2) was studied in more details in [4–6] and some other works.

A generalization of model (2) is the model described by the differential system

$$\begin{aligned} \dot{x} &= x(1 - x - \alpha_1 y - \beta_1 z) = X(x,y,z), \\ \dot{y} &= y(1 - \beta_2 x - y - \alpha_2 z) = Y(x,y,z), \\ \dot{z} &= z(1 - \alpha_3 x - \beta_3 y - z) = Z(x,y,z), \end{aligned} \tag{4}$$

where $x, y, z \geq 0$ and $\alpha_i,\ \beta_i > 0\ (1 \leq i \leq 3)$, which is called the asymmetric May–Leonard model. The dynamics of Equation (4) were studied in [6–9]. In particular, Chi, Hsu and Wu [8] studied (4) under the assumption

$$0 < \alpha_i < 1 < \beta_i\ (1 \leq i \leq 3) \tag{5}$$

and showed that under this assumption the system has a unique interior equilibrium P, which is locally asymptotically stable if

$$A_1 A_2 A_3 > B_1 B_2 B_3,$$

where $A_i = 1 - \alpha_i, \quad B_i = \beta_i - 1, \quad (1 \leq i \leq 3)$, and if

$$A_1 A_2 A_3 < B_1 B_2 B_3,$$

then P is a saddle point with a one-dimensional stable manifold. They also have shown that if $A_1 A_2 A_3 \neq B_1 B_2 B_3$, then the system does not have periodic solutions, and if

$$A_1 A_2 A_3 = B_1 B_2 B_3, \tag{6}$$

then there is a family of periodic solutions. It was shown in [7] that even if assumption (5) is dropped, the system (4) still can have a family of periodic solutions. Moreover, it was shown there, that the periodic solutions of the system do not arise as a result of Hopf bifurcations, but their existence is due to the Lyapunov theorem on holomorphic integrals.

First integrals of the May–Leonard system (2) were studied by Leach and Miritzis [10] (see also [11]), who obtained the following first integrals:

(i) $H_1 = \frac{xyz}{(x+y+z)^3}$ if $\alpha + \beta = 2$ and $\alpha \neq 1$,
(ii) $H_2 = \frac{y(x-z)}{x(y-z)}$ if $\alpha = \beta \neq 1$,
(iii) $H_3 = x/z$ and $H_4 = y/z$, which are two independent first integrals, if $\alpha = \beta = 1$.

It was shown in [4] that system (2) is completely integrable, that is, it admits two independent first integrals, if either $\alpha + \beta = 2$ or $\beta = \alpha$.

In this paper we study integrability of the asymmetric May–Leonard model (4). Using algorithms from elimination theory, we first find systems of the form in Equation (4) admitting invariant planes and invariant surfaces defined by the quadratic polynomials. Then we look for first integrals of the Darboux type constructed using these invariant surfaces and find subfamilies of (4) admitting one or two independent first integrals. As we show, the set of systems with first integrals is much larger for system (4) than for the classical May–Leonard system (2).

2. Preliminaries

In this section we recall some general results from elimination theory and the Darboux theory of integrability, which we shall use in our study.

Consider the system of differential equations

$$\begin{aligned} \dot{x} &= P(x,y,z), \\ \dot{y} &= Q(x,y,z), \\ \dot{z} &= R(x,y,z), \end{aligned} \tag{7}$$

where P, Q and R are polynomials of degree at most m, and let $\mathfrak{X}$ be the corresponding vector field,

$$\mathfrak{X} = P\frac{\partial}{\partial x} + Q\frac{\partial}{\partial y} + R\frac{\partial}{\partial z}.$$

A C^1 function

$$H : U \to \mathbb{R}$$

with $U \subset \mathbb{R}^3$, non-constant in any open subset of U is a first integral of the differential system (7) if and only if $\mathfrak{X}H \equiv 0$ in U. Let $H_1 : U_1 \to \mathbb{R}$ and $H_2 : U_2 \to \mathbb{R}$ be two first integrals of the system (7). It is said that H_1 and H_2 are functionally independent in $U_1 \cap U_2$ if their gradients are independent in all the points of $U_1 \cap U_2$ except perhaps in a zero Lebesgue measure set. Equivalently, $H_i = H_i(x,y,z)$, $i = 1,2$, are functionally independent if their Jacobian has maximal rank,

$$\text{rank}\frac{\partial(H_1, H_2)}{\partial(x,y,z)} = 2, \tag{8}$$

in all the points of $U_1 \cap U_2$ except perhaps on a zero Lebesgue measure set. System (7) is completely integrable in $\mathbb{R}^3$ if it has two independent first integrals in $\mathbb{R}^3$.

A Darboux polynomial of system (7) is a polynomial $f(x,y,z)$ such that

$$\mathfrak{X}f = \frac{\partial f}{\partial x}P + \frac{\partial f}{\partial y}Q + \frac{\partial f}{\partial z}R = Kf, \tag{9}$$

where $K(x,y,z)$ is a polynomial of degree at most $m-1$. The polynomial $K(x,y,z)$ is called the cofactor of f. It easy to see that if f is a Darboux polynomial of Equation (7), then the equation $f = 0$ defines an algebraic surface which is invariant under the flow of system (7). For this reason, f often is referred as an invariant algebraic surface of Equation (7).

A simple computation shows that if there are Darboux polynomials $f_1, f_2, ..., f_k$ with the cofactors $K_1, K_2, ..., K_k$ satisfying

$$\sum_{i=1}^{k} \lambda_i K_i = 0, \tag{10}$$

where $\lambda_1, \ldots, \lambda_k$ are some non-zero real numbers, then

$$H = f_1^{\lambda_1} \cdots f_k^{\lambda_k}, \tag{11}$$

is a first integral of (7). An integral of the form in Equation (11) is called a Darboux integral of system (7).

The ideas of the method go back to the works of Darboux [12,13]. Further developments of the approach were presented in the works of Prelle and Singer [14] and Schlomiuk [15,16]. In [14], the authors did not use the term "Darboux polynomials", but they proposed an algorithm to find first integrals using them. This algorithm was put in relation with the Darboux method in the work of Schlomiuk [15,16]. See also [17,18] for more details on the method.

To find Darboux polynomials (algebraic invariant surfaces) of system (4) we will use the following result from computational commutative algebra. Let I be an ideal in the polynomial ring $k[x_1, \ldots, x_n]$, where k is a field, and ℓ be a fixed number from the set $\{0, 1, \ldots, n-1\}$. The ℓ-th elimination ideal of I is the ideal

$$I_\ell = I \cap k[x_{\ell+1}, \ldots, x_n].$$

According to the Elimination Theorem (see, for example, [19,20]) in order to compute (for any $0 \leqslant \ell \leqslant n-1$) the ℓ-th elimination ideal I_ℓ of an ideal I in $k[x_1, \ldots, x_n]$, one can choose the lexicographic term order with

$$x_1 > x_2 > \cdots > x_n$$

on the ring $k[x_1, \ldots, x_n]$ and compute a Gröbner basis G for the ideal I with respect to this order. Then, by the Elimination theorem, the set

$$G_\ell := G \cap k[x_{\ell+1}, \ldots, x_n]$$

is a Gröbner basis for the ℓ-th elimination ideal I_ℓ. Geometrically, the elimination means projecting the variety $\mathbf{V}(I)$ of the ideal I to the affine space $k^{n-\ell}$ corresponding to the variables $x_{\ell+1}, \ldots, x_n$.

3. Darboux Polynomials of System (4)

In this section, using the Elimination Theorem, we look for Darboux polynomials of degree two for system (4). A general form of a polynomial of degree two is

$$\begin{aligned} f(x,y,z) = {} & h_{000} + h_{100}x + h_{010}y + h_{001}z + h_{200}x^2 + h_{110}xy \\ & + h_{101}xz + h_{020}y^2 + h_{011}yz + h_{002}z^2. \end{aligned} \tag{12}$$

A cofactor of any Darboux polynomials of system (7) is a polynomial of degree one which we write in the form

$$K(x,y,z) = c_0 + c_1 x + c_2 y + c_3 z. \tag{13}$$

Polynomial (12) will be a Darboux polynomial of system (4) with cofactor (13) if

$$\mathfrak{X} f = K f, \tag{14}$$

where now

$$\mathfrak{X} f := \frac{\partial f}{\partial x} X + \frac{\partial f}{\partial y} Y + \frac{\partial f}{\partial z} Z,$$

with X, Y and Z defined in (4).

Comparing the coefficients of the monomials on both sides of (14) we obtain the polynomial system

$$g_1 = g_2 = \ldots = g_{19} = g_{20} = 0,$$

where

$$
\begin{aligned}
g_1 &= -c_0 h_{000}, \\
g_2 &= -c_3 h_{000} + h_{001} - c_0 h_{001}, \\
g_3 &= -h_{001} - c_3 h_{001} + 2h_{002} - c_0 h_{002}, \\
g_4 &= -2h_{002} - c_3 h_{002}, \\
g_5 &= -c_2 h_{000} + h_{010} - c_0 h_{010}, \\
g_6 &= -\beta_3 h_{001} - c_2 h_{001} - \alpha_2 h_{010} - c_3 h_{010} + 2h_{011} - c_0 h_{011}, \\
g_7 &= -2\beta_3 h_{002} - c_2 h_{002} - h_{011} - \alpha_2 h_{011} - c_3 h_{011}, \\
g_8 &= -h_{010} - c_2 h_{010} + 2h_{020} - c_0 h_{020}, \\
g_9 &= -2h_{020} - c_2 h_{020}, \\
g_{10} &= -h_{011} - \beta_3 h_{011} - c_2 h_{011} - 2\alpha_2 h_{020} - c_3 h_{020}, \\
g_{11} &= -c_1 h_{000} + h_{100} - c_0 h_{100}, \\
g_{12} &= -\alpha_3 h_{001} - c_1 h_{001} - \beta_1 h_{100} - c_3 h_{100} + 2h_{101} - c_0 h_{101}, \\
g_{13} &= -2\alpha_3 h_{002} - c_1 h_{002} - h_{101} - \beta_1 h_{101} - c_3 h_{101}, \\
g_{14} &= -\beta_2 h_{010} - c_1 h_{010} - \alpha_1 h_{100} - c_2 h_{100} + 2h_{110} - c_0 h_{110}, \\
g_{15} &= -2\beta_2 h_{020} - c_1 h_{020} - h_{110} - \alpha_1 h_{110} - c_2 h_{110}, \\
g_{16} &= -\alpha_3 h_{011} - \beta_2 h_{011} - c_1 h_{011} - \alpha_1 h_{101} - \beta_3 h_{101} \\
&\quad - c_2 h_{101} - \alpha_2 h_{110} - \beta_1 h_{110} - c_3 h_{110}, \\
g_{17} &= -h_{100} - c_1 h_{100} + 2h_{200} - c_0 h_{200}, \\
g_{18} &= -2h_{200} - c_1 h_{200}, \\
g_{19} &= -h_{110} - \beta_2 h_{110} - c_1 h_{110} - 2\alpha_1 h_{200} - c_2 h_{200}, \\
g_{20} &= -h_{101} - \alpha_3 h_{101} - c_1 h_{101} - 2\beta_1 h_{200} - c_3 h_{200}.
\end{aligned}
\tag{15}
$$

We denote by $I = \langle g_1, g_2, ..., g_{19}, g_{20} \rangle$ the ideal generated by polynomials (15). Since computations based on the Elimination Theorem are very laborious, to simplify them we consider separately the cases $h_{000} = 1$ and $h_{000} = 0$, that is, we look separately for invariant curves $f = 0$ not passing and passing through the origin, so from now on in this section we assume that $h_{000} = 1$.

To find Darboux polynomials of system (4) of degree two, we have to determine for which values of parameters α_i, β_i $(i = 1,2,3)$ system (15) has a solution with at least one of coefficient $h_{200}, h_{002}, h_{011}, h_{020}, h_{101}, h_{110}$ different from zero. To satisfy this condition we have six options that can be written in polynomial forms as

$$
\begin{aligned}
&1 - wh_{200} = 0, \quad 1 - wh_{110} = 0, \quad 1 - wh_{101} = 0, \\
&1 - wh_{020} = 0, \quad 1 - wh_{011} = 0, \quad 1 - wh_{002} = 0,
\end{aligned}
\tag{16}
$$

respectively (where w is a new variable). For instance, to find systems of the form (4) which have surfaces with $h_{200} \neq 0$, we can compute (for example, with the routine eliminate of the computer algebra system SINGULAR [21]) the 13th elimination ideal of the ideal $I^{(1)} = \langle I, 1 - wh_{200} \rangle$, in the ring $\mathbb{Q}[w, c_0, c_1, c_2, c_3, h_{001}, h_{002}, h_{010}, h_{011}, h_{020}, h_{100}, h_{101}, h_{110}, \alpha_1, \beta_1, \alpha_2, \beta_2, \alpha_3, \beta_3]$. Denote this elimination ideal by $I_{13}^{(1)}$ and its variety by V_1 (that is, $V_1 = \mathbf{V}(I_{13}^{(1)})$). Proceeding analogously we find the other five elimination ideals $I_{13}^{(2)}, \ldots, I_{13}^{(6)}$ corresponding to the other cases of Equation (16). Denote the corresponding varieties $V_2 = \mathbf{V}(I_{13}^{(2)}), \ldots, \mathbf{V}(I_{13}^{(6)})$. It is clear that the union $V = V_1 \cup ... \cup V_6$ of these six varieties contains the set of all systems (4) having invariant surfaces of the form (12) not passing through the origin. To compute the irreducible decomposition of the variety V it is sufficient to compute the ideal $J = I_{13}^{(1)} \cap \cdots \cap I_{13}^{(6)}$, which defines the variety $V = V_1 \cup ... \cup V_6$ and then to find the irreducible decomposition of V. The intersection of ideals can be computed with the routine intersect of SINGULAR, and the irreducible decomposition of V can be found with the routine minAssGTZ [22], which is based on the algorithm of [23]. Theoretically, such computations should give all systems in family (4) having invariant surfaces of degree two. However all the routines eliminate, intersect and minAssGTZ rely on computations of many Gröbner bases, and such computations can be rarely completed when computing over the field $\mathbb{Q}$ of rational numbers for polynomials in many variables. To be able to complete our computations, we computed in the field of the finite characteristic 32003 and then lifted the resulting ideals to the ring of polynomials with rational coefficients using the rational reconstruction algorithm of [24] (a MATHEMATICA code for the algorithm can be found in [25]).

The primary decomposition of the radical of the ideal

$$J = \bigcap_{i=1}^{6} I_{13}^{(i)} \tag{17}$$

computed using the routine minAssGTZ in the field of characteristic 32003 consists of 88 ideals, that is, we have 88 irreducible components of the variety $\mathbf{V}(J)$ given in Appendix A. It means there are 88 conditions on the parameters α_i, β_i of system (4) for existence of an invariant surface of degree two not passing through the origin.

However some of these conditions give systems with the same dynamics in the phase space, since system (4) has a symmetry with respect to simple linear transformations. Namely, it is easily seen that the transformations

$$x \to z,\ y \to x,\ z \to y, \tag{18}$$

$$x \to y,\ y \to z,\ z \to x, \tag{19}$$

$$x \to y,\ y \to x,\ z \to z, \tag{20}$$

$$x \to z,\ y \to y,\ z \to z, \tag{21}$$

$$x \to x,\ y \to z,\ z \to y, \tag{22}$$

which correspond to re-labeling of the coordinate axes, do not change the shape of the system. For instance, under transformation (19) system (4) is changed into the system

$$\begin{aligned} \dot{x} &= x(1 - x - \alpha_2 y - \beta_2 z), \\ \dot{y} &= y(1 - \beta_3 x - y - \alpha_3 z), \\ \dot{z} &= z(1 - \alpha_1 x - \beta_1 y - z), \end{aligned} \tag{23}$$

which can be obtained from system (4) by the change of parameters

$$\alpha_1 \to \alpha_3,\ \beta_1 \to \beta_3,\ \alpha_2 \to \alpha_1,\ \beta_2 \to \beta_1,\ \alpha_3 \to \alpha_2,\ \beta_3 \to \beta_2. \tag{24}$$

Thus, if we have a condition on the parameters of Equation (4) under which the system has an algebraic invariant surface, another condition will be obtained by the transformation of the parameters according to rule (24). For example, as we will see below, system (4) has the invariant surface

$$f = 2 - 4x + 2x^2 - 2y + yz$$

if condition (5) of Theorem 1 is fulfilled, that is, if

$$\beta_3 = \beta_1 = \alpha_3 + 1 = \beta_2 - 3 = \alpha_2 + 1 = \alpha_1 - 1/2 = 0.$$

Applying to Equation (4) the transformation (19) we obtain that system (4) has the invariant surface

$$f = 2 - 4z + 2z^2 - 2x + xy$$

if the condition

$$\beta_2 = \beta_3 = \alpha_2 + 1 = \beta_1 - 3 = \alpha_1 + 1 = \alpha_3 - 1/2 = 0$$

holds, that is, condition (3) is changed according to Equation (24). Similarly, after substitutions (20)–(22) the conditions for existence of invariant surfaces are changed according to the rules

$$\alpha_1 \to \alpha_2,\ \beta_1 \to \beta_2,\ \alpha_2 \to \alpha_3,\ \beta_2 \to \beta_3,\ \alpha_3 \to \alpha_1,\ \beta_3 \to \beta_1, \tag{25}$$

$$\alpha_1 \to \beta_2,\ \beta_1 \to \alpha_2,\ \alpha_2 \to \beta_1,\ \beta_2 \to \alpha_1,\ \alpha_3 \to \beta_3,\ \beta_3 \to \alpha_3, \tag{26}$$

$$\alpha_1 \to \beta_3,\ \beta_1 \to \alpha_3,\ \alpha_2 \to \beta_2,\ \beta_2 \to \alpha_2,\ \alpha_3 \to \beta_1,\ \beta_3 \to \alpha_1, \tag{27}$$

$$\alpha_1 \to \beta_1,\ \beta_1 \to \alpha_1,\ \alpha_2 \to \beta_3,\ \beta_2 \to \alpha_3,\ \alpha_3 \to \beta_2,\ \beta_3 \to \alpha_2, \tag{28}$$

respectively.

We say, that two conditions for existence of invariant planes are conjugate if one can be obtained from another by means of one of transformations (24), (25)–(28). For instance, condition (3) (which is the same as condition (7) from Appendix A) and conditions (10), (19), (25), (33), (47) from Appendix A can be obtained from each other by one of the transformations (24), (25)–(28), so all these conditions are conjugate.

Note that some of the obtained 88 conditions give Darboux polynomials of degree two which are not irreducible, but they are products of two polynomials of degree one. Namely, if

(i) $\alpha_1 = \beta_1 = 0$ (condition 1 of the Appendix), then system (4) has the Darboux polynomial $(-1+x)^2$ (and the conjugate conditions are 22 and 36 from Appendix A);
(ii) $\alpha_2 = \beta_1 = \beta_2 + \alpha_1 - 2 = 0$ (condition 5 of Appendix A), then system (4) has the Darboux polynomial $(-1+x+z)^2$ (and the conjugate conditions are 44 and 78 from Appendix);
(iii) $\beta_1 + \alpha_3 - 2 = \beta_2 + \alpha_1 - 2 = \beta_3 + \alpha_2 - 2 = 0$ (condition 88 of Appendix), then system (4) has the Darboux polynomial $(-1+x+y+z)^2$.

From the analysis of the obtained 88 conditions we obtain the following result.

Theorem 1. *System (4) has an irreducible invariant surface not passing through the origin if its parameters have the values given in the following Table 1 or are conjugate to them.*

Table 1. Parameter values for systems with invariant surfaces not passing through the origin.

	α_1	α_2	α_3	β_1	β_2	β_3	Condition in Appendix A
1.	3	0	α_3	0	1/2	β_3	2
2.	3	0	α_3	0	3	β_3	4
3.	$1+\alpha_3$	−1	α_3	0	$1-\alpha_3$	0	6
4.	1/2	−1	−1	0	3	0	7
5.	−1	3/2	3	0	3	0	8
6.	1	1/2	3	0	1	3	11
7.	3	−1	1/2	0	1/2	3	12
8.	1/2	3/2	3	0	3	1/2	14
9.	3	−1	−3	0	3	3	15
10.	1/2	3/2	2	0	3	1/2	16
11.	$1-\beta_3$	$2-\beta_3$	0	0	$1+\beta_3$	β_3	17
12.	α_3-2	−1	α_3	0	$4-\alpha_3$	3	18
13.	$2-\beta_2$	3	1/2	3	β_2	1/2	53
14.	1/2	3	3	3	3	1/2	54
15.	1/2	3	α_3	$2-\alpha_3$	3	1/2	55
16.	α_1	3	3	3	$2-\alpha_1$	3	65
17.	α_3-2	3	α_3	$2-\alpha_3$	$4-\alpha_3$	3	67

Remark 1. *For instance, the first row of the table means that the parameters* α_3 *and* β_3 *can be chosen arbitrary, the other parameters satisfy the condition*

$$\alpha_1 = 3,\ \alpha_2 = \beta_1 = 0,\ \beta_2 = \frac{1}{2},$$

and this is condition 2 from Appendix A.

Proof of Theorem 1. For each case of the theorem we give below the irreducible Darboux polynomial f of degree two which defines the invariant quadratic invariant surface $f = 0$ not passing through the origin and the corresponding cofactor:

1. $f = 1 - x - 2y + y^2;\quad K = -x - 2y;$
2. $f = 1 - 2x + x^2 - 2y - 2xy + y^2;\quad K = -2(x+y);$
3. $f = 2 - 2x - 2y + yz;\quad K = -x - y;$
4. $f = 2 - 4x + 2x^2 - 2y + yz;\quad K = -2x - y;$
5. $f = 2 - 4x + 2x^2 + 2xy - 2z + xz;\quad K = -2x - z;$
6. $f = 2 - 4x + 2x^2 - 4y + 4xy + 2y^2 - 2z + xz;\quad K = -2x - 2y - z;$
7. $f = 1 - x - 2y + y^2 + yz;\quad K = -x - 2y;$
8. $f = 2 - 4x + 2x^2 - 2y - 2z + xz;\quad K = -2x - y - z;$
9. $f = 1 - 2x + x^2 - 2y - 2xy + y^2 + yz;\quad K = -2(x+y);$
10. $f = 1 - 2x + x^2 - y - z + xz;\quad K = -2x - y - z;$
11. $f = 1 - x - y - z + xz;\quad K = -x - y - z;$
12. $f = 1 - 2x + x^2 - 2y + 2xy + y^2 + yz;\quad K = -2(x+y);$
13. $f = 1 - x - y - 2z + z^2;\quad K = -x - y - 2z;$
14. $f = 1 - 2x + x^2 - y - 2z - 2xz + z^2;\quad K = -2x - y - 2z;$
15. $f = 1 - 2x + x^2 - y - 2z + 2xz + z^2;\quad K = -2x - y - 2z;$
16. $f = 1 - 2x + x^2 - 2y + 2xy + y^2 - 2z - 2xz - 2yz + z^2;\quad K = -2(x+y+z);$
17. $f = 1 - 2x + x^2 - 2y + 2xy + y^2 - 2z + 2xz - 2yz + z^2;\quad K = -2(x+y+z).$

□

4. First Integrals of System (4)

In this section we look for Darboux first integrals of the system (4), which can be constructed using the invariant surfaces obtained in the previous section.

Theorem 2. *(a) If one of conditions 1–3, 11, 12, 17 of Theorem 1 holds, then the corresponding system (4) admits at least one Darboux first integral. (b) If one of conditions 4–10, 13–16 of Theorem 1 holds, then the corresponding system (4) is completely integrable, that is, it admits two independents Darboux first integrals.*

Proof. First note that system (4) always has the following three invariant surfaces of degree one, with the respective cofactors,

$$\begin{aligned} f_1 &= x;\ K_1 = 1 - x - \alpha_1 y - \beta_1 z; \\ f_2 &= y;\ K_2 = 1 - \beta_2 x - y - \alpha_2 z; \\ f_3 &= z;\ K_3 = 1 - \alpha_3 x - \beta_3 y - z. \end{aligned} \tag{29}$$

However, in most cases it is impossible to construct Darboux first integrals using just these invariant planes and the surfaces given by Theorem 1. To find the integrals we additionally look for invariant surfaces of the form (12) with $h_{000} = 0$ using the procedure described at the beginning of Section 3. For each considered case we have to solve system (15) with $h_{000} = 0$ and parameters α_i, β_i $(i = 1,2,3)$ given by Theorem 1. Since some parameters are fixed the corresponding systems (15) are easily solved with MATHEMATICA (no need for computations with SINGULAR now).

Case (a). To prove statement (a) of the theorem, we present the Darboux first integrals for each case mentioned in the statement.

If condition (1) of Theorem 1 is satisfied the system has the form

$$\dot{x} = x(1 - x - 3y), \quad \dot{y} = y(1 - x/2 - y)y, \quad \dot{z} = z(1 - \alpha_3 x - \beta_3 y - z) \tag{30}$$

Besides the invariant surfaces f_1, f_2 and f_3 given above and the invariant surface

$$f = 1 - x - 2y + y^2 \tag{31}$$

system (30) has the following surfaces f_4, f_5 (with cofactors K_4, K_5, respectively),

$$\begin{aligned} f_4 &= x + 4y; \quad K_4 = 1 - x - y; \\ f_5 &= x + 2y - 2y^2; \quad K_5 = 1 - x - 2y. \end{aligned} \tag{32}$$

From the corresponding Equation (10) we find that $\lambda_1 = \lambda_3/2, \lambda_2 = \lambda_4, \lambda_5 = -\lambda_3 - 2\lambda_4, \lambda_6 = 0$. Thus, for arbitrary λ_3, λ_4 not both equal to zero system (30) has a Darboux first integral

$$\widetilde{H} = x^{\lambda_4} y^{\lambda_3} (x + 4y)^{\lambda_4} \left(x - 2y^2 + 2y\right)^{-\lambda_3 - 2\lambda_4} \left(-x + y^2 - 2y + 1\right)^{\frac{\lambda_3}{2}}.$$

In particular, taking $\lambda_4 = 1$ and $= \lambda_3 = 0$ we have the Darboux first integral

$$H = \frac{x(x + 4y)}{(x + 2y - 2y^2)^2}.$$

Using the same approach we obtain the following Darboux first integrals for the remaining cases:

(2) $H = \dfrac{xy}{(-x + x^2 - y - 2xy + y^2)^2}$;

(3) $H = \dfrac{(x + y - yz)^2}{x^2 + 2xy + y^2 - 2yz}$;

(11) $H = \dfrac{xz(1 - x - y - z + xz)}{(-x - y - z + 2xz)^2}$;

(12) $H = \dfrac{yz}{(-x + x^2 - y + 2xy + y^2 + yz)^2}$;

(17) $H = \dfrac{yz}{(-x + x^2 - y + 2xy + y^2 - z + 2xz - 2yz + z^2)^2}$.

Case (b). For each system of this case we present two independent Darboux first integrals.

Case (4). Besides the invariant surface f_1, f_2, f_3 given above and f of the previous theorem, we have the invariant surfaces $f_4 = 4x + y - 2z$ with the cofactor $K_4 = 1 - x - y - z$. Using these polynomials we can find the following two Darboux first integrals:

$$\begin{aligned} H_1 &= \frac{z(2 - 4x + 2x^2 - 2y + yz)}{(4x + y - 2z)}, \\ H_2 &= \frac{yz}{x^2}. \end{aligned}$$

To check if these first integrals are independent, we compute their gradients and obtain that they are

$$\begin{aligned} G_1 = \{ &\frac{4(-2 + 2x + y)(1 + x - z)z}{(4x + y - 2z)^2}, \ -\frac{2(1 + x - z)^2 z}{(4x + y - 2z)^2}, \\ &\frac{2(4x - 8x^2 + 4x^3 + y - 6xy + x^2 y - y^2 + 4xyz + y^2 z - yz^2)}{(4x + y - 2z)^2} \}, \\ G_2 = \{ &-\frac{2yz}{x^3}, \ \frac{z}{x^2}, \ \frac{y}{x^2} \}, \end{aligned}$$

respectively. Then we verify if for the Jacobian

$$J = [G_1, G_2].$$

condition (8) holds. One of 2×2 minors of the matrix J is

$$m_1 = -\frac{2z^2(x - z + 1)\,(2x^2 - 2x + yz - y)}{x^3(4x + y - 2z)}.$$

Clearly, m_1 is different from zero on the neighborhood of the origin except the set of the points where

$$xz(x - z + 1)(2x^2 - 2x + yz - y)(4x + y - 2z)^2 = 0. \tag{33}$$

Since the set defined by Equation (33) has Lebesgue measure zero, the Darboux first integrals H_1 and H_2 are independent.

Case (5). Besides the invariant surfaces f_1, f_2, f_3 given in Equation (29) and f of the previous theorem, we have the following invariant surfaces passing through the origin (with the respective cofactors):

$$\begin{aligned}
&f_4 = -4xy + 2xz + z^2; \;\; K_4 = -2(-1 + 2x + z);\\
&f_5 = 2y + z; \;\; K_5 = 1 - 3x - y - z;\\
&f_6 = 2x + 2y + z; \;\; K_6 = 1 - x - y - z;\\
&f_7 = -2x + 2x^2 + 2xy - z + xz; \;\; K_7 = 1 - 2x - z.
\end{aligned}$$

Using these polynomials we can find the following two Darboux first integrals:

$$\begin{aligned}
H_1 &= \frac{xy^2}{z^2(2x + 2y + z)},\\
H_2 &= \frac{xy^2}{(2y + z)(-2x + 2x^2 + 2xy - z + xz)^2}.
\end{aligned}$$

The gradients of them are

$$\begin{aligned}
G_1 = \{&\frac{y^2(2y + z)}{z^2(2x + 2y + z)^2}, \frac{2xy(2x + y + z)}{z^2(2x + 2y + z)^2}, -\frac{xy^2(4x + 4y + 3z)}{z^3(2x + 2y + z)^2}\},\\
G_2 = \{&-\frac{y^2(-2x + 6x^2 + 2xy + z + xz)}{(2y + z)(-2x + 2x^2 + 2xy - z + xz)^3},\\
&\frac{2xy(-2xy + 2x^2y - 2xy^2 - 2xz + 2x^2z - yz + xyz - z^2 + xz^2)}{(2y + z)^2(-2x + 2x^2 + 2xy - z + xz)^3},\\
&-\frac{xy^2(-2x + 2x^2 - 4y + 6xy - 3z + 3xz)}{(2y + z)^2(-2x + 2x^2 + 2xy - z + xz)^3}\},
\end{aligned}$$

respectively. Similarly as in the previous case, computing the minors of the Jacobian we check H_1 and H_2 are independent.

Using similar computations we get the following pairs of independent Darboux first integrals for the remaining cases:

$$\begin{aligned}
(6)\quad H_1 &= \frac{z}{x(2 - 4x + 2x^2 - 4y + 4xy + 2y^2 - 2z + xz)},\\
H_2 &= \frac{z(2x + 4y + z)}{y^2(2 - 4x + 2x^2 - 4y + 4xy + 2y^2 - 2z + xz)};\\
(7)\quad H_1 &= -\frac{x^2}{yz(-1 + x + 2y - y^2 - yz)},
\end{aligned}$$

$$H_2 = -\frac{(x-2z)^2}{z(y+z)(-1+x+2y-y^2-yz)};$$

(8) $$H_1 = \frac{xz(2-4x+2x^2-2y-2z+xz)}{(y+z)^2},$$

$$H_2 = \frac{(2x+z)(y+z)^2}{xy^2};$$

(9) $$H_1 = \frac{yz(1-2x+x^2-2y-2xy+y^2+yz)}{x^2},$$

$$H_2 = \frac{y^2z(4x-z)}{x^2(x^2-2xy+y^2+yz)};$$

(10) $$H_1 = -\frac{x(y-z+xz+z^2)}{z(-2x+2x^2-y-z+2xz)},$$

$$H_2 = \frac{y^2(x+z)}{z(2x-2x^2+y+z-2xz)(y-z+xz+z^2)};$$

(13) $$H_1 = \frac{(-x-y-2z+2z^2)^2}{z^2(1-x-y-2z+z^2)},$$

$$H_2 = \frac{xz^{2\alpha_1-2}(x+y+4z)^{2-2\alpha_1}}{y};$$

(14) $$H_1 = \frac{(-2x+2x^2-y-2z-4xz+2z^2)^2}{(x-z)^2(1-2x+x^2-y-2z-2xz+z^2)},$$

$$H_2 = \frac{x(y+4z)^2(-2x+2x^2-y-2z-4xz+2z^2)^2}{z(x-z)^4(1-2x+x^2-y-2z-2xz+z^2)^2};$$

(15) $$H_1 = \frac{y(4x+y+4z)}{(2x-2x^2+y+2z-4xz-2z^2)^2},$$

$$H_2 = \frac{x(4x+y+4z)^{1-\alpha_3}(-2x+2x^2-y-2z+4xz+2z^2)^{1+\alpha_3}}{z(x+z)^2(1-2x+x^2-y-2z+2xz+z^2)};$$

(16) $$H_1 = \frac{(x+y)z}{(-x+x^2-y+2xy+y^2-z-2xz-2yz+z^2)^2},$$

$$H_2 = \frac{1}{y^4}x^4z^{2-2\alpha_1}(1-2x+x^2-2y+2xy+y^2-2z-2xz-2yz+z^2)^{1-\alpha_1}$$
$$(-x+x^2-y+2xy+y^2-z-2xz-2yz+z^2)^{2\alpha_1-2}.$$

□

Remark 2. *Note that first two equations of (30) are independent of z, they are,*

$$\dot{x} = x(1-x-3y), \quad \dot{y} = y(1-x/2-y)y. \tag{34}$$

Therefore we cannot construct another independent first integral $H_2(x,y,z)$ of Equation (30) using only the planes $x=0$, $y=0, z=0$ and the surfaces defined by Equations (31) and (32). Indeed, since the equations of all surfaces of this case, except of $z=0$, are independent on z, if such integral would exist, it would be independent of z, but then two-dimensional system (34) would have two independent first integrals, which is impossible.

In case (2), similarly as in case (1), the system is separable into a two-dimensional system and a single first order equation, and we can construct only one Darboux first integral using the found invariant surfaces.

5. Conclusions

To summarize, we have found some Darboux first integrals of the May–Leonard system (4) which are constructed using Darboux polynomials of degree one and two. We do not know if we found all independent first integrals of system (4) which can be constructed from Darboux polynomials of degree one and two. To verify if the list is complete, we have to find Darboux polynomials of Equation (4), which define invariant algebraic surfaces passing through the origin, that is, polynomials (12) with $h_{000}=0$. A naïve expectation is that this case should be simpler, than the case $h_{000}=1$, which we have successfully investigated in this paper. However it turns out that the case $h_{000} = 0$ is computationally much more difficult and we were not able to complete computations for this case using our computational facilities. We believe that a reason for this difficulty is that since the origin is a singular point there are many invariant surfaces passing through the origin and it implies a complicated structure of the elimination ideals which we have to compute using our approach.

Author Contributions: V.A. and V.G.R. contributed for supervision, conceptualization, methodology and prepared the final version of the paper; W.F. performed computations and wrote the initial draft of the paper, N.L.S. developed the software and performed computations.

Funding: Valery Romanovski is supported by the Slovenian Research Agency (program P1-0306, project N1-0063). The second, third and forth authors acknowledge also the support by a Marie Curie International Research Staff Exchange Scheme Fellowship within the 7th European Community Framework Programme, FP7-PEOPLE-2012-IRSES-316338.

Conflicts of Interest: The authors declare no conflict of interest.

Appendix A

Here we list the irreducible components of the variety of ideals in (17), which give conditions for existence in system (4) of invariant surfaces of degree two not passing through the origin of the system:

1. $\alpha_1 = \beta_1 = 0$
2. $-(1/2) + \beta_2 = \alpha_2 = \beta_1 = -3 + \alpha_1 = 0$
3. $-3 + \beta_2 = \alpha_2 = \beta_1 = -(1/2) + \alpha_1 = 0$
4. $-3 + \beta_2 = \alpha_2 = \beta_1 = -3 + \alpha_1 = 0$
5. $\alpha_2 = \beta_1 = \beta_2 + \alpha_1 - 2 = 0$
6. $\beta_3 = -1 + \alpha_3 + \beta_2 = 1 + \alpha_2 = \beta_1 = -1 + \alpha_1 - \alpha_3 = 0$
7. $\beta_3 = 1 + \alpha_3 = -3 + \beta_2 = 1 + \alpha_2 = \beta_1 = -(1/2) + \alpha_1 = 0$
8. $\beta_3 = -3 + \alpha_3 = -3 + \beta_2 = -(3/2) + \alpha_2 = \beta_1 = 1 + \alpha_1 = 0$
9. $-3 + \beta_3 = -(3/2) + \alpha_3 = \beta_2 = 1 + \alpha_2 = \beta_1 = -3 + \alpha_1 = 0$
10. $-3 + \beta_3 = 1 + \alpha_3 = \beta_2 = -(1/2) + \alpha_2 = \beta_1 = 1 + \alpha_1 = 0$
11. $-3 + \beta_3 = -3 + \alpha_3 = -1 + \beta_2 = -(1/2) + \alpha_2 = \beta_1 = -1 + \alpha_1 = 0$
12. $-3 + \beta_3 = -(1/2) + \alpha_3 = -(1/2) + \beta_2 = 1 + \alpha_2 = \beta_1 = -3 + \alpha_1 = 0$
13. $1 + \alpha_3 = \beta_2 = -2 + \alpha_2 + \beta_3 = \beta_1 = -1 + \alpha_1 + \beta_3 = 0$
14. $-(1/2) + \beta_3 = -3 + \alpha_3 = -3 + \beta_2 = -(3/2) + \alpha_2 = \beta_1 = -(1/2) + \alpha_1 = 0$
15. $-3 + \beta_3 = 3 + \alpha_3 = -3 + \beta_2 = 1 + \alpha_2 = \beta_1 = -3 + \alpha_1 = 0$
16. $-(1/2) + \beta_3 = -2 + \alpha_3 = -3 + \beta_2 = -(3/2) + \alpha_2 = \beta_1 = -(1/2) + \alpha_1 = 0$
17. $\alpha_3 = -1 + \beta_2 - \beta_3 = -2 + \alpha_2 + \beta_3 = \beta_1 = -1 + \alpha_1 + \beta_3 = 0$
18. $-3 + \beta_3 = -4 + \alpha_3 + \beta_2 = 1 + \alpha_2 = \beta_1 = 2 + \alpha_1 - \alpha_3 = 0$
19. $1 + \beta_3 = -3 + \alpha_3 = 1 + \beta_2 = \alpha_2 = -(1/2) + \beta_1 = \alpha_1 = 0$
20. $1 + \beta_3 = -1 + \alpha_3 + \beta_2 = \alpha_2 = -2 + \alpha_3 + \beta_1 = \alpha_1 = 0$
21. $-(3/2) + \beta_3 = -3 + \alpha_3 = -3 + \beta_2 = \alpha_2 = 1 + \beta_1 = \alpha_1 = 0$
22. $\alpha_2 = \beta_2 = 0$
23. $-2 + \beta_3 = -(1/2) + \alpha_3 = -(1/2) + \beta_2 = \alpha_2 = -(3/2) + \beta_1 = -3 + \alpha_1 = 0$
24. $-3 + \beta_3 = -(1/2) + \alpha_3 = -(1/2) + \beta_2 = \alpha_2 = -(3/2) + \beta_1 = -3 + \alpha_1 = 0$
25. $1 + \beta_3 = \alpha_3 = -(1/2) + \beta_2 = \alpha_2 = 1 + \beta_1 = -3 + \alpha_1 = 0$
26. $3 + \beta_3 = -3 + \alpha_3 = -3 + \beta_2 = \alpha_2 = 1 + \beta_1 = -3 + \alpha_1 = 0$
27. $-(1/2) + \beta_3 = -3 + \alpha_3 = -3 + \beta_2 = \alpha_2 = 1 + \beta_1 = -(1/2) + \alpha_1 = 0$
28. $\alpha_3 = -1 + \beta_2 - \beta_3 = \alpha_2 = 1 + \beta_1 = -1 + \alpha_1 + \beta_3 = 0$
29. $-3 + \beta_3 = \alpha_3 = 1 + \beta_2 = \alpha_2 = -(3/2) + \beta_1 = -3 + \alpha_1 = 0$
30. $-3 + \alpha_3 = 2 + \beta_2 - \beta_3 = \alpha_2 = 1 + \beta_1 = -4 + \alpha_1 + \beta_3 = 0$
31. $-3 + \beta_3 = -3 + \alpha_3 = -1 + \beta_2 = \alpha_2 = -(1/2) + \beta_1 = -1 + \alpha_1 = 0$
32. $\beta_3 = -1 + \alpha_3 + \beta_2 = \alpha_2 = -2 + \alpha_3 + \beta_1 = -1 + \alpha_1 - \alpha_3 = 0$
33. $\beta_3 = -(1/2) + \alpha_3 = \beta_2 = 1 + \alpha_2 = -3 + \beta_1 = 1 + \alpha_1 = 0$
34. $\beta_3 = \beta_2 = 1 + \alpha_2 - \alpha_3 = -2 + \alpha_3 + \beta_1 = 1 + \alpha_1 = 0$
35. $\beta_3 = 1 + \alpha_3 = \beta_2 = -3 + \alpha_2 = -3 + \beta_1 = -(3/2) + \alpha_1 = 0$
36. $\alpha_3 = \beta_3 = 0$

37. $\beta_3 = -(1/2) + \alpha_3 = -3 + \beta_1 = \alpha_1 = 0$
38. $\beta_3 = -(1/2) + \alpha_3 = -(1/2) + \beta_2 = -2 + \alpha_2 = -3 + \beta_1 = -(3/2) + \alpha_1 = 0$
39. $\beta_3 = -(1/2) + \alpha_3 = -(1/2) + \beta_2 = -3 + \alpha_2 = -3 + \beta_1 = -(3/2) + \alpha_1 = 0$
40. $\beta_3 = -3 + \alpha_3 = -(1/2) + \beta_1 = \alpha_1 = 0$
41. $\beta_3 = -3 + \alpha_3 = -3 + \beta_1 = \alpha_1 = 0$
42. $\beta_3 = -3 + \alpha_3 = -3 + \beta_2 = -(1/2) + \alpha_2 = -(1/2) + \beta_1 = 1 + \alpha_1 = 0$
43. $\beta_3 = -3 + \alpha_3 = -3 + \beta_2 = 3 + \alpha_2 = -3 + \beta_1 = 1 + \alpha_1 = 0$
44. $\alpha_1 = \beta_1 + \alpha_3 - 2 = \beta_3 = 0$
45. $\beta_3 = -1 + \alpha_3 = -3 + \beta_2 = -3 + \alpha_2 = -1 + \beta_1 = -(1/2) + \alpha_1 = 0$
46. $\beta_3 = -3 + \beta_2 = -2 + \alpha_2 - \alpha_3 = -2 + \alpha_3 + \beta_1 = 1 + \alpha_1 = 0$
47. $-(1/2) + \beta_3 = \alpha_3 = 1 + \beta_2 = -3 + \alpha_2 = 1 + \beta_1 = \alpha_1 = 0$
48. $-(1/2) + \beta_3 = -1 + \alpha_3 = -3 + \beta_2 = -3 + \alpha_2 = -1 + \beta_1 = \alpha_1 = 0$
49. $-(1/2) + \beta_3 = \alpha_3 = \beta_2 = -3 + \alpha_2 = 0$
50. $-(1/2) + \beta_3 = 1 + \alpha_3 = \beta_2 = -3 + \alpha_2 = -3 + \beta_1 = -(1/2) + \alpha_1 = 0$
51. $-(1/2) + \beta_3 = \alpha_3 = -(3/2) + \beta_2 = -3 + \alpha_2 = -2 + \beta_1 = -(1/2) + \alpha_1 = 0$
52. $-(1/2) + \beta_3 = \alpha_3 = -(3/2) + \beta_2 = -3 + \alpha_2 = -3 + \beta_1 = -(1/2) + \alpha_1 = 0$
53. $-(1/2) + \beta_3 = -(1/2) + \alpha_3 = -3 + \alpha_2 = -3 + \beta_1 = -2 + \alpha_1 + \beta_2 = 0$
54. $-(1/2) + \beta_3 = -3 + \alpha_3 = -3 + \beta_2 = -3 + \alpha_2 = -3 + \beta_1 = -(1/2) + \alpha_1 = 0$
55. $-(1/2) + \beta_3 = -3 + \beta_2 = -3 + \alpha_2 = -2 + \alpha_3 + \beta_1 = -(1/2) + \alpha_1 = 0$
56. $-3 + \beta_3 = \alpha_3 = \beta_2 = -(1/2) + \alpha_2 = 0$
57. $-3 + \beta_3 = \alpha_3 = \beta_2 = -3 + \alpha_2 = 0$
58. $-3 + \beta_3 = -(3/2) + \alpha_3 = \beta_2 = -(1/2) + \alpha_2 = -(1/2) + \beta_1 = -2 + \alpha_1 = 0$
59. $-3 + \beta_3 = -(3/2) + \alpha_3 = \beta_2 = -(1/2) + \alpha_2 = -(1/2) + \beta_1 = -3 + \alpha_1 = 0$
60. $-3 + \beta_3 = 1 + \alpha_3 = \beta_2 = -3 + \alpha_2 = -3 + \beta_1 = 3 + \alpha_1 = 0$
61. $-3 + \beta_3 = \alpha_3 = 1 + \beta_2 = -(1/2) + \alpha_2 = -(1/2) + \beta_1 = -3 + \alpha_1 = 0$
62. $-3 + \beta_3 = \alpha_3 = 1 + \beta_2 = -3 + \alpha_2 = 3 + \beta_1 = -3 + \alpha_1 = 0$
63. $-3 + \beta_3 = -(1/2) + \alpha_3 = -(1/2) + \beta_2 = -3 + \alpha_2 = -3 + \beta_1 = -3 + \alpha_1 = 0$
64. $-3 + \beta_3 = -3 + \alpha_3 = -(1/2) + \alpha_2 = -(1/2) + \beta_1 = -2 + \alpha_1 + \beta_2 = 0$
65. $-3 + \beta_3 = -3 + \alpha_3 = -3 + \alpha_2 = -3 + \beta_1 = -2 + \alpha_1 + \beta_2 = 0$
66. $-3 + \beta_3 = -3 + \alpha_3 = -3 + \beta_2 = -(1/2) + \alpha_2 = -(1/2) + \beta_1 = -3 + \alpha_1 = 0$
67. $-3 + \beta_3 = -4 + \alpha_3 + \beta_2 = -3 + \alpha_2 = -2 + \alpha_3 + \beta_1 = 2 + \alpha_1 - \alpha_3 = 0$
68. $-3 + \beta_3 = -(1/2) + \beta_2 = -(1/2) + \alpha_2 = -2 + \alpha_3 + \beta_1 = -3 + \alpha_1 = 0$
69. $-3 + \beta_3 = -3 + \beta_2 = -3 + \alpha_2 = -2 + \alpha_3 + \beta_1 = -3 + \alpha_1 = 0$
70. $-3 + \alpha_3 + \beta_3 = \beta_2 = -2 + \alpha_2 + \beta_3 = 1 + \beta_1 - \beta_3 = \alpha_1 = 0$
71. $\alpha_3 = 1 + \beta_2 = -2 + \alpha_2 + \beta_3 = 1 + \beta_1 - \beta_3 = \alpha_1 = 0$
72. $1 + \beta_3 = \alpha_3 = -(3/2) + \beta_2 = -3 + \alpha_2 = -3 + \beta_1 = \alpha_1 = 0$
73. $1 + \beta_3 = -(1/2) + \alpha_3 = -(1/2) + \beta_2 = -3 + \alpha_2 = -3 + \beta_1 = \alpha_1 = 0$
74. $-(3/2) + \beta_3 = -3 + \alpha_3 = -2 + \beta_2 = -(1/2) + \alpha_2 = -(1/2) + \beta_1 = \alpha_1 = 0$
75. $-(3/2) + \beta_3 = -3 + \alpha_3 = -3 + \beta_2 = -(1/2) + \alpha_2 = -(1/2) + \beta_1 = \alpha_1 = 0$
76. $1 + \beta_3 = -3 + \alpha_3 = 3 + \beta_2 = -3 + \alpha_2 = -3 + \beta_1 = \alpha_1 = 0$
77. $1 + \beta_3 = -4 + \alpha_3 + \beta_2 = -3 + \alpha_2 = -2 + \alpha_3 + \beta_1 = \alpha_1 = 0$
78. $\alpha_3 = \beta_2 = \beta_3 + \alpha_1 - 2 = 0$
79. $1 + \alpha_3 = \beta_2 = -2 + \alpha_2 + \beta_3 = -3 + \beta_1 = -4 + \alpha_1 + \beta_3 = 0$
80. $-1 + \beta_3 = -(1/2) + \alpha_3 = \beta_2 = -1 + \alpha_2 = -3 + \beta_1 = -3 + \alpha_1 = 0$
81. $-1 + \beta_3 = \alpha_3 = -(1/2) + \beta_2 = -1 + \alpha_2 = -3 + \beta_1 = -3 + \alpha_1 = 0$
82. $-(1/2) + \alpha_3 = -(1/2) + \beta_2 = -2 + \alpha_2 + \beta_3 = -3 + \beta_1 = -3 + \alpha_1 = 0$
83. $-3 + \alpha_3 = -3 + \beta_2 = -2 + \alpha_2 + \beta_3 = -(1/2) + \beta_1 = -(1/2) + \alpha_1 = 0$
84. $-3 + \alpha_3 = -3 + \beta_2 = -2 + \alpha_2 + \beta_3 = -3 + \beta_1 = -3 + \alpha_1 = 0$
85. $\alpha_3 + \beta_3 = -3 + \beta_2 = -2 + \alpha_2 + \beta_3 = -2 + \beta_1 - \beta_3 = -3 + \alpha_1 = 0$
86. $\alpha_3 = 1 + \beta_2 = -2 + \alpha_2 + \beta_3 = -2 + \beta_1 - \beta_3 = -3 + \alpha_1 = 0$
87. $-3 + \alpha_3 = 2 + \beta_2 - \beta_3 = -2 + \alpha_2 + \beta_3 = -3 + \beta_1 = -4 + \alpha_1 + \beta_3 = 0$
88. $\beta_1 + \alpha_3 - 2 = \beta_2 + \alpha_1 - 2 = \beta_3 + \alpha_1 - 2 = 0.$

References

1. Lotka, A.J. Analytical note on certain rhythmic relations in organic systems. *Proc. Natl. Acad. Sci. USA* **1920**, *6*, 410–415. [CrossRef] [PubMed]
2. Volterra, V. *Lecons sur la Théorie Mathématique de la Lutte pour la Vie*; Gauthier-Villars: Paris, France, 1931.
3. May, R.M.; Leonard, W.J. Nonlinear aspects of competition between three species. *SIAM J. Appl. Math.* **1975**, *29*, 243–253. [CrossRef]
4. Blé, G.; Castellanos, V.; Llibre, J.; Quilantán, I. Integrability and global dynamics of the May–Leonard model. *Nonlinear Anal. Real World Appl.* **2013**, *14*, 280–293. [CrossRef]
5. Schuster, P.; Sigmund, K.; Wolf, R. On ω-limit for competition between three species. *SIAM J. Appl. Math.* **1979**, *37*, 49–54. [CrossRef]
6. Zeeman, M.L. Hopf bifurcations in competitive three dimensional Lotka–Volterra systems. *Dyn. Stab. Syst.* **1993**, *8*, 189–216. [CrossRef]
7. Antonov, V.; Dolićanin, D.; Romanovski, V.G.; Tóth, J. Invariant planes and periodic oscillations in the May–Leonard asymmetric model. *MATCH Commun. Math. Comput. Chem.* **2016**, *76*, 455–474.
8. Chi, C.-W.; Hsu, S.-B.; Wu, L.-I. On the asymmetric May–Leonard model of three competing species. *SIAM J. Appl. Math.* **1998**, *58*, 211–226. [CrossRef]
9. Van der Hoff, Q.; Greeff, J.C.; Fay, T.H. Defining a stability boundary for three species competition models. *Ecol. Model.* **2009**, *220*, 2640–2645. [CrossRef]
10. Leach, G.L.; Miritzis, J. Analytic behaviour of competition among three species. *J. Nonlinear Math. Phys.* **2006**, *13*, 535–548. [CrossRef]
11. Llibre, J.; Valls, C. Polynomial, rational and analytic first integrals for a family of 3-dimensional Lotka–Volterra systems. *Z. Angew. Math. Phys.* **2011**, *62*, 761–777. [CrossRef]
12. Darboux, G. Mémoire sur les équations différentielles algébriques du premier ordre et du premier degré (Mélanges). *Bull. Sci. Math.* **1878**, *2*, 60–96, 123–144, 151–200.
13. Darboux, G. De l'emploi des solutions particulières algébriques dans l'intégration des systèmes d'équations différentielles algébriques. *C. R. Math. Acad. Sci. Paris* **1878**, *86*, 1012–1014.
14. Prelle, M.J.; Singer, M.F. Elementary first integrals of differential equations. *Trans. Am. Math. Soc.* **1983**, *279*, 613–636. [CrossRef]
15. Schlomiuk, D. Algebraic and geometric aspects of the theory of polynomial vector fields. In *Bifurcations and Periodic Orbits of Vector Fields*; Schlomiuk, D., Ed.; NATO ASI Series, Series C: Mathematical and Physical Sciences; Kluwer Academic Publishers: New York, NY, USA, 1993; Volume 408, pp. 429–467.
16. Schlomiuk, D. Elementary first integrals and algebraic invariant curves of differential equations. *Expos. Math.* **1993**, *11*, 433–454.
17. Llibre, J. On the integrability of the differential systems in dimension two and of the polynomial differential systems in arbitrary dimension. *J. Appl. Anal. Comput.* **2011**, *1*, 33–52.
18. Llibre, J.; Zhang, X. On the Darboux integrability of polynomial differential systems. *Qual. Theory Dyn. Syst.* **2012**, *11*, 129–144. [CrossRef]
19. Romanovski, V.G.; Shafer, D.S. *The Center and Cyclicity Problems: A Computational Algebra Approach*; Birkhäuser: Boston, MA, USA, 2009.
20. Cox, D.; Little, J.; O'Shea, D. *Ideals, Varieties, and Algorithms: An Introduction to Computational Algebraic Geometry and Commutative Algebra*; Springer: New York, NY, USA, 1997.
21. Decker, W.; Greuel, G.-M.; Pfister, G.; Shönemann, H. SINGULAR 3-1-6—A Computer Algebra System for Polynomial Computations. 2012. Available online: http://www.singular.uni-kl.de (accessed on 15 May 2017).
22. Decker, W.; Pfister, G.; Schönemann, H.; Laplagne, S. A SINGULAR 3.0 Library for Computing the Primary Decomposition and Radical of Ideals. 2005. Available online: http://www.singular.uni-kl.de (accessed on 15 May 2017).
23. Gianni, P.; Trager, B.; Zacharias, G. Gröbner bases and primary decomposition of polynomials. *J. Symb. Comput.* **1998**, *6*, 146–167. [CrossRef]

24. Wang, P.S.; Guy, M.J.T.; Davenport, J.H. P-adic reconstruction of rational numbers. *SIGSAM Bull.* **1982**, *16*, 2–3. [CrossRef]
25. Giné, J.; Christopher, C.; Prešern, M.; Romanovski, V.G.; Shcheglova, N.L. The resonant center problem for a 2:−3 resonant cubic Lotka–Volterra system. In Proceedings of the 14th International Workshop on Computer Algebra in Scientific Computing CASC 2012, Maribor, Slovenia, 3–6 September 2012; Lecture Notes in Computer Science; Springer: Berlin/Heidelberg, Germany, 2012; Volume 7442, pp. 129–142.

© 2019 by the authors. Licensee MDPI, Basel, Switzerland. This article is an open access article distributed under the terms and conditions of the Creative Commons Attribution (CC BY) license (http://creativecommons.org/licenses/by/4.0/).

mathematics

MDPI

Article

Dini-Type Helicoidal Hypersurfaces with Timelike Axis in Minkowski 4-Space E_1^4

Erhan Güler * and **Ömer Kişi**

Department of Mathematics, Faculty of Sciences, Bartın University, 74100 Bartın, Turkey; okisi@bartin.edu.tr
* Correspondence: eguler@bartin.edu.tr; Tel.: +90-378-5011000-1521

Received: 31 January 2019; Accepted: 13 February 2019; Published: 22 February 2019

Abstract: We consider Ulisse Dini-type helicoidal hypersurfaces with timelike axis in Minkowski 4-space $\mathbb{E}_1^4$. Calculating the Gaussian and the mean curvatures of the hypersurfaces, we demonstrate some special symmetries for the curvatures when they are flat and minimal.

Keywords: Minkowski 4-space; Dini-type helicoidal hypersurface; Gauss map; timelike axis

1. Introduction

The concept of finite-type immersion of submanifolds of a Euclidean space has been known in classifying and characterizing Riemannian submanifolds [1]. Chen proposed the problem of classifying these kinds surfaces in the three-dimensional Euclidean space $\mathbb{E}^3$. A Euclidean submanifold is called Chen finite-type if its coordinate functions are a finite sum of eigenfunctions of its Laplacian Δ [1]. Hence, the idea of finite-type can be enlarged to any smooth functions on a submanifold of Euclidean or pseudo-Euclidean spaces.

Takahashi [2] obtained spheres and the minimal surfaces are the unique surfaces in $\mathbb{E}^3$ satisfying the condition $\Delta r = \lambda r$, where r is the position vector, $\lambda \in \mathbb{R}$. Ferrandez, Garay and Lucas [3] showed the surfaces of $\mathbb{E}^3$ providing $\Delta H = AH$. Here H is the mean curvature and $A \in Mat(3,3)$ are either of a right circular cylinder, or of an open piece of sphere, or minimal. Choi and Kim [4] worked the minimal helicoid with pointwise 1-type Gauss map of the first type.

Dillen, Pas, and Verstraelen [5] studied the unique surfaces in $\mathbb{E}^3$ providing $\Delta r = Ar + B$, $A \in Mat(3,3)$, $B \in Mat(3,1)$ are the spheres, the circular cylinder, the minimal surfaces. Senoussi and Bekkar [6] obtained helicoidal surfaces in $\mathbb{E}^3$ by using the fundamental forms I, II and III.

In classical surface geometry, it is well known a pair of the right helicoid and the catenoid is the unique ruled and rotational surface, which is minimal. When we look at ruled (i.e., helicoid) and rotational surfaces, we meet Bour's theorem in [7]. By using a result of Bour [7], Do Carmo and Dajczer [8] worked isometric helicoidal surfaces.

Lawson [9] defined the generalized Laplace-Beltrami operator. Magid, Scharlach and Vrancken [10] studied the affine umbilical surfaces in 4-space. Vlachos [11] introduced hypersurfaces with harmonic mean curvature in $\mathbb{E}^4$. Scharlach [12] gave the affine geometry of surfaces and hypersurfaces in 4-space. Cheng and Wan [13] studied complete hypersurfaces of 4-space with CMC. Arslan, Deszcz and Yaprak [14] obtained Weyl pseudosymmetric hypersurfaces. Arvanitoyeorgos, Kaimakamais and Magid [15] wrote that if the mean curvature vector field of M_1^3 satisfies the equation $\Delta H = \alpha H$ (α a constant), then M_1^3 has constant mean curvature in Minkowski 4-space $\mathbb{E}_1^4$. This equation is a natural generalization of the biharmonic submanifold equation $\Delta H = 0$.

General rotational surfaces in the four-dimensional Euclidean space were originated by Moore [16,17]. Ganchev and Milousheva [18] considered the analogue of these surfaces in $\mathbb{E}_1^4$. Verstraelen, Valrave, and Yaprak [19] studied the minimal translation surfaces in $\mathbb{E}^n$ for arbitrary dimension n. Kim and Turgay [20] studied surfaces with L_1-pointwise 1-type Gauss map in $\mathbb{E}^4$. Moruz and Munteanu [21] considered hypersurfaces defined as the sum of a curve and a surface whose mean curvature vanishes in $\mathbb{E}^4$.

Yoon [22] considered rotational surfaces which has a finite-type Gauss map in $\mathbb{E}^4$. Dursun [23] introduced hypersurfaces of pointwise 1-type Gauss map in Minkowski space. Dursun and Turgay [24] studied minimal, pseudo-umbilical rotational surfaces in $\mathbb{E}^4$. Arslan, Bulca and Milousheva [25] focused pointwise 1-type Gauss map of meridian surfaces in $\mathbb{E}^4$. Aksoyak and Yaylı [26] worked boost-invariant surfaces with pointwise 1-type Gauss map in $\mathbb{E}^4_1$. Also they [27] considered generalized rotational surfaces of pointwise 1-type Gauss map in $\mathbb{E}^4_2$. Güler, Magid and Yaylı [28] defined helicoidal hypersurface with the Laplace-Beltrami operator in $\mathbb{E}^4$. Furthermore, Güler, Hacısalihoğlu and Kim [29] worked rotational hypersurface with the III Laplace-Beltrami operator and the Gauss map in $\mathbb{E}^4$.

There are few works in the literature about Italian Mathematician Ulisse Dini's helicoidal surface [30] in $\mathbb{E}^3$. Moreover, Güler and Kişi [31] introduced helicoidal hypersurfaces of Dini-type with spacelike axis in $\mathbb{E}^4_1$.

In this paper, we study the Ulisse Dini-type helicoidal hypersurface with timelike axis in Minkowski 4-space $\mathbb{E}^4_1$. We give some basic notions of Minkowskian geometry, and define helicoidal hypersurface in Section 2. Moreover, we obtain the Dini-type helicoidal hypersurface timelike axis, and calculate its curvatures in the Section 3. We obtain some special symmetries in the last section.

2. Preliminaries

In this section, we will describe the notation that will be used in the paper, after we give some basic facts and basic definitions.

Let $\mathbb{E}^m_1$ be the Minkowski m-space with the Euclidean metric denoted by

$$\widetilde{g} = \langle \, , \, \rangle = \sum_{i=1}^{m-1} dx_i^2 - dx_m^2,$$

where $(x_1, x_2, \ldots, x_m)$ is a coordinate system in $\mathbb{E}^m_1$.

Consider an n-dimensional Minkowskian submanifold of the space $\mathbb{E}^m_1$. We denote Levi-Civita connections of $\mathbb{E}^m_1$ and M by $\widetilde{\nabla}$ and ∇, respectively. We will use letters X, Y, Z, W (resp., ξ, η) to show vector fields tangent (resp., normal) to M. The Gauss and the Weingarten formulas are defined by as follows:

$$\begin{aligned} \widetilde{\nabla}_X Y &= \nabla_X Y + h(X, Y), \\ \widetilde{\nabla}_X \xi &= -A_\xi(X) + D_X \xi, \end{aligned}$$

where h, D, and A are the second fundamental form, the normal connection and the shape operator of M, respectively.

The shape operator A_ξ is a symmetric endomorphism of the tangent space T_pM at $p \in M$ for each $\xi \in T_p^\perp M$. The second fundamental form and the shape operator are connected by

$$\langle h(X, Y), \xi \rangle = \langle A_\xi X, Y \rangle .$$

The Gauss and Codazzi equations are denoted, respectively, as follows:

$$\langle R(X, Y,)Z, W \rangle = \langle h(Y, Z), h(X, W) \rangle - \langle h(X, Z), h(Y, W) \rangle, \tag{1}$$

$$(\bar{\nabla}_X h)(Y, Z) = (\bar{\nabla}_Y h)(X, Z). \tag{2}$$

Here, R, R^D are the curvature tensors related with connections ∇ and D, respectively, and $\bar{\nabla} h$ is defined by

$$(\bar{\nabla}_X h)(Y, Z) = D_X h(Y, Z) - h(\nabla_X Y, Z) - h(Y, \nabla_X Z).$$

2.1. Hypersurfaces of Minkowski Space

Assume that M be an oriented hypersurface in Minkowski space $\mathbb{E}_1^n$, $\mathbf{S}$ its shape operator and x its position vector. We think about a local orthonormal frame field $\{e_1, e_2, \ldots, e_n\}$ occurring of the principal directions of M matching to the principal curvatures k_i for $i = 1, 2, \ldots n$. Let $\{\theta_1, \theta_2, \ldots, \theta\}$ be dual basis of this frame field. Then the first structural equation of Cartan is

$$d\theta_i = \sum_{i=1}^{n} \theta_j \wedge \omega_{ij}, \quad i = 1, 2, \ldots, n.$$

Here, ω_{ij} demonstrates the connection forms matching to the chosen frame field. We show the Levi-Civita connection of M and $\mathbb{E}_1^n$ by ∇ and $\widetilde{\nabla}$, respectively. Then, from the Codazzi Equation (2) we have

$$\begin{aligned} e_i(k_j) &= \omega_{ij}(e_j)(k_i - k_j), \\ \omega_{ij}(e_l)(k_i - k_j) &= \omega_{il}(e_j)(k_i - k_l) \end{aligned}$$

for distinct $i, j, l = 1, 2, \ldots, n$.

We take $s_j = \sigma_j(k_1, k_2, \ldots, k_n)$, where σ_j is the j-th elementary symmetric function given by

$$\sigma_j(a_1, a_2, \ldots, a_n) = \sum_{1 \leq i_1 < i_2 < \ldots, i_j \leq n} a_{i_1} a_{i_2} \ldots a_{i_j}.$$

We also use the following notation

$$r_i^j = \sigma_j(k_1, k_2, \ldots, k_{i-1}, k_{i+1}, k_{i+2}, \ldots, k_n).$$

By definition, we have $r_i^0 = 1$ and $s_{n+1} = s_{n+2} = \cdots = 0$.

On the other hand, we will call the function s_k as the k-th mean curvature of M. We would like to note that functions $H = \frac{1}{n} s_1$ and $K = s_n$ are called the mean and the Gauss-Kronecker curvatures of M, respectively. Particularly, M is called j-minimal if $s_j \equiv 0$ on M.

2.2. Helicoidal Hypersurfaces with Timelike Axis in Minkowskian Spaces

In this subsection, we will obtain the helicoidal hypersurfaces with timelike axis in Minkowski 4-space $\mathbb{E}_1^4$. In the rest of this paper, we will identify a vector (a,b,c,d) with its transpose.

Before we proceed, we would like to note that the definition of rotational hypersurfaces in Riemannian space forms were defined in [32]. A rotational hypersurface $M \subset \mathbb{E}_1^n$ generated by a curve C about an axis $\mathbf{r}$ does not meet C is generated by using the orbit of C under those orthogonal transformations of $\mathbb{E}_1^n$ which leave $\mathbf{r}$ pointwise fixed (See [32] remark 2.3).

A curve C rotates about the axis $\mathbf{r}$, and at the same time replaces parallel lines orthogonal to the axis $\mathbf{r}$, so that the speed of replacement is proportional to the speed of rotation. Finally, the resulting hypersurface is called the *helicoidal hypersurface* with axis $\mathbf{r}$.

Consider the particular case $n = 4$ and let C be the curve parametrized by

$$\gamma(u) = (f(u), 0, 0, \varphi(u)),$$

where f and φ are differentiable functions. If $\mathbf{r}$ is the timelike vector $(0, 0, 0, 1)$, then an orthogonal transformation of $\mathbb{E}_1^4$ that leaves $\mathbf{r}$ pointwise fixed has the form $Z(v, w)$ as follows:

$$Z(v,w)=\begin{pmatrix}\cos v\cos w & -\sin v & -\cos v\sin w & 0\\ \cos w\sin v & \cos v & -\sin v\sin w & 0\\ \sin w & 0 & \cos w & 0\\ 0 & 0 & 0 & 1\end{pmatrix},$$

and the following relations hold:

$$Z^T\varepsilon Z = Z\varepsilon Z^T=\varepsilon,\ Z\mathbf{r}^T=\mathbf{r}^T,\ \det Z=1,\ \varepsilon = diag\,(1,1,1,-1),$$

$v,w\in\mathbb{R}$. Therefore, the parametrization of the rotational hypersurface obtained by a curve C around an axis $\mathbf{r}$ is

$$\mathbf{H}(u,v,w)=Z(v,w)\gamma(u)^T+(av+bw)\,\mathbf{r}^T,$$

where $u\in I$, $v,w\in[0,2\pi]$ and pitches $a,b\in\mathbb{R}\backslash\{0\}$.

Clearly, an helicoidal hypersurface with timelike axis written as

$$\mathbf{H}(u,v,w)=\begin{pmatrix} f(u)\cos v\cos w\\ f(u)\sin v\cos w\\ f(u)\sin w\\ \varphi(u)+av+bw\end{pmatrix}. \tag{3}$$

When $w=0$, we have an helicoidal surface with timelike axis in $\mathbb{E}_1^4$.

Now we give some basic elements of the Minkowski 4-space $\mathbb{E}_1^4$. Let $\mathbf{M}=\mathbf{M}(u,v,w)$ be an isometric immersion of a hypersurface M^3 in $\mathbb{E}_1^4$. Using vectors $\overrightarrow{x}=(x_1,x_2,x_3,x_4)$, $\overrightarrow{y}=(y_1,y_2,y_3,y_4)$ and $\overrightarrow{z}=(z_1,z_2,z_3,z_4)$, the Minkowskian inner product and vector product are defined by as follows, respectively,

$$\overrightarrow{x}\cdot\overrightarrow{y}=x_1y_1+x_2y_2+x_3y_3-x_4y_4,$$

$$\begin{aligned}\overrightarrow{x}\times\overrightarrow{y}\times\overrightarrow{z}=(&x_2y_3z_4-x_2y_4z_3-x_3y_2z_4+x_3y_4z_2+x_4y_2z_3-x_4y_3z_2,\\ &-x_1y_3z_4+x_1y_4z_3+x_3y_1z_4-x_3z_1y_4-y_1x_4z_3+x_4y_3z_1,\\ &x_1y_2z_4-x_1y_4z_2-x_2y_1z_4+x_2z_1y_4+y_1x_4z_2-x_4y_2z_1,\\ &x_1y_2z_3-x_1y_3z_2-x_2y_1z_3+x_2y_3z_1+x_3y_1z_2-x_3y_2z_1).\end{aligned}$$

For a hypersurface $\mathbf{M}$ in $\mathbb{E}_1^4$, the first fundamental form matrix is $\mathbf{I}=\left(\, g_{ij}\,\right)_{3\times3}$, and $\det\mathbf{I}=\det\left(\, g_{ij}\,\right)$, and also the second fundamental form matrix is $\mathbf{II}=\left(\, h_{ij}\,\right)_{3\times3}$, and $\det\mathbf{II}=\det\left(\, h_{ij}\,\right)$, where $1\le i,j\le 3$, $g_{11}=\mathbf{M}_u\cdot\mathbf{M}_u$, $g_{12}=\mathbf{M}_u\cdot\mathbf{M}_v,\ldots,g_{33}=\mathbf{M}_w\cdot\mathbf{M}_w$, and $h_{11}=\mathbf{M}_{uu}\cdot\mathbf{G}$, $h_{12}=\mathbf{M}_{uv}\cdot\mathbf{G},\ldots,h_{33}=\mathbf{M}_{ww}\cdot\mathbf{G}$, and some partial differentials we represent are $\mathbf{M}_u=\frac{\partial\mathbf{M}}{\partial u}$, $\mathbf{M}_{uw}=\frac{\partial^2\mathbf{M}}{\partial u\partial w}$,

$$\mathbf{G}=\frac{\mathbf{M}_u\times\mathbf{M}_v\times\mathbf{M}_w}{\|\mathbf{M}_u\times\mathbf{M}_v\times\mathbf{M}_w\|}$$

is the Gauss map. $\left(\, g_{ij}\,\right)^{-1}\left(\, h_{ij}\,\right)$ gives the matrix of shape operator (i.e., Weingarten map) $\mathbf{S}=\frac{1}{\det\mathbf{I}}\left(\, s_{ij}\,\right)_{3\times3}$. Therefore, we get the Gaussian and the mean curvature formulas, respectively, as follows:

$$K=\det(\mathbf{S})=\frac{\det\mathbf{II}}{\det\mathbf{I}}, \tag{4}$$

and

$$H=\frac{1}{3}tr\,(\mathbf{S})\,. \tag{5}$$

3. Dini-Type Helicoidal Hypersurface with a Timelike Axis

Taking $f(u) = \sin u$ in (3), we define Dini-type helicoidal hypersurface with a timelike axis in $\mathbb{E}_1^4$, as follows:

$$\mathbf{D}(u,v,w) = \begin{pmatrix} \sin u \cos v \cos w \\ \sin u \sin v \cos w \\ \sin u \sin w \\ \varphi(u) + av + bw \end{pmatrix}, \tag{6}$$

where $u \in \mathbb{R}\backslash\{0\}$ and $0 \leq v, w \leq 2\pi$.

Computing the first differentials of (6) depend on u, v, w, we obtain the first quantities as follows:

$$\mathbf{I} = \begin{pmatrix} \cos^2 u - \varphi'^2 & -a\varphi' & -b\varphi' \\ -a\varphi' & \sin^2 u \cos^2 w - a^2 & -ab \\ -b\varphi' & -ab & \sin^2 u - b^2 \end{pmatrix},$$

and have

$$\det \mathbf{I} = -\sin^2 u \left\{ \varphi'^2 \sin^2 u \cos^2 w + \left[\left(b^2 - \sin^2 u \right) \cos^2 w + a^2 \right] \cos^2 u \right\},$$

where $\varphi = \varphi(u)$, $\varphi' = \frac{d\varphi}{du}$.

By using the second differentials depend on u, v, w, we have the second quantities as follows:

$$\mathbf{II} = \begin{pmatrix} -\frac{\sin^2 u \cos w(\varphi'' \cos u + \varphi' \sin u)}{\sqrt{\|\det \mathbf{I}\|}} & \frac{a \sin u \cos^2 u \cos w}{\sqrt{\|\det \mathbf{I}\|}} & \frac{b \sin u \cos^2 u \cos w}{\sqrt{\|\det \mathbf{I}\|}} \\ \frac{a \sin u \cos^2 u \cos w}{\sqrt{\|\det \mathbf{I}\|}} & \frac{\sin^2 u \cos^2 w(b \cos u \sin w - \varphi' \sin u \cos w)}{\sqrt{\|\det \mathbf{I}\|}} & -\frac{a \sin^2 u \cos u \sin w}{\sqrt{\|\det \mathbf{I}\|}} \\ \frac{b \sin u \cos^2 u \cos w}{\sqrt{\|\det \mathbf{I}\|}} & -\frac{a \sin^2 u \cos u \sin w}{\sqrt{\|\det \mathbf{I}\|}} & -\frac{\varphi' \sin^3 u \cos w}{\sqrt{\|\det \mathbf{I}\|}} \end{pmatrix},$$

and we get

$$\det \mathbf{II} = \frac{\begin{pmatrix} -\varphi'^2 \varphi'' \sin^8 u \cos u \cos^5 w + b\varphi' \varphi'' \sin^7 u \cos^2 u \sin w \cos^4 w \\ +a^2 \varphi'' \sin^6 u \cos^3 u \sin^2 w \cos w - \varphi'^3 \sin^9 u \cos^5 w \\ +b\varphi'^2 \sin^8 u \cos u \cos^4 w \sin w \\ +\left(a^2 \left(\cos^2 u \cos^2 w + \sin^2 u \sin^2 w\right) - b^2 \cos^4 u\right) \varphi' \sin^5 u \cos^2 u \cos w \\ -b\left(2a^2 + b^2 \cos^2 w\right) \sin^4 u \cos^5 u \sin w \cos^2 w \end{pmatrix}}{(\det \mathbf{I})^{3/2}}.$$

The Gauss map of a helicoidal hypersurface with a timelike axis is

$$e_{\mathbf{D}} = \frac{1}{\sqrt{\det \mathbf{I}}} \begin{pmatrix} (\varphi' \sin u \cos v \cos^2 w - a \cos u \sin v - b \cos u \cos v \sin w \cos w) \sin u \\ (\varphi' \sin u \sin v \cos^2 w + a \cos u \cos v - b \cos u \sin v \sin w \cos w) \sin u \\ (\varphi' \sin u \sin w + b \cos u \cos w) \sin u \cos w \\ \sin^2 u \cos u \cos w \end{pmatrix}.$$

Finally, we have the Gaussian curvature of a helicoidal hypersurface with a timelike axis as follows:

$$K = \frac{\alpha_1 \varphi'^2 \varphi'' + \alpha_2 \varphi' \varphi'' + \alpha_3 \varphi'' + \alpha_4 \varphi'^3 + \alpha_5 \varphi'^2 + \alpha_6 \varphi' + \alpha_7}{(\det \mathbf{I})^{5/2}},$$

where

$\alpha_1 = -\sin^8 u \cos u \cos^5 w,$
$\alpha_2 = b \sin^7 u \cos^2 u \sin w \cos^4 w,$
$\alpha_3 = a^2 \sin^8 u \cos^3 u \sin^2 w \cos w,$
$\alpha_4 = -\sin^9 u \cos^5 w,$
$\alpha_5 = b \sin^8 u \cos u \sin w \cos^4 w,$

$$\alpha_6 = \left(a^2\left(\cos^2 u\cos^2 w + \sin^2 u\sin^2 w\right) - b^2\cos^4 u\right)\sin^5 u\cos^2 u\cos w, :$$
$$\alpha_7 = -b(2a^2 + b^2\cos^2 w)\sin^4 u\cos^5 u\sin w\cos^2 w.$$

Then we calculate the mean curvature of a helicoidal hypersurface with a timelike axis as follows:

$$H = \frac{\beta_1\varphi'' + \beta_2\varphi'^3 + \beta_3\varphi'^2 + \beta_4\varphi' + \beta_5}{3(\det \mathbf{I})^{3/2}},$$

where

$$\beta_1 = -\left(\left(b^2 - \sin^2 u\right)\cos^2 w + a^2\right)\sin^4 u\cos u\cos w,$$
$$\beta_2 = -2\sin^5 u\cos^3 w,$$
$$\beta_3 = -b\sin^4 u\cos u\sin w\cos^2 w,$$
$$\beta_4 = -\left(\left(\left(b^2 + \cos^2 u\right)^2 - 1\right)\cos^2 w + a^2\left(2\cos^2 u + 1\right)\right)\sin^3 u\cos w,$$
$$\beta_5 = b(\left(b^2 - \sin^2 u\right)\cos^2 w + 2a^2)\sin^2 u\cos^3 u\sin w.$$

Therefore, we get the following theorems about flatness and minimality of the hypersurface.

Theorem 1. *Let* $\mathbf{D} : M^3 \longrightarrow \mathbb{E}^4_1$ *be an isometric immersion given by* (6). *Then* M^3 *is flat if and only if*

$$\alpha_1\varphi'^2\varphi'' + \alpha_2\varphi'\varphi'' + \alpha_3\varphi'' + \alpha_4\varphi'^3 + \alpha_5\varphi'^2 + \alpha_6\varphi' + \alpha_7 = 0. \tag{7}$$

Theorem 2. *Let* $\mathbf{D} : M^3 \longrightarrow \mathbb{E}^4_1$ *be an isometric immersion given by* (6). *Then* M^3 *is minimal if and only if*

$$\beta_1\varphi'' + \beta_2\varphi'^3 + \beta_3\varphi'^2 + \beta_4\varphi' + \beta_5 = 0. \tag{8}$$

Solving these two equations is an attractive problem.

In the next two propositions, we will use the function

$$\varphi(u) = \cos u + \log\left(\tan\frac{u}{2}\right) \tag{9}$$

as in Dini helicoidal surface used by Ulisse Dini in Euclidean 3-space, and its following derivatives

$$\varphi'(u) = \frac{\tan^2\frac{u}{2} - 2\sin u\tan\frac{u}{2} + 1}{2\tan\frac{u}{2}} \tag{10}$$

and

$$\varphi''(u) = \frac{\tan^4\frac{u}{2} - 4\cos u\tan^2\frac{u}{2} - 1}{4\tan^2\frac{u}{2}}. \tag{11}$$

Proposition 1. *Let* $\mathbf{D}$ *is Dini-type flat hypersurface with a timelike axis (i.e.* $K = 0$*) in Minkowski 4-space. Using the function* (9) *and its derivatives* (10), (11) *and substituting them into the* (7) *in Theorem 1, we obtain*

$$\sum_{i=0}^{8} A_i\tan^i\left(\frac{u}{2}\right) = 0,$$

where

$$A_8 = \alpha_1,$$
$$A_7 = -4\alpha_1\sin u + 2\alpha_2 + 2\alpha_4,$$
$$A_6 = \left(2 + 4\sin^2 u - 4\cos u\right)\alpha_1 - 4\alpha_2\sin u + 4\alpha_3 - 12\alpha_4\sin u + 4\alpha_5 u,$$
$$A_5 = \left(16\cos u - 4\right)\alpha_1\sin u + \left(-8\cos u + 2\right)\alpha_2 + \left(24\sin^2 u + 6\right)\alpha_4 - 16\alpha_5\sin u + 8\alpha_6,$$
$$A_4 = \left(-16\sin^2 u - 8\right)\alpha_1\cos u + 16\alpha_2\cos u\sin u - 16\alpha_3\cos u$$
$$+ \left(-16\sin^2 u - 24\right)\alpha_4\sin u + \left(16\sin^2 u + 8\right)\alpha_5 - 16\alpha_6\sin u + 16\alpha_7$$
$$A_3 = \left(16\cos u + 4\right)\alpha_1\sin u + \left(-8\cos u - 2\right)\alpha_2 + \left(24\sin^2 u + 6\right)\alpha_4 - 16\alpha_5\sin u + 8\alpha_6,$$

$$\begin{aligned} A_2 &= \left(-2-4\sin^2 u-4\cos u\right)\alpha_1+4\alpha_2\sin u-4\alpha_3-12\alpha_4\sin u+4\alpha_5,\\ A_1 &= 4\alpha_1\sin u-2\alpha_2+2\alpha_4,\\ A_0 &= -\alpha_1. \end{aligned}$$

Proposition 2. *Let* **D** *is Dini-type minimal helicoidal hypersurface with a timelike axis (i.e., $H=0$) in Minkowski 4-space. Using the function (9) and its derivatives (10), (11) and substituting them into the (8) in Theorem 2, we get*

$$\sum_{i=0}^{6} B_i \tan^i\left(\frac{u}{2}\right)=0,$$

where

$$\begin{aligned} B_6 &= \beta_2,\\ B_5 &= 2\beta_1-6\beta_2\sin u+2\beta_3,\\ B_4 &= \left(3+12\sin^2 u\right)\beta_2-8\beta_3\sin u+4\beta_4,\\ B_3 &= -8\beta_1\cos u-\left(12\sin u+8\sin^3 u\right)\beta_2+\left(4+8\sin^2 u\right)\beta_3-8\beta_4\sin u+8\beta_5,\\ B_2 &= \left(3+12\sin^2 u\right)\beta_2-8\beta_3\sin u+4\beta_4,\\ B_1 &= -2\beta_1-6\beta_2\sin u+2\beta_3,\\ B_0 &= \beta_2. \end{aligned}$$

Corollary 1. *From the Proposition 1, and the Proposition 2, we obtain following special symmetries of* **D***, respectively,*

$$A_8\sim A_0,\ A_7\sim A_1,\ A_6\sim A_2,\ A_5\sim A_3,$$

and

$$B_6=B_0,\ B_5\sim B_1,\ B_4=B_2,$$

where "$\sim$" means the α_i $(i=1,2,...,7)$ and β_j $(j=1,2,...,5)$ term coefficients which ignored signs, respectively, are equal.

Author Contributions: E.G. considered the idea for Dini type helicoidal hypersurface with timelike axis in the four dimensional Minkowski space. Then E.G. and Ö.K. checked and polished the draft.

Funding: This research received no external funding.

Conflicts of Interest: The authors declare that there is no conflict of interests regarding the publication of this paper.

References

1. Chen, B.Y. *Total Mean Curvature and Submanifolds of Finite Type*; World Scientific: Singapore, 1984.
2. Takahashi, T. Minimal immersions of Riemannian manifolds. *J. Math. Soc. Japan* **1966**, *18*, 380–385. [CrossRef]
3. Ferrandez, A.; Garay, O.J.; Lucas, P. On a certain class of conformally at Euclidean hypersurfaces. In *Global Analysis and Global Differential Geometry*; Springer: Berlin, Germany, 1990; pp. 48–54.
4. Choi, M.; Kim, Y.H. Characterization of the helicoid as ruled surfaces with pointwise 1-type Gauss map. *Bull. Korean Math. Soc.* **2001**, *38*, 753–761.
5. Dillen, F.; Pas, J.; Verstraelen, L. On surfaces of finite type in Euclidean 3-space. *Kodai Math. J.* **1990**, *13*, 10–21. [CrossRef]
6. Senoussi, B.; Bekkar, M. Helicoidal surfaces with $\Delta^J r = Ar$ in 3-dimensional Euclidean space. *Stud. Univ. Babeş-Bolyai Math.* **2015**, *60*, 437–448.
7. Bour, E. Theorie de la deformation des surfaces. *J. Ecole Imp. Polytech.* **1862**, *22*, 1–148.
8. Do Carmo, M.; Dajczer, M. Helicoidal surfaces with constant mean curvature. *Tohoku Math. J.* **1982**, *34*, 351–367. [CrossRef]
9. Lawson, H.B. *Lectures on Minimal Submanifolds*, 2nd ed.; Mathematics Lecture Series 9; Publish or Perish, Inc.: Wilmington, DE, USA, 1980.

10. Magid, M.; Scharlach, C.; Vrancken, L. Affine umbilical surfaces in $\mathbb{R}^4$. *Manuscr. Math.* **1995**, *88*, 275–289. [CrossRef]
11. Vlachos, T. Hypersurfaces in $\mathbb{E}^4$ with harmonic mean curvature vector field. *Math. Nachr.* **1995**, *172*, 145–169.
12. Scharlach, C. Affine geometry of surfaces and hypersurfaces in $\mathbb{R}^4$. In *Symposium on the Differential Geometry of Submanifolds*; Dillen, F., Simon, U., Vrancken, L., Eds.; University Valenciennes: Valenciennes, France, 2007; Volume 124, pp. 251–256.
13. Cheng, Q.M.; Wan, Q.R. Complete hypersurfaces of $\mathbb{R}^4$ with constant mean curvature. *Monatsh. Math.* **1994**, *118*, 171–204. [CrossRef]
14. Arslan, K.; Deszcz, R.; Yaprak, Ş. On Weyl pseudosymmetric hypersurfaces. *Colloq. Math.* **1997**, *72*, 353–361. [CrossRef]
15. Arvanitoyeorgos, A.; Kaimakamis, G.; Magid, M. Lorentz hypersurfaces in $\mathbb{E}_1^4$ satisfying $\Delta H = \alpha H$. *Ill. J. Math.* **2009**, *53*, 581–590.
16. Moore, C. Surfaces of rotation in a space of four dimensions. *Ann. Math.* **1919**, *21*, 81–93. [CrossRef]
17. Moore, C. Rotation surfaces of constant curvature in space of four dimensions. *Bull. Am. Math. Soc.* **1920**, *26*, 454–460. [CrossRef]
18. Ganchev, G.; Milousheva, V. General rotational surfaces in the 4-dimensional Minkowski space. *Turk. J. Math.* **2014**, *38*, 883–895. [CrossRef]
19. Verstraelen, L.; Valrave, J.; Yaprak, Ş. The minimal translation surfaces in Euclidean space. *Soochow J. Math.* **1994**, *20*, 77–82.
20. Kim, Y.H.; Turgay, N.C. Surfaces in $\mathbb{E}^4$ with L_1-pointwise 1-type Gauss map. *Bull. Korean Math. Soc.* **2013**, *50*, 935–949. [CrossRef]
21. Moruz, M.; Munteanu, M.I. Minimal translation hypersurfaces in $\mathbb{E}^4$. *J. Math. Anal. Appl.* **2016**, *439*, 798–812. [CrossRef]
22. Yoon, D.W. Rotation Surfaces with finite type Gauss map in $\mathbb{E}^4$. *Indian J. Pure Appl. Math.* **2001**, *32*, 1803–1808.
23. Dursun, U. Hypersurfaces with pointwise 1-type Gauss map in Lorentz-Minkowski space. *Proc. Est. Acad. Sci.* **2009**, *58*, 146–161. [CrossRef]
24. Dursun, U.; Turgay, N.C. Minimal and pseudo-umbilical rotational surfaces in Euclidean space $\mathbb{E}^4$. *Mediterr. J. Math.* **2013**, *10*, 497–506. [CrossRef]
25. Arslan, K.; Bulca, B.; Milousheva, V. Meridian surfaces in $\mathbb{E}^4$ with pointwise 1-type Gauss map. *Bull. Korean Math. Soc.* **2014**, *51*, 911–922. [CrossRef]
26. Aksoyak, F.; Yaylı, Y. Boost invariant surfaces with pointwise 1-type Gauss map in Minkowski 4-Space $\mathbb{E}_1^4$. *Bull. Korean Math. Soc.* **2014**, *51*, 1863–1874. [CrossRef]
27. Aksoyak, F.; Yaylı, Y. General rotational surfaces with pointwise 1-type Gauss map in pseudo-Euclidean space $\mathbb{E}_2^4$. *Indian J. Pure Appl. Math.* **2015**, *46*, 107–118. [CrossRef]
28. Güler, E.; Magid, M.; Yaylı, Y. Laplace Beltrami operator of a helicoidal hypersurface in four space. *J. Geom. Symmetry Phys.* **2016**, *41*, 77–95. [CrossRef]
29. Güler, E.; Hacısalihoğlu, H.H.; Kim, Y.H. The Gauss map and the third Laplace-Beltrami operator of the rotational hypersurface in 4-space. *Symmetry* **2018**, *10*, 398. [CrossRef]
30. Dini, U. Sopra le funzioni di una variabile complessa. *Annali di Matematica Pura ed Applicata* **1871**, *4*, 159–174. [CrossRef]
31. Güler, E.; Kişi, Ö. Helicoidal Hypersurfaces of Dini-Type in the Four Dimensional Minkowski Space. In Proceedings of the International Conference on Analysis and Its Applications (ICAA-2018), Kırşehir, Türkiye, 11–14 September 2018; pp. 13–18.
32. Do Carmo, M.; Dajczer, M. Rotation Hypersurfaces in Spaces of Constant Curvature. *Trans. Am. Math. Soc.* **1983**, *277*, 685–709. [CrossRef]

© 2019 by the authors. Licensee MDPI, Basel, Switzerland. This article is an open access article distributed under the terms and conditions of the Creative Commons Attribution (CC BY) license (http://creativecommons.org/licenses/by/4.0/).

mathematics

Article

Implicit Equations of the Henneberg-Type Minimal Surface in the Four-Dimensional Euclidean Space

Erhan Güler [1,*], Ömer Kişi [1] and Christos Konaxis [2]

[1] Department of Mathematics, Faculty of Sciences, Bartın University, 74100 Bartın, Turkey; okisi@bartin.edu.tr
[2] Department of Informatics and Telecommunications, National and Kapodistrian University of Athens, 15784 Athens, Greece; ckonaxis@di.uoa.gr
* Correspondence: eguler@bartin.edu.tr; Tel.: +90-378-5011000-1521

Received: 18 October 2018; Accepted: 22 November 2018; Published: 25 November 2018

Abstract: Considering the Weierstrass data as $(\psi, f, g) = (2, 1 - z^{-m}, z^n)$, we introduce a two-parameter family of Henneberg-type minimal surface that we call $\mathfrak{H}_{m,n}$ for positive integers (m, n) by using the Weierstrass representation in the four-dimensional Euclidean space $\mathbb{E}^4$. We define $\mathfrak{H}_{m,n}$ in (r, θ) coordinates for positive integers (m, n) with $m \neq 1, n \neq -1, -m + n \neq -1$, and also in (u, v) coordinates, and then we obtain implicit algebraic equations of the Henneberg-type minimal surface of values $(4, 2)$.

Keywords: Henneberg-type minimal surface; Weierstrass representation; four-dimensional space; implicit equation; degree

1. Introduction

The theory of surfaces has an important role in mathematics, physics, biology, architecture, see e.g., the classical books [1,2] and papers [3–9].

A minimal surface in the three-dimensional Euclidean space $\mathbb{E}^3$, also in higher dimensions, is a regular surface for which the mean curvature vanishes identically. See [10–27] for details. On the other hand, a Henneberg surface [4–6], also obtained by the Weierstrass representation [8,9] is well-known classical minimal surface in $\mathbb{E}^3$.

In the four-dimensional Euclidean space $\mathbb{E}^4$, a general definition of rotation surfaces was given by Moore in [28] as follows

$$X(u,t) = \begin{pmatrix} x_1(u)\cos(at) - x_2(u)\sin(at) \\ x_1(u)\cos(at) + x_2(u)\sin(at) \\ x_3(u)\cos(bt) - x_4(u)\sin(bt) \\ x_3(u)\cos(bt) + x_4(u)\sin(bt) \end{pmatrix}.$$

A more restricted case can be found in [29]:

$$W(u,t) = (x_1(u), x_2(u), r(u)\cos(t), r(u)\sin(t)).$$

It is a bit too general since the curve is not located in any subspace before rotation.

Güler and Kişi [30] studied the Weierstrass representation, the degree and the classes of surfaces in $\mathbb{E}^4$, see [31–38] for some previous work.

In this paper, we study a two-parameter family of Henneberg-type minimal surfaces using the Weierstrass representation in $\mathbb{E}^4$. We give the Weierstrass equations for a minimal surface in $\mathbb{E}^4$, and obtain two normals of the surface in Section 2.

In Section 3, we introduce complex form of the Henneberg-type minimal surface in 4-dimension, considering 3-dimension case. Then we define Henneberg-type minimal surface in the polar coordinates using real part for values (m, n) called $\mathfrak{H}_{m,n}$, where m and n are positive integers with $m \neq 1$, $n \neq -1$, $-m + n \neq -1$. We also focus on Henneberg-type minimal surface $\mathfrak{H}_{4,2}$ using the Weierstrass representation in $\mathbb{E}^4$, and give explicit parametrizations for minimal Henneberg-type surface of values $(4, 2)$.

Finally, we describe how we obtained the implicit algebraic equation of the Henneberg-type surface $\mathfrak{H}_{4,2}$, by using elimination techniques based on Groebner Basis in the software package Maple in Section 4.

2. Weierstrass Equations for a Minimal Surface in $\mathbb{E}^4$

We identify $\vec{x}$ and $\vec{x^t}$ without further comment. Let $\mathbb{E}^4 = (\{\vec{x} = (x_1, x_2, x_3, x_4)^t | x_i \in \mathbb{R}\}, \langle \cdot, \cdot \rangle)$ be the 4-dimensional Euclidean space with metric $\langle x, y \rangle = x_1y_1 + x_2y_2 + x_3y_3 + x_4y_4$.

Hoffman and Osserman [12] gave the Weierstrass equations for a minimal surface in $\mathbb{E}^4$:

$$\Phi(z) = \frac{\psi}{2}\left[1 + fg, i(1 - fg), f - g, -i(f + g)\right]. \tag{1}$$

Here, ψ is analytic and the order of the zeros of ψ must be greater than the order of the poles of f, g at each point.

$$\begin{aligned} X_x - iX_y &= \Phi(z) \\ &= [(1 + f_1g_1 - f_2g_2)x - (f_2g_1 + f_1g_2)y, \\ &\quad (f_2g_1 + f_1g_2)\,x - y + f_1g_1y - f_2g_2y, \\ &\quad (f_1 - g_1)\,x + (-f_2 + g_2)y, (f_2 + g_2)\,x + (f_1 + g_1)y] \\ &\quad -i[-y - f_1(g_2x + g_1y) + f_2(-g_1x + g_2y), \\ &\quad (-1 + f_1g_1 - f_2g_2)x - (f_2g_1 + f_1g_2)y, \\ &\quad +(-f_2 + g_2)x + (-f_1 + g_1)y, \\ &\quad (f_1 + g_1)\,x - (f_2 + g_2)y], \end{aligned}$$

where $\psi = 2z$ and $f = f_1 + if_2$, $g = g_1 + ig_2$. We set

$$\begin{aligned} w_1 &= [-(f_2g_1x + f_1g_2x - y + f_1g_1y - f_2g_2y), \\ &\quad (1 + f_1g_1 - f_2g_2)x - (f_2g_1 + f_1g_2)y, \\ &\quad -((f_2 + g_2)\,x + (f_1 + g_1)y), \\ &\quad (f_1 - g_1)\,x + (-f_2 + g_2)y] \end{aligned}$$

which is perpendicular to X_x, and

$$\begin{aligned} w_2 &= [-((-1 + f_1g_1 - f_2g_2)x - (f_2g_1 + f_1g_2)y), \\ &\quad -y - f_1(g_2x + g_1y) + f_2(-g_1x + g_2y), \\ &\quad -(f_1x + g_1x - (f_2 + g_2)y), \\ &\quad -f_2x + g_2x + (-f_1 + g_1)y] \end{aligned}$$

which is perpendicular to X_y.

So far, we see that:

$$\begin{aligned} b &= \langle X_x, w_2 \rangle \\ &= -(-1 + f_1^2 + f_2^2)(1 + g_1^2 + g_2^2)(x^2 + y^2) \\ &= -\langle X_y, w_1 \rangle, \end{aligned}$$

while

$$\begin{aligned} a &= \langle X_x, X_x \rangle \\ &= \langle X_y, X_y \rangle \\ &= \left(1+f_1^2+f_2^2\right)(1+g_1^2+g_2^2)(x^2+y^2) \\ &= \langle w_j, w_j \rangle. \end{aligned}$$

Next, we use Gram-Schmidt to find an orthonormal basis for the normal space. Let $e_1 = X_x/\sqrt{a}$ and $e_2 = X_y/\sqrt{a}$.

Then we get

$$n_1 = \sqrt{\frac{a}{a^2-b^2}}\left(w_1 + \frac{b}{a}X_y\right) \tag{2}$$

and

$$n_2 = \sqrt{\frac{a}{a^2-b^2}}\left(w_2 - \frac{b}{a}X_x\right), \tag{3}$$

where

$$\begin{aligned} a^2-b^2 &= 4\left(f_1^2+f_2^2\right)\left(x^2+y^2\right)^2\left(g_1^2+g_2^2+1\right)^2, \\ \sqrt{\frac{a}{a^2-b^2}} &= \sqrt{\frac{1+f_1^2+f_2^2}{4\left(f_1^2+f_2^2\right)(x^2+y^2)\left(g_1^2+g_2^2+1\right)}}, \\ \frac{b}{a} &= -\frac{-1+f_1^2+f_2^2}{1+f_1^2+f_2^2}, \end{aligned}$$

$$\begin{aligned} w_1 &= \begin{pmatrix} -\left(f_1g_2+f_2g_1\right)x - \left(-1+f_1g_1-f_2g_2\right)y \\ (1+f_1g_1-f_2g_2)x-(f_2g_1+f_1g_2)y \\ -\left(f_2+g_2\right)x-(f_1+g_1)y \\ \left(f_1-g_1\right)x+(-f_2+g_2)y \end{pmatrix}, \\ w_2 &= \begin{pmatrix} -((-1+f_1g_1-f_2g_2)x-(f_2g_1+f_1g_2)y) \\ -y-f_1(g_2x+g_1y)+f_2(-g_1x+g_2y) \\ -(f_1x+g_1x-(f_2+g_2)y) \\ -f_2x+g_2x+(-f_1+g_1)y \end{pmatrix}, \end{aligned}$$

$$\begin{aligned} X_x &= \begin{pmatrix} (1+f_1g_1-f_2g_2)x-(f_2g_1+f_1g_2)y \\ f_2g_1x+f_1g_2x-y+f_1g_1y-f_2g_2y \\ f_1x-g_1x+(-f_2+g_2)y \\ f_2x+g_2x+(f_1+g_1)y \end{pmatrix}, \\ X_y &= \begin{pmatrix} -\left(f_1g_2+f_2g_1\right)x+\left(-1-f_1g_1+f_2g_2\right)y \\ (-1+f_1g_1-f_2g_2)x-(f_2g_1+f_1g_2)y \\ \left(-f_2+g_2\right)x+(-f_1+g_1)y \\ \left(f_1+g_1\right)x-(f_2+g_2)y \end{pmatrix}. \end{aligned}$$

With $x = r\cos(\theta)$, $y = r\sin(\theta)$, $f_1 = 1 - r^{-m}\cos(m\theta)$, $f_2 = -r^{-m}\sin(m\theta)$, $g_1 = r^n\cos(n\theta)$, $g_2 = r^n\sin(n\theta)$ we have the following two normals:

$$n_1(r,\theta) = A\begin{pmatrix} B\sin(\theta) - r^{2m}r^n\sin((n+1)\theta) + r^m r^n\sin((m+n+1)\theta) \\ B\cos(\theta) + r^{2m}r^n\cos((n+1)\theta) - r^m r^n\cos((m+n+1)\theta) \\ -r^{2m}\sin(\theta) + r^m\sin((m+1)\theta) - Br^n\sin((n+1)\theta) \\ r^{2m}\cos(\theta) - r^m\cos((m+1)\theta) - Br^n\cos((n+1)\theta) \end{pmatrix}, \tag{4}$$

and

$$n_2(r,\theta) = A \begin{pmatrix} B\cos(\theta) - r^{2m}r^n\cos((n+1)\theta) + r^m r^n \cos((m+n+1)\theta) \\ -B\sin(\theta) - r^{2m}r^n\sin((n+1)\theta) + r^m r^n \sin((m+n+1)\theta) \\ -r^{2m}\cos(\theta) + r^m\cos((m+1)\theta) - Br^n\cos((n+1)\theta) \\ -r^{2m}\sin(\theta) + r^m\sin((m+1)\theta) + Br^n\sin((n+1)\theta) \end{pmatrix}, \tag{5}$$

where $A = \left[B\left(r^{2n}+1\right)\left(2r^{2m} - 2r^m\cos(m\theta)+1\right)\right]^{-1/2}$, $B = r^{2m} - 2r^m\cos(m\theta) + 1$.

When we check inner products of n_1 and n_2 with themselves, we get

$$\begin{aligned} \langle n_1, n_1 \rangle &= \langle n_2, n_2 \rangle \\ &= A^2\left(r^{2n}+1\right)\left(r^{2m} + r^{4m} - 2r^{3m}\cos(m\theta) + B^2\right) \\ &= 1. \end{aligned}$$

3. Henneberg Family of Surfaces $\mathfrak{H}_{m,n}$

In 3-space, the Weierstrass data of the Henneberg surface is known as $(f,g) = (1-1/z^4, z)$. In 4-space, we consider general case of it and choose $\psi = 2$, $f = 1 - 1/z^m$ and $g = z^n$ in (1). This gives

$$\Phi(z) = \left(1 + z^n - z^{n-m}, i(1 - z^n + z^{n-m}), 1 - z^{-m} - z^n, -i(1 - z^{-m} + z^n)\right). \tag{6}$$

We integrate (6) to get complex form of the family of Henneberg-type minimal surface:

$$\int \Phi(z)dz = \begin{pmatrix} z + \dfrac{z^{n+1}}{n+1} - \dfrac{z^{-m+n+1}}{-m+n+1} \\ i\left(z - \dfrac{z^{n+1}}{n+1} + \dfrac{z^{-m+n+1}}{-m+n+1}\right) \\ z - \dfrac{z^{-m+1}}{-m+1} - \dfrac{z^{n+1}}{n+1} \\ -i\left(z - \frac{z^{-m+1}}{-m+1} + \dfrac{z^{n+1}}{n+1}\right) \end{pmatrix} \tag{7}$$

with $m \neq 1, n \neq -1, -m+n \neq -1$. Therefore, we get following definition:

Definition 1. *Taking the real part of the (7), with $z = re^{i\theta}$, we obtain family of Henneberg-type minimal surface $\mathfrak{H}_{m,n}$ as follows*

$$\mathfrak{H}_{m,n}(r,\theta) = \begin{pmatrix} r\cos(\theta) + \dfrac{r^{n+1}\cos((n+1)\theta)}{n+1} - \dfrac{r^{-m+n+1}\cos((-m+n+1)\theta)}{-m+n+1} \\ -r\sin(\theta) + \dfrac{r^{n+1}\sin((n+1)\theta)}{n+1} - \dfrac{r^{-m+n+1}\sin((-m+n+1)\theta)}{-m+n+1} \\ r\cos(\theta) - \dfrac{r^{-m+1}\cos((-m+1)\theta)}{-m+1} - \dfrac{r^{n+1}\cos((n+1)\theta)}{n+1} \\ r\sin(\theta) - \dfrac{r^{-m+1}\sin((-m+1)\theta)}{-m+1} + \dfrac{r^{n+1}\sin((n+1)\theta)}{n+1} \end{pmatrix}, \tag{8}$$

where $m \neq 1, n \neq -1, -m+n \neq -1$.

Algebraic Henneberg-Type Minimal Surface $\mathfrak{H}_{4,2}$

Next, we choose $(\psi, f, g) = (2, 1 - 1/z^4, z^2)$ in (1). This means $(m,n) = (4,2)$. Hence, we can define Henneberg-type surface $\mathfrak{H}_{4,2}$ in (r,θ) and (u,v) coordinates in the four-dimensional Euclidean space.

Definition 2. *In (r,θ) coordinates, taking $m=4$, $n=2$ in (8), we have Henneberg-type minimal surface as follows:*

$$\mathfrak{H}_{4,2}(r,\theta)=\begin{pmatrix}\dfrac{r^3\cos(3\theta)}{3}+r\cos(\theta)+\dfrac{\cos(\theta)}{r}\\ \dfrac{r^3\sin(3\theta)}{3}-r\sin(\theta)-\dfrac{\sin(\theta)}{r}\\ -\dfrac{r^3\cos(3\theta)}{3}+r\cos(\theta)+\dfrac{\cos(3\theta)}{3r^3}\\ \dfrac{r^3\sin(3\theta)}{3}+r\sin(\theta)-\dfrac{\sin(3\theta)}{3r^3}\end{pmatrix}=\begin{pmatrix}x(r,\theta)\\ y(r,\theta)\\ z(r,\theta)\\ w(r,\theta)\end{pmatrix}. \tag{9}$$

With the help of following equalities

$$\begin{aligned}\frac{r^3\cos(3\theta)}{3}&=\frac{1}{3}r^3\cos^3\theta-r^3\cos\theta\sin^2\theta,\\ \frac{r^3\sin(3\theta)}{3}&=-\frac{1}{3}r^3\sin^3\theta+r^3\cos^2\theta\sin\theta,\\ \frac{\cos(3\theta)}{3r^3}&=\frac{1}{3r^3}\cos^3\theta-\frac{1}{r^3}\cos\theta\sin^2\theta,\\ \frac{\sin(3\theta)}{3r^3}&=-\frac{1}{3r^3}\sin^3\theta+\frac{1}{r^3}\cos^2\theta\sin\theta,\end{aligned}$$

and substituting

$$\frac{\cos(\theta)}{r}=\frac{u}{u^2+v^2},\quad \frac{\sin(\theta)}{r}=\frac{v}{u^2+v^2},$$

into (9), we have following definition:

Definition 3. *Henneberg-type minimal surface in (u,v) coordinates is defined by as follows:*

$$\mathfrak{H}_{4,2}(u,v)=\begin{pmatrix}\frac{1}{3}u^3-uv^2+u+\dfrac{u}{u^2+v^2}\\ -\frac{1}{3}v^3+u^2v-v-\dfrac{v}{u^2+v^2}\\ -\frac{1}{3}u^3+uv^2+u+\frac{1}{3}\dfrac{u^3}{(u^2+v^2)^3}-\dfrac{uv^2}{(u^2+v^2)^3}\\ -\frac{1}{3}v^3+u^2v+v+\frac{1}{3}\dfrac{v^3}{(u^2+v^2)^3}-\dfrac{u^2v}{(u^2+v^2)^3}\end{pmatrix}=\begin{pmatrix}x(u,v)\\ y(u,v)\\ z(u,v)\\ w(u,v)\end{pmatrix}, \tag{10}$$

where $u:=r\cos\theta$, $v:=r\sin\theta$.

Next, we see algebraic surface and its degree:

Definition 4. *With $\mathbb{R}^4=\{(x,y,z,w)\mid x,y,z,w\in\mathbb{R}\}$, the set of roots of a polynomial $f(x,y,z,w)=0$ gives an algebraic surface. An algebraic surface is said to be of degree n, when $n=\deg(f)$.*

On the other hand, we meet following lemma about an algebraic minimal surface and an algebraic curve, obtained by Henneberg:

Lemma 1. *(Henneberg [5,7]) A plane intersects an algebraic minimal surface in an algebraic curve.*

See also [16] for details.

Considering the above definition and lemma in 4-space, we obtain the following corollaries for the algebraic curves within the Henneberg-type minimal surface $\mathfrak{H}_{4,2}(u,v)$ in (10):

Corollary 1. *The implicit equation of the curve*

$$\mathfrak{H}_{4,2}(u,0)=\gamma_{4,2}(u)=\begin{pmatrix}\frac{1}{3}u^3+u+\frac{1}{u}\\ 0\\ -\frac{1}{3}u^3+u+\frac{1}{3u^3}\\ 0\end{pmatrix}$$

on the xz-plane, obtained by eliminating u and v, is as follows (see Figure 1a)

$$\begin{aligned}\gamma_{4,2}(x,z) &= -729x^6+6561x^5z-19683x^4z^2+19683x^3z^3+1458x^5-10935x^4z\\ &+26244x^3z^2-19683x^2z^3+9720x^4-32076x^3z+65610x^2z^2+6561xz^3\\ &-59049z^4-14040x^3+36936x^2z-49572xz^2-729z^3-38772x^2\\ &+72576xz-116154z^2+29016x-27000z+83240.\end{aligned}$$

Its degree is $deg(\gamma_{4,2}(x,z))=6$. Hence, the xz-plane intersects the algebraic minimal surface $\mathfrak{H}_{4,2}(u,v)$ in an algebraic curve $\gamma_{4,2}(u)$.

Corollary 2. *The implicit equation of the curve*

$$\mathfrak{H}_{4,2}(0,v)=\gamma_{4,2}(v)=\begin{pmatrix}0\\ -\frac{1}{3}v^3-v-\frac{1}{v}\\ 0\\ -\frac{1}{3}v^3+v+\frac{1}{3v^3}\end{pmatrix}$$

on the yw-plane, obtained by eliminating u and v, is as follows (see Figure 1b)

$$\begin{aligned}\gamma_{4,2}(y,w) &= 729w^3y^3-2187w^2y^4+2187wy^5-729y^6+2187w^4\\ &-8748w^3y+12636w^2y^2-3402wy^3+14823y^4\\ &+13365w^2+25623wy-41175y^2+39601,\end{aligned}$$

and we see that its degree is $deg(\gamma_{4,2}(y,w))=6$. Therefore, the yw-plane intersects the algebraic minimal surface $\mathfrak{H}_{4,2}(u,v)$ in an algebraic curve $\gamma_{4,2}(v)$.

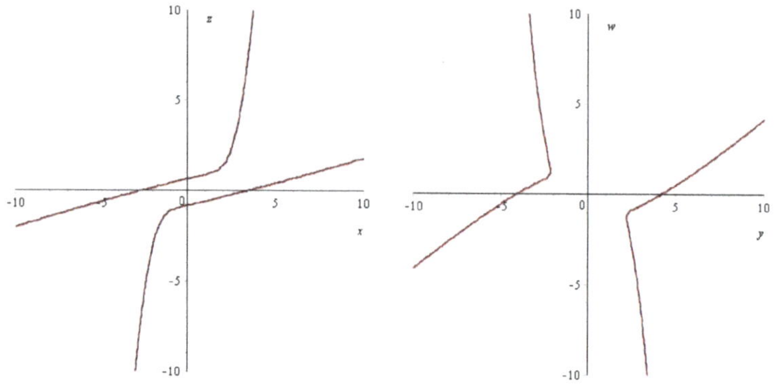

(a) (b)

Figure 1. Henneberg algebraic curves. (**a**): $\gamma_{4,2}(x,z) = 0$; (**b**): $\gamma_{4,2}(y,w) = 0$.

Next, we will focus on the implicit equation of the algebraic surface $H_{4,2}(x,y,z,w)$ and on the degree of the Henneberg-type surface $\mathfrak{H}_{4,2}(u,v)$.

By eliminating u and v of $\mathfrak{H}_{4,2}(u,v)$ using Groebner Basis in the Maple software package (see Section 4), we obtain the irreducible implicit equations of $H_{4,2}(x,y,z,w) = 0$ in the cartesian coordinates x, y, z, w. The degrees of the 125 implicit equations vary from 12 to 15. Next, we show only the leading term of one of the degree 15 implicit equations:

$$
\begin{aligned}
H_{4,2}(x,y,z,w) = \; & -2003575291140109663929868496961731353844001602123062388 14 \\
& 6921798341947018263352974811247016293579407850833661779885 \\
& 3866925524317171303746574348380455005752233355972467214402 \\
& 70054850560 \; xy^2zw^{11} + 729 \text{ other lower degree terms.}
\end{aligned}
$$

Since $deg\,(H_{4,2}) = 15$, we have that $H_{4,2}(x,y,z,w) = 0$ is an implicit algebraic Henneberg-type minimal surface in 4-space.

4. Maple Codes and Figures for Algebraic Henneberg Surface in $\mathbb{E}^4$

To compute the implicit equation of the Henneberg surface in $\mathbb{E}^4$ we have tried a series of standard techniques in elimination theory: projective (Macaulay) and sparse multivariate resultants implemented in the Maple package *multires* (The package can be found at http://www-sop.inria.fr/galaad/software/multires/multires), Maple's native implicitization command `Implicitize`, and implicitization based on Maples' native implementation of Groebner Basis. For the latter we implemented in Maple the method in [39] (Chapter 3, p. 128).

All the above methods failed to give the implicit equations in reasonable time. In particular, for the resultant methods, the bottleneck was the computation of the determinant of the huge resultant matrix.

The final and successful method we have tried was to compute the equations defining the elimination ideal using the Groebner Basis package FGb [40]. The package can be found at: https://www-polsys.lip6.fr/~jcf/FGb/index.html.

The time required to output the 125 polynomials defining the elimination ideal was under 20 s. See Figures 2 and 3 for the projections in $\mathbb{R}^3$ of the surface defined by one of these polynomials.

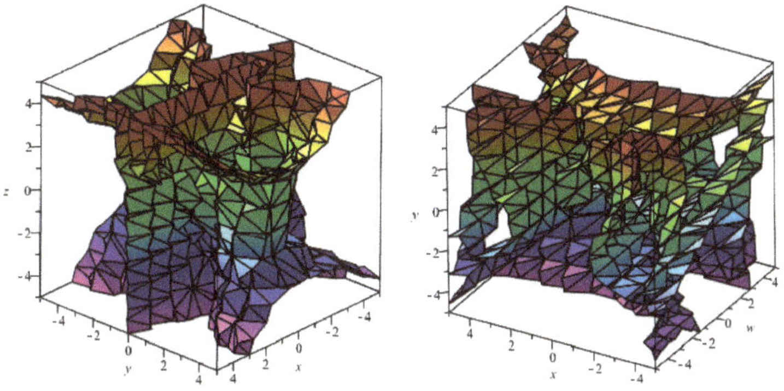

(a) (b)

Figure 2. Projection in $\mathbb{R}^3$ of a Henneberg algebraic surface. (**a**): $H_{4,2}(x,y,z)=0$; (**b**): $H_{4,2}(x,y,w)=0$.

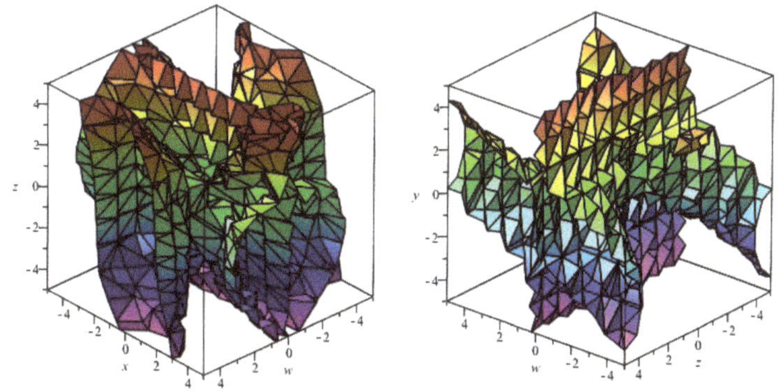

(a) (b)

Figure 3. Projection in $\mathbb{R}^3$ of a Henneberg algebraic surface. (**a**): $H_{4,2}(x,z,w)=0$; (**b**): $H_{4,2}(y,z,w)=0$.

Author Contributions: E.G. gave the idea for Henneberg type minimal surface in 4-space. Then E.G., Ö.K. and C.K. checked and polished the draft.

Funding: This research received no external funding.

Conflicts of Interest: The author declares that there is no conflict of interests regarding the publication of this paper.

References

1. Darboux, G. *Lecons sur la Theorie Generate des Surfaces III*; Gauthier-Villars: Paris, France, 1894.
2. Eisenhart, L.P. *A Treatise on the Differential Geometry of Curves and Surfaces*; Dover Publications: New York, NY, USA, 1909.
3. Bour, E. Théorie de la déformation des surfaces. *J. l'École Polytech.* **1862**, *22*, 1–148.
4. Henneberg, L. Über Salche Minimalfläche, Welche Eine Vorgeschriebene Ebene Curve sur Geodätishen Line Haben. Ph.D. Thesis, Eidgenössisches Polythechikum, Zürich, Switzerland, 1875.
5. Henneberg, L. Über diejenige minimalfläche, welche die Neilsche Parabel zur ebenen geodätischen Linie hat. *Wolf Z.* **1876**, *XXI*, 17–21.
6. Henneberg, L. Über die Evoluten der ebenen algebraischen Curven. *Wolf Z.* **1876**, *21*, 71–72.

7. Henneberg, L. Bestimmung der niedrigsten classenzahl der algebraischen minimalflachen. *Ann. Mat. Pura Appl.* **1878**, *9*, 54–57. [CrossRef]
8. Weierstrass, K. Untersuchungen über die flächen, deren mittlere Krümmung überall gleich null ist. *Preuss Akad. Wiss.* **1866**, *III*, 219–220.
9. Weierstrass, K. *Mathematische Werke*; Mayer & Muller: Berlin, Germany, 1903; Volume 3.
10. Takahashi, T. Minimal immersions of Riemannian manifolds. *J. Math. Soc. Jpn.* **1966**, *18*, 380–385. [CrossRef]
11. Osserman, R. *A Survey of Minimal Surfaces*; Van Nostrand Reinhold Co.: New York, NY, USA, 1969.
12. Hoffman, D.A.; Osserman, R. *The Geometry of the Generalized Gauss Map*; American Mathematical Society: Providence, RI, USA, 1980.
13. Lawson, H.B. *Lectures on Minimal Submanifolds*, 2nd ed.; Mathematics Lecture Series 9; Publish or Perish, Inc.: Wilmington, NC, USA, 1980; Volume I.
14. Do Carmo, M.; Dajczer, M. Helicoidal surfaces with constant mean curvature. *Tohoku Math. J.* **1982**, *34*, 351–367. [CrossRef]
15. De Oliveira, M.E.G.G. Some new examples of nonorientable minimal surfaces. *Proc. Am. Math. Soc.* **1986**, *98*, 629–636. [CrossRef]
16. Nitsche, J.C.C. *Lectures on Minimal Surfaces. Vol. 1. Introduction, Fundamentals, Geometry and Basic Boundary Value Problems*; Cambridge University Press: Cambridge, UK, 1989.
17. Small, A.J. Minimal surfaces in $\mathbb{R}^3$ and algebraic curves. *Differ. Geom. Appl.* **1992**, *2*, 369–384. [CrossRef]
18. Small, A.J. Linear structures on the collections of minimal surfaces in $\mathbb{R}^3$ and $\mathbb{R}^4$. *Ann. Glob. Anal. Geom.* **1994**, *12*, 97–101. [CrossRef]
19. Ikawa, T. Bour's theorem and Gauss map. *Yokohama Math. J.* **2000**, *48*, 173–180.
20. Ikawa, T. Bour's theorem in Minkowski geometry. *Tokyo J. Math.* **2001**, *24*, 377–394. [CrossRef]
21. Gray, A.; Abbena, E.; Salamon, S. *Modern Differential Geometry of Curves and Surfaces with Mathematica®*, 3rd ed.; Studies in Advanced Mathematics; Chapman & Hall/CRC: Boca Raton, FL, USA, 2006.
22. Güler, E.; Turgut Vanlı, A. Bour's theorem in Minkowski 3-space. *J. Math. Kyoto Univ.* **2006**, *46*, 47–63. [CrossRef]
23. Güler, E.; Yaylı, Y.; Hacısalihoğlu, H.H. Bour's theorem on the Gauss map in 3-Euclidean space. *Hacet. J. Math. Stat.* **2010**, *39*, 515–525.
24. Güler, E.; Yaylı, Y. Generalized Bour theorem. *Kuwait J. Sci.* **2015**, *42*, 79–90.
25. Ji, F.; Kim, Y.H. Mean curvatures and Gauss maps of a pair of isometric helicoidal and rotation surfaces in Minkowski 3-space. *J. Math. Anal. Appl.* **2010**, *368*, 623–635. [CrossRef]
26. Ji, F.; Kim, Y.H. Isometries between minimal helicoidal surfaces and rotation surfaces in Minkowski space. *Appl. Math. Comput.* **2013**, *220*, 1–11. [CrossRef]
27. Dierkes, U.; Hildebrandt, S.; Sauvigny, F. *Minimal Surfaces*, 2nd ed.; Springer: Berlin/Heidelberg, Germany, 2010.
28. Moore, C. Surfaces of rotation in a space of four dimensions. *Ann. Math.* **1919**, *21*, 81–93. [CrossRef]
29. Ganchev, G.; Milousheva, V. An invariant theory of surfaces in the four-dimensional Euclidean or Minkowski space. *Pliska Stud. Math. Bulg.* **2012**, *21*, 177–200.
30. Güler, E.; Kişi, Ö. Weierstrass representation, degree and classes of the surfaces in the four dimensional Euclidean space. *Celal Bayar Univ. J. Sci.* **2017**, *13*, 155–163. [CrossRef]
31. Arslan, K.; Kılıç Bayram, B.; Bulca, B.; Öztürk, G. Generalized Rotation Surfaces in $\mathbb{E}^4$. *Results Math.* **2012**, *61* 315–327. [CrossRef]
32. Xu, G.; Rabczuk, T.; Güler, E.; Wu X.; Hui, K.; Wang, G. Quasi-harmonic Bezier approximation of minimal surfaces for finding forms of structural membranes. *Comput. Struct.* **2015**, *161*, 55–63. [CrossRef]
33. Arslan, K.; Bayram, B.; Bulca, B.; Öztürk, G. On translation surfaces in 4-dimensional Euclidean space. *Acta Comment. Univ. Tartu. Math.* **2016**, *20*, 123–133. [CrossRef]
34. Güler, E.; Magid, M.; Yaylı, Y. Laplace Beltrami operator of a helicoidal hypersurface in four space. *J. Geom. Symmetry Phys.* **2016**, *41*, 77–95. [CrossRef]
35. Arslan, K.; Bulca, B.; Kosova, D. On generalized rotational surfaces in Euclidean spaces. *J. Korean Math. Soc.* **2017**, *54*, 999–1013. [CrossRef]
36. The Hieu, D.; Ngoc Thang, N. Bour's theorem in 4-dimensional Euclidean space. *Bull. Korean Math. Soc.* **2017**, *54*, 2081–2089.
37. Güler, E.; Hacısalihoğlu, H.H.; Kim, Y.H. The Gauss map and the third Laplace-Beltrami operator of the rotational hypersurface in 4-Space. *Symmetry* **2018**, *10*, 398. [CrossRef]

38. Güler, E. Isometric deformation of (m, n)-type helicoidal surface in the three dimensional Euclidean space. *Mathematics* **2018**, *6*, 226. [CrossRef]
39. Cox, D.; Little, J.; O'Shea, D. *Ideals, Varieties, and Algorithms. An Introduction to Computational Algebraic Geometry and Commutative Algebra*, 3rd ed.; Undergraduate Texts in Mathematics; Springer: New York, NY, USA, 2007.
40. Faugère, J.C. FGb: A library for computing Gröbner bases. In Proceedings of the Third International Congress Conference on Mathematical Software (ICMS'10), Kobe, Japan, 13–17 September 2010; Springer: Berlin/Heidelberg, Germany, 2010; pp. 84–87.

© 2018 by the authors. Licensee MDPI, Basel, Switzerland. This article is an open access article distributed under the terms and conditions of the Creative Commons Attribution (CC BY) license (http://creativecommons.org/licenses/by/4.0/).

mathematics

MDPI

Article

A Characterization of Projective Special Unitary Group PSU(3,3) and Projective Special Linear Group PSL(3,3) by NSE

Farnoosh Hajati [1], Ali Iranmanesh [2,*] and Abolfazl Tehranian [1]

1 Department of Mathematics, Science and Research Branch, Islamic Azad University, Tehran 14515-775, Iran; F_hajati@azad.ac.ir (F.H.); tehranian@srbiau.ac.ir (A.T.)
2 Department of Mathematics, Tarbiat Modares University, Tehran 14115-137, Iran
* Correspondence: iranmanesh@modares.ac.ir

Received: 17 May 2018; Accepted: 29 June 2018; Published: 10 July 2018

Abstract: Let G be a finite group and $\omega(G)$ be the set of element orders of G. Let $k \in \omega(G)$ and m_k be the number of elements of order k in G. Let $nse(G) = \{m_k | k \in \omega(G)\}$. In this paper, we prove that if G is a finite group such that $nse(G) = nse(H)$, where $H = PSU(3,3)$ or $PSL(3,3)$, then $G \cong H$.

Keywords: element order; number of elements of the same order; projective special linear group; projective special unitary group; simple K_n-group

1. Introduction

We devote this section to relevant definitions, basic facts about nse, and a brief history of this problem. Throughout this paper, G is a finite group. We express by $\pi(G)$ the set of prime divisors of $|G|$, and by $\omega(G)$, we introduce the set of order of elements from G. Set $m_k = m_k(G) = |\{g \in G | the\ order\ of\ g\ is\ k\}|$ and $nse(G)=\{m_k | k \in \omega(G)\}$. In fact, m_k is the number of elements of order k in G and nse(G) is the set of sizes of elements with the same order in G.

One of the important problems in group theory is characterization of a group by a given property, that is, to prove there exist only one group with a given property (up to isomorphism). A finite nonabelian simple group H is called characterizable by nse if every finite group G with $nse(G) = nse(H)$ implies that $G \cong H$.

After the monumental attempt to classify the finite simple groups, a huge amount of information about these groups has been collected. It has been noticed that some of the known simple groups are characterizable by some of their properties. Until now, different characterization are considered for some simple groups.

The twentieth century mathematician J.G. Thompson posed very interesting problem [1] .

Thompson Problem. Let $T(G)=\{(k, m_k) | k \in \omega(G), m_k \in nse(G)\}$ where m_k is the number of elements with order k. Suppose that $T(G) = T(H)$. If G is a finite solvable group, is it true that H is also necessary solvable?

Characterization of a group G by nse(G) and $|G|$, for short, deals with the number of elements of order k in the group G and $|G|$, where one must answer the question "is a finite group G, can be characterized by the set nse(G) and $|G|$?" While mathematicians might undoubtedly give many answers to such a question, the answer in Shao et al. [2,3] would probably rank near the top of most responses. They proved that if G is a simple k_i $(i = 3, 4)$ group, then G is characterizable by nse(G) and $|G|$. Several groups were characterized by nse and order. For example, in [4,5], it is proved that the Suzuki group, and sporadic groups are characterizable by nse and order. We remark here that not all groups can be characterized by their group orders and the set nse. For example, let $H_1 = C_4 \times C_4$ and $H_2 = C_2 \times Q_8$, where C_2 and C_4 are cyclic groups of order 2 and 4, respectively, and Q_8 is a quaternion group of order 8. It is easy to see that $nse(H_1) = nse(H_2) = \{1,3,12\}$ and $|H_1| = |H_2| = 16$ but $H_1 \ncong H_2$.

We know that the set of sizes of conjugacy classes has an essential role in determining the structure of a finite group. Hence, one might ask whether the set of sizes of elements with the same order has an essential role in determining the structure of a finite group. It is claimed that some simple groups could be characterized by exactly the set nse, without considering the order of group. In [6–12], it is proved that the alternating groups A_n, where $n \in \{7,8\}$, the symmetric groups S_n where $n \in \{3,4,5,6,7\}$, M_{12}, $L_2(27)$, $L_2(q)$ where $q \in \{16,17,19,23\}$, $L_2(q)$ where $q \in \{7,8,11,13\}$, $L_2(q)$ where $q \in \{17,27,29\}$, are uniquely determined by nse(G). Besides, in [13–16], it is proved that $U_3(4)$, $L_3(4)$, $U_3(5)$, and $L_3(5)$ are uniquely determined by nse(G). Recently, in [17–19], it is proved that the simple groups $G_2(4)$, $L_2(3^n)$, where $|\pi(L_2(3^n))| = 4$, and $L_2(2^m)$, where $|\pi(L_2(2^m))| = 4$, are uniquely determined by nse(G). Therefore, it is natural to ask what happens with other kinds of simple groups.

The purpose of this paper is to continue this work by considering the following theorems:

Theorem 1. *Let G be a group such that $nse(G) = nse(PSU(3,3))$. Then G is isomorphic to $PSU(3,3)$.*

Theorem 2. *Let G be a group such that $nse(G) = nse(PSL(3,3))$. Then G is isomorphic to $PSL(3,3)$.*

2. Notation and Preliminaries

Before we get started, let us fix some notations that will be used throughout the paper. For a natural number n, by $\pi(n)$, we mean the set of all prime divisors of n, so it is obvious that if G is a finite group, then $\pi(G) = \pi(|G|)$. A Sylow r-subgroup of G is denoted by P_r and by $n_r(G)$, we mean the number of Sylow r- subgroup of G. Also the largest element order of P_r is signified by $exp(P_r)$. In addition, G is called a simple K_n group if G is a simple group with $|\pi(G)| = n$. Moreover, we denote by ϕ, the Euler function. In the following, we bring some useful lemmas which be used in the proof of main results.

Remark 1. *If G is a simple K_1- group, then G is a cyclic of prime order.*

Remark 2. *If $|G| = p^a q^b$, with p and q distinct primes, and a, b non-negative integers, then by Burnside's pq-theorem, G is solvable. In particular, there is no simple K_2-groups [20].*

Lemma 1. *Let G be a group containing more than two elements. If the maximal number s of elements of the same order in G is finite, then G is finite and $|G| \le s(s^2 - 1)$ [21].*

Lemma 2. *Let G be a group. If $1 \neq n \in nse(G)$ and $2 \not| n$, then the following statements hold [12]:*

(1) $2 \mid |G|$;

(2) $m_2 = n$;

(3) *for any* $2 < t \in \omega(G)$, $m_t \neq n$.

Lemma 3. *Let G be a finite group and m be a positive integer dividing $|G|$. If $L_m(G) = \{g \in G | g^m = 1\}$, then $m \mid |L_m(G)|$ [22].*

Lemma 4. *Let G be a group and P be a cyclic Sylow p-group of G of order p^{α}. If there is a prime r such that $p^{\alpha} r \in \omega(G)$, then $m_{p^{\alpha} r} = m_r(C_G(P)) m_{p^{\alpha}}$. In particular, $\phi(r) m_{p^{\alpha}} | m_{p^{\alpha} r}$, where $\phi(r)$ is the Euler function of r [23].*

Lemma 5. *Let G be a finite group and $p \in \pi(G)$ be odd. Suppose that P is a Sylow p-subgroup of G and $n = p^s m$, where $(p, m) = 1$. If P is not cyclic group and $s > 1$, then the number of elements of order n is always a multiple of p^s [24].*

Lemma 6. *Let G be a finite group, $P \in Syl_p(G)$, where $p \in \pi(G)$. Let G have a normal series $1 \trianglelefteq K \trianglelefteq L \trianglelefteq G$. If $P \leq L$ and $p \not| |K|$, then the following hold [3]:*

(1) $N_{\frac{G}{K}}(\frac{PK}{K}) = \frac{N_G(P)K}{K}$;
(2) $|G : N_G(P)| = |L : N_L(P)|$, *that is,* $n_p(G) = n_p(L)$;
(3) $|\frac{L}{K} : N_{\frac{L}{K}}(\frac{PK}{K})|t = |G : N_G(P)| = |L : N_L(P)|$, *that is,* $n_p(\frac{L}{K})t = n_p(G) = n_p(L)$ *for some positive integer* t, *and* $|N_K(P)|t = |K|$.

Lemma 7. *Let G be a finite solvable group and $|G| = mn$, where $m = p_1^{\alpha 1} \cdots p_r^{\alpha r}$, $(m,n) = 1$. Let $\pi = \{p_1, \cdots, p_r\}$ and let h_m be the number of π-Hall subgroups of G. Then $h_m = q_1^{\beta 1} \cdots q_s^{\beta s}$ satisfies the following conditions for all $i \in \{1, 2, \cdots, s\}$ [25]:*

(1) $q_i^{\beta i} = 1\ (mod p_j)$ *for some* p_j;
(2) *The order of some chief factor of G is divisible by* $q_i^{\beta i}$.

Lemma 8. *Let the finite group G act on the finite set X. If the action is semi regular, then $|G| \mid |X|$ [26].*

Let us mention the structure of simple K_3-groups, which will be needed in Section 3.

Lemma 9. *If G is a simple K_3-group, then G is isomorphic to one of the following groups [27]: A_5, A_6, $L_2(7)$, $L_2(8)$, $L_2(17)$, $L_3(3)$, $U_3(3)$, $U_4(2)$.*

3. Main Results

Suppose G is a group such that $nse(G) = nse(H)$, where $H = PSU(3,3)$, or $PSL(3,3)$. By Lemma 1, we can assume that G is finite. Let m_n be the number of elements of order n. We notice that $m_n = k\phi(n)$, where k is the number of cyclic subgroups of order n in G. In addition, we notice that if $n > 2$, then $\phi(n)$ is even. If $n \in \omega(G)$, then by Lemma 3 and the above discussion, we have

$$\begin{cases} \phi(n) | m_n \\ n | \sum_{d|n} m_d \end{cases} \quad (1)$$

In the proof of Theorem 1 and Theorem 2, we often apply formula (1) and the above comments.

Proof of Theorem 1. Let G be a group with

$$nse(G) = nse(PSU(3,3)) = \{1, 63, 504, 728, 1008, 1512, 1728\},$$

where $PSU(3,3)$ is the projective special unitary group of degree 3 over field of order 3. The proof will be divided into a sequence of lemmas.

Lemma 10. $\pi(G) \subseteq \{2, 3, 7\}$.

Proof. First, since $63 \in nse(G)$, by Lemma 2, $2 \in \pi(G)$ and $m_2 = 63$. Let $2 \neq p \in \pi(G)$, by formula (1), $p | (1 + m_p)$ and $(p-1) | m_p$, which implies that $p \in \{3, 5, 7, 13, 19, 1009\}$. Now, we prove that $13 \notin \pi(G)$. Conversely, suppose that $13 \in \pi(G)$. Then formula (1), implies $m_{13} = 1728$. On the other hand, by formula (1), we conclude that if $2.13 \in \omega(G)$, then $m_{2.13} \in \{504, 1008, 1512, 1728\}$ and $2.13 | 1 + m_2 + m_{13} + m_{2.13} (= 2296, 2800, 3304, 3520)$. Hence, $(2.13 | 2296)$, $(2.13 | 2800)$, $(2.13 | 3304)$, or $(2.13 | 3520)$, which is a contradiction, and hence $2.13 \notin \omega(G)$. Since $2.13 \notin \omega(G)$, the group P_{13} acts fixed point freely on the set of elements of order 2, and so, by Lemma 8, $|P_{13}| | m_2$, which is a contradiction. Hence $13 \notin \pi(G)$. Similarly, we can prove that the prime numbers 19 and 1009 do not belong to $\pi(G)$. Now, we prove $5 \notin \pi(G)$. Conversely, suppose that $5 \in \pi(G)$. Then formula (1), implies $m_5 = 504$. From the formula (1), we conclude that if $3.5 \in \omega(G)$, then $m_{15} = 1512$. On the other hand, if $3.5 \in \omega(G)$, then by Lemma 4, $m_{3.5} = m_5.\phi(3).t$ for some integer t. Hence $1512 = (504)(2)t$, which is a contradiction and hence $3.5 \notin \omega(G)$. Since $3.5 \notin \omega(G)$, the group P_5 acts fixed point freely on the set of elements of order 3, and so $|P_5||m_3$, which is a contradiction. From what has already been proved, we conclude that $\pi(G) \subseteq \{2,3,7\}$. □

Remark 3. *If* $3\ ,\ 7 \in \pi(G)$, *then, by formula (1),* $m_3 = 728$ *and* $m_7 = 1728$. *If* $7^a \in \omega(G)$, *since* $m_{7^2} \notin nse(G)$, *then* $a = 1$. *By Lemma 3,* $|P_7||(1+m_7)$ *and so* $|P_7||7$. *Suppose* $7 \in \pi(G)$. *Then since* $|P_7| = 7$, $n_7 = \frac{m_7}{\phi(7)} = 3^2.2^5||G|$. *Therefore, if* $7 \in \pi(G)$, *then* $3, 2 \in \pi(G)$. *Hence, we only have to consider two proper sets* $\{2\}$, $\{2,3\}$, *and finally the whole set* $\{2,3,7\}$.

Now, we will show that $\pi(G)$ is not equal $\{2\}$ and $\{2,3\}$. For this purpose at first, we need obtain some information about elements of $\omega(G)$.

If $2^a \in \omega(G)$, then $\phi(2^a) = 2^{a-1}|m_{2^a}$ and so $0 \leq a \leq 7$.

By Lemma 3, $|P_2||(1+m_2+m_{2^2}+\cdots+m_{2^7})$ and so $|P_2||2^{10}$.

If $3^a \in \omega(G)$, then $1 \leq a \leq 4$.

Lemma 11. $\pi(G) \neq \{2\}$ *and* $\pi(G) \neq \{2,3\}$.

Proof. We claim that $\pi(G) \neq \{2\}$. Assume the contrary, that is, let $\pi(G) = \{2\}$. Since $2^8 \notin \omega(G)$, we have $\omega(G) \subseteq \{1,2,2^2,2^3,2^4,2^5,2^6,2^7\}$. Hence $|G| = 2^m = 5544 + 504k_1 + 728k_2 + 1008k_3 + 1512k_4 + 1728k_5$, where k_1, k_2, k_3, k_4, k_5 and m are non-negative integers and $0 \leq k_1 + k_2 + k_3 + k_4 + k_5 \leq 1$. Since $5544 \leq |G| = 2^m \leq 5544 + (k_1+k_2+k_3+k_4+k_5)1728$, we have $5544 \leq |G| = 2^m \leq 5544 + 1728$. Now, it is easy to check that the equation has no solution, which is a contradiction. Hence $\pi(G) \neq \{2\}$. Our next claim is that $\pi(G) \neq \{2,3\}$. Suppose, contrary to our claim, that $\pi(G) = \{2,3\}$. Since $3^5 \notin \omega(G)$, $exp(P_3) = 3, 3^2, 3^3, 3^4$.

- Let $exp(P_3) = 3$. Then by Lemma 3, $|P_3||(1+m_3)$ and so $|P_3||3^6$. We will consider six cases for $|P_3|$.

Case 1. If $|P_3| = 3$, then since $n_3 = \frac{m_3}{\phi(3)} = 2^2.7.13||G|$, $13 \in \pi(G)$, which is a contradiction.

Case 2. If $|P_3| = 3^2$, then since $exp(P_3) = 3$ and $2^7.3 \notin \omega(G)$, we have $\omega(G) \subseteq \{1,2,2^2,2^3,2^4,2^5,2^6,2^7\} \cup \{3,3.2,3.2^2,3.2^3,3.2^4,3.2^5,3.2^6\}$, and $|\omega(G)| \leq 15$. Therefore, $5544 + 504k_1 + 728k_2 + 1008k_3 + 1512k_4 + 1728k_5 = |G| = 2^a.9$, where k_1, k_2, k_3, k_4, k_5, and a are non-negative integers and $0 \leq k_1+k_2+k_3+k_4+k_5 \leq 8$. Since $5544 \leq 2^a.9 \leq 5544 + 8.1728$, we have $a = 10$ or $a = 11$.
If $a = 11$, then since $|P_2||2^{10}$, we have a contradiction.
If $a = 10$, then $3672 = 504k_1 + 728k_2 + 1008k_3 + 1512k_4 + 1728k_5$ where $0 \leq k_1+k_2+k_3+k_4+k_5 \leq 8$. By a computer calculation it is easily seen that the equation has no solution.

Case 3. If $|P_3| = 3^3$, then $5544 + 504k_1 + 728k_2 + 1008k_3 + 1512k_4 + 1728k_5 = |G| = 2^a.27$, where k_1, k_2, k_3, k_4, k_5, and a are non-negative integers and $0 \leq k_1+k_2+k_3+k_4+k_5 \leq 8$. Since $5544 \leq 2^a.27 \leq 5544 + 8.1728$, we have $a = 8$ or $a = 9$.
If $a = 8$, then $1368 = 504k_1 + 728k_2 + 1008k_3 + 1512k_4 + 1728k_5$ where $0 \leq k_1+k_2+k_3+k_4+k_5 \leq 8$. By a computer calculation, it is easily seen that the equation has no solution.
If $a = 9$, then $8280 = 504k_1 + 728k_2 + 1008k_3 + 1512k_4 + 1728k_5$ where $0 \leq k_1+k_2+k_3+k_4+k_5 \leq 8$. In this case, the equation has nine solutions. For example, $(k_1, k_2, k_3, k_4, k_5) = (1,0,3,2,1)$ is one of the solutions. We show this is impossible. Since $k_2 = 0$ and $m_3 = 728$, it follows that $m_{2^i} \neq 728$ for $1 \leq i \leq 7$. On the other hand, since $2^8 \notin \omega(G)$, $exp(P_2) = 2, 2^2, 2^3, 2^4, 2^5, 2^6, 2^7$. Hence, if $exp(P_2) = 2^i$ where $1 \leq i \leq 7$, then $|P_2||(1+m_2+m_{2^2}+\cdots+m_{2^i})$ by Lemma 3. Since $m_{2^i} \neq 728$, for $1 \leq i \leq 7$ by a computer calculation, we have $|P_2||2^7$, which is a contradiction. The same conclusion can be drawn for other solutions.

Case 4. If $|P_3| = 3^4$, then $5544 + 504k_1 + 728k_2 + 1008k_3 + 1512k_4 + 1728k_5 = |G| = 2^a.81$, where k_1, k_2, k_3, k_4, k_5, and a are non-negative integers and $0 \leq k_1 + k_2 + k_3 + k_4 + k_5 \leq 8$. Since $5544 \leq 2^a.81 \leq 5544 + 8.1728$, we have $a = 7$. If $a = 7$, then $4824 = 504k_1 + 728k_2 + 1008k_3 + 1512k_4 + 1728k_5$ where $0 \leq k_1 + k_2 + k_3 + k_4 + k_5 \leq 8$. One sees immediately that the equation has no solution.

Case 5. If $|P_3| = 3^5$, then $5544 + 504k_1 + 728k_2 + 1008k_3 + 1512k_4 + 1728k_5 = |G| = 2^a.243$ where k_1, k_2, k_3, k_4, k_5, and a are non-negative integers and $0 \leq k_1 + k_2 + k_3 + k_4 + k_5 \leq 8$. Since $5544 \leq 2^a.243 \leq 5544 + 8.1728$, we have $a = 5$ or $a = 6$.

If $a = 5$, then $2232 = 504k_1 + 728k_2 + 1008k_3 + 1512k_4 + 1728k_5$. By a computer calculation $(1, 0, 0, 0, 1)$ is the only solution of this equation. Then $|\omega(G)| = 9$, it is clear that $exp(P_2) = 2^4$ or $exp(P_2) = 2^5$. Also since $k_2 = 0$ and $m_3 = 728$, $m_{2^i} \neq 728$ for $1 \leq i \leq 7$.

If $exp(P_2) = 2^5$, then since $|G| = 2^5.3^5$, the number of Sylow 2-subgroups of G is $1, 3, 9, 27, 81, 243$ and so the number of elements of order 2 is $1, 3, 9, 27, 81,$ 243 but none of which belong to nse(G).

If $exp(P_2) = 2^4$, then $\omega(G) = \{1, 2, 2^2, 2^3, 2^4\} \cup \{3, 3.2, 3.2^2, 3.2^3\}$. Since $3.2^4 \notin \omega(G)$, it follows that the group P_3 acts fixed point freely on the set of elements of order 2^4. Hence, $|P_3||m_{2^4}$, which is a contradiction ($m_{2^4} \in \{504, 1008, 1512, 1728\}$).

If $a = 6$, then $10,008 = 504k_1 + 728k_2 + 1008k_3 + 1512k_4 + 1728k_5$. By a computer calculation, $(0, 0, 2, 3, 2)$, and $(1, 0, 0, 4, 2)$ are solutions of this equation. Since $|\omega(G)| = 14$, we have $\omega(G) = \{1, 2, 2^2, 2^3, 2^4, 2^5, 2^6\} \cup \{3, 3.2, 3.2^2, 3.2^3, 3.2^4, 3.2^5, 3.2^6\}$. We know $|G| = 2^6.3^5$. It follows that, the number of Sylow 2-subgroups of G is $1, 3, 9, 27, 81, 243$ and so the number of elements of order 2 is $1, 3, 9, 27, 81, 243$ but none of which belong to nse(G).

Case 6. Similarly, we can rule out $|P_3| = 3^6$.

- Let $exp(P_3) = 3^2$. Then by Lemma 3, $|P_3||(1 + m_3 + m_{3^2})$ and so $|P_3||3^3$ (for example when $m_9 = 1512$). We will consider two cases for $|P_3|$.

Case 1. If $|P_3| = 3^2$, then $n_3 = \frac{m_9}{\phi(9)}$, since $m_9 \in \{504, 1008, 1512, 1728\}$, $n_3 = 2^2.3.7$ or $n_3 = 2^2.7.3^2$ or $n_3 = 2^3.3.7$, and so $7 \in \pi(G)$, which is a contradiction, and if $n_3 = 2^5.3^2$, since a cyclic group of order 9 has two elements of order 3, $m_3 \leq 2^5.3^2.2 = 576$, which is a contradiction.

Case 2. If $|P_3| = 3^3$, then since $2^7.3 \notin \omega(G)$ and $2^7.3^2 \notin \omega(G)$, $|\omega(G)| \leq 22$. Therefore, $5544 + 504k_1 + 728k_2 + 1008k_3 + 1512k_4 + 1728k_5 = |G| = 2^a.27$, where k_1, k_2, k_3, k_4, k_5, and a are non-negative integers and $0 \leq k_1 + k_2 + k_3 + k_4 + k_5 \leq 15$. Since $5544 \leq 2^a.27 \leq 5544 + 15.1728$, we have $a = 8$, $a = 9$, or $a = 10$.

If $a = 8$, then $1368 = 504k_1 + 728k_2 + 1008k_3 + 1512k_4 + 1728k_5$ where $0 \leq k_1 + k_2 + k_3 + k_4 + k_5 \leq 15$. By a computer calculation, it is easily seen that the equation has no solution.

If $a = 9$, then $8280 = 504k_1 + 728k_2 + 1008k_3 + 1512k_4 + 1728k_5$ where $0 \leq k_1 + k_2 + k_3 + k_4 + k_5 \leq 15$. By a computer calculation, the equation has 22 solutions. For example, $(k_1, k_2, k_3, k_4, k_5) = (1, 0, 0, 4, 1)$. We show this solution is impossible. Since $k_2 = 0$ and $m_3 = 728$, it follows that $m_{2^i} \neq 728$, for $1 \leq i \leq 7$. On the other hand, if $2^a \in \omega(G)$, then $0 \leq a \leq 7$. By Lemma 3, we have $|P_2||(1 + m_2 + m_{2^2} + \cdots + m_{2^7})$, since $m_{2^i} \neq 728$ for $1 \leq i \leq 7$, by a computer calculation we have $|P_2||2^7$, which is a contradiction. Arguing as above, for other solutions, we have a contradiction.

Similarly, $a = 10$ can be ruled out as the above method.

- Let $exp(P_3) = 3^3$. Then by Lemma 3, $|P_3||(1 + m_3 + m_{3^2} + m_{3^3})$ and so $|P_3||3^4$ (for example when ($m_9 = 1512$ and $m_{27} = 1728$)). We will consider two cases for $|P_3|$.

Case 1. If $|P_3| = 3^3$, then $n_3 = \frac{m_{27}}{\phi(27)}$, since $m_{27} \in \{504, 1008, 1512, 1728\}$, $n_3 = 2^3.7$ or $n_3 = 2^2.7$ or $n_3 = 2^2.3.7$, and so $7 \in \pi(G)$, which is a contradiction, and if $n_3 = 2^5.3$, since a cyclic group of order 27 has two elements of order 3, $m_3 \leq 2^5.3.2 = 192$, which is a contradiction.

Case 2. If $|P_3| = 3^4$, and P_3 is not cyclic subgroup, then by Lemma 5, $27 | m_{27}$. Since $(27 \not| 504)$ and $(27 \not| 1008)$, it is understood that $m_{27} \in \{1512, 1728\}$. Since $2^7.3 \notin \omega(G)$, $2^7.3^2 \notin \omega(G)$, and $2^7.3^3 \notin \omega(G)$, $|\omega(G)| \leq 29$. Therefore $5544 + 504k_1 + 728k_2 + 1008k_3 + 1512k_4 + 1728k_5 = |G| = 2^a.81$, where k_1, k_2, k_3, k_4, k_5, and a are non-negative integers and $0 \leq k_1 + k_2 + k_3 + k_4 + k_5 \leq 22$. Since $5544 \leq 2^a.81 \leq 5544 + 22.1728$, we have $a = 7$, $a = 8$, or $a = 9$.

If $a = 7$, then $4824 = 504k_1 + 728k_2 + 1008k_3 + 1512k_4 + 1728k_5$ where $0 \leq k_1 + k_2 + k_3 + k_4 + k_5 \leq 22$. By a computer calculation, it is easily seen that the equation has no solution.

If $a = 8$, then $15192 = 504k_1 + 728k_2 + 1008k_3 + 1512k_4 + 1728k_5$ where $0 \leq k_1 + k_2 + k_3 + k_4 + k_5 \leq 22$. By a computer calculation, the equation has 22 solutions. For example, $(k_1, k_2, k_3, k_4, k_5) = (0, 0, 2, 3, 5)$. We show this solution is impossible. Since $k_2 = 0$ and $m_3 = 728$, it follows that $m_{2^i} \neq 728$, for $1 \leq i \leq 7$. On the other hand, by Lemma 3, we have $|P_2| | (1 + m_2 + m_{2^2} + \cdots + m_{2^7})$, since $m_{2^i} \neq 728$ for $1 \leq i \leq 7$, by a computer calculation we have $|P_2| | 2^7$, which is a contradiction. Assume $(k_1, k_2, k_3, k_4, k_5) = (0, 9, 0, 0, 5)$ is a solution. Since $|P_2| | (1 + m_2 + m_{2^2} + \cdots + m_{2^7})$ by Lemma 3. Indeed, $|P_2| | (1 + 63 + 504t_1 + 728t_2 + 1008t_3 + 1512t_4 + 1728t_5)$ where t_1, t_2, t_3, t_4, t_5, are non-negative integers and $0 \leq t_1 + t_2 + t_3 + t_4 + t_5 \leq 6$. Since $k_1 = 0$, $k_2 = 9$, and $k_3 = 0$, $0 \leq t_1 \leq 1$, $0 \leq t_2 \leq 10$, and $0 \leq t_3 \leq 1$. Since $k_4 = 0$ and $m_{27} = 1512$ or 1728, $t_4 = 0$. Also $k_5 = 5$, and thus $0 \leq t_5 \leq 6$. By an easy calculation, this is impossible. Arguing as above, for other solutions, we have a contradiction.

If $a = 9$, then $35928 = 504k_1 + 728k_2 + 1008k_3 + 1512k_4 + 1728k_5$ where $0 \leq k_1 + k_2 + k_3 + k_4 + k_5 \leq 22$. By a computer calculation, it is easily seen that the equation has no solution.

- Let $exp(P_3) = 3^4$. Then by Lemma 3, $|P_3| | (1 + m_3 + m_{3^2} + m_{3^3} + m_{3^4})$ and so $|P_3| | 3^4$ (for example when ($m_9 = 504$, $m_{27} = 1008$, and $m_{81} = 1728$)).

  If $|P_3| = 3^4$, then $n_3 = \frac{m_{81}}{\phi(81)}$, since $m_{81} \in \{1512, 1728\}$, $n_3 = 3.7$ or $n_3 = 2^5$. If $n_3 = 3.7$, then $7 \in \pi(G)$ which is a contradiction. If $n_3 = 2^5$, since a cyclic group of order 81 has two elements of order 3, then $m_3 \leq 2^5.2$, which is a contradiction.

□

Remark 4. *According to Lemmas 10 and 11, Remark 3 we have* $\pi(G) = \{2, 3, 7\}$.

Lemma 12. $G \cong PSU(3, 3)$.

Proof. First, we show that $|G| = |PSU(3, 3|$. From the above arguments, we have $|P_7| = 7$. Since $3.7 \notin \omega(G)$, the group P_3 acts fixed point freely on the set of elements of order 7, and so $|P_3| | m_7$. Hence $|P_3| | 3^3$. Likewise, $2.7 \notin \omega(G)$, and so $|P_2| | 2^6$. Hence, we have $|G| = 2^m.3^n.7$. Since $5544 = 2^3.3^2.7.11 \leq 2^m.3^n.7$, we conclude that $|G| = 2^6.3^3.7$ or $|G| = 2^5.3^3.7$. The proof is completed by showing that there is no group such that $|G| = 2^6.3^3.7$ and $nse(G) = nse(PSU(3, 3))$. First, we claim that G is a non-solvable group. Suppose that G is solvable, since $n_7 = \frac{m_7}{\phi(7)} = 2^5.3^2$, by Lemma 7, $2^5 \equiv 1 \ (mod 7)$, which is a contradiction. Therefore, G is a non-solvable group and $7^2 \not| |G|$. Hence, G has a normal series $1 \trianglelefteq N \trianglelefteq H \trianglelefteq G$, such that N is a maximal solvable normal subgroup of G and $\frac{H}{N}$ is a non-solvable minimal normal subgroup of $\frac{G}{N}$. Indeed, $\frac{H}{N}$ is a non-abelian simple K_3-group, and so by Lemma 9, $\frac{H}{N}$ is isomorphic to $L_2(7)$ or $L_2(8)$. Suppose that $\frac{H}{N} \cong L_2(7)$. We know $n_7(L_2(7)) = 8$. From Lemma 6, we have $n_7(\frac{H}{N})t = n_7(G)$, and so, $n_7(G) = 8t$ for some integer t. On the other hand, since $n_7(G) | 2^6.3^3$ and $n_7(G) = 1 + 7k$, we have $n_7(G) = 1$, $n_7(G) = 8$,

$n_7(G) = 36$, $n_7(G) = 64$, or $n_7(G) = 288$. If $n_7(G) = 36$, then since $36 = 8t$ has no integer solution, we have a contradiction. Similarly, if $\frac{H}{N} \cong L_2(8)$, we have a contradiction. As a result, $|G| = 2^5.3^3.7 = |PSU(3,3)|$. Hence $|G| = |PSU(3,3)|$, and by assumption, $nse(G) = nse(PSU(3,3))$, so by [2], $G \cong PSU(3,3)$ and the proof is completed. □

The remainder of this section will be devoted to the proof of Theorem 2.

Proof of Theorem 2. Let G be a group with

$$nse(G) = nse(PSL(3,3)) = \{1, 117, 702, 728, 936, 1404, 1728\},$$

where $PSL(3,3)$ is the projective special linear group of degree 3 over field of order 3. The proof will be divided into a sequence of lemmas.

Lemma 13. $\pi(G) \subseteq \{2,3,13\}$.

Proof. First, since $117 \in nse(G)$, by Lemma 2, $2 \in \pi(G)$ and $m_2 = 117$. Applying formula (1), we obtain $\pi(G) \subseteq \{3,5,7,13,19,937\}$. Now, we prove that $7 \notin \pi(G)$. Conversely, suppose that $7 \in \pi(G)$. Then formula (1), implies $m_7 = 1728$. From the formula (1), we conclude that if $2.7 \in \omega(G)$, then $m_{14} = 702$. On the other hand, if $2.7 \in \omega(G)$, then by Lemma 4, $m_{2.7} = m_7.\phi(2).t$ for some integer t. Hence $702 = 1728t$, which is a contradiction and hence $2.7 \notin \omega(G)$. Since $2.7 \notin \omega(G)$, the group P_7 acts fixed point freely on the set of elements of order 2 of G. Hence, by Lemma 8, $|P_7| | m_2$, which is a contradiction. In the same manner, we can see that $5 \notin \pi(G)$. Now, we prove $19 \notin \pi(G)$. Conversely, suppose that $19 \in \pi(G)$. Then formula (1), implies $m_{19} \in \{702, 1728\}$. On the other hand, by formula (1), we conclude that if $2.19 \in \omega(G)$, then $m_{2.19} \in \{702, 936, 1404, 1728\}$. Now, if $m_{19} = 702$, then $2.19 | 1 + m_2 + m_{19} + m_{2.19} (= 1522, 1756, 2224, 2548)$, which is a contradiction, and if $m_{19} = 1728$, $2.19 | 1 + m_2 + m_{19} + m_{2.19} (= 2548, 2782, 3250, 3574)$ which is a contradiction. Hence $2.19 \notin \omega(G)$. Since $2.19 \notin \omega(G)$, the group P_{19} acts fixed point freely on the set of elements of order 2 of G, and so $|P_{19}| | m_2.$, which is a contradiction. Similarly, we can prove that $937 \notin \pi(G)$. From what has already been proved, we conclude that $\pi(G) \subseteq \{2,3,13\}$. □

Remark 5. *If* $3, 13 \in \pi(G)$, *then* $m_3 = 728$ *and* $m_{13} = 1728$. *If* $(13)^a \in \omega(G)$, *since* $m_{(13)^2} \notin nse(G)$, *then* $a = 1$. *By Lemma 3,* $|P_{13}| | 1 + m_{13}$ *and so* $|P_{13}| | 13$. *Suppose* $13 \in \pi(G)$. *Then since* $|P_{13}| = 13$, $n_{13} = \frac{m_{13}}{\phi(13)} = 3^2.2^4 | |G|$.*Therefore, if* $13 \in \pi(G)$, *then* $3, 2 \in \pi(G)$. *Hence, we only have to consider two proper sets* $\{2\}$, $\{2,3\}$, *and finally the whole set* $\{2,3,13\}$.

Now, we will show that $\pi(G)$ is not equal $\{2\}$ and $\{2,3\}$. For this purpose at first, we need obtain some information about elements of $\omega(G)$.

If $2^a \in \omega(G)$, then, by formula (1), we have $0 \leq a \leq 4$.

By Lemma 3, $|P_2| | (1 + m_2 + m_{2^2} + \cdots + m_{2^4})$ and so $|P_2| | 2^4$.

If $3^a \in \omega(G)$, then $1 \leq a \leq 4$.

Lemma 14. $\pi(G) \neq \{2\}$ *and* $\pi(G) \neq \{2,3\}$.

Proof. We claim that $\pi(G) \neq \{2\}$. Assume the contrary, that is, let $\pi(G) = \{2\}$. Then $|\omega(G)| \leq 5$. Since, nse(G) has seven elements and $|\omega(G)| \leq 5$, we have a contradiction. Hence $\pi(G) \neq \{2\}$.
Our next claim is that $\pi(G) \neq \{2,3\}$. Suppose, contrary to our claim, that $\pi(G) = \{2,3\}$. Since $3^5 \notin \omega(G)$, $exp(P_3) = 3, 3^2, 3^3, 3^4$.

- Let $exp(P_3) = 3$. Then by Lemma 3, $|P_3| | (1 + m_3)$ and so $|P_3| | 3^6$. We will consider six cases for $|P_3|$.

Case 1. If $|P_3| = 3$, then since $n_3 = \frac{m_3}{\phi(3)} = 2.7.13 | |G|$, $7 \in \pi(G)$, which is a contradiction.

Case 2. If $|P_3| = 3^2$, then since $exp(P_3) = 3$ and $3.2^5 \notin \omega(G)$, $|\omega(G)| \leq 10$. Therefore $5616 + 702k_1 + 728k_2 + 936k_3 + 1404k_4 + 1728k_5 = |G| = 2^a.9$ where k_1, k_2, k_3, k_4, k_5, and a are non-negative integers and $0 \leq k_1 + k_2 + k_3 + k_4 + k_5 \leq 3$. Since $5616 \leq 2^a.9 \leq 5616 + 3.1728$, we have $a = 10$.
If $a = 10$, then since $|P_2||2^4$, we have a contradiction. Similarly, we can rule out other cases.

- Let $exp(P_3) = 3^2$. Then by Lemma 3, $|P_3||(1 + m_3 + m_{3^2})$ and $|P_3||3^3$ (for example when $m_9 = 702$). We will consider two cases for $|P_3|$.
  Case1. If $|P_3| = 3^2$, then $n_3 = \frac{m_9}{\phi(9)}||G|$, since $m_9 \in \{702, 936, 1404, 1728\}$, $n_3 = 3^2.13$, $n_3 = 2^2.13.3$, or $n_3 = 2.3^2.13$, and so $13 \in \pi(G)$, which is a contradiction, and if $n_3 = 2^5.3^2$, since a cyclic group of order 9 has two elements of order 3, $m_3 \leq 2^5.3^2.2 = 576$, which is a contradiction.
  Case 2. If $|P_3| = 3^3$, then since $exp(P_3) = 3^2$, $3.2^5 \notin \omega(G)$, and $3^2.2^5 \notin \omega(G)$, $|\omega(G)| \leq 15$. Therefore $5616 + 702k_1 + 728k_2 + 936k_3 + 1404k_4 + 1728k_5 = |G| = 2^a.27$ where k_1, k_2, k_3, k_4, k_5, and a are non-negative integers and $0 \leq k_1 + k_2 + k_3 + k_4 + k_5 \leq 8$. Since $5616 \leq 2^a.27 \leq 5616 + 8.1728$, we have $a = 8$ or $a = 9$, which is a contradiction.
- Let $exp(P_3) = 3^3$. Then by Lemma 3, $|P_3||(1 + m_3 + m_{3^2} + m_{3^3})$ and $|P_3||3^5$ (for example when $m_9 = 702$ and $m_{27} = 1728$). We will consider tree cases for $|P_3|$.
  Case 1. If $|P_3| = 3^3$, then $n_3 = \frac{m_{27}}{\phi(27)}$, since $m_{27} \in \{702, 1404, 1728\}$, $n_3 = 3.13$, or $n_3 = 2.3.13$, and so $13 \in \pi(G)$, which is a contradiction, and if $n_3 = 2^5.3$, since a cyclic group of order 27 has two elements of order 3, $m_3 \leq 2^5.3.2 = 192$, which is a contradiction.
  Case 2. If $|P_3| = 3^4$, then since $exp(P_3) = 3^3$, $3.2^5 \notin \omega(G)$, $3^2.2^5 \notin \omega(G)$, and $3^3.2^5 \notin \omega(G)$, $|\omega(G)| \leq 20$. Therefore $5616 + 702k_1 + 728k_2 + 936k_3 + 1404k_4 + 1728k_5 = |G| = 2^a.81$ where k_1, k_2, k_3, k_4, k_5, and a are non-negative integers and $0 \leq k_1 + k_2 + k_3 + k_4 + k_5 \leq 13$. Since $5616 \leq 2^a.81 \leq 5616 + 13.1728$, we have $a = 7$ or $a = 8$, which is a contradiction. In the same way, we can rule out the case $|P_3| = 3^5$
- Let $exp(P_3) = 3^4$. Then by Lemma 3, $|P_3||(1 + m_3 + m_{3^2} + m_{3^3} + m_{3^4})$ and $|P_3||3^5$ (for example when $m_9 = 1404$, $m_{27} = m_{81} = 1728$).We will consider two cases for $|P_3|$.
  Case 1. If $|P_3| = 3^4$, then $n_3 = \frac{m_{81}}{\phi(81)}$, since $m_{81} \in \{702, 1404, 1728\}$, $n_3 = 13$ or $n_3 = 13.2$ and so $13 \in \pi(G)$, which is a contradiction. If $n_3 = 2^5$, since a cyclic group of order 81 has two elements of order 3, then $m_3 \leq 2^5.2$ which is a contradiction.
  Case 2. If $|P_3| = 3^5$, since $exp(P_3) = 3^4$, $3.2^5 \notin \omega(G)$, $3^2.2^5 \notin \omega(G)$, $3^3.2^5 \notin \omega(G)$, and $3^4.2^5 \notin \omega(G)$, $|\omega(G)| \leq 25$. Therefore, $5616 + 702k_1 + 728k_2 + 936k_3 + 1404k_4 + 1728k_5 = |G| = 2^a.243$ where k_1, k_2, k_3, k_4, k_5, and a are non-negative integers and $0 \leq k_1 + k_2 + k_3 + k_4 + k_5 \leq 18$. Since $5616 \leq 2^a.243 \leq 5616 + 18.1728$, we have $a = 5$ or $a = 6$ or $a = 7$, which is a contradiction.

□

Remark 6. *According to Lemmas 13 and 14, and Remark 5, we have* $\pi(G) = \{2, 3, 13\}$.

Lemma 15. $G \cong PSL(3, 3)$.

Proof. We show that $|G| = |PSL(3, 3|$. From the above arguments, we have $|P_{13}| = 13$. Since $2.13 \notin \omega(G)$, it follows that, the group P_2 acts fixed point freely on the set of elements of order 13, and so $|P_2||m_{13}$. Hence, $|P_2||2^6$. Likewise, $3.13 \notin \omega(G)$, and so $|P_3||3^3$. and so $|P_2||m_{13}$. Hence, $|P_2||2^6$. Likewise, $3.13 \notin \omega(G)$, and so $|P_3||3^3$. Hence we have $|G| = 2^m.3^n.13$.

Since $5616 = 2^4.3^3.13 \leq 2^m.3^n.13$, we conclude that $|G| = 2^6.3^3.13$, $|G| = 2^6.3^2.13$, $|G| = 2^5.3^3.13$, or $|G| = 2^4.3^3.13$. The proof is completed by showing that there is no group such that $|G| = 2^6.3^3.13$, $|G| = 2^6.3^2.13$, or $|G| = 2^5.3^3.13$, and $nse(G) = nse(PSL(3, 3))$. First, we show that there is no group such that $|G| = 2^6.3^3.13$ and $nse(G) = nse(PSL(3, 3))$. We claim that G is a non-solvable group. Suppose that G is a solvable group, since $n_{13} = \frac{m_{13}}{\phi(13)} = 2^4.3^2$, by Lemma 7, $2^4 \equiv 1\ (mod 13)$, which is a contradiction. Therefore G is a non-solvable group and $(13)^2 \nmid |G|$. Hence, G has a normal series

$1 \trianglelefteq N \trianglelefteq H \trianglelefteq G$, such that N is a maximal solvable normal subgroup of G and $\frac{H}{N}$ is a non-solvable minimal normal subgroup of $\frac{G}{N}$. Indeed, $\frac{H}{N}$ is a non-abelian simple K_3-group, and so by Lemma 9 $\frac{H}{N}$ is isomorphic to one of the simple K_3 groups. In fact, $\frac{H}{N} \cong L_3(3)$. We know $n_{13}(L_3(3)) = 144$. From Lemma 6, we have $n_{13}(\frac{H}{N})t = n_{13}(G)$, and so $n_{13}(G) = 144t$ for some integer t. On the other hand, since $n_{13}(G) | 2^6.3^3$ and $n_{13}(G) = 1 + 13k$, we have $n_{13}(G) = 1$, $n_{13}(G) = 27$, or $n_{13}(G) = 144$. If $n_{13}(G) = 27$, then since $27 = 144t$ has no integer solution, we have a contradiction. Similarly, we can rule out the case $|G| = 2^5.3^3.13$ and $nse(G) = nse(PSL(3,3))$. Finally, we have to show that there is no group such that $|G| = 2^6.3^2.13$ and $nse(G) = nse(PSL(3,3))$. By Lemma 7, it is easy to check that G is a non-solvable group, and $(13)^2 \not| |G|$. Hence, G has a normal series $1 \trianglelefteq N \trianglelefteq H \trianglelefteq G$, such that N is a maximal solvable normal subgroup of G and $\frac{H}{N}$ is a non-solvable minimal normal subgroup of $\frac{G}{N}$. Indeed, $\frac{H}{N}$ is a non-abelian simple K_3-group, and so by Lemma 9 $\frac{H}{N}$ is isomorphic to $L_3(3)$. Therefore $|H| = |N| 2^4.3^3.13$, which is a contradiction. As a result, $|G| = 2^4.3^3.13 = |PSL(3,3)|$. Hence $|G| = |PSL(3,3)|$ and by assumption, $nse(G) = nse(PSL(3,3))$, so by [2], $G \cong PSL(3,3)$ and the proof is completed. □

4. Conclusions

In this paper, we showed that the groups $PSU(3,3)$ and $PSL(3,3)$ are characterized by nse. Further investigations are needed to answer "is a group G isomorphic to $PSU(3,q)$ ($q > 8$ is a prime power) if and only if $nse(G) = nse(PSU(3,q))$?" and "is a group G isomorphic to $PSL(3,q)$ ($q > 8$ is a prime power) if and only if $nse(G) = nse(PSL(3,q))$?". In future work, these questions will be considered.

Author Contributions: All authors contributed equally on writing this paper. All authors have read and have approved the final manuscript.

Funding: This research received no external funding.

Acknowledgments: The authors would like to express their deep gratitude to the referees for their helpful comments and valuable suggestion for improvment of this paper. Part of this research work was done while the second author was spending his sabbatical leave at the Department of Mathematics of University of California, Berkeley. This author expresses his thanks for the hospitality and facilities provided by Department of Mathematics of UCB.

Conflicts of Interest: The authors declare no conflict of interest.

References

1. Shi, W.. A new characterization of sporadic simple groups. In *Group Theory, Proceedings of the 1987 Singapore Conference on Group Theory, Singapore, 8–9 June 1987*; Walter de Gruyter: Berlin, Germany, 1989; pp. 531–540.
2. Shoa, C.; Shi, W.; Jiang, Q. A characterization of simple K_3-groups. *Adv. Math.* **2009**, *38*, 327–330.
3. Shoa, C.; Shi,W.; Jiang,Q. Characterization of simple K_4-groups. *Front. Math. China* **2008**, *3*, 355–370. [CrossRef]
4. Iranmanesh, A.; Parvizi Mosaed, H.; Tehranian, A. Characterization of Suzuki group by nse and order of group. *Bull. Korean Math. Soc.* **2016**, *53*, 651–656. [CrossRef]
5. Khalili Asboei, A.; Salehi Amiri, S.S.; Iranmanesh, A.; Tehranian, A. A characterization of sporadic simple groups by nse and order. *J. Algebra Appl.* **2013**, *12*. [CrossRef]
6. Khalili Asboei, A.; Salehi Amiri, S.S.; Iranmanesh, A.; Tehranian, A. A new characterization of A_7, A_8. *An. St. Univ. Ovidius Constanta* **2013**, *21*, 43–50. [CrossRef]
7. Khalili Asboei, A.; Salehi Amiri, S.S.; Iranmanesh, A. A new characterization of Symmetric groups for some n. *Hacet. J. Math. Stat.* **2013**, *43*, 715–723.
8. Khalili Asboei, A.; Salehi Amiri, S.S.; Iranmanesh, A. A new note on characterization of a Mathieu group of degree 12. *Southeast Asian Bull. Math.* **2014**, *38*, 383–388.
9. Khalili Asboei, A. A new characterization of $PSL(2,27)$. *Bol. Soc. Paran. Mat.* **2014**, *32*, 43–50. [CrossRef]
10. Khalili Asboei, A.; Salehi Amiri, S.S.; Iranmanesh, A. A new characterization of PSL(2,q) for some q. *Ukr. Math. J.* **2016**, *67*, 1297–1305. [CrossRef]

11. Khatami, M.; Khosravi, B.; Akhlaghi, Z. A new characterization for some linear groups. *Monatsh. Math.* **2011**, *163*, 39–50. [CrossRef]
12. Shoa, C.; Jiang, Q. Characterization of groups $L_2(q)$ by nse where $q \in \{17, 27, 29\}$. *Chin. Ann. Math.* **2016**, *37B*, 103–110. [CrossRef]
13. Chen, D. A characterization of PSU(3,4) by nse. *Int. J. Algebra Stat.* **2013**, *2*, 51–56. [CrossRef]
14. Liu, S. A characterization of $L_3(4)$. *Sci. Asia* **2013**, *39*, 436–439. [CrossRef]
15. Liu, S. A characterization of projective special unitary group $U_3(5)$ by nse. *Arab J. Math. Sci.* **2014**, *20*, 133–140. [CrossRef]
16. Liu, S. A characterization of projective special linear group $L_3(5)$ by nse. *Ital. J. Pure Appl. Math.* **2014**, *32*, 203–212.
17. Jahandideh Khangheshlaghi, M.; Darafsheh, M.R. Nse characterization of the Chevalley group $G_2(4)$. *Arabian J. Math.* **2018**, *7*, 21–26. [CrossRef]
18. Parvizi Mosaed, H.; Iranmanesh, A.; Tehranian, A. Nse characterization of simple group $L_2(3^n)$. *Publ. Instit. Math. Nouv. Ser.* **2016**, *99*, 193–201. [CrossRef]
19. Parvizi Mosaed, H.; Iranmanesh, A.; Foroudi Ghasemabadi, M.; Tehranian, A. A new characterization of simple group $L_2(2^m)$. *Hacet. J. Math. Stat.* **2016**, *44*, 875–886.
20. Kurzweil, H.; Stellmacher, B. *The Theory of Finite Groups an Introduction*; Springer: New York, NY, USA, 2004 .
21. Shen, R.; Shoa, C.; Q. Jiang, Q.; Shi., W.; Mazurov, V. A new characterization of A_5. *Monatsh. Math.* **2010**, *160*, 337–341. [CrossRef]
22. Frobenius, G. Verallgemeinerung der Sylowschen Satze. *Berl. Ber.* **1895**, *2*, 981–993.
23. Shoa, C.; Jiang, Q. A new characterization of some linear groups by nse. *J. Algebra Its Appl.* **2014**, *13*. [CrossRef]
24. Miller, G.A. Addition to a theorem due to Frobenius. *Bull. Am. Math. Soc.* **1904**, *11*, 6–7. [CrossRef]
25. Hall, M. *The Theory of Groups*; Macmillan: New York, NY, USA, 1959.
26. Passman, D. *Permutation Groups*; W. A. Benjamin: New York, NY, USA, **1968.**
27. Herzog, M. On finite simple groups of order divisible by three primes only. *J. Algebra* **1968**, *10*, 383–388. [CrossRef]

© 2018 by the authors. Licensee MDPI, Basel, Switzerland. This article is an open access article distributed under the terms and conditions of the Creative Commons Attribution (CC BY) license (http://creativecommons.org/licenses/by/4.0/).

mathematics

MDPI

Article

Quantum Information: A Brief Overview and Some Mathematical Aspects

Maurice R. Kibler [1,2,3]

[1] CNRS/IN2P3, Institut de Physique Nucléaire, 69622 Villeurbanne, France; m.kibler@ipnl.in2p3.fr
[2] Faculté des Sciences et Technologies, Université Claude Bernard Lyon 1, 69622 Villeurbanne, France
[3] Université de Lyon, 69361 Lyon, France

Received: 23 October 2018; Accepted: 20 November 2018; Published: 22 November 2018

Abstract: The aim of the present paper is twofold. First, to give the main ideas behind quantum computing and quantum information, a field based on quantum-mechanical phenomena. Therefore, a short review is devoted to (i) *quantum bits* or qubits (and more generally *qudits*), the analogues of the usual bits 0 and 1 of the classical information theory, and to (ii) two characteristics of quantum mechanics, namely, *linearity*, which manifests itself through the superposition of qubits and the action of unitary operators on qubits, and *entanglement* of certain multi-qubit states, a resource that is specific to quantum mechanics. A, second, focus is on some mathematical problems related to the so-called *mutually unbiased bases* used in quantum computing and quantum information processing. In this direction, the construction of mutually unbiased bases is presented via two distinct approaches: one based on the group SU(2) and the other on Galois fields and Galois rings.

Keywords: linearity; superposition; entanglement; mutually unbiased bases; SU(2); Galois fields; Galois rings

1. Introduction

In the present days, there is a growing interest for the field of *quantum information* and *quantum computing*. Such a field emerged at the beginning of the 1980s when Feynman and other scientists asked the question: is it possible to simulate the behaviour of a quantum system by using a classical computer? Then, the question evolved towards how to use quantum systems to do computations. This led to the idea of a quantum computer based on quantum physics with the hope to solve problems that would be intractable or difficult to solve with a classical computer. A fact in favour of a quantum computer is the law by Moore according to which the size of electronic and spintronic devices for a classical computer should approach 10 nm in 2020, the scale where quantum effects become important. The field of quantum information and quantum computing is at the crossroads of experimental and theoretical quantum physical sciences (physics and chemistry), discrete mathematics and informatics with the aim of building a quantum computer. We note in passing that physics, mathematics, informatics and engineering have already greatly benefited from the enormous amount of works achieved along the line of quantum information and quantum computing.

The unit of classical information is the bit (possible values 0 and 1). In a quantum computer, classical bits (0 and 1) are replaced by *quantum bits* or *qubits* (that interpolate in some sense between 0 and 1). The most general qubit is a normalized vector $|\psi\rangle$ in the two-dimensional Hilbert space $\mathbb{C}^2$

$$|\psi\rangle = a|0\rangle + b|1\rangle, \quad |a|^2 + |b|^2 = 1, \quad a \in \mathbb{C}, \quad b \in \mathbb{C} \tag{1}$$

where $|0\rangle$ and $|1\rangle$ are the elements of an orthonormal basis in $\mathbb{C}^2$. The result of a measurement of $|\psi\rangle$ is not deterministic since it gives $|0\rangle$ or $|1\rangle$ with the probability $|a|^2$ or $|b|^2$, respectively. The consideration of N qubits leads to work in the 2^N-dimensional Hilbert space $\mathbb{C}^{2^N}$. Note that the notion of qubit, corresponding to $\mathbb{C}^2$, is a particular case of the one of *qudit*, corresponding to $\mathbb{C}^d$ (d not necessarily in the form 2^N). A system of N qudits is associated with the Hilbert space $\mathbb{C}^{d^N}$. In this connection, the techniques developed for finite-dimensional Hilbert spaces are of paramount importance in quantum computation and quantum computing.

From a formal point of view, a quantum computer is a system producing qubits, the state of which can be controlled and manipulated via unitary transformations. These transformations correspond to the product of elementary unitary operators called *quantum gates* (the analogues of the logic gates of a classical computer) acting on one, two or more qubits. Measurement of the qubits out-coming from a *quantum circuit* of quantum gates yields the result of a (quantum) computation. In other words, a realization of quantum information processing can be performed by preparing a quantum system in a quantum state, then submitting this state to unitary transformations and, finally, reading the outcome from a measurement.

The two basic characteristics of quantum mechanics used in a quantum computer are *linearity* (principle of superposition of quantum states) and *entanglement*. The superposition principle gives resources: the quantum computer can be in several states at the same time. This leads to a massive quantum parallelism with a speed up of computations (for N qubits, 2^N computations can be achieved in parallel through the use of *quantum algorithms*). Entanglement, i.e., the fact that certain quantum systems made of two or more sub-systems behave as an indissociable entity, is at the root of quantum computing and *quantum teleportation*. In quantum mechanics, each measurement on a quantum system perturbs the system and the superposition principle makes impossible to duplicate a quantum state (*no-cloning theorem*). The two latter points and the use of the so-called *mutually unbiased bases* (MUBs), to be defined in Section 3, are the basic ingredients of quantum cryptography (illustrated by the BB84 protocol, the first protocol of quantum cryptography).

The aim of this paper is to present to a community of computer engineers and mathematicians the basic grounds of quantum information and quantum computing as well as some mathematical aspects and related open problems.

This paper is organized as follows. Section 2 deals with the general framework of quantum information and quantum computing (i.e., information and computing based on quantum physics): some of the concepts and ideas evoked above are further described. In Section 3, we address some mathematical aspects of quantum information; in particular, we review some of the methods for constructing mutually unbiased bases (more precisely, methods based on the group SU(2) and on Galois rings and Galois fields). Sections 2 and 3 are mainly based on References [1,2], respectively. References [3–77] constitute an incomplete list (in chronological order) of original works of relevance for an in-depth study of Sections 2 and 3. Finally, the reader will find in Reference [78] some calculations with the help of the Python language illustrating the derivation of mutually unbiased bases according to the methods described in Section 3.

2. The General Framework of Quantum Information and Quantum Computing

2.1. Quantum Mechanics in a Few Words

Classical physics does not apply in the microscopic world. It is not appropriate for describing, explaining and predicting physical and chemical phenomena at the atomic and sub-atomic level. The convenient theory for quantum systems (i.e., molecules, atoms, nuclei and elementary particles) is quantum mechanics, an extension of the old quantum theory mainly due to Planck, Einstein, Bohr and Sommerfeld (the word *quantum* comes from the fact that the energy exchanges between light and matter occur in a quantized form). Quantum mechanics, which is often used in conjunction with some other theories like relativity and quantum field theory, can be presented in two equivalent ways: *wave mechanics* initiated by de Broglie and Schrödinger and *matrix mechanics* pioneered by Heisenberg, Born and Jordan. It is not our purpose to list in detail the postulates of quantum mechanics. We shall restrict ourselves with four aspects of the Copenhagen interpretation which are indispensable in quantum information and quantum computing.

- In both presentations of quantum mechanics, the state of a closed quantum system is described by a vector (in matrix mechanics) or a wave function (in wave mechanics), noted $|\psi\rangle$ in both cases, belonging to a finite or infinite Hilbert space $\mathcal{H}$.
- In quantum information and quantum computing, the space $\mathcal{H}$ is finite-dimensional (isomorphic to $\mathbb{C}^2$ for qubits or $\mathbb{C}^d$ for qudits) and the (normalized) vector $|\psi\rangle$, defined up to a phase factor, can be the result (arising from an evolution or transformation of a vector $|\psi'\rangle$)

$$|\psi\rangle = U|\psi'\rangle$$

  of the action of a unitary operator U (or quantum gate) on $|\psi'\rangle$. (We are not concerned here with dynamical systems for which the time evolution of ψ in the wave picture is given by the Schrödinger equation, in the non-relativistic case, or the Dirac equation, in the relativistic case, two linear equations.)
- In quantum information and quantum computing, $|\psi\rangle$ is given by a linear combination of the eigenvectors of an observable in the matrix formulation. An observable $\mathcal{A}$ is associated with a measurable physical quantity (energy, position, impulsion, spin, etc.). It is represented by a self-adjoint operator A acting on the space $\mathcal{H}$. The possible outcomes of a measurement of an observable $\mathcal{A}$ are the real eigenvalues of the operator A. Measurement in quantum mechanics exhibits a probabilistic nature. More precisely, if (in the case of the finite-dimensional Hilbert space $\mathcal{H} = \mathbb{C}^d$)

$$|\psi\rangle = \sum_{n=0}^{d-1} c_n|\varphi_n\rangle, \quad c_n \in \mathbb{C} \tag{2}$$

  where the φ_n given by

$$A|\varphi_i\rangle = \lambda_i|\varphi_i\rangle, \quad i = 0, 1, \cdots, d-1$$

  are the orthormalized eigenvectors of A, then a measurement of $\mathcal{A}$ will give λ_k with the probability

$$|c_k|^2 = |\langle\varphi_k|\psi\rangle|^2$$

  where $\langle\varphi_k|\psi\rangle$ stands for the inner product of $|\psi\rangle$ by $|\varphi_k\rangle$ (we suppose that the spectrum of A is non-degenerate). Hence, before measurement, the quantum system is in several states being a linear combination of the states $|\varphi_n\rangle$ and, after measurement, the quantum system is in a well-defined state $|\varphi_k\rangle$. Measurement leads to a reduction of the wave packet or wave function collapse. In terms of measurement of qudits, what precedes can be formulated as follows. Let $|\psi\rangle$ as given by Equation (2) be a qudit describing a quantum system before measurement. A measurement of $|\psi\rangle$ in a basis $\{\varphi_i\rangle : i = 0, 1, \cdots, d-1\}$ of $\mathbb{C}^d$ yields the state

$$\frac{\langle\varphi_i|\psi\rangle}{\sqrt{\langle\psi|\varphi_i\rangle\langle\varphi_i|\psi\rangle}}|\varphi_i\rangle = \frac{\langle\varphi_i|\psi\rangle}{|\langle\varphi_i|\psi\rangle|}|\varphi_i\rangle$$

  with the probability

$$p(i) = |\langle\psi|\varphi_i\rangle|^2$$

  Observe that the factor $\langle\varphi_i|\psi\rangle|\langle\varphi_i|\psi\rangle|^{-1}$ is a simple phase factor without importance. By way of example, in the case of $\mathbb{C}^2$, measurement of the qubit $|\psi\rangle = a|0\rangle + b|1\rangle$ in the basis $\{|0\rangle, |1\rangle\}$ of $\mathbb{C}^2$ yields $|0\rangle$ or $|1\rangle$ (up to unimportant phase factors) with the probabilities $|a|^2$ or $|b|^2$, respectively.

- A postulate of quantum mechanics of considerable interest in quantum information and quantum computing concerns the description of a system composed of several sub-systems. The state vector for the system is build from tensors products of the state vectors of the various sub-systems. This may lead to entangled vector states for the composite system. Entanglement constitutes another important resource for quantum information and quantum computing besides the linearity and the non deterministic nature of quantum mechanics. As an example, suppose we have a system of qubits made of two two-level sub-systems. The Hilbert space for the system is $\mathcal{H} = \mathbb{C}^4 \sim \mathbb{C}^2 \otimes \mathbb{C}^2$, where the first and second $\mathbb{C}^2$ corresponds to the first and second sub-systems, respectively. By the tensor product, we can take

$$\{|0\rangle_1 \otimes |0\rangle_2,\ |0\rangle_1 \otimes |1\rangle_2,\ |1\rangle_1 \otimes |0\rangle_2,\ |1\rangle_1 \otimes |1\rangle_2\}$$

as a basis for $\mathbb{C}^4$, where the indices 1 and 2 refer to the first and the second qubits, respectively. Two kinds of states can be considered in $\mathbb{C}^4$, namely separable or non entangled states as

$$|\psi_s\rangle = |0\rangle_1 \otimes \frac{1}{2}(|0\rangle_2 + \sqrt{3}|1\rangle_2)$$

and non separable or entangled states as

$$|\psi_{ns}\rangle = \frac{1}{\sqrt{2}}(|0\rangle_1 \otimes |1\rangle_2 + |1\rangle_1 \otimes |0\rangle_2)$$

For the non entangled state $|\psi_s\rangle$, measurement of the qubit 1 yields $|0\rangle_1$ with the probability 1 while measurement of the qubit 2 leads either to $|0\rangle_2$ with the probability $\frac{1}{4}$ or to $|1\rangle_2$ with the probability $\frac{3}{4}$; therefore, the result of a measurement for one qubit does not depend on the result of a measurement for the other qubit. The situation turns out to be entirely different for the entangled state $|\psi_{ns}\rangle$: a measurement of the first qubit leads either to $|0\rangle_1$ with the probability $\frac{1}{2}$ or to $|1\rangle_1$ with the probability $\frac{1}{2}$; once one of the two results has been obtained, we immediately know what would be the result if we perform a measurement on the second qubit; it is thus unnecessary to make a measurement on the second qubit and this may be sum up as follows:

$$\begin{aligned} \text{result of a measurement of qubit 1} &\Rightarrow \text{state of qubit 2 (without measurement)} \\ |0\rangle_1 &\Rightarrow |1\rangle_2 \\ |1\rangle_1 &\Rightarrow |0\rangle_2 \end{aligned}$$

and conversely

$$\begin{aligned} \text{result of a measurement of qubit 2} &\Rightarrow \text{state of qubit 1 (without measurement)} \\ |1\rangle_2 &\Rightarrow |0\rangle_1 \\ |0\rangle_2 &\Rightarrow |1\rangle_1 \end{aligned}$$

Entanglement may also occur for more than two qubits. For entangled states, there are strong correlations between the results of measurements of the qubits. This effect is essential for quantum information and quantum computing.

Unfortunately, "something is rotten in the state of Denmark" (where the Copenhagen interpretation developed). In fact, entanglement is also an inconvenience: entanglement of qubits with their environment leads to errors. This is known as the effect of decoherence an important drawback for the building of a quantum computer. One way to fight against errors due to decoherence and other effects of noise is to develop *quantum error-correcting codes*.

2.2. Qubits and Qudits

2.2.1. Qubits

Let

$$B_2 = \{|0\rangle, |1\rangle\}$$

be an orthonormal basis called the computational basis of the Hilbert space $\mathbb{C}^2$. Any normalized (to unity) vector $|\psi\rangle$, see Equation (1), in $\mathbb{C}^2$ is called a quantum bit or qubit. From the quantum mechanical point of view, a qubit describes a state of a two-level quantum system. In the absence of measurement (and decoherence), the state $|\psi\rangle$ is a superposition of $|0\rangle$ and $|1\rangle$. A measurement of the state $|\psi\rangle$ yields either $|0\rangle$ (with the probability $|a|^2$) or $|1\rangle$ (with the probability $|b|^2$). Therefore, the superposition of the states $|0\rangle$ and $|1\rangle$ is lost after the measurement. In matrix form, we take

$$|0\rangle = \begin{pmatrix} 1 \\ 0 \end{pmatrix}, \quad |1\rangle = \begin{pmatrix} 0 \\ 1 \end{pmatrix}, \quad |\psi\rangle = \begin{pmatrix} a \\ b \end{pmatrix}$$

From a group-theoretical point of view, $|0\rangle$ and $|1\rangle$ can be considered as the basis vectors for the fundamental irreducible representation $\left(\frac{1}{2}\right)$ of SU(2), in the chain SU(2) $\supset$ U(1), with

$$|0\rangle = |\frac{1}{2}, \frac{1}{2}\rangle, \quad |1\rangle = |\frac{1}{2}, -\frac{1}{2}\rangle \tag{3}$$

in the notations of quantum angular momentum theory.

The state $|\psi\rangle$ can be associated with a point (x, y, z, t) of the sphere S^3 in $\mathbb{R}^4$ according to

$$\mathbb{C}^2 \to S^3 \; : \; a|0\rangle + b|1\rangle \mapsto (x, y, z, t)$$

with $a = x + iy$ and $b = z + it$. In fact, the point (x, y, z, t) can be visualized as a point $(1, \theta, \varphi)$ of the sphere S^2 in $\mathbb{R}^3$, referred to as the Bloch sphere, since ψ can be re-written as

$$|\psi\rangle = \cos\frac{\theta}{2}|0\rangle + \mathrm{e}^{\mathrm{i}\varphi}\sin\frac{\theta}{2}|1\rangle, \quad 0 \le \theta \le \pi, \quad 0 \le \varphi < 2\pi \tag{4}$$

up to a global multiplicative phase factor. The application

$$S^3 \to S^2 \; : \; (x, y, z, t) \mapsto (1, \theta, \varphi)$$

corresponds to the first Hopf fibration $S^3 \xrightarrow{S^1} S^2$ of compact fibre S^1. Any qubit as given by Equation (4) can be represented by a point on the Bloch sphere. Table 1 gives the correspondence between some remarkable qubits $|\psi\rangle$ and points on the Bloch sphere. Any unitary transformation acting on a qubit $|\psi\rangle$ corresponds to a rotation around an axis passing through the centre of the Bloch sphere.

Table 1. Correspondence between qubits $|\psi\rangle = \cos\frac{\theta}{2}|0\rangle + \mathrm{e}^{\mathrm{i}\varphi}\sin\frac{\theta}{2}|1\rangle$ and points ($\xi = \sin\theta\cos\varphi$, $\eta = \sin\theta\sin\varphi$, $\zeta = \cos\theta$) of the Bloch sphere S^2 in $\mathbb{R}^3$.

$\lvert\psi\rangle$	$\lvert 0\rangle$	$\lvert 1\rangle$	$\frac{1}{\sqrt{2}}(\lvert 0\rangle + \lvert 1\rangle)$	$\frac{1}{\sqrt{2}}(\lvert 0\rangle - \lvert 1\rangle)$	$\frac{1}{\sqrt{2}}(\lvert 0\rangle + \mathrm{i}\lvert 1\rangle)$	$\frac{1}{\sqrt{2}}(\lvert 0\rangle - \mathrm{i}\lvert 1\rangle)$
(ξ, η, ζ)	$(0,0,1)$	$(0,0,-1)$	$(1,0,0)$	$(-1,0,0)$	$(0,1,0)$	$(0,-1,0)$

Note that the sets

$$B_0 = \left\{ \frac{|0\rangle + |1\rangle}{\sqrt{2}}, \frac{|0\rangle - |1\rangle}{\sqrt{2}} \right\}, \quad B_1 = \left\{ \frac{|0\rangle + \mathrm{i}|1\rangle}{\sqrt{2}}, \frac{|0\rangle - \mathrm{i}|1\rangle}{\sqrt{2}} \right\}, \quad B_2 = \{|0\rangle, |1\rangle\} \tag{5}$$

appearing in Table 1 are three orthonormal bases of the space $\mathbb{C}^2$. In addition, the vectors in B_0, B_1 and B_2 are eigenvectors of the Pauli matrices σ_1, σ_2 and σ_3 (defined in Equation (9) below), respectively. The bases B_0, B_1 and B_2 constitute the simplest example of the so-called MUBs to be studied in Section 3.

2.2.2. Qudits

The generalisation from the two-dimensional Hilbert space $\mathbb{C}^2$ to the d-dimensional Hilbert space $\mathbb{C}^d$ ($d > 2$) is immediate. Given an orthonormal basis (called the computational basis)

$$B_d = \{|n\rangle : n = 0, 1, \cdots, d-1\} \tag{6}$$

of $\mathbb{C}^d$, any normalized vector

$$|\psi\rangle = \sum_{n=0}^{d-1} c_n |n\rangle, \quad \sum_{n=0}^{d-1} |c_n|^2 = 1, \quad c_i \in \mathbb{C}, \quad i = 0, 1, \cdots, d-1$$

is called a qudit. From the point of view of quantum mechanics, the states $|n\rangle$ can be realized as generalized angular momentum states with

$$|n\rangle = |j, m\rangle, \quad n = j - m, \quad d = 2j + 1 \tag{7}$$

where for fixed j, the index m takes the values $-j, -j+1, \cdots, j$. This yields the correspondence

$$|0\rangle = |j, j\rangle, \quad |1\rangle = |j, j-1\rangle, \quad \cdots, \quad |d-1\rangle = |j, -j\rangle$$

between qudits and angular momentum states. (Let us recall that the *angular momentum state* $|j, m\rangle$ is a common eigenstate of the square J^2 of a generalized angular momentum and of the z-component J_z of the angular momentum.) Therefore, $|\psi\rangle$ can be re-written

$$|\psi\rangle = \sum_{m=-j}^{j} d_{j-m} |j, m\rangle$$

in the angular momentum basis $\{|j, m\rangle : m = -j, -j+1, \cdots, j\}$. For instance, a qutrit $|\psi\rangle$ can be written

$$|\psi\rangle = c_0|0\rangle + c_1|1\rangle + c_2|2\rangle$$

in the ternary basis $\{|0\rangle, |1\rangle, |2\rangle\}$ or

$$|\psi\rangle = d_2|1, -1\rangle + d_1|1, 0\rangle + d_0|1, 1\rangle$$

in the balanced basis $\{|1, -1\rangle, |1, 0\rangle, |1, 1\rangle\}$ associated with the angular momentum $j = 1$.

2.2.3. Qudits with $d = 2^N$

In the case where $d = 2^N$, the corresponding qudits can be obtained from tensor products. For example, for $d = 4$ a basis of $\mathbb{C}^4 \sim \mathbb{C}^2 \otimes \mathbb{C}^2$ is

$$|0\rangle \otimes |0\rangle = \begin{pmatrix}1\\0\end{pmatrix} \otimes \begin{pmatrix}1\\0\end{pmatrix} = \begin{pmatrix}1\\0\\0\\0\end{pmatrix}, \quad |0\rangle \otimes |1\rangle = \begin{pmatrix}1\\0\end{pmatrix} \otimes \begin{pmatrix}0\\1\end{pmatrix} = \begin{pmatrix}0\\1\\0\\0\end{pmatrix}$$

$$|1\rangle \otimes |0\rangle = \begin{pmatrix}0\\1\end{pmatrix} \otimes \begin{pmatrix}1\\0\end{pmatrix} = \begin{pmatrix}0\\0\\1\\0\end{pmatrix}, \quad |1\rangle \otimes |1\rangle = \begin{pmatrix}0\\1\end{pmatrix} \otimes \begin{pmatrix}0\\1\end{pmatrix} = \begin{pmatrix}0\\0\\0\\1\end{pmatrix}$$

Then, the most general quartit $|\psi\rangle$ is made of the superposition of tensor products of two qubits. In detail, we have

$$|\psi\rangle = a|0\rangle \otimes |0\rangle + b|0\rangle \otimes |1\rangle + c|1\rangle \otimes |0\rangle + d|1\rangle \otimes |1\rangle$$

where $a, b, c, d \in \mathbb{C}$ (usually, in $|i\rangle \otimes |j\rangle$ the state $|i\rangle$ refers to the first qubit and $|j\rangle$ to the second).

It is interesting to remark that the vectors $|\psi\rangle$ for $d = 2$, 2^2 and 2^3 are associated with the Hopf fibrations $S^3 \xrightarrow{S^1} S^2$ (connected to complex numbers), $S^7 \xrightarrow{S^3} S^4$ (connected to quaternions) and $S^{15} \xrightarrow{S^7} S^8$ (connected to octonions). Entanglement for $d = 2^2$ and 2^3 can be discussed in terms of fibrations on spheres [21]. In the same vein, we may ask the question of the interest for entanglement of Cayley-Dickson algebras for $d = 2^N$ with $N > 3$ and of fibrations on hyperboloids [13].

2.3. Physical Realizations of Qubits

According to R. Landauer, information is physical so that qubits are realised by quantum systems, more specifically by two-level quantum systems, the qubits $|0\rangle$ and $|1\rangle$ corresponding to two different (energy) levels. We shall not be concerned here with the physical realization of qubits (and qudits). It is enough to say that any two-level quantum system may be considered as a qubit. Therefore, qubits can be carried out by nuclear spins, ultra-cold trapped ions, neutral atoms and Bose-Einstein condensates, two different polarizations of a photon, and Josephson tunnel nanojunctions. For instance, in nuclear magnetic resonance, the nuclear spins of an atom in an organic molecule can be aligned (giving the state $|0\rangle$) or anti-aligned (giving the state $|1\rangle$) with an applied constant magnetic field; in generalized angular momentum terminology, we have the quantum states given by Equation (3) and corresponding to the spin $j = \frac{1}{2}$. Similarly, for an ion cooled and trapped by electric fields in a cavity, qubits can be implemented as electronic states (ground state for $|0\rangle$, excited state for $|1\rangle$). Vibrational states can also be used for realizing qubits (zero-phonon state for $|0\rangle$, one-phonon state for $|1\rangle$).

2.4. Entanglement

2.4.1. Generalities

Entanglement occurs only in quantum physics. It has no analogue in classical physics. The notion of entanglement goes back to the famous paper by Einstein, Poldosky and Rosen. In quantum physics, two (or more than two) particles are said to be entangled if the quantum state of each particle depends of the quantum state(s) of the other(s) or cannot be described independently of the quantum state(s) of the other(s). In other words, there exist correlations between the physical properties of a system of entangled particles. More generally, two entangled sub-systems S_1 and S_2 are not independent so that the global system $\{S_1, S_2\}$ must be considered as a whole even after separation by an arbitrary distance. Then, a measurement made on one sub-system gives an information on the other (without measurement on the other sub-system). On the contrary, for a non entangled system consisting of two sub-systems, a measurement on one sub-system does not give in general an information on the other sub-system.

As an example, let us consider a system consisting of two particles, system having a total spin equal to 0. If the spin of one particle is measured to be $\frac{1}{2}$ on a certain axis, then we know (without any measurement) that the spin on the other particle on the same axis is $-\frac{1}{2}$ because

$$0 = \frac{1}{2} - \frac{1}{2}$$

The two particles are not independent, even after separation. They still behave like an indivisible system of spin 0.

Entanglement contradicts the principle of locality. There is non locality in the sense that what happens in some place depends of what happens in another place. Indeed, quantum mechanics is a non local, non deterministic and linear physical theory.

2.4.2. Entanglement of Qubits

In quantum information, the notion of entanglement occurs for multi-qubit systems. Let us consider a two-qubit system. There are two possibilities.

- The system is non entangled (or separable); it is then described by a state $|\psi_s\rangle \in \mathbb{C}^2 \otimes \mathbb{C}^2$ such that

$$|\psi_s\rangle = (a|0\rangle + b|1\rangle) \otimes (c|0\rangle + d|1\rangle)$$

  which can be re-written as

$$|\psi_s\rangle = ac|0\rangle \otimes |0\rangle + ad|0\rangle \otimes |1\rangle + bc|1\rangle \otimes |0\rangle + bd|1\rangle \otimes |1\rangle$$

  where $a|0\rangle + b|1\rangle$ and $c|0\rangle + d|1\rangle$ refer to the first and second qubit, respectively.
- The system is entangled (or non separable); it is then described by a state $|\psi_{ns}\rangle \in \mathbb{C}^4$ such that

$$|\psi_s\rangle = A|0\rangle \otimes |0\rangle + B|0\rangle \otimes |1\rangle + C|1\rangle \otimes |0\rangle + D|1\rangle \otimes |1\rangle$$

  cannot be written as the tensor product of two qubits in $\mathbb{C}^2$.

It is clear that a necessary and sufficient condition for an arbitrary two-qubit state

$$|\psi\rangle = \alpha|0\rangle \otimes |0\rangle + \beta|0\rangle \otimes |1\rangle + \gamma|1\rangle \otimes |0\rangle + \delta|1\rangle \otimes |1\rangle$$

of $\mathbb{C}^4$ to be non entangled is

$$\alpha\delta - \beta\gamma = 0$$

Therefore, if $\alpha\delta - \beta\gamma \neq 0$, then the state is entangled. The degree of entanglement of an arbitrary normalized two-qubit state $|\psi\rangle$ is characterized by the concurrence defined by

$$C = |\alpha\delta - \beta\gamma|, \quad 0 \leq C \leq \frac{1}{2} \tag{8}$$

Non entangled states correspond to $C = 0$, maximally entangled states to $C = \frac{1}{2}$. (A maximally entangled state is such that the density operator for each qubit is half the identity operator; it corresponds to a maximum value of the entropy.) Equation (8) can be straightforwardly generalized to the case

$$|\psi\rangle = \sum_{i=0}^{d-1} \sum_{j=0}^{d-1} a_{ij} |i\rangle \otimes |j\rangle$$

of two qudits for which the concurrence C is defined as

$$C = \det(a_{ij}), \quad 0 \leq C \leq \frac{1}{\sqrt{d^d}}$$

in agreement with Equation (8) for $d = 2$.

Example 1. *Let us consider the four states ($\oplus$ stands for the addition modulo 2)*

$$|\beta_{xy}\rangle = \frac{1}{\sqrt{2}}[|0\rangle \otimes |y\rangle + (-1)^x|1\rangle \otimes |y \oplus 1\rangle], \quad x, y = 0, 1$$

called Bell states (in reference to the work on the so-called Bell inequalities) or EPR pairs (in reference to the paper by Einstein, Poldosky and Rosen). As a particular case

$$|\beta_{01}\rangle = \frac{1}{\sqrt{2}}(|0\rangle_1 \otimes |1\rangle_2 + |1\rangle_1 \otimes |0\rangle_2)$$

where the first qubit (qubit 1) and the second one (qubit 2) are clearly emphasized in order to avoid confusion. The result of a measurement of the qubit 1 gives

- *either $|0\rangle_1$ (with the probability $\frac{1}{2}$) so that the qubit 2 is a priori (without measurement) in the state $|1\rangle_2$*
- *or $|1\rangle_1$ (with the probability $\frac{1}{2}$) so that the qubit 2 is a priori (without measurement) in the state $|0\rangle_2$*

but no measurement can lead to both qubits 1 and 2 in the same state ($|0\rangle$ or $|1\rangle$). The result of a measurement of the qubit 1 provides information on the qubit 2 and reciprocally. It is then unnecessary to make a measurement of one qubit once the result of the measurement of the other is known. Similar conclusions can be obtained for the three other Bell states β_{00}, β_{10} and β_{11}. The four Bell states are maximally entangled (they correspond to $C = \frac{1}{2}$).

In passing note that

$$|\beta_{xy}\rangle = (-1)^{xy}[(\sigma_1)^y(\sigma_3)^x] \otimes \sigma_0|\beta_{00}\rangle$$

where σ_0, σ_1 and σ_3 are three of the four Pauli matrices

$$\sigma_0 = \begin{pmatrix} 1 & 0 \\ 0 & 1 \end{pmatrix}, \quad \sigma_1 = \begin{pmatrix} 0 & 1 \\ 1 & 0 \end{pmatrix}, \quad \sigma_3 = \begin{pmatrix} 1 & 0 \\ 0 & -1 \end{pmatrix}, \quad \sigma_2 = \mathrm{i}\sigma_1\sigma_3 = \begin{pmatrix} 0 & -\mathrm{i} \\ \mathrm{i} & 0 \end{pmatrix} \tag{9}$$

Thus, any Bell state $|\beta_{xy}\rangle$ can be obtained from $|\beta_{00}\rangle$.

Example 2. *Let us consider the separable state*

$$|\psi\rangle = (a|0\rangle + b|1\rangle) \otimes \frac{1}{\sqrt{5}}(|0\rangle + 2|1\rangle) = \frac{1}{\sqrt{5}}(a|0\rangle \otimes |0\rangle + 2a|0\rangle \otimes |1\rangle + b|1\rangle \otimes |0\rangle + 2b|1\rangle \otimes |1\rangle)$$

tensor product of two normalized qubits. A measurement of the first qubit gives either $|0\rangle$ with the probability $|a|^2 = |\frac{a}{\sqrt{5}}|^2 + |\frac{2a}{\sqrt{5}}|^2$ or $|1\rangle$ with the probability $|b|^2 = |\frac{b}{\sqrt{5}}|^2 + |\frac{2b}{\sqrt{5}}|^2$ while a measurement of the second qubit gives either $|0\rangle$ with the probability $\frac{1}{5} = |\frac{a}{\sqrt{5}}|^2 + |\frac{b}{\sqrt{5}}|^2$ or $|1\rangle$ with the probability $\frac{4}{5} = |\frac{2a}{\sqrt{5}}|^2 + |\frac{2b}{\sqrt{5}}|^2$. Therefore, a measurement on one qubit does not provide information on the other qubit (the state $|\psi\rangle$ corresponds to $C = 0$).

It is important to realize that entanglement of qubits (as in Example 1) and more generally of qudits has no analogue for classical bits. To be clear, the bits in 00 or 01 or 10 or 11 are not correlated. This is not the case for the quantum bits in any of the Bell states β_{xy}.

2.5. Quantum Gates

2.5.1. One-Qubit Gates

In a classical computer, bits are handled with the help of logic gates (there exist seven basic logic gates: AND, OR, XOR, NOT, NAND, NOR, and XNOR). A quantum computer processes qubits arranged in registers. It is equipped with quantum gates which perform unitary transformations on qubits. Quantum gates can be represented by unitary matrices. Table 2 gives some examples of quantum gates [G] for one-qubit systems together with their matrix representations G. The actions of the one-qubit gates of Table 2 on the qubit $|x\rangle$ (with $x = 0$ or 1) are given by

$$|x\rangle \to [\mathrm{I}] \to |x\rangle, \quad |x\rangle \to [\mathrm{NOT}] \to |x \oplus 1\rangle$$
$$|x\rangle \to [\mathrm{S}_\theta] \to \mathrm{e}^{\mathrm{i}x\theta}|x\rangle, \quad |x\rangle \to [\mathrm{H}] \to \frac{1}{\sqrt{2}}(|0\rangle + (-1)^x|1\rangle) \equiv \frac{1}{\sqrt{2}}(|x \oplus 1\rangle + (-1)^x|x\rangle)$$

(as an example, the quantum circuit $|x\rangle \to [\mathrm{S}_\theta] \to \mathrm{e}^{\mathrm{i}x\theta}|x\rangle$ is described by the action $S_\theta|x\rangle = \mathrm{e}^{\mathrm{i}x\theta}|x\rangle$). Therefore, by linearity

$$a|0\rangle + b|1\rangle \to [\mathrm{NOT}] \to b|0\rangle + a|1\rangle$$
$$a|0\rangle + b|1\rangle \to [\mathrm{S}_\theta] \to a|0\rangle + \mathrm{e}^{\mathrm{i}\theta}b|1\rangle$$
$$a|0\rangle + b|1\rangle \to [\mathrm{H}] \to \frac{1}{\sqrt{2}}(a+b)|0\rangle + \frac{1}{\sqrt{2}}(a-b)|1\rangle$$
$$a|0\rangle + b|1\rangle \to [\mathrm{H}] \to [\mathrm{H}] \to a|0\rangle + b|1\rangle$$

(the last circuit reflects that $H^2 = I$). Note that the most general qubit can be obtained from the sequence $[\mathrm{H}] \to [\mathrm{S}_{2\theta}] \to [\mathrm{H}] \to [\mathrm{S}_{\frac{\pi}{2}+\varphi}]$ of one-qubit gates since

$$|0\rangle \to [\mathrm{H}] \to [\mathrm{S}_{2\theta}] \to [\mathrm{H}] \to [\mathrm{S}_{\frac{\pi}{2}+\varphi}] \to \cos\theta|0\rangle + \mathrm{e}^{\mathrm{i}\varphi}\sin\theta|1\rangle$$

or

$$S_{\frac{\pi}{2}+\varphi}HS_{2\theta}H|0\rangle = \cos\theta|0\rangle + \mathrm{e}^{\mathrm{i}\varphi}\sin\theta|1\rangle$$

up to the phase factor $\mathrm{e}^{\mathrm{i}\theta}$.

Table 2. Four basic quantum gates for one-qubit systems; the gates [I] and [NOT] also denoted [X] are associated with the Pauli matrices σ_0 or I and σ_1 or σ_x, respectively; the two other Pauli matrices σ_2 or σ_y and σ_3 or σ_z define two further one-qubit gates denoted as [Y] and [Z], respectively.

Gate [G]	Identity Gate [I]	Not Gate [NOT]	Phase Gate [S$_\theta$]	Hadamard Gate [H]
matrix form G	$I = \begin{pmatrix} 1 & 0 \\ 0 & 1 \end{pmatrix}$	$NOT = \begin{pmatrix} 0 & 1 \\ 1 & 0 \end{pmatrix}$	$S_\theta = \begin{pmatrix} 1 & 0 \\ 0 & \mathrm{e}^{\mathrm{i}\theta} \end{pmatrix}$	$H = \frac{1}{\sqrt{2}}\begin{pmatrix} 1 & 1 \\ 1 & -1 \end{pmatrix}$

2.5.2. Multi-Qubit Gates

Quantum gates for two-qubit systems are important. For example, let us mention the controlled-NOT gate [$\mathrm{C}_{\mathrm{NOT}}$] defined via

$$|x\rangle \otimes |y\rangle \to [\mathrm{C}_{\mathrm{NOT}}] \to |x\rangle \otimes |y \oplus x\rangle$$

or in operator form

$$C_{NOT}|x\rangle \otimes |y\rangle = |x\rangle \otimes |y \oplus x\rangle$$

where the first input qubit $|x\rangle$ and the second input qubit $|y\rangle$ are called control qubit and target qubit, respectively. Here, the corresponding quantum circuit has two inputs ($|x\rangle$ and $|y\rangle$) and two outputs ($|x\rangle$ and $|y \oplus x\rangle$). In matrix form, we have the permutation matrix

$$C_{NOT} = \begin{pmatrix} 1 & 0 & 0 & 0 \\ 0 & 1 & 0 & 0 \\ 0 & 0 & 0 & 1 \\ 0 & 0 & 1 & 0 \end{pmatrix}$$

Clearly, $(C_{NOT})^2 = I$. Note that

$$C_{NOT}|x\rangle \otimes |0\rangle = |x\rangle \otimes |x\rangle \tag{10}$$

where $x = 0$ or 1; however, this result does not mean that an arbitrary state $|\psi\rangle = a|0\rangle + b|1\rangle$ can be cloned by using the gate $[\mathrm{C_{NOT}}]$ since we generally have (see Section 2.6)

$$C_{NOT}|\psi\rangle \otimes |0\rangle \neq |\psi\rangle \otimes |\psi\rangle$$

to be compared with Equation (10). Note also that

$$|x\rangle \otimes |y\rangle \rightarrow [\mathrm{H} \otimes \mathrm{I}] \rightarrow [\mathrm{C_{NOT}}] \rightarrow |\beta_{xy}\rangle$$

or

$$|\beta_{xy}\rangle = C_{NOT}(H \otimes I)|x\rangle \otimes |y\rangle$$

that shows the interest of the gate $[\mathrm{C_{NOT}}]$ for producing Bell states (i.e., entangled states) from non entangled states. (By $[\mathrm{H} \otimes \mathrm{I}]$, we mean that the quantum gates [H] and [I] act on $|x\rangle$ and $|y\rangle$, respectively. Hence, $H \otimes I$ stands for the direct product of the matrices H and I.)

More generally, the quantum gate $[\mathrm{U_f}]$ is defined through

$$|x\rangle \otimes |y\rangle \rightarrow [\mathrm{U_f}] \rightarrow |x\rangle \otimes |y \oplus f(x)\rangle$$

or in an equivalent way

$$U_f|x\rangle \otimes |y\rangle = |x\rangle \otimes |y \oplus f(x)\rangle$$

where f stands for the function $f : \{0, 1\} \rightarrow \{0, 1\}$. Clearly, $(U_f)^2 = I$.

Another important two-qubit gate is the controlled phase gate $[\mathrm{CP}_\theta]$ such that

$$|x\rangle \otimes |y\rangle \rightarrow [\mathrm{CP}_\theta] \rightarrow |x\rangle \otimes \mathrm{e}^{\mathrm{i}xy\theta}|y\rangle$$

or

$$CP_\theta|x\rangle \otimes |y\rangle = |x\rangle \otimes \mathrm{e}^{\mathrm{i}xy\theta}|y\rangle$$

with

$$CP_\theta = \begin{pmatrix} 1 & 0 & 0 & 0 \\ 0 & 1 & 0 & 0 \\ 0 & 0 & 1 & 0 \\ 0 & 0 & 0 & \mathrm{e}^{\mathrm{i}\theta} \end{pmatrix}$$

Note that

$$[\mathrm{C_{NOT}}] = [\mathrm{I} \otimes \mathrm{H}] \rightarrow [\mathrm{CP}_{\frac{\pi}{2}}] \rightarrow [\mathrm{CP}_{\frac{\pi}{2}}] \rightarrow [\mathrm{I} \otimes \mathrm{H}]$$

so that the gate $[\mathrm{C_{NOT}}]$ can be obtained from the gates $[\mathrm{I} \otimes \mathrm{H}]$ and $[\mathrm{CP}_{\frac{\pi}{2}}]$.

There exist other two-qubit gates. Moreover, use is also made of n-qubit gates ($n > 2$). The advantage of the quantum gates over the classical logic gates is that all the quantum gates are reversible or invertible due to the unitary property of the matrices representing quantum gates; this is not always the case for classical logic gates.

The preceding examples are sufficient for illustrating how works the algorithm set up by Deutsch and Jozsa [1].

2.5.3. Quantum Computing Algorithms

The Deutsch-Jozsa algorithm addresses the following problem: to find with only one measurement if the function

$$f : \{0,1\}^{\otimes n} \to \{0,1\}$$

is constant or balanced (f is balanced means either $f(0) = 0$ and $f(1) = 1$ or $f(0) = 1$ and $f(1) = 0$; f is constant means $f(0) = f(1) = 0$ or 1). The classical algorithm requires $2^{n-1} + 1$ evaluations of f whereas only one measurement is necessary in order to get the answer. For $n = 1$, the proof based on the quantum circuit $[\mathrm{H} \otimes \mathrm{H}] \to [\mathrm{U_f}] \to [\mathrm{H} \otimes \mathrm{I}]$ of two-qubit gates is as follows. It is easy to show that

$$|0\rangle \otimes |1\rangle \to [\mathrm{H} \otimes \mathrm{H}] \to [\mathrm{U_f}] \to [\mathrm{H} \otimes \mathrm{I}] \to |x\rangle \otimes |y\rangle$$

alternatively

$$|x\rangle \otimes |y\rangle = (H \otimes I)U_f(H \otimes H)|0\rangle \otimes |1\rangle$$

where

$$\begin{aligned} |x\rangle \otimes |y\rangle &= \pm|0\rangle \otimes \frac{1}{\sqrt{2}}(|0\rangle - |1\rangle) \text{ if } f \text{ is constant} \\ |x\rangle \otimes |y\rangle &= \pm|1\rangle \otimes \frac{1}{\sqrt{2}}(|0\rangle - |1\rangle) \text{ if } f \text{ is balanced} \end{aligned}$$

Then, the result of a single measurement of the first output qubit can be

$$\begin{cases} |0\rangle \Rightarrow f \text{ is constant} \\ \text{or} \\ |1\rangle \Rightarrow f \text{ is balanced} \end{cases}$$

Therefore, a single measurement (instead of two in the classical case) is sufficient for getting the answer. The Deutsch-Jozsa algorithm is of little interest. However, it shows the superiority of the quantum approach on the classical one (namely, only one measurement instead of $2^{n-1} + 1$ evaluations in the general case where $f : \{0,1\}^{\otimes n} \to \{0,1\}$).

Let us briefly mention two other historical algorithms, viz, the Shor algorithm and the Grover algorithm [1]. The Shor algorithm concerns the search of the period of a periodic function and is used for the factorization of a composite integer into prime factors. It constitutes an alternative to the classical RSA code. The Grover algorithm makes it possible to find an item in an unstructured data basis consisting of n entries; the quantum speed up for this algorithm is $n \to \sqrt{n}$ ($\mathrm{O}(n)$ researches for the classical case and $\mathrm{O}(\sqrt{n})$ for the quantum case). The two preceding algorithms are based on the massive quantum parallelism. They formally show the superiority of a (still hypothetical) quantum computer on a classical one. The present evolution is towards quantum cryptography.

2.6. No-Cloning Theorem

We may ask the question: does there exist a unitary operator (or quantum gate) U such that

$$U|\psi\rangle \otimes |0\rangle = |\psi\rangle \otimes |\psi\rangle \tag{11}$$

where $|\psi\rangle = a|0\rangle + b|1\rangle$ is an arbitrary qubit. As a consequence of the linearity of quantum mechanics, the answer is no: it is not possible to clone an arbitrary qubit $|\psi\rangle$ [8]. This result can be proved in the following way. Suppose that there exists U such that Equation (11) is true. Then, by linearity

$$\begin{aligned} U|\psi\rangle \otimes |0\rangle &= U(a|0\rangle + b|1\rangle) \otimes |0\rangle \\ &= U(a|0\rangle \otimes |0\rangle + b|1\rangle \otimes |0\rangle) \\ &= aU|0\rangle \otimes |0\rangle + bU|1\rangle \otimes |0\rangle \\ &= a|0\rangle \otimes |0\rangle + b|1\rangle \otimes |1\rangle \end{aligned} \tag{12}$$

On another side, we have

$$\begin{aligned} U|\psi\rangle \otimes |0\rangle &= |\psi\rangle \otimes |\psi\rangle \\ &= (a|0\rangle + b|1\rangle) \otimes (a|0\rangle + b|1\rangle) \\ &= a^2|0\rangle \otimes |0\rangle + ab(|0\rangle \otimes |1\rangle + |1\rangle \otimes |0\rangle) + b^2|1\rangle \otimes |1\rangle \end{aligned} \tag{13}$$

Compatibility between Equations (12) and (13) yields

$$a^2 = a\ (\Rightarrow\ a = 0, 1), \quad b^2 = b\ (\Rightarrow\ b = 0, 1), \quad ab = 0\ (\Rightarrow\ a = 0 \text{ or } b = 0)$$

The sole solutions are ($a = 1,\ b = 0$) and ($a = 0,\ b = 1$) in agreement with Equation (10). There are no solution in the general case. This proves the no-cloning theorem (a theorem that does not have an analogue in classical information).

Another way to understand this result is to realize that in order to clone an arbitrary state $|\psi\rangle = a|0\rangle + b|1\rangle$ one must measure it so that one gets $|0\rangle$ or $|1\rangle$, two states that differ from $|\psi\rangle$ in general.

2.7. Quantum Teleportation

It is not possible to clone an arbitrary quantum state. However, it is feasible to teleporte it, i.e., to transfer it from one place to another without an effective transportation. In other words, without a material transportation of a qubit, it is possible to transmit at distance the information contained in the qubit. We shall not deal here with some physical device making teleportation possible. We shall rather limit ourselves to the corresponding quantum algorithm [15].

Suppose someone, Alice, wants to send a qubit $|\psi\rangle = a|0\rangle + b|1\rangle$ (for which she does not know a and b) to somebody, Bob, by a quantum circuit and the possibility of using a classical communication channel. The only requirement for Bob and Alice is to dispose of and EPR pair $|\beta_{00}\rangle$, the first qubit of which belongs to Alice and the second one to Bob. Thus, the entry $|\varphi_0\rangle$ of the quantum circuit is

$$\begin{aligned} |\varphi_0\rangle &= |\psi\rangle \otimes |\beta_{00}\rangle \\ &= (a|0\rangle_1 + b|1\rangle_1) \otimes \frac{1}{\sqrt{2}}(|0\rangle_2 \otimes |0\rangle_3 + |1\rangle_2 \otimes |1\rangle_3) \\ &= \frac{1}{\sqrt{2}}\left[a|0\rangle_1 \otimes (|0\rangle_2 \otimes |0\rangle_3 + |1\rangle_2 \otimes |1\rangle_3) + b|1\rangle_1 \otimes (|0\rangle_2 \otimes |0\rangle_3 + |1\rangle_2 \otimes |1\rangle_3)\right] \\ &= \frac{1}{\sqrt{2}}\left[a(|0\rangle_1 \otimes |0\rangle_2 \otimes |0\rangle_3 + |0\rangle_1 \otimes |1\rangle_2 \otimes |1\rangle_3) + b(|1\rangle_1 \otimes |0\rangle_2 \otimes |0\rangle_3 + |1\rangle_1 \otimes |1\rangle_2 \otimes |1\rangle_3)\right] \end{aligned}$$

where qubits 1 and 2 refer to the Alice qubit and qubit 3 to the Bob qubit. Then, Alice sends her qubits to a controlled-NOT gate producing the state

$$|\varphi_1\rangle = \frac{1}{\sqrt{2}}\left[a(|0\rangle_1 \otimes |0\rangle_2 \otimes |0\rangle_3 + |0\rangle_1 \otimes |1\rangle_2 \otimes |1\rangle_3) + b(|1\rangle_1 \otimes |1\rangle_2 \otimes |0\rangle_3 + |1\rangle_1 \otimes |0\rangle_2 \otimes |1\rangle_3)\right]$$
$$= \frac{1}{\sqrt{2}}\left[a|0\rangle_1 \otimes (|0\rangle_2 \otimes |0\rangle_3 + |1\rangle_2 \otimes |1\rangle_3) + b|1\rangle_1 \otimes (|1\rangle_2 \otimes |0\rangle_3 + |0\rangle_2 \otimes |1\rangle_3)\right]$$

Next, qubit 1 goes to an Hadamard gate giving

$$|\varphi_2\rangle = \frac{1}{2}\left[a(|0\rangle_1 + |1\rangle_1) \otimes (|0\rangle_2 \otimes |0\rangle_3 + |1\rangle_2 \otimes |1\rangle_3) + b(|0\rangle_1 - |1\rangle_1) \otimes (|1\rangle_2 \otimes |0\rangle_3 + |0\rangle_2 \otimes |1\rangle_3)\right]$$

which can be re-arranged as

$$|\varphi_2\rangle = \frac{1}{2}\left[(|0\rangle_1 \otimes |0\rangle_2) \otimes (a|0\rangle_3 + b|1\rangle_3) + (|0\rangle_1 \otimes |1\rangle_2) \otimes (a|1\rangle_3 + b|0\rangle_3)\right.$$
$$+ \left.(|1\rangle_1 \otimes |0\rangle_2) \otimes (a|0\rangle_3 - b|1\rangle_3) + (|1\rangle_1 \otimes |1\rangle_2) \otimes (a|1\rangle_3 - b|0\rangle_3)\right]$$

Measurement of qubits 1 and 2 by Alice can give

$$|0\rangle_1 \otimes |0\rangle_2 \text{ with the probability } \tfrac{1}{4}, \quad |0\rangle_1 \otimes |1\rangle_2 \text{ with the probability } \tfrac{1}{4}$$
$$|1\rangle_1 \otimes |0\rangle_2 \text{ with the probability } \tfrac{1}{4}, \quad |1\rangle_1 \otimes |1\rangle_2 \text{ with the probability } \tfrac{1}{4}$$

Suppose Alice gets $|0\rangle_1 \otimes |0\rangle_2$. Then, she communicates this result to Bob by a classical channel (telephone or mail). Thus, Bob knows that $|\psi\rangle$ is $a|0\rangle_3 + b|1\rangle_3$. Should Alice have got $|0\rangle_1 \otimes |1\rangle_2$ or $|1\rangle_1 \otimes |0\rangle_2$ or $|1\rangle_1 \otimes |1\rangle_2$, then Bob would obtain $a|0\rangle_3 + b|1\rangle_3$ after the use of the gates [X] or [Z] or [T] with $T = ZX$ on the states $a|1\rangle_3 + b|0\rangle_3$ or $a|0\rangle_3 - b|1\rangle_3$ or $a|1\rangle_3 - b|0\rangle_3$, respectively. In all cases, the qubit $|\psi\rangle = a|0\rangle + b|1\rangle$ has been teleported. This proof shows that entanglement (via the EPR pair) plays a crucial role in teleportation.

3. Some Mathematical Aspects: Mutually Unbiased Bases

3.1. Introducing MUBs

3.1.1. Generalities about MUBs

Unitary operator bases in the Hilbert space $\mathbb{C}^d$ are of pivotal importance for quantum information and quantum computing as well as for quantum mechanics in general. The interest for unitary operator bases started with the seminal work by Schwinger [5]. In this connection, MUBs play a key role in quantum information and quantum computing. Two distinct orthonormal bases of $\mathbb{C}^d$ are said to be unbiased if and only if the modulus of the inner product of any vector of one basis with any vector of the other one is equal to $\frac{1}{\sqrt{d}}$ (see the detailed definition in Section 3.1.2).

MUBs proved to be useful in classical information theory (network communication protocols) [17,47]. They play an important role in quantum mechanics as for the discrete Wigner function [11,29,34,42,43,55,62], for the solution of the Mean King problem [20,26,33,34,43], for the understanding of the Feynman path integral formalism [57,63] and potentially for studies of the Weyl-Heisenberg group in connection with quantum optics. MUBs are of central importance in quantum information theory as for instance in quantum state tomography (deciphering an unknown quantum state) [38,56,77], quantum cryptography (secure quantum key exchange) [9,25] and quantum teleportation [15]. Along this line, measurements corresponding to MUBs are appropriate for an optimal determination of the density matrix of a quantum system and the use of MUBs ensure the maximum of security for quantum communication (especially in the BB84 quantum cryptography protocol). Let us also mention that MUBs are connected with the notion of maximal entanglement of quantum states a result of great importance for quantum computing.

Here, it is not our purpose to give some details about all the applications listed above. The interested reader may consult the quoted original references for a full description of each application. It is enough to say that a central common point to all the applications is given by Equation (15) that reflects the uniform probability nature of the results of measurements using MUBs. This is especially obvious in the BB84 protocol where the probability of detection of Eve (a spy) on a quantum communication channel between Alice and Bob is maximum when Alice and Bob use MUBs.

There exist numerous ways of constructing sets of MUBs (e.g., see [58,64,65]). Most of them are based on discrete Fourier transform over Galois fields and Galois rings [2,14,17,28–30,36,41,72], discrete Wigner distribution [11,29,34,42,55], generalized Pauli spin matrices [22,23,27,30], mutually orthogonal Latin squares [33,35], graph theory [74], finite and projective geometries [49,61], convex polytopes [40], complex projective 2-designs [19,39,67], quantum angular momentum theory [44], group theoretical methods [24,45,50,53], discrete phase states [68] and Hadamard matrices [73]. In this section, from quantum theory of angular momentum theory (or, in mathematical terms, from the Lie algebra A_1 of the group SU(2) or SU$(2,\mathbb{C})$ or SL$(2,\mathbb{C})$) we shall derive a formula for a complete set of MUBs in dimension p with p prime. Moreover, we shall construct complete sets of MUBs in dimension p^m with p prime and m positive integer from the additive characters of the Galois field $\mathbb{GF}(p^m)$ for p odd and of the Galois ring $\mathbb{GR}(2^2, m)$ for $p = 2$.

3.1.2. Definition of MUBs

Definition 1. *Let B_a and B_b two distinct orthonormal bases*

$$B_a = \{|a\alpha\rangle \ : \ \alpha = 0, 1, \cdots, d-1\}, \quad B_b = \{|b\beta\rangle \ : \ \beta = 0, 1, \cdots, d-1\}$$

of the Hilbert space $\mathbb{C}^d$. The bases B_a and B_b $(a \neq b)$ are said to be unbiased if and only if

$$\forall \alpha \in \mathbb{Z}_d, \ \forall \beta \in \mathbb{Z}_d : |\langle a\alpha | b\beta \rangle| = \frac{1}{\sqrt{d}} \tag{14}$$

where $\langle \, | \, \rangle$ denotes the inner product of $\mathbb{C}^d$ [5,6,10,11]. In other words, the inner product $\langle a\alpha | b\beta \rangle$ has a modulus independent of α and β. The relation

$$|\langle a\alpha | b\beta \rangle| = \delta_{a,b}\delta_{\alpha,\beta} + \frac{1}{\sqrt{d}}(1 - \delta_{a,b})$$

makes it possible to describe both the cases $B_a = B_b$ and $B_a \neq B_b$.

As a typical example, the bases B_0, B_1 and B_2 of $\mathbb{C}^2$, see Equation (5), constitute a set of three MUBS whose basis vectors are specific qubits.

3.1.3. Well-Known Results about MUBs

The main results concerning MUBs are [6,14,19,35,37]:

1. MUBs are stable under unitary or anti-unitary transformations. More precisely, if two unbiased bases undergo the same unitary or anti-unitary transformation, they remain mutually unbiased.
2. The number $N(d)$ of MUBs in $\mathbb{C}^d$ cannot exceed $d + 1$. Thus

$$N(d) \leq d + 1$$

3. The maximum number $d + 1$ of MUBs is attained when d is a power p^m $(m \geq 1)$ of a prime number p. Thus

$$N(p^m) = p^m + 1$$

4. When d is a composite number, $N(d)$ is not known but it can be shown that

$$3 \leq N(d) \leq d+1$$

As a more accurate result, for $d = \prod_i p_i^{m_i}$ with p_i prime and m_i positive integer, we have

$$\min(p_i^{m_i}) + 1 \leq N(d) \leq d+1$$

By way of illustration, let us mention the following cases.

- In the particular composite case $d = 6 = 2 \times 3$, we have

$$3 \leq N(6) \leq 7$$

and it was conjectured that $N(6) = 3$. Indeed, in spite of an enormous amount of computational works, no more than three MUBs were found for $d = 6$.
- For $d = 15 = 3 \times 5$ and $d = 21 = 3 \times 7$, there are at least four MUBs.
- For $d = 676 = 2^2 \times 13^2$, we have

$$2^2 + 1 = 5 \leq N(676) \leq 677$$

but it is known how to construct at least six MUBs.

A set of $d+1$ MUBs in $\mathbb{C}^d$ is referred to as a complete set. Such sets exist for $d = p^m$ (p prime, m positive integer) and this result opens the way to establish a link between MUBs and Galois fields and/or Galois rings.

For d composite (different from a power of a prime), the question to know if there exist complete sets in dimension d, i.e., to know if $N(d)$ can be equal to $d+1$, is still an open problem (in 2018). Indeed, for d different from a power of a prime, it was conjectured (SPR conjecture [32]) that the problem of the existence of a set of $d+1$ MUBs in $\mathbb{C}^d$ is equivalent to the problem of whether there exist a projective plane of order d. As another conjecture for d composite (different from a power of a prime), the problem of the existence of a set of $d+1$ MUBs in $\mathbb{C}^d$ is equivalent to the one of the existence of a decomposition of the Lie algebra of SU(d) into $d+1$ Cartan subalgebras of dimension $d-1$.

3.1.4. Interests of MUBs

MUBs are or relevance in advanced quantum mechanics. From a very general point of view, MUBs are closely connected to the principle of complementarity introduced by Bohr in the early days of quantum mechanics. This principle, quite familiar in terms of observables like position and momentum, tells that for two non-commuting observables, if we have a complete knowledge of one observable, then we have a total uncertainty of the other. Equation (14) indicates that the development in the basis B_a of any vector of the basis B_b is such that each vector of B_a appears in the development with the probability $\frac{1}{d}$. This is especially interesting when translated in terms of measurements, the bases B_a and B_b corresponding to the (non-degenerate) eigenvectors of two non-commuting observables.

A significance of MUBs in terms of quantum measurements can be seen as follows. Let A and B be two non-degenerate (i.e., with multiplicity-free eigenvalues) self-adjoint (or hermitian) operators associated with two observables $\mathcal{A}$ and $\mathcal{B}$ of a quantum system with the Hilbert space $\mathbb{C}^d$ of dimension d. Suppose that the eigenvectors of A and B yield two unbiased bases B_a and B_b, respectively. When the quantum system is prepared in an eigenvector $|b\beta\rangle$ of the observable B, no information can be obtained from a measurement of the observable A. This result follows from the development in the basis B_a of any vector of the basis B_b

$$|b\beta\rangle = \sum_{\alpha=0}^{d-1} |a\alpha\rangle\langle a\alpha|b\beta\rangle$$

which shows that the d probabilities

$$|\langle a\alpha|b\beta\rangle|^2 = \frac{1}{d}, \quad \alpha, \beta = 0, 1, \cdots, d-1 \tag{15}$$

of obtaining any state vector $|a\alpha\rangle$ in a measurement of A are equal.

Indeed, the two operators A and B do not commute. The two corresponding observables $\mathcal{A}$ and $\mathcal{B}$ are said to be complementary (Bohr's principle of complementarity introduced in the early days of quantum mechanics): a precise knowledge of one of them implies a total uncertainty of the other (or, all possible results of measurements of the other one are equally probable). This can be made more explicit through the generalized Heisenberg uncertainty principle. Let A and B be two hermitian operators associated with two observables and $|\psi\rangle$ a vector of $\mathbb{C}^d$. The generalized Heisenberg uncertainty principle can be expressed as

$$\Delta A \Delta B \geq \frac{1}{2}|\langle\psi|[A, B]_-|\psi\rangle|$$

where $[A, B]_- = AB - BA$ and ΔO stands for the standard deviation

$$\Delta O = \sqrt{\langle\psi|O^2|\psi\rangle - \langle\psi|O|\psi\rangle^2}$$

of the operator $O = A$ or B. (The most familiar example is for d infinite. The position $A = x$ and the momentum $B = p_x$, along the x direction, of a particle are complementary observables. They satisfy the commutation relations $[x, p_x]_- = i\hbar$, where $\hbar$ is the Planck constant. Hence, $\Delta x \Delta p_x \geq \frac{1}{2}\hbar$ so that more precise is Δx more imprecise is Δp_x and *vice versa*.) Therefore, if A and B correspond to observables generating MUBs, then a precise knowledge of A yields a complete indeterminacy of B and *vice versa*.

Note that

$$d + 1 = \frac{d^2 - 1}{d - 1}$$

is the number of different measurements to fully determine a quantum state for a quantum system in dimension d. (This follows from the fact that a $d \times d$ density matrix, that is to say an Hermitian matrix with a trace equal to 1, contains $d^2 - 1$ real parameters and each measurement gives $d - 1$ real parameters.) Note also that $d^2 - 1$ and $d - 1$ are the number of generators and the rank of the special unitary group SU(d) in d dimensions, respectively, and that for $d = p$ (prime number) their ratio $p + 1$ is the number of disjoint sets of $p - 1$ commuting generators of SU(p).

The rest of the paper is structured in the following way. In Section 3.2, we give a complete solution, based on a nonstandard approach to the Lie algebra of the group SU(2) (equivalently, to the quantum theory of angular momentum), for the construction of MUBs in the case where $d = p$ is a prime number. Further developments are discussed in Section 3.3 in relation with Weyl pairs. Sections 3.4 and 3.5 are concerned with the construction of MUBs from Galois fields (for $d = p^m$, a power of an odd prime number) and Galois rings (for $d = 2^m$, a power of the even prime number), respectively. (See Refs. [31,46,48] for the formalism of Galois quantum systems.)

3.2. Group-Theoretical Construction of MUBs

3.2.1. Standard Basis for SU(2)

Equation (7) shows that the vectors $|n\rangle$ (with $n = 0, 1, \cdots, d-1$) of the computational basis (6) can be viewed as the basis vectors $|j, m\rangle$ (with $m = j, j-1, \cdots, -j$) for the irreducible representation (j) of SU(2) in the chain SU(2) $\supset$ U(1). In the language of group theory (and quantum angular momentum theory), the vector $|j, m\rangle$ is a common eigenvector of the Casimir operator J^2 (the square of an angular momentum) and of a Cartan generator J_z (the z component of the angular momentum) of the Lie algebra A_1 of the group $\mathrm{SU}(2)$. More precisely, we have the eigenvalue equations

$$J^2|j,m\rangle = j(j+1)|j,m\rangle, \quad J_z|j,m\rangle = m|j,m\rangle$$

with the orthonormality relations

$$\langle j,m|j,m'\rangle = \delta_{m,m'}, \quad m,m' = j, j-1, \cdots, -j$$

In other words, the computational basis B_d can be visualized as the basis

$$B_{2j+1} = \{|j,m\rangle \ : \ m = j, j-1, \cdots, -j\}$$

known as the standard basis for the irreducible representation (j) of $\mathrm{SU}(2)$ or the angular momentum basis corresponding to the angular momentum quantum number j, referred to as spin angular momentum for $j = \frac{1}{2}$.

3.2.2. Nonstandard Bases for SU(2)

As far as the representation theory of $\mathrm{SU}(2)$ is concerned, we can replace the complete set $\{J^2, J_z\}$ by another complete set of two commuting operators. For instance, we may consider the set $\{J^2, v_a\}$, where the unitary operator v_a is defined by

$$v_a|j,m\rangle = \begin{cases} |j,-j\rangle & \text{if} \quad m = j \\ \omega^{(j-m)a}|j,m+1\rangle & \text{if} \quad m = j-1, j-2, \cdots, -j \end{cases}$$

where

$$\omega = \mathrm{e}^{\mathrm{i}\frac{2\pi}{2j+1}}$$

is a primitive $(2j+1)$-th root of unity and a is a fixed parameter in the ring $\mathbb{Z}_{2j+1}$. The operator v_a takes its origin in a polar decomposition of the two generators $E_\pm = J_\pm$ of the group $\mathrm{SU}(2)$. For fixed a, the common eigenvectors of J^2 and v_a provide an alternative basis to that given by the common eigenstates of J^2 and J_z. This can be made precise by the following result.

Proposition 1. *For fixed j and a (with $2j \in \mathbb{N}^*$ and $a \in \mathbb{Z}_{2j+1}$), the $2j+1$ common eigenvectors of J^2 and v_a can be taken in the form*

$$|j\alpha;a\rangle = \frac{1}{\sqrt{2j+1}} \sum_{m=-j}^{j} \omega^{\frac{1}{2}(j+m)(j-m+1)a+(j+m)\alpha}|j,m\rangle$$

with $\alpha = 0, 1, \cdots, 2j$. The corresponding eigenvalues of v_a are given by

$$v_a|j\alpha;a\rangle = \omega^{ja-\alpha}|j\alpha;a\rangle$$

Then, the spectrum of v_a is non-degenerate.

The inner product

$$\langle j\alpha;a|j\beta;a\rangle = \delta_{\alpha,\beta}, \quad \alpha,\beta = 0, 1, \cdots, 2j$$

shows that for fixed j and a

$$B_a = \{|j\alpha; a\rangle \ : \ \alpha = 0, 1, \cdots, 2j\}$$

is an orthonormal set which provides a nonstandard basis for the irreducible representation (j) of $\mathrm{SU}(2)$. For fixed j, there exists $2j+1$ orthonormal bases B_a since a can take $2j+1$ distinct values $(a = 0, 1, \cdots, 2j)$.

3.2.3. Bases in Quantum Information

We now go back to quantum information. By introducing

$$|a\alpha\rangle = |j\alpha; a\rangle$$

together with the change of notations (7), the eigenvectors of v_a can be written as

$$|a\alpha\rangle = \frac{1}{\sqrt{d}} \sum_{n \in \mathbb{Z}_d} \omega^{\frac{1}{2}(n+1)(d-n-1)a-(n+1)\alpha} |n\rangle$$

where $\omega = \mathrm{e}^{\mathrm{i}\frac{2\pi}{d}}$. The vector $|a\alpha\rangle$ satisfies the eigenvalue equation

$$v_a |a\alpha\rangle = \omega^{\frac{1}{2}(d-1)a-\alpha} |a\alpha\rangle$$

For fixed d and a, each eigenvector $|a\alpha\rangle$ is a linear combination of the qudits $|0\rangle, |1\rangle, \cdots, |d-1\rangle$ and the basis

$$B_a = \{|a\alpha\rangle \ : \ \alpha = 0, 1, \cdots, d-1\}$$

is an alternative to the computational basis B_d. For fixed d, we therefore have $d+1$ remarkable bases of the d-dimensional space $\mathbb{C}^d$, namely, B_d and B_a for $a = 0, 1, \cdots, d-1$.

The operator v_a can be represented by a d-dimensional unitary matrix V_a. The matrix V_a, built on the basis B_d with the ordering $0, 1, \cdots, d-1$ for the lines and columns, reads

$$V_a = \begin{pmatrix} 0 & \omega^a & 0 & \cdots & 0 \\ 0 & 0 & \omega^{2a} & \cdots & 0 \\ \vdots & \vdots & \vdots & \cdots & \vdots \\ 0 & 0 & 0 & \cdots & \omega^{(d-1)a} \\ 1 & 0 & 0 & \cdots & 0 \end{pmatrix}$$

The eigenvectors of V_a are

$$\phi(a\alpha) = \frac{1}{\sqrt{d}} \sum_{n \in \mathbb{Z}_d} \omega^{\frac{1}{2}(n+1)(d-n-1)a-(n+1)\alpha} \phi_n$$

with $\alpha = 0, 1, \cdots, d-1$, where ϕ_n with $n = 0, 1, \cdots, d-1$ are the column vectors

$$\phi_0 = \begin{pmatrix} 1 \\ 0 \\ \vdots \\ 0 \end{pmatrix}, \quad \phi_1 = \begin{pmatrix} 0 \\ 1 \\ \vdots \\ 0 \end{pmatrix}, \quad \cdots, \quad \phi_{d-1} = \begin{pmatrix} 0 \\ 0 \\ \vdots \\ 1 \end{pmatrix}$$

representing the qudits $|0\rangle, |1\rangle, \cdots, |d-1\rangle$, respectively. The vectors $\phi(a\alpha)$ satisfy the eigenvalue equation

$$V_a \phi(a\alpha) = \omega^{\frac{1}{2}(d-1)a-\alpha} \phi(a\alpha)$$

with the orthonormality relation

$$\phi(a\alpha)^{\dagger} \phi(a\beta) = \delta_{\alpha,\beta}$$

for $\alpha, \beta = 0, 1, \cdots, d-1$.

The matrix V_a can be diagonalized by means of the d-dimensional matrix H_a of elements

$$(H_a)_{n\alpha} = \frac{1}{\sqrt{d}} \omega^{\frac{1}{2}(n+1)(d-n-1)a-(n+1)\alpha}$$

with the lines and columns of H_a arranged from left to right and from top to bottom in the order $n, \alpha = 0, 1, \cdots, d-1$. Indeed, by introducing the $d \times d$ permutation matrix

$$P = \begin{pmatrix} 1 & 0 & 0 & \cdots & 0 & 0 \\ 0 & 0 & 0 & \cdots & 0 & 1 \\ 0 & 0 & 0 & \cdots & 1 & 0 \\ \vdots & \vdots & \vdots & \cdots & \vdots & \vdots \\ 0 & 0 & 1 & \cdots & 0 & 0 \\ 0 & 1 & 0 & \cdots & 0 & 0 \end{pmatrix}$$

we can check that

$$(H_a P)^{\dagger} V_a (H_a P) = \omega^{\frac{1}{2}(d-1)a} \begin{pmatrix} \omega^0 & 0 & \cdots & 0 \\ 0 & \omega^1 & \cdots & 0 \\ \vdots & \vdots & \cdots & \vdots \\ 0 & 0 & \cdots & \omega^{d-1} \end{pmatrix}$$

from which we recover the eigenvalues of V_a. Note that the complex matrix H_a is a unitary matrix for which each entry has a modulus equal to $\frac{1}{\sqrt{d}}$. Thus, H_a is a generalized Hadamard matrix. This establishes a connection between MUBs and Hadamard matrices [35,51,52,60,64,66,73].

3.2.4. MUBs for $d = p$ (p Prime)

Going back to the case where d is arbitrary, we now examine an important property for the couple (B_a, B_d) and its generalization to couples (B_a, B_b) with $b \neq a$ $(a, b = 0, 1, \cdots, d-1)$. For fixed d and a, we verify that

$$|\langle n|a\alpha\rangle| = \frac{1}{\sqrt{d}}, \quad n, \alpha = 0, 1, \cdots, d-1$$

which shows that B_a and B_d are two unbiased bases of the Hilbert space $\mathbb{C}^d$.

Other examples of unbiased bases can be obtained for $d = 2$ and 3. We easily check that the bases B_0 and B_1 for $d = 2$ are unbiased. Similarly, the bases B_0, B_1 and B_2 for $d = 3$ are mutually unbiased. Therefore, by taking into account the computational basis B_d, we end up with $d + 1 = 3$ MUBs for $d = 2$ and $d + 1 = 4$ MUBs for $d = 3$. This is in agreement with the general result according to which, in dimension d, the maximum number $d + 1$ of MUBs is attained when d is a prime number or a power of a prime number. The results for $d = 2$ and 3 can be generalized through the following proposition.

Proposition 2. *For $d = p$, p a prime number, the bases $B_0, B_1, \cdots, B_p$ form a complete set of $p+1$ MUBs. The p^2 vectors $|a\alpha\rangle$, with $a, \alpha = 0, 1, \cdots, p-1$, of the bases $B_0, B_1, \cdots, B_{p-1}$ are given by a single formula, namely*

$$|a\alpha\rangle = \frac{1}{\sqrt{p}} \sum_{n \in \mathbb{F}_p} \omega^{\frac{1}{2}(n+1)(p-n-1)a-(n+1)\alpha} |n\rangle, \quad \omega = e^{i\frac{2\pi}{p}} \tag{16}$$

that gives the p basis vectors for each basis B_a. In matrix form, $|a\alpha\rangle$ and $|n\rangle$ are replaced by $\phi(a\alpha)$ and ϕ_n, respectively.

Proof. First, the computational basis B_p is clearly unbiased to any of the p bases $B_0, B_1, \cdots, B_{p-1}$. Second, let us consider

$$\langle a\alpha|b\beta\rangle = \frac{1}{p} \sum_{k=0}^{p-1} e^{i\frac{\pi}{p}\{(a-b)k^2+[(b-a)p+2(\beta-\alpha)]k\}}$$

for $b \neq a$. The inner product $\langle a\alpha|b\beta\rangle$ can be rewritten by making use of the generalized quadratic Gauss sum [18]

$$S(u, v, w) = \sum_{k=0}^{|w|-1} e^{i\frac{\pi}{w}(uk^2+vk)}$$

where u, v and w are integers such that u and w are co-prime, uw is non-vanishing and $uw + v$ is even. This leads to

$$\langle a\alpha|b\beta\rangle = \frac{1}{p} S(u, v, w), \quad u = a - b, \quad v = -(a-b)p - 2(\alpha - \beta), \quad w = p$$

It can be shown that $|S(u, v, w)| = \sqrt{p}$. Consequently

$$|\langle a\alpha|b\beta\rangle| = \frac{1}{\sqrt{p}}$$

for $b \neq a$ and $\alpha, \beta = 0, 1, \cdots, p-1$. This completes the proof. □

In many of the papers dealing with the construction of MUBs for $d = p$ a prime number or $d = p^m$ a power of a prime number, the explicit derivation of the bases requires the diagonalization of a set of matrices. Equation (16) arises from the diagonalization of a single matrix. It allows to derive in one step the $p(p+1)$ vectors (or qupits, i.e., qudits with $d = p$) of a complete set of $p+1$ MUBs in $\mathbb{C}^p$ via a single formula easily encodable on a classical computer.

Note that, for d arbitrary, the inner product $\langle a\alpha|b\beta\rangle$ can be rewritten as

$$\langle a\alpha|b\beta\rangle = \left(H_a{}^\dagger H_b\right)_{\alpha\beta}$$

in terms of the generalized Hadamard matrices H_a and H_b. In the case where $d = p$ is a prime number, we find that

$$\left|\left(H_a{}^\dagger H_b\right)_{\alpha\beta}\right| = |\langle a\alpha|b\beta\rangle| = \frac{1}{\sqrt{p}}$$

Therefore, the product $H_a{}^\dagger H_b$ is another generalized Hadamard matrix [64].

Finally note that the passage, given by Equation (16), from the computational basis $B_p = \{|n\rangle : n = 0, 1, \cdots, p-1\}$ to the the basis $B_0 = \{|0\alpha\rangle : \alpha = 0, 1, \cdots, p-1\}$ corresponds to a discrete Fourier transform. Similarly, the passage from the basis B_p to the the basis $B_a = \{|a\alpha\rangle : \alpha = 0, 1, \cdots, p-1\}$ with $a = 1, 2, \cdots, p-1$ corresponds to a *quadratic discrete Fourier transform*.

Example 3. $d = 2$. *In this case, relevant for a spin* $j = \frac{1}{2}$ *or for a qubit, we have* $\omega = e^{i\pi}$ *and* $a, \alpha \in \mathbb{F}_2$. *The matrices of the operators* v_a *are*

$$V_0 = \begin{pmatrix} 0 & 1 \\ 1 & 0 \end{pmatrix} = \sigma_1, \quad V_1 = \begin{pmatrix} 0 & -1 \\ 1 & 0 \end{pmatrix} = -i\sigma_2$$

The $d + 1 = 3$ *MUBs* B_0, B_1 *and* B_2 *are the following:*

$$\begin{aligned}
B_0: &\quad |00\rangle = \frac{|0\rangle + |1\rangle}{\sqrt{2}} = \frac{1}{\sqrt{2}}\begin{pmatrix} 1 \\ 1 \end{pmatrix}, \quad |01\rangle = -\frac{|0\rangle - |1\rangle}{\sqrt{2}} = -\frac{1}{\sqrt{2}}\begin{pmatrix} 1 \\ -1 \end{pmatrix} \\
B_1: &\quad |10\rangle = i\frac{|0\rangle - i|1\rangle}{\sqrt{2}} = \frac{i}{\sqrt{2}}\begin{pmatrix} 1 \\ -i \end{pmatrix}, \quad |11\rangle = -i\frac{|0\rangle + i|1\rangle}{\sqrt{2}} = -\frac{i}{\sqrt{2}}\begin{pmatrix} 1 \\ i \end{pmatrix} \\
B_2: &\quad |0\rangle = \begin{pmatrix} 1 \\ 0 \end{pmatrix}, \quad |1\rangle = \begin{pmatrix} 0 \\ 1 \end{pmatrix}
\end{aligned}$$

to be compared with Equation (5).

Example 4. $d = 3$. *This case corresponds to an angular momentum* $j = 1$ *or to a qutrit. Here, we have* $\omega = e^{i\frac{2\pi}{3}}$ *and* $a, \alpha \in \mathbb{F}_3$. *The matrices of the operators* v_a *are*

$$V_0 = \begin{pmatrix} 0 & 1 & 0 \\ 0 & 0 & 1 \\ 1 & 0 & 0 \end{pmatrix}, \quad V_1 = \begin{pmatrix} 0 & \omega & 0 \\ 0 & 0 & \omega^2 \\ 1 & 0 & 0 \end{pmatrix}, \quad V_2 = \begin{pmatrix} 0 & \omega^2 & 0 \\ 0 & 0 & \omega \\ 1 & 0 & 0 \end{pmatrix}$$

The $d + 1 = 4$ *MUBs* B_0, B_1, B_2 *and* B_3 *are the following:*

$$\begin{aligned}
B_0: &\quad |00\rangle = \frac{|0\rangle + |1\rangle + |2\rangle}{\sqrt{3}}, \quad |01\rangle = \frac{\omega^2|0\rangle + \omega|1\rangle + |2\rangle}{\sqrt{3}}, \quad |02\rangle = \frac{\omega|0\rangle + \omega^2|1\rangle + |2\rangle}{\sqrt{3}} \\
B_1: &\quad |10\rangle = \frac{\omega|0\rangle + \omega|1\rangle + |2\rangle}{\sqrt{3}}, \quad |11\rangle = \frac{|0\rangle + \omega^2|1\rangle + |2\rangle}{\sqrt{3}}, \quad |12\rangle = \frac{\omega^2|0\rangle + |1\rangle + |2\rangle}{\sqrt{3}} \\
B_2: &\quad |20\rangle = \frac{\omega^2|0\rangle + \omega^2|1\rangle + |2\rangle}{\sqrt{3}}, \quad |21\rangle = \frac{\omega|0\rangle + |1\rangle + |2\rangle}{\sqrt{3}}, \quad |22\rangle = \frac{|0\rangle + \omega|1\rangle + |2\rangle}{\sqrt{3}} \\
B_3: &\quad |0\rangle, \quad |1\rangle, \quad |2\rangle
\end{aligned}$$

This can be transcribed in terms of column vectors as follows:

$$\begin{aligned}
B_0: &\quad |00\rangle = \frac{1}{\sqrt{3}}\begin{pmatrix} 1 \\ 1 \\ 1 \end{pmatrix}, \ |01\rangle = \frac{1}{\sqrt{3}}\begin{pmatrix} \omega^2 \\ \omega \\ 1 \end{pmatrix}, \ |02\rangle = \frac{1}{\sqrt{3}}\begin{pmatrix} \omega \\ \omega^2 \\ 1 \end{pmatrix} \\
B_1: &\quad |10\rangle = \frac{1}{\sqrt{3}}\begin{pmatrix} \omega \\ \omega \\ 1 \end{pmatrix}, \ |11\rangle = \frac{1}{\sqrt{3}}\begin{pmatrix} 1 \\ \omega^2 \\ 1 \end{pmatrix}, \ |12\rangle = \frac{1}{\sqrt{3}}\begin{pmatrix} \omega^2 \\ 1 \\ 1 \end{pmatrix} \\
B_2: &\quad |20\rangle = \frac{1}{\sqrt{3}}\begin{pmatrix} \omega^2 \\ \omega^2 \\ 1 \end{pmatrix}, \ |21\rangle = \frac{1}{\sqrt{3}}\begin{pmatrix} \omega \\ 1 \\ 1 \end{pmatrix}, \ |22\rangle = \frac{1}{\sqrt{3}}\begin{pmatrix} 1 \\ \omega \\ 1 \end{pmatrix} \\
B_3: &\quad |0\rangle = \begin{pmatrix} 1 \\ 0 \\ 0 \end{pmatrix}, \quad |1\rangle = \begin{pmatrix} 0 \\ 1 \\ 0 \end{pmatrix}, \quad |2\rangle = \begin{pmatrix} 0 \\ 0 \\ 1 \end{pmatrix}
\end{aligned}$$

To close this section, note that it is not necessary to treat separately the cases p odd and p even: Equation (16) for $|a\alpha\rangle$ is valid both for p even prime ($p = 2$) and for p odd prime. In the case where p is odd, there exists a useful alternative formula to Equation (16) as shown in the next section.

3.2.5. MUBs for $d = p$ (p Odd Prime)

In the special case where $d = p$ is an odd prime number, the formula

$$|a\alpha\rangle' = \frac{1}{\sqrt{p}} \sum_{n \in \mathbb{F}_p} \omega^{(an+\alpha)n} |n\rangle, \quad \omega = e^{i\frac{2\pi}{p}} \tag{17}$$

provides an alternative to Equation (16). Indeed, it can be shown that

$$B_a{}' = \{|a\alpha\rangle' \ : \ \alpha = 0, 1, \cdots, p-1\}$$

where a can take any of the values $0, 1, \cdots, p-1$ constitutes an orthonormal basis of $\mathbb{C}^d$ and that the p bases $B_a{}'$ ($a = 0, 1, \cdots, p-1$) form, with the computational basis B_p, a complete set of $p+1$ MUBs. The proof, based on the properties of Gauss sums, is analogous to that given in Section 3.2.4.

It is to be emphasized that for p even prime ($p = 2$) the bases $B_0{}'$, $B_1{}'$ and B_2 do not form a complete set of MUBs while the proposition given in Section 3.2.4 is valid for p odd prime and equally well for p even prime. The interest of Equation (17) is that it can be easily extended in the case where $\mathbb{F}_p$ is replaced by the Galois field $\mathbb{GF}(p^m)$ with $m > 1$.

3.2.6. MUBs for d Power of a Prime

We may ask what becomes the proposition in Section 3.2.4 when the prime number p is replaced by an arbitrary (not prime) number d. In this case, Equation (16), with p replaced by d, does not provide a complete set of $d+1$ MUBs. However, it is easy to verify that the bases B_0, B_1 and B_d are three MUBs in $\mathbb{C}^d$, in agreement with the well-known result according to which the number of MUBs in $\mathbb{C}^d$, with d arbitrary, is greater than or equal to 3.

Equation (16) for $\mathbb{C}^p$ can be used for deriving a complete set of $p^m + 1$ MUBs in $\mathbb{C}^{p^m}$ (p prime and $m \geq 2$) by tensor products of order m of vectors in $\mathbb{C}^p$. The general case is very much involved. Hence, we shall limit ourselves to the case $d = 2^2$.

The case $d = 4$ corresponds to the spin angular momentum $j = \frac{3}{2}$. The four bases B_a for $a = 0, 1, 2, 3$ consisting of the vectors $|a\alpha\rangle$ calculated for $d = 4$ from Section 3.2.3 and the computational basis B_4 do not constitute a complete set of $d+1 = 5$ MUBs. Nevertheless, it is possible to find $d+1 = 5$ MUBs because $d = 2^2$ is the power of a prime number. Indeed, another way to deal with the search for MUBs in $\mathbb{C}^4$ is to consider two systems of qubits associated with the spin angular momenta $j_1 = \frac{1}{2} \Leftrightarrow d_1 = p = 2$ and $j_2 = \frac{1}{2} \Leftrightarrow d_2 = p = 2$. Then, bases of $\mathbb{C}^4$ can be constructed from tensor products $|a\alpha\rangle \otimes |b\beta\rangle$ which are eigenvectors of the operator $v_a \otimes v_b$, where v_a corresponds to the first system of qubits and v_b to the second one. Obviously, the set

$$B_{ab} = \{|a\alpha\rangle \otimes |b\beta\rangle \ : \ \alpha, \beta = 0, 1\}$$

is an orthonormal basis of $\mathbb{C}^4$. Four of the five MUBs for $d = 2^2 = 4$ can be constructed from the various bases B_{ab}. It is evident that B_{00} and B_{11} are two unbiased bases since the modulus of the inner product of $|1\alpha'\rangle \otimes |1\beta'\rangle$ by $|0\alpha\rangle \otimes |0\beta\rangle$ is

$$|\langle 0\alpha|1\alpha'\rangle\langle 0\beta|1\beta'\rangle| = \frac{1}{\sqrt{4}} = \frac{1}{\sqrt{d}}$$

A similar result holds for the two bases B_{01} and B_{10}. However, the four bases B_{00}, B_{11}, B_{01} and B_{10} are not mutually unbiased. A possible way to overcome this no-go result is to keep the bases B_{00}

and B_{11} intact and to re-organize the vectors inside the bases B_{01} and B_{10} in order to obtain four MUBs. We are thus left with the four bases

$$W_{00} \equiv B_{00}, \quad W_{11} \equiv B_{11}, \quad W_{01}, \quad W_{10}$$

which together with the computational basis B_4 give five MUBs. In detail, we have

$$\begin{aligned}
W_{00} &= \{|0\alpha\rangle \otimes |0\beta\rangle \ : \ \alpha, \beta = 0, 1\} \\
W_{11} &= \{|1\alpha\rangle \otimes |1\beta\rangle \ : \ \alpha, \beta = 0, 1\} \\
W_{01} &= \{\lambda|0\alpha\rangle \otimes |1\beta\rangle + \mu|0\alpha \oplus 1\rangle \otimes |1\beta \oplus 1\rangle \ : \ \alpha, \beta = 0, 1\} \\
W_{10} &= \{\lambda|1\alpha\rangle \otimes |0\beta\rangle + \mu|1\alpha \oplus 1\rangle \otimes |0\beta \oplus 1\rangle \ : \ \alpha, \beta = 0, 1\}
\end{aligned}$$

where the addition $\oplus$ should be understood modulo 4; furthermore

$$\lambda = \frac{1-\mathrm{i}}{2}, \quad \mu = \frac{1+\mathrm{i}}{2}$$

and the vectors of type $|a\alpha\rangle$ are given by Equation (16). As a résumé, only two formulas are necessary for obtaining the $d^2 = 16$ vectors $|ab; \alpha\beta\rangle$ for the bases W_{ab}, namely

$$\begin{aligned}
W_{00}, W_{11} &: \ |aa; \alpha\beta\rangle = |a\alpha\rangle \otimes |a\beta\rangle \\
W_{01}, W_{10} &: \ |aa \oplus 1; \alpha\beta\rangle = \lambda|a\alpha\rangle \otimes |a \oplus 1\beta\rangle + \mu|a\alpha \oplus 1\rangle \otimes |a \oplus 1\beta \oplus 1\rangle
\end{aligned}$$

for all a, α, β in $\mathbb{F}_2$. A simple development of W_{00}, W_{11}, W_{01} and W_{10} gives the following expressions.

The W_{00} basis:

$$\begin{aligned}
|00;00\rangle &= \frac{1}{2}(|0\rangle \otimes |0\rangle + |0\rangle \otimes |1\rangle + |1\rangle \otimes |0\rangle + |1\rangle \otimes |1\rangle) \\
|00;01\rangle &= \frac{1}{2}(|0\rangle \otimes |0\rangle - |0\rangle \otimes |1\rangle + |1\rangle \otimes |0\rangle - |1\rangle \otimes |1\rangle) \\
|00;10\rangle &= \frac{1}{2}(|0\rangle \otimes |0\rangle + |0\rangle \otimes |1\rangle - |1\rangle \otimes |0\rangle - |1\rangle \otimes |1\rangle) \\
|00;11\rangle &= \frac{1}{2}(|0\rangle \otimes |0\rangle - |0\rangle \otimes |1\rangle - |1\rangle \otimes |0\rangle + |1\rangle \otimes |1\rangle)
\end{aligned}$$

or in column vectors

$$\frac{1}{2}\begin{pmatrix}1\\1\\1\\1\end{pmatrix}, \quad \frac{1}{2}\begin{pmatrix}1\\-1\\1\\-1\end{pmatrix}, \quad \frac{1}{2}\begin{pmatrix}1\\1\\-1\\-1\end{pmatrix}, \quad \frac{1}{2}\begin{pmatrix}1\\-1\\-1\\1\end{pmatrix}$$

The W_{11} basis:

$$\begin{aligned}
|11;00\rangle &= \frac{1}{2}(|0\rangle \otimes |0\rangle + \mathrm{i}|0\rangle \otimes |1\rangle + \mathrm{i}|1\rangle \otimes |0\rangle - |1\rangle \otimes |1\rangle) \\
|11;01\rangle &= \frac{1}{2}(|0\rangle \otimes |0\rangle - \mathrm{i}|0\rangle \otimes |1\rangle + \mathrm{i}|1\rangle \otimes |0\rangle + |1\rangle \otimes |1\rangle) \\
|11;10\rangle &= \frac{1}{2}(|0\rangle \otimes |0\rangle + \mathrm{i}|0\rangle \otimes |1\rangle - \mathrm{i}|1\rangle \otimes |0\rangle + |1\rangle \otimes |1\rangle) \\
|11;11\rangle &= \frac{1}{2}(|0\rangle \otimes |0\rangle - \mathrm{i}|0\rangle \otimes |1\rangle - \mathrm{i}|1\rangle \otimes |0\rangle - |1\rangle \otimes |1\rangle)
\end{aligned}$$

or in column vectors

$$\frac{1}{2}\begin{pmatrix}1\\ \mathrm{i}\\ \mathrm{i}\\ -1\end{pmatrix},\quad \frac{1}{2}\begin{pmatrix}1\\ -\mathrm{i}\\ \mathrm{i}\\ 1\end{pmatrix},\quad \frac{1}{2}\begin{pmatrix}1\\ \mathrm{i}\\ -\mathrm{i}\\ 1\end{pmatrix},\quad \frac{1}{2}\begin{pmatrix}1\\ -\mathrm{i}\\ -\mathrm{i}\\ -1\end{pmatrix}$$

The W_{01} basis:

$$\begin{aligned}
|01;00\rangle &= \frac{1}{2}(|0\rangle\otimes|0\rangle + |0\rangle\otimes|1\rangle - \mathrm{i}|1\rangle\otimes|0\rangle + \mathrm{i}|1\rangle\otimes|1\rangle)\\
|01;11\rangle &= \frac{1}{2}(|0\rangle\otimes|0\rangle - |0\rangle\otimes|1\rangle + \mathrm{i}|1\rangle\otimes|0\rangle + \mathrm{i}|1\rangle\otimes|1\rangle)\\
|01;01\rangle &= \frac{1}{2}(|0\rangle\otimes|0\rangle - |0\rangle\otimes|1\rangle - \mathrm{i}|1\rangle\otimes|0\rangle - \mathrm{i}|1\rangle\otimes|1\rangle)\\
|01;10\rangle &= \frac{1}{2}(|0\rangle\otimes|0\rangle + |0\rangle\otimes|1\rangle + \mathrm{i}|1\rangle\otimes|0\rangle - \mathrm{i}|1\rangle\otimes|1\rangle)
\end{aligned}$$

or in column vectors

$$\frac{1}{2}\begin{pmatrix}1\\ 1\\ -\mathrm{i}\\ \mathrm{i}\end{pmatrix},\quad \frac{1}{2}\begin{pmatrix}1\\ -1\\ \mathrm{i}\\ \mathrm{i}\end{pmatrix},\quad \frac{1}{2}\begin{pmatrix}1\\ -1\\ -\mathrm{i}\\ -\mathrm{i}\end{pmatrix},\quad \frac{1}{2}\begin{pmatrix}1\\ 1\\ \mathrm{i}\\ -\mathrm{i}\end{pmatrix}$$

The W_{10} basis:

$$\begin{aligned}
|10;00\rangle &= \frac{1}{2}(|0\rangle\otimes|0\rangle - \mathrm{i}|0\rangle\otimes|1\rangle + |1\rangle\otimes|0\rangle + \mathrm{i}|1\rangle\otimes|1\rangle)\\
|10;11\rangle &= \frac{1}{2}(|0\rangle\otimes|0\rangle + \mathrm{i}|0\rangle\otimes|1\rangle - |1\rangle\otimes|0\rangle + \mathrm{i}|1\rangle\otimes|1\rangle)\\
|10;01\rangle &= \frac{1}{2}(|0\rangle\otimes|0\rangle + \mathrm{i}|0\rangle\otimes|1\rangle + |1\rangle\otimes|0\rangle - \mathrm{i}|1\rangle\otimes|1\rangle)\\
|10;10\rangle &= \frac{1}{2}(|0\rangle\otimes|0\rangle - \mathrm{i}|0\rangle\otimes|1\rangle - |1\rangle\otimes|0\rangle - \mathrm{i}|1\rangle\otimes|1\rangle)
\end{aligned}$$

or in column vectors

$$\frac{1}{2}\begin{pmatrix}1\\ -\mathrm{i}\\ 1\\ \mathrm{i}\end{pmatrix},\quad \frac{1}{2}\begin{pmatrix}1\\ \mathrm{i}\\ -1\\ \mathrm{i}\end{pmatrix},\quad \frac{1}{2}\begin{pmatrix}1\\ \mathrm{i}\\ 1\\ -\mathrm{i}\end{pmatrix},\quad \frac{1}{2}\begin{pmatrix}1\\ -\mathrm{i}\\ -1\\ -\mathrm{i}\end{pmatrix}$$

The computational basis:

$$|0\rangle\otimes|0\rangle,\quad |0\rangle\otimes|1\rangle,\quad |1\rangle\otimes|0\rangle,\quad |1\rangle\otimes|1\rangle$$

or in column vectors

$$\begin{pmatrix}1\\ 0\\ 0\\ 0\end{pmatrix},\quad \begin{pmatrix}0\\ 1\\ 0\\ 0\end{pmatrix},\quad \begin{pmatrix}0\\ 0\\ 1\\ 0\end{pmatrix},\quad \begin{pmatrix}0\\ 0\\ 0\\ 1\end{pmatrix}$$

It is to be noted that the vectors of the bases W_{00} and W_{11} are not entangled (i.e., each vector is the tensor product of two vectors) while the vectors of the bases W_{01} and W_{10} are entangled (i.e., each vector is not the tensor product of two vectors). In fact, all the state vectors for W_{01} and W_{10} are maximally entangled (the entanglement entropy is maximum for W_{01} and W_{10} and vanishes for W_{00} and W_{11}).

Generalization of the formulas given above for two systems of qubits can be obtained in more complicated situations (two systems of qupits, three systems of qubits, etc.). The generalization of the bases W_{00} and W_{11} is immediate. The generalization of W_{01} and W_{10} can be achieved by taking linear combinations of vectors such that each linear combination is made of vectors corresponding to the same eigenvalue of the relevant tensor product of operators of type v_a.

3.3. Weyl Pairs

3.3.1. Shift and Phase Operators

Let us go back to the case d arbitrary. The matrix V_a can be decomposed as

$$V_a = XZ^a, \quad a = 0, 1, \cdots, d-1$$

where

$$X = \begin{pmatrix} 0 & 1 & 0 & \cdots & 0 \\ 0 & 0 & 1 & \cdots & 0 \\ \vdots & \vdots & \vdots & \cdots & \vdots \\ 0 & 0 & 0 & \cdots & 1 \\ 1 & 0 & 0 & \cdots & 0 \end{pmatrix}, \quad Z = \begin{pmatrix} 1 & 0 & 0 & \cdots & 0 \\ 0 & \omega & 0 & \cdots & 0 \\ 0 & 0 & \omega^2 & \cdots & 0 \\ \vdots & \vdots & \vdots & \cdots & \vdots \\ 0 & 0 & 0 & \cdots & \omega^{d-1} \end{pmatrix}, \quad \omega = e^{i\frac{2\pi}{d}}$$

The matrices X and Z satisfy

$$Z\phi_n = \omega^n \phi_n, \; n = 0, 1, \cdots, d-1, \quad X\phi_n = \phi_{n-1 \bmod d} = \begin{cases} \phi_{d-1}, \; n = 0 \\ \phi_{n-1}, \; n = 1, 2, \cdots, d-1 \end{cases}$$

The linear operators corresponding to the matrices X and Z are known in quantum information as flip or shift and clock or phase operators, respectively. The unitary matrices X and Z ω-commute in the sense that

$$XZ - \omega ZX = O_d$$

In addition, they satisfy

$$X^d = Z^d = I_d$$

where I_d and O_d are the d-dimensional unity and zero matrices, respectively. The last two equations show that X and Z constitute a so-called Weyl pair [3].

Note that the Weyl pair (X, Z) can be deduced from the master matrix V_a via

$$X = V_0, \quad Z = {V_0}^{\dagger} V_1$$

which shows a further interest of the matrix V_a. Indeed, the matrix V_a condensates all that can be done with the matrices X and Z. This has been seen in Section 3.2.4 with the derivation of a single formula for the determination from V_a of a complete set of $p+1$ MUBs when $d = p$ is prime whereas many other determinations of such a complete set needs repeated use of the matrices X and Z.

A connection between X and Z can be deduced from the expression of $(H_aP)^\dagger V_a(H_aP)$ given in Section 3.2.3. By taking $a = 0$, we obtain

$$(H_0P)^\dagger X(H_0P) = Z \Leftrightarrow X = (H_0P)Z(H_0P)^\dagger$$

where H_0 is the matrix of a discrete Fourier transform that allows to pass from the vectors ϕ_n ($n = 0, 1, \cdots, d-1$) to the vector $\phi(0, \alpha)$ according to

$$\phi(0,\alpha) = \sum_{n\in\mathbb{Z}_d} (H_0)_{n\alpha}\, \phi_n = (-1)^\alpha \frac{1}{\sqrt{d}} \sum_{n\in\mathbb{Z}_d} \mathrm{e}^{-\mathrm{i}\frac{2\pi}{d}n\alpha} \phi_n$$

cf. the expression of $\phi(a, \alpha)$ in Section 3.2.3.

3.3.2. Generalized Pauli Matrices

For d arbitrary, let us define the matrices

$$U_{ab} = X^a Z^b, \quad a, b \in \mathbb{Z}_d$$

The matrices U_{ab} belong to the unitary group $\mathrm{U}(d)$. The d^2 matrices U_{ab} are called *generalized Pauli matrices* in dimension d. They satisfy the trace relation

$$\mathrm{tr}\left({U_{ab}}^\dagger U_{a'b'} \right) = d\, \delta_{a,a'}\, \delta_{b,b'}$$

Thus, the set $\{U_{ab} \ : \ a, b \in \mathbb{Z}_d\}$ of unitary matrices is an orthogonal set with respect to the Hilbert-Schmidt inner product. Consequently, the d^2 pairwise orthogonal matrices U_{ab} can be used as a basis of $\mathbb{C}^{d\times d}$.

Example 5. *The case $d = 2 \Leftrightarrow j = \frac{1}{2}$ ($\Rightarrow \omega = \mathrm{e}^{\mathrm{i}\pi}$ and $a, b = 0, 1$) corresponds to the two-dimensional ordinary Pauli matrices of quantum mechanics. The matrices X^aZ^b are*

$$I_2 = X^0Z^0 = \begin{pmatrix} 1 & 0 \\ 0 & 1 \end{pmatrix}, \ X = X^1Z^0 = \begin{pmatrix} 0 & 1 \\ 1 & 0 \end{pmatrix}, \ Z = X^0Z^1 = \begin{pmatrix} 1 & 0 \\ 0 & -1 \end{pmatrix}, \ Y = X^1Z^1 = \begin{pmatrix} 0 & -1 \\ 1 & 0 \end{pmatrix}$$

so that the matrices X and Z generate the ordinary Pauli matrices. Indeed, we have

$$I_2 = \sigma_0, \quad X = V_0 = \sigma_1, \quad Y = XZ = V_1 = -i\sigma_2, \quad Z = \sigma_3$$

in terms of the usual (Hermitian and unitary) Pauli matrices.

Example 6. *The case $d = 3 \Leftrightarrow j = 1$ ($\Rightarrow \omega = \mathrm{e}^{\mathrm{i}\frac{2\pi}{3}}$ and $a, b = 0, 1, 2$) yields nine three-dimensional matrices. More precisely, the matrices X and Z generate $I_3 = X^0Z^0$ and*

$$X = V_0, \quad X^2, \quad Z, \quad Z^2, \quad XZ = V_1, \quad X^2Z^2, \quad XZ^2 = V_2, \quad X^2Z$$

In the detail, the matrices X^aZ^b are

$$X^0Z^0 = \begin{pmatrix} 1 & 0 & 0 \\ 0 & 1 & 0 \\ 0 & 0 & 1 \end{pmatrix}, \quad X^0Z^1 = \begin{pmatrix} 1 & 0 & 0 \\ 0 & \omega & 0 \\ 0 & 0 & \omega^2 \end{pmatrix}, \quad X^0Z^2 = \begin{pmatrix} 1 & 0 & 0 \\ 0 & \omega^2 & 0 \\ 0 & 0 & \omega \end{pmatrix}$$

$$X^1Z^0 = \begin{pmatrix} 0 & 1 & 0 \\ 0 & 0 & 1 \\ 1 & 0 & 0 \end{pmatrix}, \quad X^1Z^1 = \begin{pmatrix} 0 & \omega & 0 \\ 0 & 0 & \omega^2 \\ 1 & 0 & 0 \end{pmatrix}, \quad X^1Z^2 = \begin{pmatrix} 0 & \omega^2 & 0 \\ 0 & 0 & \omega \\ 1 & 0 & 0 \end{pmatrix}$$

$$X^2Z^0 = \begin{pmatrix} 0 & 0 & 1 \\ 1 & 0 & 0 \\ 0 & 1 & 0 \end{pmatrix}, \quad X^2Z^1 = \begin{pmatrix} 0 & 0 & \omega^2 \\ 1 & 0 & 0 \\ 0 & \omega & 0 \end{pmatrix}, \quad X^2Z^2 = \begin{pmatrix} 0 & 0 & \omega \\ 1 & 0 & 0 \\ 0 & \omega^2 & 0 \end{pmatrix}$$

They constitute a natural extension in dimension $d = 3$ of the usual Pauli matrices.

3.3.3. Weyl Pair and Groups

For arbitrary d, the Weyl pair ($X = V_0$, $Z = V_0^\dagger V_1$) is a basic ingredient for generating the Pauli group P_d in d dimensions and the Lie algebra of the linear group $\mathrm{GL}(d, \mathbb{C})$ in d dimensions, groups of central interest in group theory, quantum mechanics and quantum information.

The Pauli group. For arbitrary d, let us define the matrices

$$V_{abc} = \omega^a U_{bc} = \omega^a X^b Z^c, \quad a, b, c \in \mathbb{Z}_d, \quad \omega = \mathrm{e}^{\mathrm{i}\frac{2\pi}{d}}$$

The matrices V_{abc} are unitary and satisfy

$$\mathrm{tr}\left(V_{abc}{}^{\dagger} V_{a'b'c'} \right) = \omega^{a'-a}\, d\, \delta_{b,b'}\, \delta_{c,c'}$$

In addition, we have the following result.

Proposition 3. *The set $\{V_{abc} \ : \ a, b, c \in \mathbb{Z}_d\}$ is a finite group of order d^3, denoted P_d, for the internal law (matrix multiplication)*

$$V_{abc} V_{a'b'c'} = V_{a''b''c''}, \quad a'' = a + a' - cb', \quad b'' = b + b', \quad c'' = c + c'$$

It is a non-commutative (for $d \geq 2$) nilpotent group with nilpotency class equal to 3.

The group P_d is called the Pauli group in dimension d. It is of considerable importance in quantum information, especially for quantum computation and for quantum error-correcting codes. The group P_d is a sub-group of the unitary group $\mathrm{U}(d)$. The normalizer of P_d in $\mathrm{U}(d)$ is called Clifford group (denoted as C_d) in d dimensions. More precisely, C_d is the set $\{U \in \mathrm{U}(d) \ : \ UP_dU^\dagger = P_d\}$ endowed with matrix multiplication. The Pauli group P_d as well as any other invariant sub-group of C_d are useful for quantum error-correcting codes in the case of N-qubit systems corresponding to $d = 2^N$.

Moreover, the Pauli group is connected to the Heisenberg-Weyl group. In fact, the group P_d corresponds to a discretization of the Heisenberg-Weyl group $HW(\mathbb{R})$. From an abstract point of view, the group $HW(\mathbb{R})$ is the set $S = \{(x, y, z) \ : \ x, y, z \in \mathbb{R}\}$ equipped with the internal law $S \times S \to S$ defined via

$$(x, y, z)(x', y', z') = (x + x' - zy', y + y', z + z')$$

This group is a non-commutative Lie group of order 3. It is non-compact and nilpotent with a nilpotency class equal to 3. The passage from $HW(\mathbb{R})$ to P_d amounts to replace the infinite field $\mathbb{R}$ by the finite ring $\mathbb{Z}_d$ so that $HW(\mathbb{R})$ gives $HW(\mathbb{Z}_d) \equiv P_d$.

The three generators of $HW(\mathbb{R})$ are

$$H = \frac{1}{\mathrm{i}} \frac{\partial}{\partial x}, \quad Q = \frac{1}{\mathrm{i}} \frac{\partial}{\partial y}, \quad P = \frac{1}{\mathrm{i}} \left(\frac{\partial}{\partial z} - y \frac{\partial}{\partial x} \right)$$

They satisfy the commutation relations

$$[Q, P]_- = \mathrm{i}H, \quad [P, H]_- = 0, \quad [H, Q]_- = 0$$

Therefore, the Lie algebra $hw(\mathbb{R})$ of $HW(\mathbb{R})$ is a three-dimensional nilpotent Lie algebra with nilpotency class equal to 3. The commutation relations of Q, P and H are reminiscent of the Heisenberg commutation relations. As a matter of fact, the Heisenberg commutation relations correspond to an infinite-dimensional irreducible representation by Hermitian matrices of $hw(\mathbb{R})$. The Lie algebra $hw(\mathbb{R})$ also admits finite-dimensional irreducible representations at the price to abandon the Hermitian character of the representation matrices.

The linear group. The Weyl pair consisting of the generalized Pauli matrices X and Z in d dimensions can be used for constructing a basis of the Lie algebra of $\mathrm{U}(d)$. More precisely, we have the two following propositions.

Proposition 4. *For arbitrary d, the set $\{X^a Z^b \ : \ a, b \in \mathbb{Z}_d\}$ forms a basis for the Lie algebra $gl(d, \mathbb{C})$ of the linear group $GL(d, \mathbb{C})$ or for the Lie algebra $u(d)$ of the unitary group $U(d)$. The Lie brackets of $gl(d, \mathbb{C})$ in such a basis are*

$$[X^a Z^b, X^e Z^f]_- = \sum_{i \in \mathbb{Z}_d} \sum_{j \in \mathbb{Z}_d} (ab, ef; ij) X^i Z^j$$

with the structure constants

$$(ab, ef; ij) = \delta_{i,a+e} \delta_{j,b+f} \left(\omega^{-be} - \omega^{-af} \right)$$

where $a, b, e, f, i, j \in \mathbb{Z}_d$.

Note that the commutator $[U_{ab}, U_{ef}]_- = U_{ab} U_{ef} - U_{ef} U_{ab}$ and the anti-commutator $[U_{ab}, U_{ef}]_+ = U_{ab} U_{ef} + U_{ef} U_{ab}$ of U_{ab} and U_{ef} are given by

$$[U_{ab}, U_{ef}]_\pm = \left(\omega^{-be} \pm \omega^{-af} \right) U_{ij}, \quad i = a + e, \quad j = b + f$$

Consequently, $[U_{ab}, U_{ef}]_- = 0$ if and only if $af - be = 0$ (mod d) and $[U_{ab}, U_{ef}]_+ = 0$ if and only if $af - be = \frac{1}{2}d$ (mod d). Therefore, all anti-commutators $[U_{ab}, U_{ef}]_+$ are different from 0 if d is an odd integer.

Proposition 5. *For $d = p$, with p a prime number, the simple Lie algebra $sl(p, \mathbb{C})$ of the special linear group $SL(p, \mathbb{C})$ or its compact real form $su(d)$ of the special unitary group $SU(d)$ can be decomposed into a sum of $p + 1$ Abelian subalgebras of dimension $p - 1$*

$$\mathrm{sl}(p, \mathbb{C}) = \mathcal{V}_0 \oplus \mathcal{V}_1 \oplus \cdots \oplus \mathcal{V}_p$$

where each of the $p + 1$ subalgebras $\mathcal{V}_0, \mathcal{V}_1, \cdots, \mathcal{V}_p$ is a Cartan subalgebra generated by a set of $p - 1$ commuting matrices.

A similar result holds for $d = p^m$, a power of a prime number [7,12,16,53,64].

The decomposition of $\mathrm{sl}(p, \mathbb{C})$, called orthogonal decomposition of $\mathrm{sl}(p, \mathbb{C})$, is trivial for $p = 2$. In fact, for $p = 2$ we have the following decomposition

$$\mathrm{su}(2) = \sigma_1 \oplus \sigma_2 \oplus \sigma_3$$

in terms of vector space sum.

3.3.4. MUBs and the Special Linear Group

According to the orthogonal decomposition proposition, in the case where $d = p$ is a prime number (even or odd), the set $\{X^a Z^b \,:\, a, b \in \mathbb{Z}_p\} \setminus \{X^0 Z^0\}$ of cardinality $p^2 - 1$ can be partitioned into $p + 1$ subsets containing each $p - 1$ commuting matrices.

As an example, let us consider the case $d = 5$. For this case, we are left with the six following sets of four commuting matrices

$$\mathcal{V}_0 = \{01, 02, 03, 04\}, \quad \mathcal{V}_1 = \{10, 20, 30, 40\}, \quad \mathcal{V}_2 = \{11, 22, 33, 44\}$$
$$\mathcal{V}_3 = \{12, 24, 31, 43\}, \quad \mathcal{V}_4 = \{13, 21, 34, 42\}, \quad \mathcal{V}_5 = \{14, 23, 32, 41\}$$

where ab is used as an abbreviation of $X^a Z^b$.

More generally, for $d = p$ with p prime, the $p + 1$ sets of $p - 1$ commuting matrices are easily seen to be

$$\begin{aligned}
\mathcal{V}_0 &= \{X^0 Z^a \,:\, a = 1, 2, \cdots, p-1\} \\
\mathcal{V}_1 &= \{X^a Z^0 \,:\, a = 1, 2, \cdots, p-1\} \\
\mathcal{V}_2 &= \{X^a Z^a \,:\, a = 1, 2, \cdots, p-1\} \\
\mathcal{V}_3 &= \{X^a Z^{2a} \,:\, a = 1, 2, \cdots, p-1\} \\
&\vdots \\
\mathcal{V}_{p-1} &= \{X^a Z^{(p-2)a} \,:\, a = 1, 2, \cdots, p-1\} \\
\mathcal{V}_p &= \{X^a Z^{(p-1)a} \,:\, a = 1, 2, \cdots, p-1\}
\end{aligned}$$

Each of the $p + 1$ sets $\mathcal{V}_0, \mathcal{V}_1, \cdots, \mathcal{V}_p$ can be put in a one-to-one correspondence with one basis of the complete set of $p + 1$ MUBs. In fact, $\mathcal{V}_0$ is associated with the computational basis while $\mathcal{V}_1, \mathcal{V}_2, \cdots, \mathcal{V}_p$ are associated with the p remaining MUBs in view of

$$V_a \in \mathcal{V}_{a+1} = \{X^b Z^{ab} \,:\, b = 1, 2, \cdots, p-1\}, \quad a = 0, 1, \cdots, p-1$$

More precisely, we have

$$Z \in \mathcal{V}_0, \quad X \in \mathcal{V}_1, \quad XZ \in \mathcal{V}_2, \quad \cdots, \quad XZ^{p-1} \in \mathcal{V}_p$$

The eigenvectors of the $p + 1$ unitary operators

$$Z, \quad X, \quad XZ, \quad \cdots, \quad XZ^{p-1}$$

generate $p + 1$ MUBs (one basis is associated with each of the $p + 1$ operators).

3.4. Galois Field Approach to MUBs

The existence of a complete set of $p^m + 1$ MUBS in $\mathbb{C}^{p^m}$ (p prime and m positive integer) is an indication of a possible utility of Galois fields and Galois rings for the construction of MUBs in $\mathbb{C}^{p^m}$ (p prime, $m \geq 2$). Indeed, the passage from the case $d = p$ to the case $d = p^m$ (p prime, $m \geq 2$) can be achieved by considering the Galois field $\mathbb{GF}(p^m)$ for p odd prime and the Galois ring $\mathbb{GR}(2^2, m)$ for $p = 2$ [2,28]. In this section, we shall deal with the construction of a complete set of $p^m + 1$ MUBs in $\mathbb{C}^{p^m}$, corresponding to the case of m qupits, via the use of the Galois field $\mathbb{GF}(p^m)$ for p odd prime and m greater than 1.

3.4.1. The Computational Basis

We first have to define the computational basis B_{p^m} in the framework of $\mathbb{GF}(p^m)$, p odd prime and $m \geq 2$. The vectors of the basis B_{p^m} of the Hilbert space $\mathbb{C}^{p^m}$ can be labeled by the elements x of the Galois field $\mathbb{GF}(p^m)$. This can be done in two ways according to as the elements x are taken in the monomial form ($x = 0$, α^ℓ with $\ell = 1, 2, \cdots, p^m - 1$) or in the polynomial form ($x = [x_0 x_1 \cdots x_{m-1}]$ with $x_0, x_1, \cdots, x_{m-1} \in \mathbb{F}_p$). In both cases, we have

$$B_{p^m} = \{|0\rangle \text{ or } \phi_0, \quad |1\rangle \text{ or } \phi_1, \quad \cdots, \quad |p^m - 1\rangle \text{ or } \phi_{p^m-1}\}$$

in terms of vectors or column vectors. More precisely, this can be achieved as follows.

- In the monomial form, we define the vectors of B_{p^m} via the correspondences

$$x = 0 \mapsto |0\rangle \text{ or } \phi_0, \quad x = \alpha^\ell \mapsto |\ell\rangle \text{ or } \phi_\ell \text{ with } \ell = 1, 2, \cdots, p^m - 1$$

  where α is a primitive element of $\mathbb{GF}(p^m)$.
- In the polynomial form, we can range the vectors of B_{p^m} in the order $0, 1, \cdots, p^m - 1$ by adopting the lexicographical order for the elements $[x_0 x_1 \cdots x_{m-1}]$.

These notations are reminiscent of those employed for the computational basis

$$B_p = \{|0\rangle \text{ or } \phi_0, \quad |1\rangle \text{ or } \phi_1, \quad \cdots, \quad |p-1\rangle \text{ or } \phi_{p-1}\}$$

corresponding to the limit case $m = 1$.

3.4.2. Shift and Phase Operators for $\mathbb{GF}(p^m)$

The notion of Weyl pair can be extended to any Galois field $\mathbb{GF}(p^m)$ with p (even or odd) prime and $m \geq 2$. Let x and y be two elements of $\mathbb{GF}(p^m)$ and ϕ_y be the basis column vector of B_{p^m} associated with y. For fixed x, we define the matrices $\hat{X}_x$ (shift operators) and $\hat{Z}_x$ (phase operators) via the actions

$$\hat{X}_x \phi_y = \phi_{y-x}, \quad \hat{Z}_x \phi_y = \chi(xy) \phi_y = e^{i \frac{2\pi}{p} \mathrm{Tr}(xy)} \phi_y$$

where y is arbitrary. One easily verifies the properties

$$\hat{X}_{x+y} = \hat{X}_x \hat{X}_y = \hat{X}_y \hat{X}_x, \quad \hat{Z}_{x+y} = \hat{Z}_x \hat{Z}_y = \hat{Z}_y \hat{Z}_x$$

and

$$\hat{X}_x \hat{Z}_y - \chi(xy) \hat{Z}_y \hat{X}_x = O_{p^m}, \quad \chi(xy) = e^{i \frac{2\pi}{p} \mathrm{Tr}(xy)}$$

In the limit case $m = 1$ (i.e., for the base field $\mathbb{F}_p$) the matrices

$$X = \hat{X}_1, \quad Z = \hat{Z}_1$$

corresponding to $x = y = 1$ satisfy

$$XZ - e^{i \frac{2\pi}{p}} ZX = O_p$$

to be compared with the relations satisfied by the Weyl pair (X, Z) defined in Section 3.3.1.

3.4.3. Bases in the Frame of $\mathbb{GF}(p^m)$

We might use the Weyl pair (X_x, Z_y) defined in the framework of $\mathbb{GF}(p^m)$, see Section 3.4.2, for determining a complete set of p^m+1 MUBs in $\mathbb{C}^{p^m}$ in a way similar to that used for $m=1$ with the help of the matrix V_a for a in $\mathbb{F}_p$. However, it is quicker to start from Equation (17) giving MUBs in $\mathbb{C}^p$ in order to generate a formula for $\mathbb{C}^{p^m}$ giving back Equation (17) in $\mathbb{C}^p$ in the limit case $m=1$. In this direction, a possible way to pass from the basis vector

$$\frac{1}{\sqrt{p}} \sum_{x \in \mathbb{F}_p} \mathrm{e}^{\mathrm{i}\frac{2\pi}{p}(ax+\alpha)x} |x\rangle$$

of $\mathbb{C}^p$ to a basis vector of $\mathbb{C}^{p^m}$ is to replace

$$\mathrm{e}^{\mathrm{i}\frac{2\pi}{p}(ax+\alpha)x}, \quad a, \alpha, x \in \mathbb{F}_p$$

by

$$\chi(ax^2+\alpha x) = \mathrm{e}^{\mathrm{i}\frac{2\pi}{p}\mathrm{Tr}(ax^2+\alpha x)}, \quad a, \alpha, x \in \mathbb{GF}(p^m)$$

where χ is the canonical additive character of $\mathbb{GF}(p^m)$. This yields the two following propositions.

Proposition 6. *For p odd prime and $m \geq 2$, the set*

$$B_a = \{|a\alpha\rangle \, : \, \alpha \in \mathbb{GF}(p^m)\}$$

where

$$|a\alpha\rangle = \frac{1}{\sqrt{p^m}} \sum_{x \in \mathbb{GF}(p^m)} \mathrm{e}^{\mathrm{i}\frac{2\pi}{p}\mathrm{Tr}(ax^2+\alpha x)} |x\rangle, \quad a \in \mathbb{GF}(p^m)$$

constitutes an orthonormal basis of $\mathbb{C}^{p^m}$.

Proof. See the proof of the next proposition. □

Note that for $m=1$

$$\mathrm{Tr}(ax^2+\alpha x) = ax^2+\alpha x$$

so that the vector $|a\alpha\rangle$ coincides with the vector $|a\alpha\rangle'$ derived in Section 3.2.5. This explains why we chose to extend Equation (17) valid for $\mathbb{C}^p$ to the case $\mathbb{C}^{p^m}$. Indeed, the same kind of extension applied to Equation (16) is not possible since $\mathrm{Tr}[\frac{1}{2}n(p-n)a+n\alpha]$ does not make sense.

3.4.4. MUBs in the Frame of $\mathbb{GF}(p^m)$

Proposition 7. *For p odd prime and $m \geq 2$, the p^m bases B_a, a ranging in $\mathbb{GF}(p^m)$, constitute with the computational basis B_{p^m} a complete set of p^m+1 MUBs in $\mathbb{C}^{p^m}$.*

Proof. Let $|a\alpha\rangle$ and $|b\beta\rangle$ two vectors belonging to the bases B_a and B_b, respectively. We have

$$\langle a\alpha|b\beta\rangle = \frac{1}{p^m} \sum_{x \in \mathbb{GF}(p^m)} \mathrm{e}^{\mathrm{i}\frac{2\pi}{p}\mathrm{Tr}[(b-a)x^2+(\beta-\alpha)x]}, \quad a, b, \alpha, \beta \in \mathbb{GF}(p^m)$$

By using [2,4,18]

$$\left| \sum_{x \in \mathbb{GF}(p^m)} \mathrm{e}^{\mathrm{i}\frac{2\pi}{p}\mathrm{Tr}(ux^2+vx)} \right| = \sqrt{p^m}, \quad u \in \mathbb{GF}(p^m)^*, \quad v \in \mathbb{GF}(p^m)$$

(valid for p odd prime), we obtain

$$|\langle a\alpha|b\beta\rangle| = \begin{cases} \delta_{\alpha,\beta} \text{ if } b = a \\ \\ \frac{1}{\sqrt{p^m}} \text{ if } b \neq a \end{cases}$$

or in compact form

$$|\langle a\alpha|b\beta\rangle| = \delta_{a,b}\delta_{\alpha,\beta} + \frac{1}{\sqrt{p^m}}(1 - \delta_{a,b})$$

which shows that B_a is an orthonormal basis and that the couple (B_a, B_b) with $b \neq a$ is a couple of unbiased bases. Of course, each basis B_a is unbiased to the computational basis B_{p^m}. We thus end up with a total of $p^m + 1$ MUBs as desired. □

The previous result applies in the limit case $m = 1$ for which we recover the $p + 1$ MUBs in $\mathbb{C}^p$.

3.5. Galois Ring Approach to MUBs

In dimension $d = 2^m$, $m \geq 2$, the use of the Galois field $\mathbb{GF}(2^m)$ for constructing a complete set of $2^m + 1$ MUBs in $\mathbb{C}^{2^m}$ according to the method employed in Section 3.4 for $d = p^m$, p odd prime, would lead to a no-win situation because $\gcd(2, 2^m) \neq 1$ (while $\gcd(2, p^m) = 1$ for p odd prime). For $d = 2^m$, which corresponds to the case of m qubits, we can use the Galois ring $\mathbb{GR}(2^2, m)$, denoted R_{4^m} too, for constructing MUBs in $\mathbb{C}^{2^m}$.

3.5.1. Bases in the Frame of $\mathbb{GR}(2^2, m)$

We start with the residue class ring

$$\mathbb{GR}(2^2, m) = \mathbb{Z}_{2^2}[\xi]/\langle P_m(\xi)\rangle$$

where $P_m(x)$ is a monic basic irreducible polynomial of degree m (i.e., its restriction $\overline{P_m(x)} = P_m(x)$ modulo 2 is irreducible over $\mathbb{Z}_2$). The 2^m vectors of the computational basis B_{2^m} are labeled by the 2^m elements of the Teichmüller set T_m associated with the ring $\mathbb{Z}_{2^2}[\xi]/\langle P_m(\xi)\rangle$. Thus

$$B_{2^m} = \{|x\rangle \ : \ x \in T_m\}$$

(the set T_m and the ring $\mathbb{GR}(2^2, m)$ contain 2^m and 4^m elements, respectively).

Proposition 8. *For a and α in T_m, let*

$$|a\alpha\rangle = \frac{1}{\sqrt{2^m}} \sum_{x \in T_m} \chi[(a + 2\alpha)x]|x\rangle = \frac{1}{\sqrt{2^m}} \sum_{x \in T_m} \mathrm{e}^{\mathrm{i}\frac{2\pi}{4}\mathrm{Tr}(ax+2\alpha x)}|x\rangle = \frac{1}{\sqrt{2^m}} \sum_{x \in T_m} \mathrm{i}^{\mathrm{Tr}(ax+2\alpha x)}|x\rangle$$

where χ is an additive character vector of $\mathbb{GR}(2^2, m)$ and the trace takes its values in $\mathbb{Z}_4$. For fixed a in T_m, the set

$$B_a = \{|a\alpha\rangle \ : \ \alpha \in T_m\}$$

constitutes an orthonormal basis of $\mathbb{C}^{2^m}$.

Proof. See the proof of the next proposition. □

Note that for $m = 1$

$$\mathrm{Tr}(ax + 2\alpha x) = ax + 2\alpha x$$

so that

$$|a\alpha\rangle = \frac{1}{\sqrt{2}} \sum_{x \in \mathbb{F}_2} \mathrm{i}^{ax+2\alpha x} |x\rangle \tag{18}$$

to be compared with the vector

$$|a\alpha\rangle = \frac{1}{\sqrt{2}} \sum_{x \in \mathbb{F}_2} \mathrm{e}^{\mathrm{i}\frac{2\pi}{2}[\frac{1}{2}ax(2-x)+\alpha x]} |1-x\rangle = \frac{1}{\sqrt{2}} \sum_{x \in \mathbb{F}_2} \mathrm{i}^{ax(2-x)+2\alpha x} |1-x\rangle \tag{19}$$

given by Equation (16). In view of the fact that

$$\mathrm{i}^{ax+2\alpha x} = \mathrm{i}^{ax(2-x)+2\alpha x}$$

for $x = 0$ and $x = 1$, the two vectors $|a\alpha\rangle$ in Equations (18) and (19) are the same up to an interchange of the vectors $|0\rangle$ and $|1\rangle$. □

3.5.2. MUBs in the Frame of $\mathbb{GR}(2^2, m)$

Proposition 9. *The 2^m bases B_a, with $m \geq 2$ and a ranging in the Teichüller set T_m associated with the Galois ring $\mathbb{GR}(2^2, m)$, constitute with the computational basis B_{2^m} a complete set of $2^m + 1$ MUBs in $\mathbb{C}^{2^m}$.*

Proof. Let $|a\alpha\rangle$ and $|b\beta\rangle$ two vectors belonging to the bases B_a and B_b, respectively. We have

$$\langle a\alpha|b\beta\rangle = \frac{1}{2^m} \sum_{x \in T_m} \mathrm{e}^{\mathrm{i}\frac{\pi}{2}\mathrm{Tr}[(b-a+2\beta-2\alpha)x]}$$

By using [2,4,18]

$$\left| \sum_{x \in T_m} \mathrm{e}^{\mathrm{i}\frac{\pi}{2}\mathrm{Tr}(ux)} \right| = \begin{cases} 0 \text{ if } u \in 2T_m,\ u \neq 0 \\ 2^m \text{ if } u = 0 \\ \sqrt{2^m} \text{ otherwise} \end{cases}$$

we obtain

$$|\langle a\alpha|b\beta\rangle| = \begin{cases} \delta_{\alpha,\beta} \text{ if } b = a \\ \frac{1}{\sqrt{2^m}} \text{ if } b \neq a \end{cases}$$

or in compact form

$$|\langle a\alpha|b\beta\rangle| = \delta_{a,b}\delta_{\alpha,\beta} + \frac{1}{\sqrt{2^m}}(1 - \delta_{a,b})$$

which shows that B_a is an orthonormal basis and that the couple (B_a, B_b) with $b \neq a$ is a couple of unbiased bases. Of course, each basis B_a is unbiased to the computational basis B_{2^m}. We thus end up with a total of $2^m + 1$ MUBs and we are done. □

The previous result applies in the limit case $m = 1$ for which we can recover the $2 + 1$ MUBs in $\mathbb{C}^2$.

3.5.3. One-Qubit System

For $m = 1$, the $2^m = 2$ vectors of the computational basis B_2 are labeled with the help of the two elements of the Teichmüller set $T_1 = \mathbb{Z}_2$ of the Galois ring $\mathbb{GR}(2^2, 1) = \mathbb{Z}_{2^2}$. Thus, the basis B_2 is

$$B_2 \ : \ |0\rangle = \begin{pmatrix} 1 \\ 0 \end{pmatrix}, \quad |1\rangle = \begin{pmatrix} 0 \\ 1 \end{pmatrix}$$

The vectors $|a\alpha\rangle$ of the basis B_a ($a \in T_1$) are given by (see Section 3.5.1)

$$|a\alpha\rangle = \frac{1}{\sqrt{2}} \sum_{x=0}^{1} \mathrm{i}^{(a+2\alpha)x} |x\rangle, \quad \alpha \in T_1 = \{0, 1\}$$

This yields the two unbiased bases

$$B_0 \ : \ |00\rangle = \frac{|0\rangle + |1\rangle}{\sqrt{2}}, \quad |01\rangle = \frac{|0\rangle - |1\rangle}{\sqrt{2}}$$
$$B_1 \ : \ |10\rangle = \frac{|0\rangle + \mathrm{i}|1\rangle}{\sqrt{2}}, \quad |11\rangle = \frac{|0\rangle - \mathrm{i}|1\rangle}{\sqrt{2}}$$

which, together with the computational basis B_2, form a complete set of $2 + 1 = 3$ MUBs in $\mathbb{C}^2$. Note that the bases B_0 and B_1 are in agreement (up to phase factors and a rearrangement of the vectors inside B_1) with the bases B_0 and B_1 derived in Section 3.2.4.

3.5.4. Two-Qubit System

For $m = 2$, the $2^m = 4$ vectors of the computational basis B_4 are labeled with the help of the four elements of the Teichmüller set $T_2 = \{0, \beta^1, \beta^2 = 3 + 3\beta, \beta^3 = 1\}$ of the Galois ring $\mathbb{GR}(2^2, 2)$ (here, we use β instead of α in order to avoid confusion with the index α in $|a\alpha\rangle$). Thus, the basis B_4 is

$$B_4 \ : \ |0\rangle = \begin{pmatrix} 1 \\ 0 \\ 0 \\ 0 \end{pmatrix}, \ |\beta^1 \,\mathrm{or}\, 1\rangle = \begin{pmatrix} 0 \\ 1 \\ 0 \\ 0 \end{pmatrix}, \ |\beta^2 \,\mathrm{or}\, 2\rangle = \begin{pmatrix} 0 \\ 0 \\ 1 \\ 0 \end{pmatrix}, \ |\beta^3 \,\mathrm{or}\, 3\rangle = \begin{pmatrix} 0 \\ 0 \\ 0 \\ 1 \end{pmatrix}$$

The vectors $|a\alpha\rangle$ of the basis B_a ($a = 0$, β^1 or 1, β^2 or 2, β^3 or 3) are given by (see Section 3.5.1)

$$|a\alpha\rangle = \frac{1}{2} \sum_{x \in T_2} \mathrm{i}^{\mathrm{Tr}(ax+2\alpha x)} |x\rangle, \quad \alpha \in T_2 = \{0, \beta^1, \beta^2 = 3 + 3\beta, \beta^3 = 1\}$$

with

$$\mathrm{Tr}(ax + 2\alpha x) = ax + 2\alpha x + \phi(ax + 2\alpha x)$$

where ϕ is the generalized Frobenius map $\mathbb{GR}(2^2, 2) \to \mathbb{GR}(2^2, 2)$. The correspondence between the indexes a, α in $|a\alpha\rangle$ and the elements $0, \beta^1, \beta^2, \beta^3$ of T_2 is as follows

$$0 \leftrightarrow a \text{ or } \alpha = 0, \ \beta^1 \leftrightarrow a \text{ or } \alpha = 1, \ \beta^2 \leftrightarrow a \text{ or } \alpha = 2, \ \beta^3 \leftrightarrow a \text{ or } \alpha = 3$$

This yields the four unbiased bases

$$B_0 \ : \ |00\rangle = \frac{1}{2}\begin{pmatrix}1\\1\\1\\1\end{pmatrix}, |01\rangle = \frac{1}{2}\begin{pmatrix}1\\-1\\1\\-1\end{pmatrix}, |02\rangle = \frac{1}{2}\begin{pmatrix}1\\1\\-1\\-1\end{pmatrix}, |03\rangle = \frac{1}{2}\begin{pmatrix}1\\-1\\-1\\1\end{pmatrix}$$

$$B_1 \ : \ |12\rangle = \frac{1}{2}\begin{pmatrix}1\\-\mathrm{i}\\1\\\mathrm{i}\end{pmatrix}, |11\rangle = \frac{1}{2}\begin{pmatrix}1\\\mathrm{i}\\-1\\\mathrm{i}\end{pmatrix}, |13\rangle = \frac{1}{2}\begin{pmatrix}1\\\mathrm{i}\\1\\-\mathrm{i}\end{pmatrix}, |10\rangle = \frac{1}{2}\begin{pmatrix}1\\-\mathrm{i}\\-1\\-\mathrm{i}\end{pmatrix}$$

$$B_2 \ : \ |21\rangle = \frac{1}{2}\begin{pmatrix}1\\1\\-\mathrm{i}\\\mathrm{i}\end{pmatrix}, |22\rangle = \frac{1}{2}\begin{pmatrix}1\\-1\\\mathrm{i}\\\mathrm{i}\end{pmatrix}, |20\rangle = \frac{1}{2}\begin{pmatrix}1\\-1\\-\mathrm{i}\\-\mathrm{i}\end{pmatrix}, |23\rangle = \frac{1}{2}\begin{pmatrix}1\\1\\\mathrm{i}\\-\mathrm{i}\end{pmatrix}$$

$$B_3 \ : \ |33\rangle = \frac{1}{2}\begin{pmatrix}1\\\mathrm{i}\\\mathrm{i}\\-1\end{pmatrix}, |32\rangle = \frac{1}{2}\begin{pmatrix}1\\-\mathrm{i}\\\mathrm{i}\\1\end{pmatrix}, |31\rangle = \frac{1}{2}\begin{pmatrix}1\\\mathrm{i}\\-\mathrm{i}\\1\end{pmatrix}, |30\rangle = \frac{1}{2}\begin{pmatrix}1\\-\mathrm{i}\\-\mathrm{i}\\-1\end{pmatrix}$$

We thus end up with $4 + 1 = 5$ bases (B_0 to B_4) which form a complete set of MUBs in $\mathbb{C}^4$. Note that the bases B_0, B_1, B_2 and B_3 coincide with the bases W_{00}, W_{10}, W_{01} and W_{11} derived from tensor products, respectively; for the purpose of comparison, the vectors $|a\alpha\rangle$ are listed in the same order for each of the couples (B_0, W_{00}), (B_1, W_{10}), (B_2, W_{01}) and (B_3, W_{11}), see Section 3.2.6.

4. Closing Remarks

During the last two decades, quantum information and quantum computing have been the object of considerable progresses both in theoretical and experimental physical sciences, scientific engineering, discrete mathematics and quantum informatics. In the present days, there exit several quantum computer languages and, although quantum devices are mainly developed in academic and private laboratories, the scientific community has access to some quantum computers (e.g., access to the 5-qubit quantum computer of the IBM Quantum Experience [79]) and to quantum simulators (e.g., access to the 41-qubit ATOS Quantum Learning Machine [80]). In the medium term, the accent shall be put, among others, on (i) the development of new quantum algorithms that outperform classical ones, (ii) the production of qubits robust to decoherence (with coherence time greater than 500 ms), (iii) the increase of the lifetime of quantum memories, (iv) the development of quantum networks working over a few thousands of kilometres (v) the realization of 50–100 qubit computers, and (vi) the test of quantum supremacy. There is a long way before the realization of a universal quantum computer!

From the side of the mathematical aspects of MUBs, some further developments and a few open problems should be mentioned. It would be interesting to see if Cayley-Dickson algebras of dimension $d = 2^N$ could be used for providing a geometrical approach to entanglement of N qubits with $N > 3$. Furthermore, the problem of the determination of the maximum number $N(d)$ of MUBs in composite dimension d is still an unsolved problem (except in the case where d is a power of a prime number). The two conjectures listed in Section 3.1.3 do not very much help, probably because they lead to two equivalent problems for which the solutions are as difficult to find as those of the initial problem. As far as the second conjecture is concerned, the recent work [76] on orthogonal decompositions of $\mathrm{sl}(n, R)$ over a finite commutative ring with identity R is very appealing. Finally, even in the simplest case where $d = 6$, the maximum number $N(6)$ of MUBs is not known (to the best of the author knowledge). However, for $d = 6$ there are numerous numerical evidences that $N(6) = 3$ [19,37,52,54,59,60,70,71]. The number $N(6) = 3$ is equal indeed to the number of *weak* mutually unbiased bases associated with the smallest prime divisor of 6 (the recently introduced notion of weak MUBs in dimension d corresponds to the Definition (14) where $\sqrt{d}$ is replaced by $\sqrt{f}$ where f is a prime divisor of d [69,75]).

Author Contributions: The author confirms to be the sole contributor of this paper.

Acknowledgments: This paper was presented at the 20th International Workshop on Computer Algebra in Scientific Computing (CASC 2018). The author wishes to thank Vladimir P. Gerdt (Dubna) for his kind invitation to give an invited talk at CASC 2018 and Andreas Weber (Bonn) for his encouragement to put the text of the talk in a form convenient for a community of computer engineers and mathematicians. He is also indebted to Wolfram Koepf (Kassel) and François Boulier (Lille) for their logistic help during the preparation of this paper. Finally, the author thanks the Referees for their remarks and suggestions.

Conflicts of Interest: The author declares no conflict of interest.

References

1. Nielsen, M.A.; Chuang, I.L. *Quantum Computation and Quantum Information*; Cambridge University Press: Cambridge, UK, 2003.
2. Kibler, M.R. *Galois Fields and Galois Rings Made Easy*; ISTE Press–Elsevier: London/Oxford, UK, 2017.
3. Weyl, H. *The Theory of Groups and Quantum Mechanics*; Dover Publications: New York, NY, USA, 1931.
4. Weil, A. On some exponential sums. *Proc. Natl. Acad. Sci. USA* **1948**, *34*, 204–207. [CrossRef] [PubMed]
5. Schwinger, J. Unitary operator bases. *Proc. Natl. Acad. Sci. USA* **1960**, *46*, 570–579. [CrossRef] [PubMed]
6. Ivanović, I.D. Geometrical description of quantal state determination. *J. Phys. A Math. Gen.* **1981**, *14*, 3241–3245. [CrossRef]
7. Kostrikin, A.I.; Kostrikin, I.A.; Ufnarovskiĭ, V.A. Orthogonal decompositions of simple Lie algebras (type A_n). *Trudy Mat. Inst. Steklov* **1981**, *158*, 105–120. (In Russian)
8. Wootters, W.K.; Zurek, W.H. A single quantum cannot be cloned. *Nature* **1982**, *299*, 802. [CrossRef]
9. Bennett, C.H.; Brassard, G. Quantum cryptography: Public key distribution and coin tossing. In Proceedings of the IEEE International Conference on Computers, Systems, and Signal Processing, Bangalore, India, 10–12 December 1984; pp. 175–179.
10. Wootters, W.K. Quantum mechanics without probability amplitudes. *Found. Phys.* **1986**, *16*, 391–405. [CrossRef]
11. Wootters, W.K. A Wigner function formulation of finite-state quantum mechanics. *Ann. Phys. (N. Y.)* **1987**, *176*, 1–21. [CrossRef]
12. Patera, J.; Zassenhaus, H. The Pauli matrices in n dimensions and finest gradings of simple Lie algebras of type A_{n-1}. *J. Math. Phys.* **1988**, *29*, 665–673. [CrossRef]
13. Lambert, D.; Kibler, M. An algebraic and geometric approach to non-bijective quadratic transformations. *J. Phys. A Math. Gen.* **1988**, *21*, 307–343. [CrossRef]
14. Wootters, W.K.; Fields, B.D. Optimal state-determination by mutually unbiased measurements. *Ann. Phys. (N. Y.)* **1989**, *191*, 363–381. [CrossRef]
15. Bennett, C.H.; Brassard, G.; Crépeau, C.; Jozsa, R.; Peres, A.; Wootters, W.K. Teleporting an unknown quantum state via dual classical and Einstein-Podolsky-Rosen channels. *Phys. Rev. Lett.* **1993**, *70*, 1895. [CrossRef] [PubMed]
16. Kostrikin, A.I.; Tiep, P.H. *Orthogonal Decompositions and Integral Lattices*; Walter de Gruyter: Berlin, Germany, 1994.
17. Calderbank, A.R.; Cameron, P.J.; Kantor, W.M.; Seidel, J.J. $\mathbb{Z}_4$–Kerdock codes, orthogonal spreads, and extremal Euclidean line-sets. *Proc. Lond. Math. Soc.* **1997**, *75*, 436–480. [CrossRef]
18. Berndt, B.C.; Evans, R.J.; Williams, K.S. *Gauss and Jacobi Sums*; Wiley: New York, NY, USA, 1998.
19. Zauner, G. Quantendesigns: Grundzüge einer Nichtcommutativen Designtheorie. Bachelor's Thesis, University of Wien, Wien, Austria, 1999.
20. Englert, B.-G.; Aharonov, Y. The mean king's problem: Prime degrees of freedom. *Phys. Lett. A* **2001**, *284*, 1–5. [CrossRef]
21. Mosseri, R.; Dandoloff, R. Geometry of entangled states, Bloch spheres and Hopf fibrations. *J. Phys. A Math. Gen.* **2001**, *34*, 10243–10252. [CrossRef]
22. Bandyopadhyay, S.; Boykin, P.O.; Roychowdhury, V.; Vatan, F. A new proof for the existence of mutually unbiased bases. *Algorithmica* **2002**, *34*, 512–528.

23. Lawrence, J.; Brukner, C.; Zeilinger, A. Mutually unbiased binary observable sets on N qubits. *Phys. Rev. A* **2002**, *65*, 032320. [CrossRef]
24. Chaturvedi, S. Aspects of mutually unbiased bases in odd prime power dimensions. *Phys. Rev. A* **2002**, *65*, 044301. [CrossRef]
25. Cerf, N.J.; Bourennane, M.; Karlsson, A.; Gisin, N. Security of quantum key distribution using *d*-level systems. *Phys. Rev. Lett.* **2002**, *88*, 127902. [CrossRef] [PubMed]
26. Aravind, P.K. Solution to the King's problem in prime power dimensions. *Z. Naturforsch.* **2003**, *58*, 85–92. [CrossRef]
27. Lawrence, J. Mutually unbiased bases and trinary operator sets for N qutrits. *Phys. Rev. A* **2004**, *70*, 012302. [CrossRef]
28. Klappenecker, A.; Rötteler, M. Constructions of mutually unbiased bases. *Lect. Notes Comput. Sci.* **2004**, *2948*, 137–144.
29. Gibbons, K.S.; Hoffman, M.J.; Wootters, W.K. Discrete phase space based on finite fields. *Phys. Rev. A* **2004**, *70*, 062101. [CrossRef]
30. Pittenger, A.O.; Rubin, M.H. Mutually unbiased bases, generalized spin matrices and separability. *Linear Algebr. Appl.* **2004**, *390*, 255–278. [CrossRef]
31. Vourdas, A. Quantum systems with finite Hilbert space. *Rep. Prog. Phys.* **2004**, *67*, 267–320. [CrossRef]
32. Saniga, M.; Planat, M.; Rosu, H. Mutually unbiased bases and finite projective planes. *J. Opt. B Quantum Semiclass. Opt.* **2004**, *6*, L19–L20. [CrossRef]
33. Hayashi, A.; Horibe, M.; Hashimoto, T. Mean king's problem with mutually unbiased bases and orthogonal Latin squares. *Phys. Rev. A* **2005**, *71*, 052331. [CrossRef]
34. Paz, J.P.; Roncaglia, A.J.; Saraceno, M. Qubits in phase space: Wigner-function approach to quantum-error correction and the mean-king problem. *Phys. Rev. A* **2005**, *72*, 012309. [CrossRef]
35. Wocjan, P.; Beth, T. New construction of mutually unbiased bases in square dimensions. *Quantum Inf. Comput.* **2005**, *5*, 93–101.
36. Archer, C. There is no generalization of known formulas for mutually unbiased bases. *J. Math. Phys.* **2005**, *46*, 022106. [CrossRef]
37. Grassl, M. On SIC-POVMs and MUBs in dimension 6. In Proceedings of the ERATO Conference on Quantum Information Science (EQIS'04), Tokyo, Japan, 1–5 September 2004; pp. 60–61.
38. Grassl, M. Tomography of quantum states in small dimensions. *Electron. Notes Discret. Math.* **2005**, *20*, 151–164. [CrossRef]
39. Klappenecker, A.; Rötteler, M. Mutually unbiased bases are complex projective 2-designs. In Proceedings of the 2005 IEEE International Symposium on Information Theory, Adelaide, Australia, 4–9 September 2005; pp. 1740–1744.
40. Bengtsson, I.; Ericsson, A.A. Mutually unbiased bases and the complementary polytope. *Open Syst. Inf. Dyn.* **2005**, *12*, 107–120. [CrossRef]
41. Durt, T. About mutually unbiased bases in even and odd prime power dimensions. *J. Phys. A Math. Gen.* **2005**, *38*, 5267–5283. [CrossRef]
42. Pittenger, A.O.; Rubin, M.H. Wigner functions and separability for finite systems. *J. Phys. A Math. Gen.* **2005**, *38*, 6005–6036. [CrossRef]
43. Durt, T. About the Mean King's problem and discrete Wigner distributions. *Int. J. Mod. Phys. B* **2006**, *20*, 1742–1760. [CrossRef]
44. Kibler, M.R. Angular momentum and mutually unbiased bases. *Int. J. Mod. Phys. B* **2006**, *20*, 1792–1801. [CrossRef]
45. Kibler, M.R.; Planat, M. A SU(2) recipe for mutually unbiased bases. *Int. J. Mod. Phys. B* **2006**, *20*, 1802–1807. [CrossRef]
46. Vourdas, A. Galois quantum systems, irreducible polynomials and Riemann surfaces. *J. Math. Phys.* **2006**, *47*, 092104. [CrossRef]
47. Heath, R.W.; Strohmer, T.; Paulraj, A.J. On quasi-orthogonal signatures for CDMA systems. *IEEE Trans. Inf. Theory* **2006**, *52*, 1217–1226. [CrossRef]
48. Vourdas, A. Quantum systems in finite Hilbert space: Galois fields in quantum mechanics. *J. Phys. A Math. Theor.* **2007**, *40*, R285–R331. [CrossRef]

49. Klimov, A.B.; Romero, J.L.; Björk, G.; Sánchez-Soto, L.L. Geometrical approach to mutually unbiased bases. *J. Phys. A Math. Theor.* **2007**, *40*, 3987–3998. [CrossRef]
50. Šulc, P.; Tolar, J. Group theoretical construction of mutually unbiased bases in Hilbert spaces of prime dimensions. *J. Phys. A Math. Theor.* **2007**, *40*, 15099. [CrossRef]
51. Aschbacher, M.; Childs, A.M.; Wocjan, P. The limitations of nice mutually unbiased bases. *J. Algebr. Comb.* **2007**, *25*, 111–123. [CrossRef]
52. Bengtsson, I.; Bruzda, W.; Ericsson, A.A.; Larsson, J.-A.A.; Tadej, W.; Zyczkowski, K. Mutually unbiased bases and Hadamard matrices of order six. *J. Math. Phys.* **2007**, *48*, 052106. [CrossRef]
53. Boykin, P.O.; Sitharam, M.; Tiep, P.H.; Wocjan, P. Mutually unbiased bases and orthogonal decompositions of Lie algebras. *Quantum Inf. Comput.* **2007**, *7*, 371–382.
54. Butterley, P.; Hall, W. Numerical evidence for the maximum number of mutually unbiased bases in dimension six. *Phys. Lett. A* **2007**, *369*, 5–8. [CrossRef]
55. Björk, G.; Romero, J.L.; Klimov, A.B.; Sánchez-Soto, L.L. Mutually unbiased bases and discrete Wigner functions. *J. Opt. Soc. Am. B* **2007**, *24*, 371–378. [CrossRef]
56. Klimov, A.B.; Muñoz, C.; Fernández, A.; Saavedra, C. Optimal quantum-state reconstruction for cold trapped ions. *Phys. Rev. A* **2008**, *77*, 060303(R). [CrossRef]
57. Svetlichny, G. Feynman's integral is about mutually unbiased bases. *arXiv* **2008**, arXiv:0708.3079v3.
58. Kibler, M.R. Variations on a theme of Heisenberg, Pauli and Weyl. *J. Phys. A Math. Theor.* **2008**, *41*, 375302. [CrossRef]
59. Brierley, S.; Weigert, S. Maximal sets of mutually unbiased quantum states in dimension six. *Phys. Rev. A* **2008**, *78*, 042312. [CrossRef]
60. Brierley, S.; Weigert, S. Constructing mutually unbiased bases in dimension six. *Phys. Rev. A* **2009**, *79*, 052316. [CrossRef]
61. Appleby, D.M. SIC-POVMS and MUBS: Geometrical relationships in prime dimension. In Proceedings of the AIP Conference, Foundations of Probability and Physics-5, San Diego, CA, USA, 26–31 May 2009; Volume 1101, pp. 223–232.
62. Albouy, O. The isotropic lines of $\mathbb{Z}_d^2$. *J. Phys. A Math. Theor.* **2009**, *42*, 072001. [CrossRef]
63. Tolar, J.; Chadzitaskos, G. Feynman's path integral and mutually unbiased bases. *J. Phys. A Math. Theor.* **2009**, *42*, 245306. [CrossRef]
64. Kibler, M.R. An angular momentum approach to quadratic Fourier transform, Hadamard matrices, Gauss sums, mutually unbiased bases, the unitary group and the Pauli group. *J. Phys. A Math. Theor.* **2009**, *42*, 353001. [CrossRef]
65. Durt, T.; Englert, B.-G.; Bengtsson, I.; Zyczkowski, K. On mutually unbiased bases. *Int. J. Quantum Inf.* **2010**, *8*, 535–640. [CrossRef]
66. Diţă, P. Hadamard matrices from mutually unbiased bases. *J. Math. Phys.* **2010**, *51*, 072202. [CrossRef]
67. Zauner, G. Quantum designs: Foundations of a noncommutative design theory. *Int. J. Quantum Inf.* **2011**, *9*, 445–507. [CrossRef]
68. Daoud, M.; Kibler, M.R. Phase operators, phase states and vector phase states for SU_3 and $SU_{2,1}$. *J. Math. Phys.* **2011**, *52*, 082101. [CrossRef]
69. Shalaby, M.; Vourdas, A. Weak mutually unbiased bases. *J. Phys. A Math. Theor.* **2012**, *45*, 052001. [CrossRef]
70. McNulty, D.; Weigert, S. The limited role of mutually unbiased product bases in dimension six. *J. Phys. A Math. Theor.* **2012**, *45*, 102001. [CrossRef]
71. McNulty, D.; Weigert, S. All mutually unbiased product bases in dimension six. *J. Phys. A Math. Theor.* **2012**, *45*, 135307. [CrossRef]
72. Ghiu, I. Generation of all sets of mutually unbiased bases for three-qubit systems. *Phys. Scr.* **2013**, *153*, 014027. [CrossRef]
73. Goyeneche, D. Mutually unbiased triplets from non-affine families of complex Hadamard matrices in dimension 6. *J. Phys. A Math. Theor.* **2013**, *46*, 105301. [CrossRef]
74. Spengler, C.; Kraus, B. Graph-state formalism for mutually unbiased bases. *Phys. Rev. A* **2013**, *88*, 052323. [CrossRef]
75. Olupitan, T.; Lei, C.; Vourdas, A. An analytic function approach to weak mutually unbiased bases. *Ann. Phys. (N. Y.)* **2016**, *371*, 1–19. [CrossRef]

76. Sriwongsa, S.; Zou, Y.M. Orthogonal abelian Cartan subalgebra decomposition of sl_n over a finite commutative ring. *Linear Multilinear Algebra* **2018**. [CrossRef]
77. Rao, H.S.S.; Sirsi, S.; Bharath, K. Mutually disjoint, maximally commuting set of physical observables for optimum state determination. *arXiv* **2018**, arXiv:1809.06762.
78. Trifa, Y. Utilisation et construction de bases mutuellement non biaisées en théorie de l'information quantique. In *Rapport de Stage, IPN Lyon—ENS Lyon*; IPN: Lyon, France; ENS: Lyon, France, 2018.
79. IBM Quantum Experience. Available online: https://quantumexperience.ng.bluemix.net/qx/experience (accessed on 21 November 2018).
80. ATOS Quantum Learning Machine. Available online: https://atos.net/en/insights-and-innovation/quantum-computing/atos-quantum (accessed on 21 November 2018).

© 2018 by the author. Licensee MDPI, Basel, Switzerland. This article is an open access article distributed under the terms and conditions of the Creative Commons Attribution (CC BY) license (http://creativecommons.org/licenses/by/4.0/).

MDPI
St. Alban-Anlage 66
4052 Basel
Switzerland
Tel. +41 61 683 77 34
Fax +41 61 302 89 18
www.mdpi.com

Mathematics Editorial Office
E-mail: mathematics@mdpi.com
www.mdpi.com/journal/mathematics

www.ingramcontent.com/pod-product-compliance
Lightning Source LLC
LaVergne TN
LVHW071357070326
832902LV00028B/4642